D0556720

MODERN WALES

MODERN WALES

WALES

A Concise History
c. 1485–1979

GARETH ELWYN JONES

Senior Lecturer in History, Department of Education,
University College of Swansea

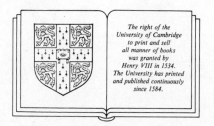

The right of the
University of Cambridge
to print and sell
all manner of books
was granted by
Henry VIII in 1534.
The University has printed
and published continuously
since 1584.

CAMBRIDGE UNIVERSITY PRESS
Cambridge
London   New York   New Rochelle
Melbourne   Sydney

Published by the Press Syndicate of the University of Cambridge
The Pitt Building, Trumpington Street, Cambridge CB2 1RP
32 East 57th Street, New York, NY 10022, USA
296 Beaconsfield Parade, Middle Park, Melbourne 3206, Australia

First published 1984

Printed in Great Britain by the University Press, Cambridge

Library of Congress catalogue card number: 84–9590

British Library cataloguing in publication data

Jones, Gareth Elwyn
Modern Wales.
1. Wales – History
I. title
942.9   DA720

ISBN 0 521 24232 0 hard covers
ISBN 0 521 28544 5 paperback

To K, B and M

CONTENTS

PREFACE

The outstanding feature of work on the history of Wales in recent years has been the extent and quality of the research which has been undertaken. Much of that research has, fortunately, found its way into print in articles, essays, monographs and a few general texts. However, we are not yet in that desirable position in which the author of a new book on Welsh history need apologise for its appearance. It follows that this book is not intended to replace anything; its purpose is to supplement the resources available to all those interested in studying Welsh history.

I have attempted to analyse the main changes which have occurred in Wales over the last five hundred years. Constraints of space meant that there have had to be some sacrifices. Treatment of many topics is less detailed than I would have wished and I have paid scant attention to the history of the Welsh outside Wales. However, I have tried to stress, more than has been usual in Welsh history texts, the economic and social background to political, religious and educational changes.

This structure, and the content on which it rests, would have been impossible were it not for the extensive and excellent research which has borne fruit in theses, journals and books during the last thirty years or so. My own research is limited to specialist aspects of the sixteenth, nineteenth and twentieth centuries. For the rest I am indebted to others. In a work which carries no footnotes it is impossible for me to discharge that debt adequately; all I can do is to thank in general terms the many historians from whose work I have learned so much.

My hope is that those who read the book will be prompted to go to other historians and, beyond them, to some of the printed and manuscript sources on which historical generalisations rest. I hope to encourage an early stage of this process by including a short selection from the more easily accessible printed primary sources, though these documents are also intended to amplify the text. There is no conventional bibliography; booklists abound in varying sizes. Again in the hope of stimulating personal investigation into some aspect of the nation's past, there is a very general introduction to some of the resources available and their location.

In writing this book I have received the most generous help from many friends and colleagues. I am much indebted to Peggy George, Trevor Herbert and Prys Morgan. It is highly likely that without David Howell's encouragement and invaluable assistance the book would never have been started, let alone completed. It was my great good fortune that, as a student at University College, Swansea, I was taught Welsh history by three of Wales's finest historians. They have continued to teach me ever since, not least in connection with this book. To say that I owe much to Ieuan Gwynedd Jones, Kenneth O. Morgan and Glanmor Williams is a considerable understatement.

Finally my thanks go to William Davies and the staff of the Cambridge University Press for the consideration and kindness they have shown me in the process of seeing the book into print.

University College of Swansea   GARETH ELWYN JONES
November 1983

1. The counties of Wales, 1543 to 1973

Edward I's Principalities 1282
Statute of Rhuddlan 1284

Welsh-Norman Marcher Lordships
Act of Union - 1536

2. Main places mentioned in the text

PART ONE

1485–1780

1

THE ECONOMY

Introduction

There was no independent Welsh state at the end of the fifteenth century. In the tenth century Hywel Dda's authority reached to all Wales except the south-east, though the unity he imposed was precarious. Three centuries later a substantial part of Wales had been united under Llywelyn the Great, Prince of Gwynedd, whose overlordship over most of Wales had been accepted at Aberdyfi in 1216, though his hegemony, too, was limited. For a time it seemed as if his grandson, Llywelyn ap Gruffydd, might be more successful. Henry III acknowledged him as Prince of Wales in 1267. So the conquest of Wales by the English in the thirteenth century saw the end of a substantial political independence which flowered again, briefly, with the exploits of Owain Glyndŵr in the early fifteenth century. At least from the conquest in 1282–3 by Edward I, consolidated by the Statute of Rhuddlan, 1284 and the circle of monumental concentric castles around North Wales, there were many shared political and governmental institutions in England and Wales, based on the authority of the English king and marcher lords. Yet distinctions of a differently rooted society remained and the divide, blurred by conquest, was in practice still marked.

No great natural frontier ran from north to south, though the eighth-century Offa's Dyke bordered the central mountain ranges of Wales. So, when the Norman marcher lords progressed westwards into Wales in the eleventh and twelfth centuries they did so mainly along the great rivers and the southern coastal routes where land was low-lying and fertile. Along the north–south border they established their marcher lordships and there, and along the southern coast, the manorial system was firmly planted, with its characteristic Norman churches, castles, and nucleated farming villages. Along with a

3

feudal economic structure went a distinctively Anglo-Norman system of defence and administration centred on the castle. The influence of the Welsh princes was mainly to be found in the medieval Welsh principalities of Powys, Deheubarth and particularly, Gwynedd where traditional social structures and relationships persisted. In those areas of Wales, studded with mountain ranges and upland plateaux, with inhospitably high rainfall and low temperatures, political independence was vested in the Welsh princes for two centuries after the Norman conquest. With the Edwardian conquest a Principality was created in which the king's authority covered the shires of Anglesey, Caernarfon, Merioneth, Cardigan and Carmarthen. By the end of the thirteenth century a new divide existed in Wales, between shired Principality and the march with its quasi-independent lordships; and this was to remain until the reign of Henry VIII. Both areas still owed something to their princely origins, since both shire and marcher lordship were often based on ancient divisions. Either might coincide with a former independent *gwlad* as with Cardiganshire, while in the north, four *cantrefi* constituted the county of Caernarfonshire. Indeed, continuity was maintained in the union legislation of 1536–43 when, for example, the new county of Brecon was based on the original Welsh *cantref* of Brycheiniog.

In various ways their history continued to condition the Welsh. The area west of Offa's Dyke coincided roughly with a linguistic divide, for the Welsh spoke their own ancient language. The influential among them were sustained by a vital historical mythology. They regarded themselves as the true inheritors of the whole island of Britain, descendants of Brutus the Trojan, defeated by the Saxons, but only by treachery. In the Middle Ages Geoffrey of Monmouth provided them with high hopes for the future, a revival to be brought about by some new Arthur. Such notions were eagerly taken up by the influential Welsh bards, and continued to sustain the Welsh even after the conquest of 1282. Owain Glyndŵr's failure did not damp down such notions and indeed Henry Tudor would profit from this tradition.

Even the Welsh system of naming was distinctive – by patronymics, or abbreviated genealogies, rather than the Anglo-Norman system of surnames. Inhabitants of the sparsely populated, straggling settlements of Wales had no need to adopt surnames, though the estate-centred gentry of the sixteenth century accepted them eagerly.

Population

The Welsh method of personal identification is one reason why assessing population structure and change is particularly difficult. To the traditional problems of lack of adequate sources such as the absence of censuses before the nineteenth century and incomplete parish registers, is allied difficulty of identification which makes the technique of family reconstitution impossible. Our data for earlier centuries make possible only the most hazardous generalisations.

Estimates of the population of Wales in 1300 vary from about 180,000 to 250,000 but such estimates are little more than informed guesses. The Black Death after 1349 decimated the population, though here again the evidence is sparse. The population had recovered to possibly 250,000 by the early sixteenth century, compared with $2\frac{1}{2}$ to 3 million in England. Again bearing in mind that the historian is generalising from, for example, taxation returns or ecclesiastical records, it would seem that the population of Wales grew steadily between 1500 and 1750 (490,000), so that by the time of the first census of 1801 numbers had risen to about 580,000. The most likely pattern seems to be that of substantial growth from 1500 to mid seventeenth century (380,000), followed by stagnation till the end of the century, whereupon growth resumed, but more modestly.

Population increase was probably irregular over Wales, with the remoter and harsher rural areas expanding at a slower rate than the more prosperous border lands and southern lowlands. The greater concentrations of population naturally lay in those areas which had been colonised by the Normans, where they had established their manorial structure with its emphasis on mixed farming, feudal tenures and the growth of towns or villages. The Principality of Wales and the Welshries of the march extended over greater areas of less friendly territory, accommodated a far sparser population and relied on a pastoral, more traditionally Welsh, economic structure.

The Welsh were a predominantly rural and scattered population at the end of the fifteenth century, though naturally the density varied and there were greater concentrations in parts of the southern and eastern areas and along the North Wales coast. This was particularly true of the market towns, serving the market and craft needs of the surrounding rural areas. Towns such as Caernarfon or Carmarthen, serving relatively rich country areas, prospered in the

sixteenth and seventeenth centuries, while those towns whose
function had been predominantly defensive, decayed. Tudor legislation provided important administrative functions for some towns as
centres for holding the courts of Great Sessions – Brecon, Denbigh,
Carmarthen and Caernarfon. Swansea, Cardiff or Haverfordwest
were ports and served modestly prosperous agricultural areas. The
population of towns roughly doubled in Swansea or Caernarfon, but
the scale was still small. Elizabethan Brecon or Carmarthen had
populations of about 2,000. Towards the end of the eighteenth
century there were hints of the dramatic changes which dominated
the nineteenth century. In Holywell, Newtown, Pontypool, Neath,
Swansea and, most dramatically, Merthyr Tydfil, population had
started to increase due to industrialisation. Holywell, strategically
placed in the North Wales coalfield, was a major town by the 1770s.
By 1801 Merthyr Tydfil, with a population of 8,000, was larger than
a major regional centre like Carmarthen. Population growth and
distribution were to be revolutionised by industrialisation.

Gentry estates

In pre-industrial Wales wealth lay in land. After the Norman
conquest land was in the hands of the Norman lords, the Church and
the native Welsh. With Norman penetration came a manorial
structure, though there was considerable diversity of settlement,
tenure and agricultural practice, but the characteristic villeinage
system embraced the native Welsh bondmen. In the areas which
remained under Welsh control, either in the marches or under the
princes, the tendency was towards a society of freemen.

Native Welsh freemen held land collectively, as kinsmen, in *gwely*
or resting-place tenure. Gavelkind, division of land among all the
family heirs, characterised the *gwely* system though it was practised
in Kent and East Anglia as well as Wales. The system was breaking
down by the beginning of the fourteenth century. The native
landholding system had come under pressure, particularly after the
Edwardian conquest when Edward I was concerned to maximise his
revenue and traditional payments in kind were commuted to money
payments. With the co-operative structure of landholding undermined, pressure mounted for the acquisition and consolidation of
individual estates. Both the Black Death and the Glyndŵr revolt made

the land market more fluid and hastened the process of transformation, though of course it was a process which took centuries. By the
fourteenth century can be discerned the origin of many of those
substantial gentry estates which were often consolidated in the
fifteenth century. The second half of the fifteenth century, particularly, provided further opportunities, and by the end of that century
there were many gentry estates in existence. The economic organisation of the Norman manor had been modified, though its significance
as a tenurial unit remained. In the Welshries the system of gavelkind
had been undermined. The new order which was consolidated in
sixteenth-century Wales was, in barest essentials, similar to that
which obtained in England. Wealth – and power – were based on land
owned by the aristocracy – few in Wales – and the gentry. That land
was leased out by a variety of tenures, and estates were kept intact
as they passed to the eldest son, a practice brought about not by Henry
VIII's legislation but by long-term economic influences. The
emergence of a gentry class in Wales, as in other European countries
at this time, was of profound significance, both within Wales and
outside.

In the early sixteenth century the major landowners tended to be
identifiably Welsh, whatever their diverse origins. Some were
descended from Welsh princes or members of their courts; some had
originally held office in the Principality of Wales; others served
marcher lords and prospered. Many were Norman or English in
origin, particularly in the lowland areas. Office-holding, trade or war
had enabled other families to progress. Those Welshmen who had
been in royal service had often prospered. There were wider opportunities for estate-building in the sixteenth century, while traditional
avenues remained. Following the dissolution of the monasteries the
amount of crown land on the market greatly increased. The best of
Margam Abbey land in Glamorgan was acquired by Sir Rhys Mansel
who had grasped his opportunity through service to Henry VIII in
his Irish wars. Monastic land was not all immediately sold off and
crown land was on the market throughout the century. Time-
honoured expedients such as judicious marriages remained important
– when Sir Thomas Gamage of Coity, near Bridgend, died without
male heir in Elizabeth's reign suitors for his heiress, grand-daughter
Barbara Gamage, were numerous, influential and very keen to
acquire her estate.

Land was also concentrated into fewer hands by an inexorable process of engrossment and enclosure. Extensive enclosure of freehold land meant that by the early seventeenth century many manors were almost completely enclosed by hedge or ditch, though in others the old open-field system remained throughout that century, and about a quarter of Welsh land was still common by the end of the eighteenth century.

Enclosure consolidated estates but it was also a defensive measure. There was a severe inflation in the sixteenth century, with some prices rising fivefold. The most defenceless groups – the labourers of town and country – could not withstand consequent pressures since rises in wages never matched those in prices. Begging and vaga-bondage increased and poor-law legislation became essential. But even once prosperous estates were under pressure and there were always land-hungry neighbours ready to pounce. So, analysis of the consolidation of estates is scarcely separable from that of their protection. Wise estate-management, husbanding of resources, pro-viding surplus produce for an increasing population were all essential. Resort to a variety of courts was common. Sir John Wynn, who inherited the Gwydir estates in Caernarfonshire in 1580, was found guilty by the council in the marches of using violence to eject tenants and was fined, initially, 1,000 marks. Similar cases concerning Welsh gentry from all counties occurred in the courts of Star Chamber, Requests and Chancery.

In the centuries between union and industrialisation Wales was a land in which economic resources were dominated by the gentry. There were few members of the aristocracy. Most important were the Earls of Worcester, resident at Raglan but with extensive lands in other parts of Wales, including Gower; and the Earls of Pembroke, particularly important from the mid sixteenth century, based in Cardiff but soon to leave Wales for Wilton. As absentee landlords they were particularly vulnerable; the fourth Earl of Worcester claimed in 1590 to have lost 3,000 acres to one thousand of his tenants. He exaggerated, but it was a significant claim, hinting at the size of the estates involved. The Earl of Pembroke remained the largest landowner in Glamorgan – he was lord of six boroughs and thirty-six manors.

The gentry were a far from homogeneous class. There were those of large estates and commensurate prestige – the Wynns of Gwydir, the Maurices of Clennenau, the Bulkeleys in Anglesey, the Salusburys of Llewenni, the Vaughans in Breconshire, the Perrots of Carew, the Griffiths of Penrhyn, the Herberts of Cardiff and the Mansels of Margam. Such gentry were lords of numerous manors, farmed many hundreds of acres and reckoned their estate revenues in many hundreds of pounds in the sixteenth century. At the other end of the scale there were gentry worse off than prosperous yeomen, though it is impossible to quantify the amount of land which either might farm. Yeomen farmers in Wales normally farmed smaller holdings than their English counterparts but their larger acreages distinguished them from the ordinary farmer and gave them some buffer against the exigencies of poor harvest or drought. The Welsh gentry remained generally poorer than their English counterparts. Very few estates in Caernarfonshire or Merioneth yielded the £1,000 per annum of a first-rate English estate in the 1670s, though in Glamorgan about fifteen families could count on this level of income. The wealthiest Welsh gentry – the Morgans of Tredegar, for instance – could count on a wholly exceptional £3,000 to £4,000 per annum at this date.

Large estates in Wales were farmed under a variety of tenures. Manorial tenures, whether freehold, customary or leasehold, survived, with freehold tenures of land held in perpetuity common in the Welsh areas and customary tenures in Normanised areas. Commonest of the customary tenures was copyhold but the form of tenure most encouraged by landlords during the sixteenth century was leasehold, normally for three lives. Tenants with even the smallest holdings were more secure than landless labourers who worked for a wage which, in real terms, fell steadily, particularly in the inflationary sixteenth century, with the rise in population making their bargaining position yet weaker. They lived at subsistence level and spent the greatest proportion of their wages on food and drink.

Gentry estates survived for centuries, despite inflationary pressures and the turmoils of Civil War and Commonwealth. Yet there was constant modification of the landowning pattern. Some estates were sequestered under the Commonwealth in the seventeenth century. Some new landed families emerged at the same time. It was, however, in the eighteenth century that far more substantial changes occurred in the ranks of the gentry and a more obvious demarcation became evident between the largest landowners and those with more modest resources. The traditional methods of estate extension – purchase,

lease, exchange, engrossment, judicious marriage – continued and
there was an increasing tendency for small estates to be absorbed into
larger units. While some families with their origins in the fifteenth
century survived to the end of the eighteenth and beyond, there was
a remarkable transformation in gentry ranks. The Vaughan estate
of Golden Grove, at 40,000 acres, one of the great estates of South
Wales, was disposed of to John Campbell, Lord Cawdor. A remarkable
social change caused the failure of the male line in family after
family. The age of gentry marriage in the eighteenth century became
far later than in the sixteenth and seventeenth centuries and the size
of families smaller. As a result, in eighteenth-century Monmouthshire
the male line failed in about half the gentry families, in Glamorgan
it had failed in ten of the twelve leading families by 1780.
Consequently many estates were taken over by families with no
previous Welsh connections. The Margam estate, acquired by Sir
Rhys Mansel of Penrice after the dissolution of the monasteries, was
inherited by a Wiltshire rector. Another consequence was that estates
were concentrated in fewer hands as they were acquired by existing
landowning families. By the end of the eighteenth century great
estates not only survived but had often been augmented. Their
fifteenth- and sixteenth-century creators, in South Wales and in at
least some of the North Wales counties, had often disappeared. There
was more evident conspicuous wealth concentrated in the hands of
fewer families and a concomitant social cleavage between this small
class of anglicised families and smaller landowners, while exploitation
of estates through agricultural improvement and development of
mineral resources trebled income on some great estates.

Farming practices

It was the geography of Wales which largely determined how
agricultural land was exploited. Extensive areas of the country, over
700 feet above sea level, inaccessible, infertile, with high humidity
and high temperature loss during the growing season, were inimical
to any arable farming. A concentration on pastoral farming was
inevitable in upland Wales, that area which saw least pressure from
Norman invaders, least anglicisation and least agricultural
improvement in succeeding centuries. The pattern of Norman
manorial penetration, from eastern lowlands into southern lowlands,

was repeated in many waves of English agricultural influences in later centuries. Here was a light loam soil, well-drained, fertile, the basis of high yield and high income from colonisers, Norman or English. Here were 'pleasant meadows and...pastures, the plains fruitful and apt for tillage, bearing abundance of all kinds of grain'.

Stock-rearing characterised the farming of the hill areas, upland Glamorgan and Pembrokeshire, Denbighshire, Caernarfonshire and Montgomeryshire, for example. Beef and dairy cattle were always centrally important while sheep were reared for their wool, meat, tallow and skins. Horse-breeding became more important in the seventeenth century as horses tended to replace oxen for ploughing. Cereals were grown in upland areas where possible. Oats were a hardy crop and particularly important for winter feeding. In lowland Wales mixed farming was characteristic, with the emphasis in the most fertile areas on the cultivation of wheat, barley and oats. Herds of cattle might be thirty to eighty strong in the sixteenth century, complemented by upwards of 500 sheep although a few estates had three times this number. Dairy cattle, for breeding and the production of milk, cheese and butter, were remunerative. Store cattle were important and oxen were kept as draught animals. Small numbers of horses, pigs and poultry were found in lowland and upland areas, while the demesne of larger estates saw deer herds for venison, orchards for fruit, and the cultivation of vegetables. Flax and hemp, essential for spinning, were also grown in small quantities.

George Owen of Henllys, whose sixteenth-century description of Pembrokeshire is so informative, criticised primitive techniques of soil preparation and the relative unimportance of corn in a predominantly pastoral economy. He mentioned the use of lime, highly thought of as a fertiliser, and sea-sand and seaweed in soil preparation. Lime was still widely used in the eighteenth century but, by then, improving landlords were preoccupied with bringing more land into cultivation by drainage and improving yields. By that time the border lands and coastal areas saw some experiments in the four-year rotation of crops – turnips, clover, barley, wheat – and in cross-breeding and pedigree herds. Welsh agriculture remained conservative, both in implements and techniques, but from the 1750s county agricultural societies sprouted in Breconshire, Glamorgan, Cardiganshire and Pembrokeshire. The wealthier landowners benefited most since they could best afford to implement new ideas. They had become 'improvement-

1485–1780

minded', turning their attention not only to better methods of land cultivation but bettering transport facilities too. By 1780 this mentality was widespread in Wales, linking gentry, stewards, professional men and industrialists. There was more intensive exploitation of estates and, with increasing absentee landlordism in the eighteenth century, the role of the estate steward was crucial, both in management and improvement. Many astute stewards became gentry in their own right.

It remains impossible to generalise about the Welsh estate in the eighteenth century, since there was such diversity of resources and practice. Certainly, rents were raised considerably in the second half of the century, particularly by the lesser gentry. While there was some capital investment, it was not sufficient to exploit estates to maximum potential. And farm building remained neglected, with landowners in general expending less than 10 per cent of their income on it. Similarly, while there were improvements in methods of husbandry by the greater gentry, particularly in their home farms, minor gentry tended to be more conservative and did not insist on more advanced farming methods in tenants' leases. Landed families did play some part in industrial development by leasing land and providing some capital.

There was a quickening in the pace of economic change in the eighteenth century and consequently new tensions arose. Privileges of medieval origin seemed increasingly anachronistic. In Gower the Duke of Beaufort, heir to lands and rights from marcher lordship days transmitted through the Earls of Worcester, enjoyed such dues as treasure trove and rights to goods from wrecks. Far more significantly, he had rights to common land which had been subject to steady encroachment since Tudor times. Local landowners, now well aware of the potential of mineral rights, were not to yield up this land without a battle, fought in quarter sessions and court of Chancery.

The wool and leather industries

The economic concern of the vast majority of the population before the Industrial Revolution was the land, and the industries and trade associated with it. The industry which involved most people – indeed all as consumers – was the woollen industry. Cattle- and sheep-rearing were the basis of the Welsh economy and cloth manufacture the staple industry, producing flannel and generally rough, coarse cloth. Spinning and weaving were domestic activities, practised in the homes of all ranks of society. Part of the purpose was to produce clothes for immediate personal use but, from the fourteenth century, a largely local activity was transformed into a commercial venture, and fulling of cloth became a mechanised process. Indeed, Welsh cloth went to Brittany, Flanders, Spain and Portugal in medieval times. An act of 1562 allowed the Shrewsbury Drapers' Company a monopoly in selling Welsh cloth and, although it was not always effective, it did lead to better organisation of an expanding industry. Local weavers provided rough cloth and depended on the specialist skills available in Oswestry and Shrewsbury for finishing. The Shrewsbury monopoly, theoretically terminated by an act of 1624, in practice remained because Welsh cloth-workers were not sufficiently prosperous to forego the cash immediately available from merchants. Only towards the end of the eighteenth century did more Welsh – and English – factors enter the Welsh wool market as employers, paying the formerly self-employed craftsmen a piece-work wage.

The Welsh woollen industry had once been located largely in the boroughs – Cardiff and Carmarthen were staple towns and Carmarthen, until the second half of the sixteenth century, a major cloth-exporting port. It was at this time that the centre of gravity of the industry was changing from West Wales to mid and North Wales, where it was a rural rather than borough industry, located in the counties of Merioneth, Montgomery, Denbigh, Monmouth and Pembroke, with the former three dominant. A flourishing domestic and international trade continued. Wool products were sold locally in fairs as well as by merchants in Oswestry and Shrewsbury. Hats, stockings and a range of other clothing were naturally always in demand and their manufacture was a vital source of income in the rural economy. Exports of Welsh cloth went mainly from Bristol and London in increasing quantities in the sixteenth and early seventeenth centuries to France, Spain, Italy and the Netherlands.

The industry remained largely cottage-oriented before the end of the eighteenth century when new machine technologies transformed it. Carding, spinning and weaving had been done by part-time, independent, but very poor, textile workers, mainly women, and the industry was normally associated with farming. Fulling had been the only mechanised process. Now carding-mills were often combined with fulling-mills near sources of water and, after 1810, the revolutionary spinning jenny came to North Wales. Despite some factory organisation in Merioneth from mid eighteenth century the industry remained under-capitalised.

Exports of woollen products increased in the second half of the eighteenth century. From Barmouth and Aberdovey, for example, Welsh woollen products went to various parts of the world via Liverpool, London and Chester. The product of many a *noson gwau* (knitting evening), when stockings were knitted by men, women and children, proceeded to America and the West Indies, an export industry valued at £18,000 by 1780.

Less important than wool, but significant in a pastoral economy, was the leather industry. In sixteenth- and seventeenth-century Swansea, for example, there were more apprentices in the leather trade than in any other, involved in processing cattle and sheep skins into boots, shoes, gloves or saddles. The processes of tanning, particularly, were very highly skilled and leather-workers tended to be prosperous members of the community.

Iron and tinplate

Although early modern Wales had an overwhelmingly rurally based economy the metal and coal industries which brought the country to the forefront of world economic development in the nineteenth century had their origins in medieval times. There was a substantial increase in metal-working in the sixteenth century and on the estates of crown, lay landlords and monasteries (before their dissolution) existed a consciousness of the value of minerals. Under Henry VIII a commission appointed to survey likely sites for metal-working in Wales listed thirty-three, the majority in Glamorgan. The king needed guns, cannon and shot, since he was heavily dependent for these on continental sources.

Although the Welsh iron industry in the sixteenth and seventeenth centuries was not nearly as important as that of Sussex and Kent, 1,000 lb of ore were being mined each day at Llantrisant in 1531, and produced 1 cwt of wrought-iron when smelted in nearby furnaces. There were technological improvements in the Tudor period – bellows worked by water-wheel, for example – which allowed increased production. In 1567, 300 tons of iron plates were shipped from Cardiff to be converted into steel at Robertsbridge in Sussex. By the end of the sixteenth century there was a network of furnaces and forges in Glamorgan, particularly in the Taff valley where already some of the foundations had been laid for expansion in the following centuries. There were numerous sites of mining and production in Carmarthenshire and Pembrokeshire, too. Production at this stage was, of course, on a very small scale and gentry families were often associated with these enterprises as they increasingly realised the value of minerals on their estates. Both before and after the Civil War they were involved in iron-working and coal-prospecting, with Sir Humphrey Mackworth's enterprises in the Neath area in the late seventeenth century the most remarkable for breadth of entrepreneurial vision and technical innovation.

From the 1570s the export of iron-ordnance was sufficiently important to be controlled by law, though this did not stop illegal exports. Excellent guns were made in Cardiff with iron from the Radyr-Pentyrch works and in the sixteenth and early seventeenth centuries there were four accusations of illegal export made against the owners, the Mathew family of Radyr. More constructively, iron-plate was required for a multifarious range of products – from hoops for wheels to ploughshares. Since iron was originally hammered out by hand, the rolling-mill, which came to Britain in the early seventeenth century, represented an important breakthrough, and by the end of that century Capel Hanbury had introduced a water-powered rolling-mill in his Pontypool works where his iron furnace was producing cast-iron, bar-iron, rolled-plate and rod-iron. Later, Pontypool was at the centre of experiments in tinplate manufacture, made by dipping iron and steel into baths of molten tin. In 1728 Payne invented a rolling method of preparing plate which replaced the hammering out of iron to the required thickness, and in essence, this continued as the technology for Welsh tinplate manufacture until Ebbw Vale stripmill opened in 1939. By 1800 the tinplate works of Glamorgan and Carmarthenshire were the focal point of the British tinplate industry.

Well before the disruption caused in the iron industry by the Civil War of the seventeenth century there was apprehension over the amount of timber having to be felled to provide charcoal fuel. Indeed, as early as 1602, the council in the marches had the power to forbid its use. Then, within a generation of the Restoration, technical and commercial developments combined to change the industry from that of individual ownership of furnaces and forges to small group partnerships with the capacity for combining numbers of units of production and putting more extensive capital resources into meeting expanding market needs. Until the mid eighteenth century charcoal remained the fuel of the blast-furnace but coal was increasingly used for forging iron and this entailed a gradual shift in the location of forges towards the coalfields. Glamorgan remained a prime area for iron-working, with, for example the Radyr–Pentyrch works which restarted in 1740, and the Melingruffydd iron and tinplate works, which started in mid eighteenth century in the lower Taff valley and prospered because of demand resulting from the American War of Independence and the French wars. But there were furnaces and forges in many other Welsh counties in the eighteenth century, including the Neath and Tawe valleys, Brecon, Kidwelly, Carmarthen, Whitland and the Gwili valley. Before the Civil War Sir Thomas Myddelton had established an iron-works on his Chirk estate and Charles Lloyd smelted iron at Bersham near Wrexham from about 1717. From 1720 there were interesting experiments there in smelting iron with coked coal, but methods of iron manufacture in Wales remained traditional throughout the eighteenth century. Despite Darby's discovery of the potential of coal for iron-smelting early in the century its adoption was slow. For example in south-east Wales in 1788 there were seven charcoal furnaces and eight coke-fired, though by the end of the century the picture had changed markedly. After 1761, when John Wilkinson had taken over from his father and set up foundries for producing precision pistons, cylinders and boilers the Bersham works played a part in another vital technological development, the Boulton and Watt engine.

By the last quarter of the eighteenth century the iron industry was a large-scale, widespread industry in Wales. The great iron-works across the heads of the South Wales valleys were particularly prominent – Hirwaun, Dowlais, Plymouth, Cyfarthfa, Sirhowy, with gentry involvement again crucial in founding some of these enterprises, but the South- and North-Wales coalfields were studded with iron-works.

Coal

Wales was richer in coal deposits than haematite ore, with extensive
fields in the north-east and in the south. Coal was mined as early as
the thirteenth century in Flintshire and Glamorgan, and in the
sixteenth century the mining of outcrop coal from shallow pits
increased, to be used mainly for domestic fuel. George Owen of
Henllys commented on the increasing use of Pembrokeshire's
anthracite or 'stone-coal' for heating. He recorded that it burned
without smoke, was slow-burning and very different from the
'running' soft coal found further east. He said that it was the chief
domestic fuel in Pembrokeshire, though actually even by the end of
the seventeenth century it was popular only in those areas adjacent
to coalfields, with wood and peat remaining the favoured fuels in
most rural areas. Even so, there was increased trade in coal in the
Tudor period, with coal being transported in twenty to thirty-ton
ships from a variety of Welsh ports, including Swansea and Neath,
as well as from the great port of Bristol in the seventeenth century.
It was destined for Ireland, western England and France, particularly.

At this stage coal-mining was on a very small scale and seasonal.
Pits were not deep, coal was dug out by pick and shovel and problems
of water and firedamp severely restricted the scale of operations.
What prompted expansion towards the end of the sixteenth century
was that prejudice against coal as a domestic fuel lessened, so that
it became the main fuel in towns by the early seventeenth century,
and there was increased anxiety over the denuding of forest areas
for industrial charcoal. New mines were opened in Flintshire,
Denbighshire and Glamorgan and in 1638–9, for example, over
10,000 tons of coal were shipped to Ireland from Flintshire, sent from
Chester and neighbouring ports. There was something of the order
of a fourteenfold growth in the century to 1640. As with the iron
industry, astute gentry profited – the Myddeltons of Chirk, for
example, were involved in coal-mining enterprises at Brymbo and
Rhos. In South Wales, coal was mined in Carmarthenshire and
Pembrokeshire, though the most important areas of mining were
around Neath and Gower where there was easy access to the sea for
the coastal and export trade, with gentry families once again being
involved in its exploitation. Only towards the end of the seventeenth
century were future momentous developments heralded in South

Wales with the sinking of pits in the interior of Glamorgan and Monmouthshire. In the Neath area the gentry families of Evans, Seys and Bussey Mansell, William Leyshon and William Phillips profited particularly from the major stimulus provided by the growth in export demand in the later sixteenth and early seventeenth centuries, with coal being shipped to Normandy, Brittany and the Channel Islands, as well as to the west coast of England. By the 1670s about 10,000 tons per annum were exported from the Neath mines, though demand fluctuated greatly. In the early eighteenth century Sir Thomas Mansel wanted to dismiss miners at his Baglan and Briton Ferry mines, while the men begged to be kept on until exports picked up.

After 1686, when Sir Humphrey Mackworth married into the Evans family of the Gnoll, he dominated the substantial coal industry there. He re-negotiated mineral rights, improved the pits, built a tramway from pits to quay and made Neath one of the most important centres of the coal industry in Wales in the late seventeenth and early eighteenth centuries. In doing so he did not please the other local gentry–coalowners, the Mansels of Briton Ferry and of Margam. Some of their clashes ended in riot.

Conditions under which coal was mined were always dangerous, particularly as timber-lined mines were sunk deeper – from about 100 feet in the Tudor period to about 360 feet in the early seventeenth century. Ladders led to the bottom of the shaft whence galleries led off, with their roofs supported by unmined coal – the pillar and stall method. The coal, mined by candlelight, was taken by wheelbarrow or sledge by men, women or boys to be loaded into baskets and hauled to the surface by a windlass worked by three or four men. The colliers themselves often ascended and descended clinging to windlass rope, though by the eighteenth century the windlass had given way in some places to a cog-and-rung gin worked by a horse circling the shaft head. Transport was normally by packhorse, though Mackworth built a tramway of wooden rails in Neath in 1699 and by mid eighteenth century a tramway served the Mansel collieries in Swansea also. The major constraint on development remained the problem of drainage, with water having to be brought to the surface by windlass or led away by adits. Real progress was only possible when mechanical pumps came into use in the eighteenth century – there was one in use in Mansel's Swansea pits in 1717.

Colliers worked in constant danger, particularly as pits deepened. There were roof falls, the dangers of laddering or winding-gear being defective and constant problems with explosive gas. In 1673, for example, there was a serious explosion at Mostyn colliery, Flintshire, and the bigger scale of mining in the eighteenth century increased the frequency and scale of accidents. In 1787 a gas explosion killed seventeen hewers in a Llansamlet pit. The tragedies of Welsh coal-mining were an established feature of life by now.

Non-ferrous metals

Lead, like iron and coal, had been mined in medieval Wales but in very small quantities. The main areas worked were north Cardiganshire and Flintshire. In the early Tudor period there was more activity – three mines were opened in Llantrisant, Glamorgan, for example. Techniques of mining were primitive – two men to mine the ore, one to take the ore to the foot of the mine-shaft, one to haul it to the surface. After 1583 lead mines in Cardiganshire were developed systematically, particularly by Hugh Myddelton who paid a rent of £400 per annum. The Cardiganshire mines were eventually taken over by Thomas Bushell who established a mint at Aberystwyth to coin Cardiganshire silver, though the mint transferred to Shrewsbury in the Civil War. Bushell's mines in Cardiganshire were reputed to be worth £5,000 per annum in the early seventeenth century. However it was Sir Carbery Pryse of Gogerddan who, at the end of the seventeenth century, successfully challenged the crown monopoly of metals which yielded silver. As a result an Act of Parliament of 1693 limited the crown's right to that of buying ore at a fixed price within thirty days of it being mined. A year after the relevant Act of 1693 Sir Carbery Pryse died and his company passed to Sir Humphrey Mackworth of Neath who, as we have seen, was also involved in mining coal and in metal industries. In the 1730s there was a further burst of activity in Cardiganshire with the rediscovery of old silver deposits.

Lead mines were worked in Pembrokeshire from the early seventeenth century and in the north there were extensive workings in Montgomery, Flintshire and Caernarfonshire. The Wynn family of Gwydir were involved in the exploitation of minerals on their estates from the end of the sixteenth century and re-established an interest in lead-mining after it had been completely disrupted by the Civil War. By the end of the seventeenth century, gentry exploitation of minerals on their lands had resulted in Flintshire becoming a particularly significant lead-producing area, with the Mostyns and the Grosvenors closely involved. Indeed by that time gentry speculation, as well as merchant speculation, was contributing towards making the metal industries more highly organised. It was in Flintshire that the reverberatory furnace – allowing coal to be used in the smelting of lead – was widely developed and the industry continued to expand in the eighteenth century, with the Halkyn mountain mines becoming particularly important.

The history of the lead-mining industry from the sixteenth to the eighteenth century was a chequered one. As demand fluctuated production was spasmodic and during the Civil War virtually ceased. There were many failed ventures and a variety of technical problems, of which the drainage of surplus water was the worst. Even the adits and horse gins which alleviated it were expensive remedies. Transport difficulties from the normally remote mines were extreme. Local gentry, though keen to exploit the potential wealth of their estates, often did not have sufficient capital to support long-term ventures. Individual lessees, then company lessees, had greater resources. The London Lead Company had extensive workings in eighteenth-century Flintshire as well as a network of smelters to process the ore. The company was able to invest in capital equipment and to treat its workers reasonably by linking wages to the cost of living. But lead-mining was a dangerous and debilitating job. There was the danger of rock falls and, more insidious, the effects of working in constantly damp conditions. Labour was plentiful, so wages stayed low, and in the remoter areas workers had to live at the mines for all but weekends. With English entrepreneurial activity increasingly important in the eighteenth century more English skilled labour was brought in, so that local labour tended to be confined to the unskilled tasks. This influx of skilled and managerial labour helped in Flintshire for example, to change the structure of local communities.

The manufacture of copper in the sixteenth century was in the hands of the Company of Mines Royal established in 1568. Its main areas of activity were Cumberland and Cornwall but in 1584 it was decided to transport Cornish ore to Neath for smelting. Neath was accessible from the sea and had ample supplies of coal, increasingly used for copper-smelting. A large smelter was built, capable of processing 560 tons of ore per week, but it was never used to capacity as the Neath operation was dogged with difficulties. Indeed, during the second half of the seventeenth century, copper-smelting virtually stopped not only in Neath but also over the rest of England and Wales. After 1693, with the crown monopoly exploded, mining resumed and copper was in demand for frequent issues of copper coinage. From the 1690s copper was mined by Sir Carbery Pryse at Esgairhir in Cardiganshire and later this unsuccessful enterprise was restarted by Sir Humphrey Mackworth. In the eighteenth century the focal point of the copper-mining industry was Parys mountain in Anglesey where there were important finds of ore in the 1760s, to be exploited first by the Parys Mines Company, then the Mona Mine Company. The manager of the Mona Company was Thomas Williams who used the resources of Anglesey copper to undercut Cornish prices and eventually enforce a marketing and pricing policy on the industry. For part of the last two decades of the eighteenth century Anglesey was producing 40 per cent of British copper.

Copper-smelting was even more important in Wales. It was Sir Humphrey Mackworth's involvement in the coal, lead and copper industries which made Neath such an important centre and by 1689 he had built a lead- and copper-smelter there, with ores brought from Cornwall and Cardiganshire to Neath quay, then by canal to the smelter. Mackworth spent nearly £17,000 between 1698 and 1708 on smelting facilities in Neath. The copper-smelter alone, with its two furnaces, two water-wheels and six stamping machines, was a major enterprise by contemporary standards, but, as we have seen, formed only part of a Mackworth industrial network in Neath, comprising coal-mining, lead- and silver-smelting and waterway and tramway construction. He was a prime example, in the pre-industrial revolution period, of landed gentleman and industrial entrepreneur who exercised a traditional role in the community by virtue of his landed status, reinforced by commercial success. He held office locally, was a Member of Parliament and used his position to wring various commercial concessions from Neath borough. Just as in the Tudor period, success on Mackworth's scale provoked bitter rivalry among neighbouring gentry, and led to physical violence. Some of

Mackworth's men were kidnapped by employees of Thomas Mansel of Baglan and Briton Ferry and some of Mansel's armed servants forced their way into Mackworth's estate on one occasion.

In 1717 copper-smelting started in Llangyfelach, near Swansea, another location enjoying access to the sea and to ample supplies of coal. Ore came from Cornwall in such quantities that Swansea works were smelting half of Britain's copper by mid eighteenth century. The leading entrepreneur here was Chauncey Townsend, a London merchant. During the century more than a dozen copper-works were established on either side of the river Tawe as it meandered down from Ynystawe through Llansamlet, Landore and Hafod. By the end of the century this area was to be the copper-smelting centre of Britain, with the capital having been provided largely by London and Bristol merchants. Stimulated, like other industries, by the Seven Years War and the American War of Independence, exports of copper rose from under 9,000 tons in 1750 to over 47,000 tons in 1780. Copper-smelting required high technical skills which were, at first, brought in to Wales while the less skilled tasks were allocated to local labour, though by the end of the century an adequately skilled local labour force existed for all requirements.

The pace of change

There were no obvious indications, even in mid eighteenth-century Wales, that developments amounting to an industrial revolution would soon be in train – no sign of the necessary expansion in demand for iron and coal, no obvious large supplies of capital available, no clear breakthrough in the problems of transport difficulties and costs. Yet by the end of the century expansion was dramatic. From the 1750s Britain's wars were crucial in this, with copper, lead, zinc, iron and tinplate all being needed. It was significant that many of the gentry closely involved in developing industry supported the colonial Seven Years War and the American War of Independence which provided a much expanded market for the metal industries' products, though these metals were also fulfilling an increasing range of domestic functions.

One vital element in the ability to increase demand was a series of inventions. In the late seventeenth century, for example, methods of smelting lead and copper with coal were discovered and, soon after, copper-and lead-works were established in the Neath and Swansea area. These industries stimulated coal production and transport improvements, with experiments in waterways and tramways. Iron production expanded spectacularly from the 1760s. With ample supplies of iron-ore available along the northern rim of the South Wales coalfield, the general location of the iron industry was determined by the availability of raw material. Previously, as we have seen, iron had been smelted in many areas of South Wales with charcoal, which limited production since an acre of trees was required to smelt three tons of iron. The use of charcoal imposed severe limitations on growth as the fuel had to be transported increasing distances to a more static industry. In 1704 six-sevenths of the £3 13s 8d which it cost to produce a ton of pig-iron in a works near Clydach were spent on charcoal. Then, in 1709, came Abraham Darby's technical breakthrough, enabling iron to be smelted by using coke. In the 1750s the process was taken up at the Hirwaun and then the Dowlais works, and the development of the iron-works at the heads of the South Wales valleys followed. The great Merthyr works were complemented by the Monmouthshire works at Tredegar, Sirhowy, Beaufort, Ebbw Vale and Blaenavon in the 1760s and 1770s. By 1788 there were fifteen iron furnaces with eight being fuelled by coke. Twenty-three years later there were fifty-three coke furnaces and more crucial inventions had been made. Since the iron industry was located in a most inaccessible part of Wales, improved access to the sea was crucial. In the 1790s began the canal building which was to alleviate this problem. The metal industries comprised the early stage of the industrial revolution in Wales, stimulating all aspects of economic activity – agriculture, shipping, coal – and at the same time producing that new social configuration which was ultimately to transform Welsh society and politics.

Trade

Out of the economic life of town and country grew a pattern of trade and a mercantile structure. In agricultural products, such as butter, there was an important trade, with substantial exports to Ireland. The South Wales trade, particularly, centred on the port of Bristol. The cattle trade was crucial, the cattle-drovers who took their herds of cattle from all parts of Wales every year were often relatively wealthy men, able to earn more than £100 per annum in the seventeenth century. Such were the capital resources of some of them that they lent money and acted as bankers. When the Civil War ended, a war which had been disastrous for certain sectors of the economy, M.P.s voted £3,000 to drovers for the loss they had incurred. They bought their cattle at markets and fairs all over Wales, had the animals marked and shod, then set off for London, Bristol and the Midlands with droves 300 to 400 strong along their own established routes dotted with shoeing stations and inns. The cattle were taken particularly to London or home counties fairs, before being fattened up for slaughter at Smithfield. On their journeys the drovers often took letters and settled financial transactions in London for Welsh clients.

The towns of Wales were focal points for the trade arising from the associated rural area. Apart from their administrative role in some cases, the chief importance of the Welsh towns lay in their economic activities as centres of trade, fairs, markets, shops and craft products. Some were also ports with a coastal and export trade. At town markets the products of the surrounding agricultural areas were sold – corn, meat, cloth, general produce. There were large weekly or monthly markets for the sale of livestock. Major market towns also held fairs twice or three times a year for the large-scale sale of animals, though goods like hats and gloves were on sale at the same time. At such times shopkeepers prospered – butchers, bakers, vintners and fishmongers. Particularly important, and prosperous, were those involved in the leather and woollen trades – tanners, saddlers, glovers, shoemakers. In the cloth trade there were hatters and seamstresses who processed cloth finished by weavers, dyers and tuckers. In the ports shipbuilding and fishing were important. All the resulting trade was regulated by a complex of regulations governing quality, cleanliness and fair trading, although the by-laws of boroughs were often regarded in a similarly cavalier fashion to the laws of the realm.

Waterborne trade

The most efficient and economical method of transport until the nineteenth century was by water – river and sea; and here most Welsh counties were in an advantageous position with so many of them bordering the sea. In the south, Glamorgan and Pembrokeshire were important trading counties, with a flourishing coastal trade in wool, butter, hides, cattle, iron and coal. Links with Bristol were vital, since Bristol was the largest city in western England, with a population of 12,000 by 1600, and itself a major consumer of agricultural produce from South Wales. Cattle and sheep were shipped across the Bristol Channel, then taken by drovers to Bristol and west-country fairs. The great port of Bristol also sent Welsh goods to Ireland, France and Spain, while Welsh wool was also exported from London. Western and northern ports, Beaumaris and Milford Haven, for example, also served Ireland, exporting butter, coal and slate and taking in fish, flax and, increasingly, timber in return. Chester, in the north, and Swansea, in the south, were important centres for the export of coal to Ireland and the continent. The coal trade to France in the sixteenth century became more important than the wool trade so that the coal-exporting ports also found themselves centres for the import of salt and wines. Coal exports from Swansea grew from about 1,800 tons in 1551–60 to about 3,000 tons in 1591–1600, although the trade was adversely affected by increased taxes in the 1620s and 1630s. All this activity, then, was on a small scale. A cargo of 20 to 30 tons was sizeable, indeed in 1635 there was only one ship of over 200 tons in South Wales. Maritime activity in North Wales was less, with few people earning a living from the sea, but fish, butter and slate were channelled to Chester, Liverpool and Dublin by North Wales merchants.

In theory, sea-going trade was closely regulated since customs revenues formed a vital part of the monarch's revenue. In practice there was no satisfactory check on Welsh ports until Elizabeth's reign. In many parts of Wales before this the crown rarely received its dues. In Glamorgan and Monmouthshire, for example, if any tolls were paid at all on the export of butter and hides, they went to the Earls of Pembroke and Worcester who controlled the coast. In Elizabeth's reign, three head ports were designated for Wales, Chester, Milford and Cardiff. Customs officers, in theory, controlled access to imports in those areas of coast under their control, and customs houses were built in large ports. Evasion of tunnage and poundage remained widespread, particularly when the influence of local aristocracy or gentry was strong. The Welsh coast was studded with creeks and small ports ideally suiting access for the small boats of the day. Even the head ports were by no means immune. Leather and butter were

illegally exported from Cardiff, for example, as was iron ordnance to
Spain in the later sixteenth century. Customs officers were themselves
sometimes corrupt. They could be bribed to issue blank warrants,
deny access to customs houses or merely turn a blind eye. Once at
sea merchant shipping had to face pirates. Cardiff enjoyed a dubious
notoriety here in Elizabethan times, being the centre of the activities
of John Callice, one of the most prolific of Elizabethan pirates, who
enjoyed the protection of some notable gentry families. But there
were many involved in illegal trade, with ships from France and
Spain, particularly, carrying cargoes of salt or wine, highly vulnerable. In port, unloaded with the connivance of officials, the goods
were sold and distributed. The Privy Council grew increasingly
anxious and mounted a series of investigations but even investigating
commissioners were sometimes in league with pirates. In the seventeenth century the threat was different. Turkish pirates, using Irish
bases, preyed on shipping in the Bristol Channel and the Irish sea with
devastating effect. Piracy was eventually brought under control but
smuggling of a variety of valuable products, tea, coffee, wine and
tobacco, for example, reached its peak in the eighteenth century and
provided a yet more intractable problem for government.

Roads

Transport of goods by road was inefficient, hazardous and expensive
throughout the period. Indeed this is one of the important reasons
why the land-locked parts of the South Wales coalfield, with its
iron-ore deposits, had not been exploited to a greater degree before
the eighteenth century.

Transport of goods by land was, perforce, mainly by packhorse –
expensive, inefficient and slow. The condition of the roads in Wales
was extremely bad. Their upkeep was the responsibility of the parish,
through a system of statutory labour which it was difficult to enforce.
The best roads had been built by the Romans, but they were few in
Wales. The major land trade, therefore, was in cattle, with the
drovers using their own routes to the Midlands and London. These
routes went from east to west across Wales. From Wrexham,
Shrewsbury, Leominster, Hereford and Monmouth they took roughly
parallel westerly courses fanning out into the Llŷn peninsula in the

north and the Pembrokeshire peninsula in the south. Again, the needs of the Irish trade were paramount, so there were westerly routes in the north and south. In the north, for example, the road ran from Chester to Holyhead via Denbigh and Caernarfon.

In mid eighteenth century the state of Welsh roads was appalling – a catalogue of unmade surfaces, prohibitive depths of mud, ways blocked by rocks and debris. The situation had long been regarded as intolerable since private travel and trade were greatly inhibited. The North Wales route to Holyhead, the major link with Ireland, did receive some attention because it was important to both British and Irish governments. Both gentlemen estate-owners and industrialists were increasingly convinced of the necessity for action. Monmouth-shire gentry, either individually or through private subscription, improved roads, but action was centred mainly in the iron- and slate-industry areas. Anthony Bacon transformed the track between Merthyr and Cardiff into a road in 1767, and Lord Penrhyn built a road between his quarry at Bethesda and Bangor in 1786.

The first turnpikes came to Wales in 1752, covering the road from Shrewsbury to Wrexham. The turnpike trusts were not intended to replace the old road system but to supplement it. They embodied a localised, piecemeal approach to road improvement, were often under-financed and presided over roads which were often in a very poor state of repair. Even so, trusts set up as a result of Acts of Parliament and dependent on tolls for revenue eventually served much of Wales. A section of the Chester–Holyhead road was completed by 1759 and the Brecon to Tavernspite road by 1763. There were north–south routes, as well, from Pembroke to Bangor and a mid-Wales route north from Llanelli. The process took many years and the roads were expensive to use. There was no standardisa-tion of tolls and no limits on the number of gates. In the 1760s, in Glamorgan, although five different trusts were operating the improvements in Welsh roads should not be exaggerated. Arthur Young, on his travels along the trust road between Chepstow and Cardiff in 1768 was unimpressed: 'mere rocky lanes, full of hugeous stones as big as one's horse, and abominable holes'. But there were improvements. A voluntary organisation surveyed the major east–west road in South Wales and put pressure on parishes to make improvements. Road improvements came with coach services. A service ran between Chester and Holyhead from 1776 and from Shrewsbury to London from 1780. By the end of the eighteenth century there were links between Milford, Cardiff, Bristol and London, though travel by coach was still restricted, and roads remained highly inadequate for the kinds of demands being made on them with increasing economic activity.

2

SOCIETY

Aristocracy and gentry

At the apex of Welsh society were the aristocracy and the gentry. The aristocracy with influence in Tudor Wales were generally absentee – the Earls of Leicester, Essex and Pembroke – though the Earls of Worcester were based at Raglan castle. The situation did not change radically in the seventeenth and eighteenth centuries. The Worcesters, created Dukes of Beaufort in 1682, remained powerful, as did the Pembrokes, but aristocratic estates in Wales were normally part of far larger estates in England. In the eighteenth century the four greatest estates were owned by the Dukes of Beaufort, who lived in Badminton, the Earl of Plymouth, whose main estates were on the Welsh border, Lord Mountstuart, later Bute, who had important Scottish estates and the Mansel Talbots at Margam.

The most powerful social group in Wales were the gentry who had emerged in the fifteenth century and often consolidated their position in the sixteenth with judicious purchases of land, office-holding and intermarriage. They were the main employers of labour, both for their estates and their houses and, in many counties, lay impropriation gave them a strong hold on the Church. Their origins were diverse – Welsh, Norman and English. Many who had originally come from outside Wales – the Bulkeleys, Thelwalls, Salusburys or Aubreys – had become assimilated into Welsh society by the sixteenth century. The permanence of many families from sixteenth to eighteenth century is impressive – the Wynns of Caernarfonshire, or the Stradlings of Glamorgan, for example – yet ranks changed markedly during the eighteenth century as changing patterns of family size and age of marriage saw the male line of family after family fail. In the sixteenth century gradations of gentry were relatively less marked than in the eighteenth, with degrees of greater and lesser gentry merging into each other. Many Tudor gentry were small fry by comparison with their English counterparts and were a much more diffuse class. They were sustained by their genealogies, often justified, often fabricated, since gentry status was more dependent on ancestry, less dependent on wealth than in England. Being of ancient family was not only looked on as an advantage by the gentry, but also assumed special importance in Wales for historic reasons – the centrality of the bardic role in a society based on kindred; and social reasons – the relative poverty of Welsh squires compared with their English counterparts. There were impressive family trees in Wales as a result. The Mansels of Margam in Glamorgan were endowed with a fictional Norman ancestor. The Salusburys of Denbighshire traced their roots back to Adam of Salzburg, Sir John Wynn of Gwydir to the princes of medieval Wales. By the eighteenth century concern with ancestry was less pronounced in a society with a more obvious oligarchy of great families whose estates had been augmented at the expense of lesser gentry. The domination of the wealthiest gentry – the Bulkeleys of Anglesey, the Vaughans of Hengwrt and Corsygedol, the Mostyns of Flint, the Hanmers, the Williams Wynns, the Pryses of Gogerddan, the Philipps of Cwmgwili, the Morgans of Tredegar – was a vital feature of eighteenth-century Wales. And even if landed wealth in Wales was less marked than in England there were some families who were wealthy by any standards. In Charles I's reign there were a dozen gentry in Glamorgan with estates worth more than £1,000 per annum and a dozen more with estates yielding between £500 and £1,000 per annum; there were at least three in Anglesey in the former category and five in the latter. Into the eighteenth century the substantial squires were worth £1,000 per annum and the Wynns or the Morgans of Tredegar owned estates worth over £3,000 per annum.

Residences and lifestyles

In the Tudor period the diversity of gentry resources was reflected in their residences. Some families lived in Norman castles. Sir John Perrot's residence was Carew castle in Pembrokeshire which he transformed into a suitable Tudor dwelling house, with comfort now more relevant than defence. St Donat's castle, home of the Stradling family, a large and impressive thirteenth-century castle, was substantially altered in the sixteenth century, with an additional wing of sleeping quarters. Some monastic houses provided the basis for a Tudor building, while St Fagan's castle, near Cardiff, an elegant, quintessentially Elizabethan dwelling of the 1580s, was a fine example of the new manor house with elegant gables, leaded windows and tall chimneys. Such mansions, usually built of stone with tiled roofs, normally had halls, living chambers, kitchens, pantries, cellars, brew houses and corn houses. In the Elizabethan period interiors became more lavish, with ceilings replacing open roofs and oak panelling becoming fashionable. Staircases of oak connected hall with upper rooms and valuable glass replaced shutters in the windows. Large, open fireplaces were often ornamented with stone-patterned surrounds and some Welsh houses had galleries in the main room where bards and musicians entertained. During the sixteenth century the wealthier families attended far more to comfort and luxury. Furniture was normally made of ash or walnut while the great four-poster beds of the time might be of oak or walnut or wainscot, with canopies and draperies of silk. Carpets, of Turkish, Irish or Scottish make, became increasingly popular. Table-ware was normally of pewter, though the richer houses boasted silver. The more prosperous gentry were able to cultivate a luxurious lifestyle for themselves, and their often large families, in the Tudor and Stuart period, through the efforts of numerous servants working on the estate, providing wood, cultivating the kitchen garden, tending fires, with perhaps half a dozen at work in the kitchen. Outside the house there were increasing concessions to luxury. Normally there would be a kitchen garden providing herbs and, beyond, a large park. Parks, too, were partly functional, partly ornamental, and might include lakes, fish-ponds, dovecotes, eyries and, particularly, deer-parks for providing venison. When the Duke of Beaufort made his progress through Wales in 1684 one of his party commented on the extra-ordinary size and fatness of the deer at Margam. Some estates boasted two parks, for red and fallow deer, providing meat and sport in the form of deer-hunting. Exotic imports of spices and wines added to the appeal of home-produced food, and entertainment was certainly available in some Tudor households – Sir Edward Stradling had his own harpist, Thomas Pritchard.

While the richest of Wales's gentry aspired to such a lifestyle the middling and lower ranks of gentry had to be content with rather more modest standards. They still attempted to impress by building new houses, but on a modest scale. Here, too, there were changes during the Tudor period as the large hall open to the roof tended to give way to two-storey houses of box-frame construction, with stairs and fireplaces. Local materials and local building customs still decreed that there was enormous variety of size, style and construction.

From the relative luxury of the hall house and its successor, domestic conditions reflected degrees of wealth or poverty. The poorest of people lived in earth-floored cottages of one room or in the outbuildings of farms where they were employed. A little more superior was the long house with its living areas and animal space adjoining. Here comfort and hygiene were at something of a premium. Depending on local materials walls might be of mud or clay, with timber supports, roofs thatched, except in parts of North Wales where slate was plentiful, holes in the walls for windows. In Pembrokeshire, farmhouses were usually of stone and, where English influence was strong, stone buildings or wattle and daub walls were frequent. The more substantial yeoman would aspire to latticed windows and, often, two storeys in a house comprising living quarters of hall and parlour serviced by a kitchen. But he might live in a far simpler farmhouse with one living room, an attic for sleeping and the simplest of oak furnishings – stools, settles, chests and a round table. Cottages for labourers remained, for centuries, of the meanest – one room, mud-floored and walled, and often with straw or rushes at one end for bedding. Straw mattresses or truckle beds were relative luxuries.

The discrepancy in lifestyle between the classes increased during the eighteenth century, reflecting the evolution of a smaller, more homogeneous, wealthy gentry class. Just as this class increased its estate and income, and looked more closely to England for standards of taste, so this was reflected in building. Many families either built new mansions or rebuilt old houses to ape these standards. Inevitably more modest in scale than the great English houses of the eighteenth century, classical houses did make an appearance in Wales and others contained a mixture of styles, like Thomas Johnes's part-gothic, part-classical house at Hafod. This was originally constructed by Baldwin of Bath, enlarged by Nash and rebuilt by Baldwin after fire damage in 1807. It was basically gothic but in the grounds was found a mixture of Doric temples, pagodas and grottoes. One of the richest of the Glamorgan gentry, Thomas Mansel Talbot, built the beautiful, classical orangery at Margam and a villa at Penrice. The orangery, built in the 1780s, was to accommodate not only a variety of orange and lemon trees but also the statues acquired by Talbot on the gentleman's mandatory grand tour of Europe. It was the longest building of its kind in the world, 275 feet long. The Penrice villa cost well over £4,000 to build, with craftsmen being brought in from Gloucestershire and Somerset.

The parklands of great estates were often landscaped in line with current practice – with lakes, trees, earth banks and stoneworks. The interiors of great houses changed, too. Elegant furniture by Sheraton and others came from London into the richest houses. The traditional walnut – and certainly oak – were superseded by mahogany. Oak panelling tended to give way to wallpaper. Wilton carpets, elaborate four-poster beds and cotton curtains were acquired for Penrice manor house in the 1770s, for example. Hospitality in the great houses became yet more institutionalised than it had been in the Tudor period, but its scale had always been substantial. The social round, by the eighteenth century, reflected the tightening of the gentry circle and the increased attractions of London and Bath. The Parliamentary season in London required Members of Parliament to reside there for its duration and leave their estates in the hands of professional stewards, compounding the growing cleavage between gentry and community and providing these stewards with enormous power and good prospects. Many bought land and entered the ranks of the gentry themselves. The distinction in gentry lifestyle was sometimes further accentuated by ostentatious gambling or conspicuous indulgence in the fripperies of contemporary high society – among gentlemen and their wives. This had to be at the expense of the estate and, ultimately, tenants. But the process of alienation, which can in any case be exaggerated, was not primarily the result of absenteeism. Eighteenth-century society was often brutal and some of the gentry were no exception. While there were men of refinement and taste there was also drunkenness. Some were downright tyrants, others were removed from the ranks of justices of the peace for rioting. There were philanthropists, but far more money was spent on gambling than on charity. The domination of the gentry over their tenants was complete. There was opposition to enclosures and, at the end of the century, food riots and threatening letters to justices but these were reactions to specific situations, never a threat to the social order.

The gentry remained focal points of village community life – to their tenants and other village inhabitants. With some exceptions they were paternalistically involved in the welfare of the community. Their birthdays were celebrated with food and drink which they provided. There were exceptions. Sir Herbert Lloyd of Peterwell in Cardiganshire terrorised his tenants and got a neighbour hanged for sheep-stealing because Lloyd wanted his land. Less dramatically, court records indicate that some landlords were ruthless in raising rents or using force to eject tenants who prevented the consolidation or extension of estates. Literary sources, too, indicate that landlords were often seen as grasping and exploiting. Yet the centre of the gentleman's orbit remained his native county in the majority of cases. He played a central role in local government. The chief county family provided the lord lieutenant, while lower down the social scale came the offices of sheriff and justice of the peace. The highspot of local society by the eighteenth century was the meeting of Great Sessions, a judicial, administrative and social occasion, though the numbers of justices attending fell off considerably during the course of the century.

The gulf between the gentry, particularly the greater gentry, and tenant farmers and small freeholders was immense – in wealth, lifestyle and social position, and the gulf grew yet larger in the eighteenth century, particularly since there was no substantial yeoman class in Wales. Demographic changes, allied with a modernised outlook among the wealthier gentry, conspired by mid century to produce a new ruling gentry elite whose concerns militated against the community leadership which their predecessors had often exercised. Their interests were now more commercial, impelling them to an enhanced interest in government and foreign policies which furthered their interests. Increasingly, these gentlemen opposed traditional tenant attitudes and rights which cut across this new commercialism. Tensions increased and the social gulf widened.

Country and town

The great majority of Welsh people lived on the land in pre-industrial times. The communities in which they lived were small, isolated and introspective in general. Life was harsh, dominated by the necessity to tease a living from unfriendly soil at a time when knowledge of crop and animal husbandry was unscientific. Poor road transport was another deterrent to mobility. The local community therefore provided the focus for economic and social and recreational life, with its own customs and folklore, its resentment and suspicion of strangers. Traditions gave the community cohesion. Tradition meant reluctance to change, even when change in agricultural practice was urged by the gentry, but it was an essential element in a society in which knowledge of nature came from experience not experiment. Knowledge of the soil, the weather, animal disease, for example, was not lacking, but it depended on a lore built up over the generations. That lore was inevitably credulous. It encompassed a belief in witchcraft which was very pervasive, though without the excesses of persecution evident periodically in England. Witchcraft provided some key to the future, and to the mysteries of the present, to the diseases which affected animals and humans with which people lived constantly and about which they could do so little.

People were at the mercy of the elements because their existence was dominated by the quality of the harvest. Excesses of drought or, far more likely, wind and rain meant disaster and even, if repeated a few years, starvation. The malnutrition resulting from a bad harvest made the population even more susceptible to diseases such as plague, typhus and smallpox. Even when harvests were good, ordinary people had a dietary deficiency resulting from eating mainly cereal food, with very little meat, vegetables and fruit.

As we shall see, life in the country, dominated as it was by work from dawn till dusk, was not without its lighter side, its merrymaking and enjoyment, on Sundays and Saints' Days. There was the consolation of the tavern, and quantities of ale at weddings and funerals, dancing to *crwth* and harp on the village green and a variety of sports for the participant, the observer and the gambler.

While Wales in this period was predominantly a rural country, and towns remained tiny by modern standards, they did play an increasingly important part. The magnetism of two urban centres outside Wales is obvious. From Tudor times the Welsh went to London in increasing numbers and from all social classes. They were welcomed at court, particularly under the Tudors, and many prospered, for example, David Owen, who was Henry VIII's chief carver, and Lewis Caerleon, his doctor. There were others of national reputation, like Sir Edward Carne who was a member of Henry VIII's great mission to Rome. There were merchants and tradesmen who made their fortune and many more who ended up in London's slums.

In the sixteenth and seventeenth centuries Ludlow was a town of considerable significance to some of the governing families of Wales because it was the meeting place of the council in the marches. As a result Ludlow became a social as well as an administrative centre, bearing some of the features of the London court scene. During the presidencies of Sir Henry Sidney in Elizabeth I's reign and that of his successor, the second Earl of Pembroke, Ludlow's social life was impressive. Banquets and masques, especially, were the social concomitants to administration and the dispensation of justice. But the social glitter diminished towards the end of Elizabeth's reign when the council became a hotbed of intrigue between Pembroke and the Earl of Essex, as the latter fought for a power base in Wales. In 1633 the Earl of Bridgwater became Lord President, determined to restore Ludlow's former glories. A year of festivities culminated in the performance of Milton's masque, *Comus* in 1644, but it was only eight years before the council in the marches went the way of the other prerogative courts, and when it was revived under Charles II it performed merely as a court of justice.

Within Wales itself the rural–urban dichotomy should not be too sharply emphasised. The town depended on its rural environment for food and the rural areas relied on the marketing function of the town. Despite the occasional presence of, and general participation by, the gentry in the running of town affairs, especially in the election of borough representatives in Parliament through the contributory borough system, the Welsh towns had a corporate existence and with their growth a small, but growing, identifiable middling and artisan class developed. The regular markets and fairs, with trade in cattle and sheep and the related rural industries of tanning, shoemaking, gloving and manufacture of farm implements, together with the whole commercial framework of shops and stalls which supported this trade, meant that a small commercial, merchant element emerged. The more successful craftsmen had some local power, too, though it should not be exaggerated. Local gentry usually controlled borough parliamentary representation and often influenced town government through pressure on borough freemen. Even so, town government was run by its freemen who, through the guild system, had a monopoly of trade and manufacture within the borough. They elected the town council and the chief officer – mayor or portreeve, perhaps, with alderman and bailiffs to serve him. The monopoly of the guilds and the rules of apprenticeship were not watertight. Despite the Statute of Artificers of 1563, which stipulated that a craftsman had to serve a seven-year apprenticeship – and this was supplemented in some towns by their own regulations – there were many unlicensed practitioners of various trades. Out of the commercial life of the towns came an increasingly complex trade and the occasional commercial fortune, but this would be translated as a matter of course into the purchase of land, since status was integrally associated with the size of an estate.

There were few sizeable towns in Wales until the early nineteenth century. At the beginning of the eighteenth century the largest town was Wrexham, with a population of about 3,000. Most towns – Cardiff, Brecon, Swansea, Carmarthen – had not increased markedly over their size in the sixteenth century, with populations between 1,000 and 2,000. By the end of the eighteenth century some of these towns had grown rapidly – Wrexham to about 8,000, Swansea to about 6,000. Despite their relatively small size they played a vital part in the economic and social life of Wales. They were the centres for regular fairs – Wrexham and Carmarthen were the most important in the eighteenth century – and travelling pedlars came in to sell their wares. Many of the town shops were permanent. There were improved amenities such as paving and lighting in places. In addition to the market function some towns were administrative centres and played host to the courts of sessions – Carmarthen, Brecon, Caernarfon and Denbigh. Growth in Swansea was of a different kind, resulting from its increasing popularity as a resort and from its industrial growth. Indeed, by the end of the eighteenth century, industrialisation had already affected some parts dramatically. Merthyr Tydfil was one of the largest towns in Wales in 1801, with a population of over 7,700. This was the first stage in the process of urban development south of Brecon which was to work its way

down to Cardiff in such dramatic fashion during the nineteenth
century. The major towns were supplemented by smaller market
towns, with populations up to 1,000 or so – Pwllheli or Llandeilo,
for example.

As we shall see in Part II, town life after the industrial revolution
was often extremely unpleasant. It is not always appreciated that this
was a perpetuation, admittedly accentuated, of conditions in pre-
industrial towns. Towns were normally dirty, badly drained and full
of rubbish. There was no adequate water supply. On fair days and
market days, held normally two or three times a week, there could
be theft, violence and general disorder. Towns did hold some
attraction but they were not pleasant places in which to live in
pre-industrial Wales.

The middling ranks

Throughout the period there was a middle stratum in society and,
although during the sixteenth and seventeenth centuries there was
not a greatly significant class of commercial or professional people,
numbers grew in the eighteenth century. With expansion in towns
and trade there were more merchants – for instance wool merchants
established small factories in towns such as Dolgellau – and with the
growth of the iron industry a range of people involved in the
commercial life of Merthyr became an important political and social
force.

In the countryside there were subtle gradations beneath the ranks
of gentry to encompass yeomen farmers, with estates of perhaps a
minimum of fifty acres, and small farmers, with estates of perhaps
five to fifty acres. While the small farmer was constantly preoccupied
with earning a hard living from the soil, and played little part in
ordering the society around him, the yeoman farmer aspired to
holding some office, perhaps that of constable, and if fortunate,
climbing to gentry status. Yeomen, particularly from the seventeenth
century, were normally literate and provided a readership for an
expanding book market.

In countryside and in towns there was a variety of craftsmen,
workers in wood, metal and leather, weavers, thatchers and, later,
clockmakers. They often combined their craft with work on the land
and increasingly played an influential part in Welsh cultural life as

literate dissenters. The traditional trade in cattle-droving expanded and drovers founded banks in places closely involved in the trade such as Llandovery. Many of the drovers, despite their arduous existence, involving hard physical work in all weathers, found time to act as cultural links with London, bringing home tunes for Welsh ballad writers, for instance.

There were as many varieties of merchant as of craftsman. They varied from the important merchants dealing with their compeers in Bristol or London to the growing numbers of shopkeepers and small traders dealing in a range of commodities from books to candles and, increasingly in the eighteenth century, incurring the wrath of their fellows in the community as they were accused of exploitation.

There was also a range of professional people, increasingly evident by the eighteenth century. The vicar of the parish was of similar social class to the gentry, indeed often of gentry family, especially in those many instances where lay patronage gave the squire the right to nominate to a living. But there were many very poor livings in Wales and curates often lived in some poverty, as we shall see in chapter five. Dissenting ministers in the seventeenth and eighteenth centuries often came from the ranks of craftsmen.

Doctors were few – in the late seventeenth century there were only three in the diocese of St David's – though their numbers grew in the eighteenth century. Again there were usually links with the gentry, though medicine was still not a prestigious profession in the eighteenth century. Lawyers were far thicker on the ground since litigation over land and other kinds of property was such an important feature throughout the period. By the seventeenth century some of the gentry had legal agents in London, but Ludlow and the smaller towns of Wales were well served. Land transactions, wills and marriage settlements were always staple elements in the law practices centred in towns. In related areas land agents and surveyors were required increasingly for the survey of estates, and architects for designing new buildings. In the eighteenth century, as absenteeism on great estates became more common, estate stewards became important and acquired considerable authority. They acquired estates and gentry status themselves in some instances. Judges, lawyers and estate stewards, almost inevitably, were not popular in the community at large since they were normally the instruments whereby a process of justice and administration, ordered by the greatest in the community, biased towards the service of the greatest in the community, was administered.

The status and remuneration of teachers varied. Some, masters in grammar schools, were well paid, but there were few such schools in Wales and they were relatively poorly endowed. Generally, teaching was a low-status profession, though less so towards the second half of the eighteenth century. But Griffith Jones's circulating school masters were paid a pitiful £3 to £4 per annum. Even this was considerably more than the wage a labourer might earn.

The poor and the treatment of poverty

The bulk of the population consisted of the labouring classes and those without any means of support. One-third to one-half of the population in the sixteenth century lived at subsistence level, so that poverty, whether associated with very low wages, bad harvests, bad health, unemployment, physical or mental shortcomings or old age, was endemic. For labourers, with their wages officially held down by statute in Elizabeth's reign, and approximating to 6d per day, life was desperately hard. The physical conditions under which the labourers worked, and slept, were conducive to disease. In the late seventeenth century, many were literate enough to read Bibles and other devotional literature, yet very rarely could they aspire to anything other than a life of toil. With ill-health or old age they were forced to rely on the support of the community or poor relief; though with the support of the community so pronounced in Wales, organised parish relief was implemented generally only in the second half of the eighteenth century.

Disadvantage began at birth. Infant mortality was very high, although this was true also for gentry families. Expectation of life at the end of the seventeenth century was probably around the mid thirties, with disease most likely to strike the poorer classes, particularly those diseases associated with malnutrition – typhus, scrofula, tuberculosis, dysentery and even smallpox. The gentry could afford physicians, although their remedies could be worse than the illness, since bleeding the patient was one of the main treatments.

The tradition of the Middle Ages was that the relief of the poor and alms-giving were the concern of the family, the community, the

---

church and the monastery, with the wives of the gentry, particularly, expected to make their contribution, too. Monastic alms-giving had fallen off by the early sixteenth century and, of course, soon disappeared altogether. This was in part responsible for the increase in poverty and vagrancy during the sixteenth century but the main reason was the extreme inflation, combined with a rise in population. By Elizabeth's reign there was anxiety in the government. Begging had increased rapidly as pressure on land had increased. Agricultural labourers always lived on the edge of poverty but a series of bad harvests might reduce a farmer with a few acres to penury. Soldiers and sailors who had seen service in Ireland and had perhaps been wounded, added to these numbers. There were ablebodied poor who preferred to beg, and in Wales the authorities viewed with suspicion the minstrels who wandered around the countryside with their songs and dances. One enterprising entrepreneur in Elizabeth's reign was Robert ap John of Denbigh who organised legless and armless beggars into a team patrolling the county and collected a commission from them.

The conditions under which the poor existed were extremely harsh. Annual lists, compiled by petty constables of the parish and high constables of the hundred, recorded unemployed servants, labourers, vagabonds, and poor people supported by the parish. The impotent poor – orphans, handicapped, old – were supported to a degree by private charity. Vagrants, increasing in numbers through the inflationary sixteenth and early seventeenth centuries, were punished. They might be whipped, branded or sent to a house of correction in the nearest county town. The few poor given licences to beg by justices of the peace deemed themselves fortunate, and if such beggars were not always well treated the licence was normally respected. It might even be reinforced by some contact between justices, as when Sir Nicholas Arnold informed Sir Edward Stradling of St Donat's that some poor man had been given a 'placard for pity and charity's sake' to beg in Glamorgan and Gloucestershire. The attitude of authority was normally far more stern. Basic tenets were that a vagrant should be returned to the parish of birth where possible, that there should be a punishment of flogging and that no charitable relief should be given, though for humanitarian reasons parish constables did not always enforce the law and there was some charitable relief. *Ad hoc* relief was no answer and the problem was compounded because the poorest had little alternative other than to steal, even though the penalty was death. The incidence of theft therefore increased. The other result was that the government was forced to legislate in the great Poor Laws, culminating in that of 1601. Impotent poor were to be given charity provided by a poor rate and supplemented by voluntary contributions given in parish churches. The ablebodied poor were supposed to be given work organised by the parish authorities, with any refusal to work to be punished by flogging or imprisonment. Legislation on the statute book did not always mean its implementation. In Wales communities were expected to look after their own according to tradition. In the seventeenth century only Monmouthshire of all the Welsh counties, indeed a county whose administrative position at that time was ambiguous, levied a poor rate. Such rates were not levied in Anglesey and Caernarfonshire until the 1760s. Only in the 1730s were places provided where the poor could be put to work. Until then the Church continued in its focal position of collecting money and administering charitable bequests. There were many of these. William Evans, merchant tailor, native of Breconshire but living in London, gave £100 for the relief of poor clothiers in Brecon. Gabriel Goodman, Dean of Westminster, provided a hospital for the poor in Ruthin in 1590, to house ten men and two women. The native gentry, too, were expected to play an important part.

The lot of the poor changed little over the period. There was a dramatic increase in their numbers in the eighteenth century, an increase of about 20 per cent from 1750 to 1801. With increasing pressure on land, the small farmers' lot tended to be depressed to that of farm labourers. The condition of the latter as they hired their labour for six months or a year was entirely at the whim of the hirer who took them on at hiring fairs. If married, and lucky, labourers might aspire to a tied cottage, but these were few. Unmarried employees, men and women, lived in; the men usually in an outbuilding such as a barn or hay loft. Only towards the end of the eighteenth century did sizeable pockets of an industrial workforce develop, in the iron- and cloth-manufacturing industries.

Money remained a scarce commodity through the eighteenth century and only towards its end did the development of country banks stimulate the fuller development of a money economy. Wages and rents were still often paid in kind. Again, towards the end of the century the lot of paupers deteriorated as the conventional mechanisms of charity and poor relief broke down. Parishes had always been anxious to ensure that relief was only given to those born within their boundaries; such provisions were now more rigidly enforced – often cruelly. Inflationary pressures had continued, although not at the rate of the sixteenth century. In the eighteenth century, the steady price rise to 1750, increasing in the following decades, was generally matched by wages. From the 1750s to the 1790s butter and wheat doubled in price. Rents soared. By 1780 a pattern of greater poverty and a much higher poor rate had set in, with the poor subsisting on a diet of potatoes, porridge, goat milk and barley bread and attempting to supplement their income with casual labour in small tanneries or mining-works. But the diet of the poor had always been meagre in the extreme. At the end of the seventeenth century labourers in Montgomeryshire, for example, lived on cereals and bread, eating virtually no meat. In recent years of bad harvests mortality rates were high, not due to direct starvation but to the cumulative effects of malnutrition. Life expectation remained low, infant mortality high. Housing conditions for poor families had changed little over three centuries, with cottages in the poorest areas of makeshift timber frames supporting mud walls and roofs thatched with rushes. It seems likely that in the second half of the eighteenth century wages were so depressed that there was some supplementation from parishes on the Speenhamland model. It has been argued recently that the old Poor Law was reasonably effective until swamped by industrialisation. It provided a range of unemployment benefits, family allowances, provision of housing and outdoor relief. But however alleviated, and provision varied enormously from area to area, the lot of the very poor was utterly demoralising.

It is hardly surprising that crime was common, with many petty crimes arising out of sheer desperation. Crimes were dealt with by justices of the peace, by courts of quarter sessions and, with more serious crimes, by courts of great sessions. Most charges were for larceny, with cattle and horse-stealing also common. In the Brecon circuit in the eighteenth century 14 per cent of cases were for burglary and house-breaking, 6 per cent for murder. Most convicted murderers were labourers and most were hanged. Punishments were savage, particularly for crimes involving property. Stealing could be punished by death, though courts tended not to impose the ultimate penalty. Typical punishment for stealing was transportation, usually for periods of seven to fourteen years. Such crimes as stealing from church, forgery or riot could result in hanging but again pardons were granted extensively.

Language, culture and recreation

The distinction apparent in Wales between the lives of landowners and landless, particularly between the more prosperous landed gentry and others, is evident in cultural life too. At the upper reaches of society there was the time, money and often the inclination to nourish a rich cultural life, though again changes occurred between the sixteenth and eighteenth centuries. In the Tudor period, gentry patronage of the bards continued. Lewis Morgannwg visited the homes of many gentry in North and South Wales in the first half of the sixteenth century, including those of Sir Rhys ap Thomas, the Stradling family and branches of the Herbert family in Monmouthshire. He composed poems in honour of the Earls of Worcester and was Sir Edward Stradling's household bard. He was welcomed at the home of Sir William Griffith of Penrhyn and composed a fine poem in praise of Sir Richard Bulkeley of Beaumaris. Meurig Dafydd regarded himself as the household bard of the Lewis family of Y Fan in Caerphilly, and composed poems to many Glamorgan gentry families. Bards not only composed poems but copied manuscripts which they and their patrons collected, often to be placed in increasingly impressive gentry libraries. It is not easy to judge the quality of literary appreciation among the gentry, but they paid for the *cywyddau* which were composed for them and some of the higher clergy joined with them in judging bardic entries at literary meetings. Patronage of the bards continued in the seventeenth century but overall in the sixteenth century there had been a decline in bardism and in the scale of gentry patronage. This may have been partly due to the high rate of inflation in the Tudor period which must have meant increasing strains over the many years of apprenticeship which the bards had to serve. Further, the bards viewed the consequences of the printing press with apprehension and they were criticised by sixteenth-century reformers for looking to the classical poetry of the medieval period for inspiration rather than adapting their work to meet the religious challenges of the Reformation.

The prose tradition was more secure in the sixteenth century than the poetic. Gentry, bards and professional copyists collected manuscripts, and sometimes gentry scholarship and a vested interest in elaborate pedigrees produced important works, as with Sir Edward Stradling's manuscript, 'The Winning of Glamorgan', fabricated but fascinating. Stradling is an interesting example of the Renaissance gentleman in Wales. He was educated at Oxford, then travelled on the continent and visited Rome. He was in contact with scholars and historians at Elizabeth's court. He was an avid collector of manuscripts, particularly those of the dissolved monasteries, was fascinated by the history of his family and his native county. Thomas Williams of Trefriw called Stradling the chief patron of the Welsh language in the southern part of Wales. He paid for the publication of Dr Sion Dafydd Rhys's Welsh grammar in 1592, again betraying the concern of contemporary humanists that Welsh should develop into a fit vehicle for the transmission of renaissance ideas. This was one of a series of Welsh grammars published from Elizabeth's reign, the finest being that of an outstanding Welsh scholar of the early seventeenth century, Dr John Davies of Mallwyd, published in 1621. When Sir Edward Stradling died fifty copies of Rhys's grammar were bequeathed to Davies, and fifty more left to Stradling's heir to distribute to other gentry for preservation. Stradling's library at St Donat's contained a wide range of manuscripts and printed books to which many other scholars sought access. His own story of the conquest of Glamorgan was incorporated into Dr David Powell's *Historie of Cambria*, which was a defence of traditional views of Welsh history against the attempts of Polydore Vergil to cast doubt upon the validity of Geoffrey of Monmouth's *History of the Kings of Britain* which attributed to the ancient British such a remarkable history. Stradling wrote in English but a copy of his work was made in Welsh. Stradling's record, exceptional but not unique, was one of humanist preoccupations – interest in history and the Welsh language, fascination with family history, patronage of the bards. His concern, and that of many gentry scholars, with writing and purchasing books was highly significant. There had been vital developments in the late fifteenth and early sixteenth centuries. First, the centrally important invention of printing resulted in books being available to the gentry, though certainly not to the mass of the population. Second, Protestant leaders were extremely anxious to provide scriptural and other religious writings in Welsh. Third, Welsh humanists were equally anxious to make Welsh a language worthy of the new humanism and to this end produced grammars and dictionaries.

There is, therefore, no question of Sir Edward Stradling or Sir John Wynn of Gwydir, for example, abandoning the language and the cultural traditions of Wales. Indeed that culture was enriched by being brought into contact with wider European ideas, as well as being rooted, through talented, original antiquarianism, in the local community, so cementing community allegiances. Many gentry were widely read in philosophy, religion and geography, as well as being skilled students of manuscripts.

Such scholars as Richard Davies, Gruffydd Robert, Thomas Huet, William Morgan and Edmwnd Prys encountered a variety of humanistic ideas at the universities. One was that vernacular languages needed to be regularised, fostered and developed. Both English and Welsh were regarded as inferior vehicles for the trans-mission of the highest ideas, an inadequate substitute for Latin. But the religious changes of the Reformation demanded the availability of the Bible in the vernacular. English was regarded as adequate from about the middle of the sixteenth century and Salesbury and others would have endorsed the provision of English religious texts for the Welsh if they could have been understood. The religious needs of the Welsh were paramount, however, and demanded that Welsh would have to be employed for scholarly purposes, especially for the translation of the Bible. Welsh had certainly once been a language of learning and, although there were now problems to be overcome, both Salesbury and Gruffydd Robert felt that Welsh could even surpass other vernaculars. It was in this context that scholarly religious work in Welsh was so important – gospels and epistles in the Prayer Book, the New Testament, the Bible, various grammars and dictionaries.

The anglicising influences at work in Wales from the sixteenth century are, however, undeniable. The language clauses of the 1536 Act of Union did not mean that Welsh ceased forthwith to play any part in administration and justice. In a country where the great majority were monoglot Welsh, evidence, interrogations and depo-sitions had to be made in Welsh and interpreters were sometimes called on even in the major London courts. Still, the language in which records were kept was mainly English, partly Latin, never

Welsh. While Welsh was the normal spoken language of the people, even in Monmouthshire, written communication between the gentry was in English. The sixteenth-century gentry had not detached themselves from the roots of their society but their increased involvement in government did bring them closer into the orbit of Ludlow and London. From Elizabeth's reign there was an increasing tendency for Members of Parliament to stay in London for the season. The higher education of the gentry took place outside Wales, at Oxford, Cambridge or the Inns of Court. Increasingly in the sixteenth and seventeenth centuries Welsh gentry, particularly heiresses, married into English families. Marriage contracts had little to do with romance or compatibility, much to do with the size of estate and position in society, although in the eighteenth century the notion of romantic marriage became fashionable. So the anglicisation of the Welsh gentry slowly proceeded. They were a numerically small class – by the eighteenth century the numbers of the greater gentry were fewer still – but their role in society was crucial. In the century or so after the Civil War, changes in the social structure were reflected in changes in attitude to the Welsh language and its literature. As the ranks of the lesser gentry approximated more closely in income, lifestyle and resources to those of well-off yeomen after 1660, and a more closely knit group of wealthy gentry emerged, so this prosperous oligarchy dominated Welsh life more completely. They monopolised parliamentary representation, ran local government, and exercised complete economic control over their tenantry.

The eighteenth-century gentry were not the philistines they are sometimes depicted as being, although they probably spent more on gambling than on charity. They helped publish books and a few carried on a traditional patronage – William Bulkeley of Brynddu and William Vaughan of Corsygedol, for example. But even among gentry-scholars the concerns of the eighteenth century were very different from those of the sixteenth as they cultivated interests indistinguishable often, from those of their English counterparts. They collected paintings and books. Some used their libraries and acquired considerable reputations – Thomas Johnes of Hafod as a translator, Thomas Pennant as botanist and zoologist. Increasingly, the London and Bath seasons came to dominate the social round and from London they acquired notions of current taste. These standards, in literature, science, architecture, travel, furniture, dress (for men and women) were those of polite society outside Wales. It was not fashionable in the age of the Enlightenment to be parochial or to use the Welsh language. A cultural cleavage consolidated a social divide. This phenomenon of popular, oral cultural tradition being abandoned by the upper classes, and dialect being relegated to use by the lower strata of society was found in other parts of Europe, Scotland, Norway and Bohemia, in the seventeenth and eighteenth centuries. In Wales as, for example, in Hungary, an upper-class and lower-class language developed. In Wales the majority of the population continued to speak Welsh and, increasingly, to read it. This was particularly true in the eighteenth century as the circulating school movement spread over Wales and consolidated the hold already exercised by the Welsh Bible.

The outlook for the Welsh language itself seemed bleak in the eighteenth century as it had long since ceased to be the language of leaders of society. It had been saved in the sixteenth century because it had become the language of religion but attitudes in the Church to things Welsh were far less sympathetic two centuries later. That Welsh was the language of the circulating schools, based on the Bible, and of Methodism, allowed it to survive at popular level but its future as a literary language was far more problematic without the sympathy and patronage of either landed or clerical establishment.

Scholarly gentry interest in Welsh manuscripts and the Welsh past, evident in so many instances in the Tudor period, had evaporated by the eighteenth century and this left a dangerous void. The gentry still held manuscripts, though these were appreciated now for their commercial value rather than as a scholarly resource. Moreover, former historical traditions had proved impossible to maintain. The great prophetic themes of medieval Wales that forecast the advent of a liberator to avenge English defeats, a leader who would restore the island of Britain to its original and rightful inhabitants ousted from their land by Saxon treachery and English conquest, had been met to bardic satisfaction in the person of the part-Welsh Henry Tudor. With him the Welsh historical tradition merged with that of England, though, as we shall see in chapter five, parts of it relating to the early conversion of the Welsh to Christianity were skilfully used to fortify the Protestant church in Wales in Elizabeth's reign. With the decline in bardism, the anglicisation of the gentry and the increased supply of printed books, the outlook for a distinctively Welsh literary and historical tradition seemed distinctly bleak. By the eighteenth century not only were the gentry concerned to reflect the manners of polite English society but also ordinary Welsh people had lost many of their traditional folk customs as Dissent and Methodism eroded them; traditional music and dancing, for example, were frowned on.

In these seemingly unpropitious circumstances the picture was not, however, entirely gloomy. In the second half of the seventeenth century the printing presses produced more devotional literature associated with educational movements, as we shall see in chapter five. Over five hundred titles were published between 1660 and 1730. After 1695 it became possible to establish printing presses outside London, Oxford and Cambridge. The range of Welsh books diversified from presses in Shrewsbury, the vale of Teifi and Carmarthen.

Patronage of the bards, the days of the household bard, had disappeared, yet there was poetic achievement with the work of, for example, Edward Morris at the end of the seventeenth century, and Goronwy Owen and William Williams, Pantycelyn, in the eighteenth. The latter's hymns were lyrical creations of genius. Copying of manuscripts proceeded in the early eighteenth century among lesser gentry in north-east Wales and among professional copyists in Cardiganshire.

Certainly much of the prose of the period was produced for restricted religious purposes but was sometimes of the first rank, as with Charles Edwards's *Y Ffydd Ddi-ffuant* (1677) and Ellis Wynne's *Gweledigaethau y Bardd Cwsc* (1704). Pamphlets were produced throughout the seventeenth and eighteenth centuries, predominantly religious in the earlier period, giving way to political pamphleteering in the later eighteenth century.

A far more remarkable feature of the eighteenth century, attracting the evocative label of a Renaissance, was the emergence of first-rate scholars working outside Wales who rediscovered the language, literature and music of medieval Wales and, in so doing, were responsible for a literary and antiquarian revival of the utmost importance. They were caught up in a general eighteenth-century antiquarian interest which focussed on the Welsh language and the history of Wales, since legends of Welsh origins associated with the myth of the Trojan, Brutus, and Geoffrey of Monmouth's account still had influence. Indeed they were given fresh life in Theophilus Evans's *Drych y Prif Oesoedd*, published in 1716. The greatest of the late seventeenth- and early eighteenth-century Welsh scholars was Edward Lhuyd who became keeper of the Ashmolean museum in Oxford. His range of interests was amazing. His plan was to publish many Welsh manuscripts housed in gentry residences in Wales and this led to a study of Celtic philology. He edited Welsh texts, recorded archaeological remains and different dialects. Lewis Morris, one of three literary Anglesey brothers who set out to rediscover the work of the medieval bards, kept Lhuyd's plans alive and one of the Morris circle, Evan Evans, copied a range of manuscripts as well as producing important books on early Welsh poetry. Lhuyd's ideas were more extensively reflected in the work of Dr William Owen-Pughe – who produced an edited text of the poems of the great poet of medieval Wales, Dafydd ap Gwilym. Pughe also produced a dictionary and worked extensively on Welsh manuscripts. Pughe's contributions, like so much eighteenth-century cultural activity, emanated from London and was made possible by the patronage of London–Welsh businessmen. The London societies, particularly the Gwyneddigion, made possible the publication of medieval poetry and produced Pughe's edition of Dafydd ap Gwilym's poems.

The eighteenth century also saw the rediscovery of Welsh history, seemingly subsumed into dynastic British history with the advent of the Tudors. Again it was Edward Lhuyd who provided the Welsh with an independent and vital vision of their history. His fascination with antiquities and his literary work coalesced in his *Archaeologia Britannica*, published in 1707, to demonstrate the links between the Welsh language, Breton, Cornish and Celtic ancient Britain. Lhuyd and his followers therefore endowed Wales with a most impressive historical pedigree, so making Wales and its history objects of fascination. That fascination was encouraged later in the century by descriptions of Wales like those of Thomas Pennant's *Tours in Wales* published from 1778. Without obvious sources of patronage, without any formal educational structure, the outlook for the Welsh language and culture was transformed quite remarkably in the eighteenth century. It seemed at the beginning of that century that the Welsh language as a means of written, scholarly communication was of little consequence, that no independent historical tradition was sustainable. By the end of it the Welsh language, traditions and culture were the object of interest and scholarly study even if that scholarship was not always based on a firm foundation of fact.

Other areas of 'high culture' were affected by lack of patronage. The gentry, from the sixteenth century, had family portraits painted and this continued. The fashion for collecting old masters became more prevalent in the following century. Painting became a rather more popular occupation in the eighteenth century but, without patronage, few from Wales could afford to train in London. During the second half of the century Welsh landscapes, particularly the mountains, attracted artists and tourists because theories of landscape beauty stressed the appeal of mountainous regions. One Welsh artist, Richard Wilson, returned from an Italian visit in 1750 with an idealised view of landscape which he proceeded to impose on the many Welsh views he painted with such talent.

At a less elevated level the recreations of different classes of society echoed their social differences. Gambling was one of the few shared interests, although it took rather different forms. In the Tudor period gambling was outlawed for the lower ranks of society because of its association with ale-houses which were often centres of violence. Even so, it was endemic in private and in public, and the authorities could do little to prevent it. Gentry who owned herds of deer were able to hunt. Some kept their own hawks which had to be carefully protected from poachers. Tennis was another sport favoured by the upper classes. In the eighteenth century horse-racing developed a formal organisation and acquired enhanced popularity.

The sports of ordinary people were rather different. Football, without restrictions on numbers, could be fatal and George Owen's description of 'knappan' as played outdoors in Elizabethan Pembrokeshire is frightening. It was a contest between the young men of two parishes who, without limit on numbers, attempted to get a wooden ball soaked in tallow into a goal, though without any rules governing the means by which it reached that end. It was physically dangerous and sometimes landed participants in court on a charge of riot. Archery was a popular pastime made compulsory at one stage because of the training it provided in local defence.

Despite the growth of puritanism and Interregnum efforts to bring light to a 'dark corner of the land' such recreations were largely unaffected. Neither government commissioners nor itinerant preachers had eradicated knappan, wrestling, football, cockfighting, tennis, bowls, quoits and skittles. Dancing to pipers, fiddlers or harpists, and dancing round the maypole reappeared with the

Restoration. Much to the chagrin and genuine concern of Dissenters, and often equally puritanical Anglicans, many of these activities took place in the churchyard on Sundays, and fulminations against sabbath-breaking were a constant theme of late seventeenth- and early eighteenth-century sermons.

Equally offensive to the Puritan conscience was the prevalence of drunkenness, inevitable in a society where the water supply could not be trusted and taverns provided some warmth, comfort, company and, above all, relief from the constant round of work. There was always an ample supply of drink in fairs and markets, family-based revels, christenings and wakes.

Changes did take place in popular culture in Wales during the eighteenth century as Dissent and Methodism exercised a growing influence in moderating and even obliterating such activities as dancing to the music of piper and harpist. Yet a rich variety of popular traditions and recreations remained. Particularly popular in North Wales was the *anterliwt*, a verse play performed by itinerant players on an improvised stage of a wagon floor. Content varied from jokes to moralistic social comment but Methodist opinion was not impressed. However, these plays, often doggerel, rich in horseplay, did help fill a gap created by the demise of a bardic culture even if the fashion for them was short-lived in face of opposition. There was little enough relief from the round of work from dawn to dusk, six days a week. Harvesting saw corporate endeavour and corporate drinking and dancing when the task was complete. Other community occasions brought a welcome break. Wedding customs served a social purpose in that the traditional giving of gifts enabled a couple to start married life with some material possessions. Married couples thus incurred a debt which was repaid at the weddings of other couples. People from the neighbourhood were summoned to a wedding in ritual fashion by the bidder, a custom which survived into the twentieth century in a few districts.

If marital infidelity followed, the community imposed its own sanctions by means which spanned the centuries. An effigy of the offender was dressed, placed on a chair, mounted on a ladder and paraded round the streets. This custom of *ceffyl pren* was most evident in south-west Wales, though it occurred in many parts, and although it tended to die out in the nineteenth century, as the law superseded community action, it does have fascinating links, as we shall see in chapter nine, with the direct disciplinary action taken by followers of Rebecca and by the Scotch Cattle against those who undermined their extra-legal discipline. Such resemblances anchor both movements in the community of the old Wales rather than in the new Wales of the later nineteenth century. Funerals were social events growing out of solemn religious observance but turning into the revelry of the wake. The wedding bidder's function now changed as he requested members of the community to provide food, drink and gifts of money.

Gradually the influence of Methodism became more pervasive and popular customs, saints' day revelries, drinking bouts, wakes, dancing round the maypole were modified. Minstrelsy and dancing were anathema and puritan attitudes accelerated a change which was affecting Welsh music anyway, as old musical manuscripts became unintelligible and traditional instruments like harp, *pibgorn* and *crwth* were replaced by new kinds of instruments fashionable in England. The richer eighteenth-century gentry played spinnets, flutes and harpsichords rather than the harp. Rough sports came in for condemnation. Dissent and Methodism may not have been numerically strong in the late seventeenth and early eighteenth century but members were sufficiently influential in their communities to modify greatly patterns of popular culture.

Interest in things Welsh was increasingly inspired in the eighteenth century by London Welshmen, clergy, gentry, businessmen and artisans, since there was no urban centre in Wales of anything like similar significance. The Honourable and Loyal Society of Ancient Britons, founded in 1715, achieved virtually nothing for Wales, but the Cymmrodorion Society, started in 1751, was concerned with propagating a variety of ideas ranging from the practical, encouraging new methods of farming, or new ideas in manufacturing, to the cultural, although its importance lay more in the ideas it kept alive than its achievements. Later, the Gwyneddigion, the most democratic of the societies, sponsored the publication of Welsh manuscripts, participated in the political debate of the 1780s and 1790s and took over the revived Eisteddfod in 1789. These societies were significant too, in that they reflected the lack of cultural leadership from within Wales itself and the new social groupings influential in Wales. The Morris brothers, for example, were members of a middle class which, though small, was growing in significance.

By 1780 the nature of cultural activity had changed greatly from the concerns of the early Tudor period. The fecund concern with the Welsh past stemmed from very different motives from those which had impelled the Tudor gentry to construct the pedigrees of their families so diligently. The activities of the London societies indicated a different social order, a new leadership, as well as a remarkable revival of interest in things past.

3

LOCAL GOVERNMENT AND THE STATE

The problem of government

The accounts we have of conditions of law and order in fifteenth-century Wales are not happy ones. The views of two sixteenth-century authors have been particularly influential. Both Sir John Wynn of Gwydir, in his *History of the Gwydir Family*, and George Owen of Henllys, in his *Description of Pembrokeshire*, were concerned to depict Wales in the pre-Tudor period in the worst light. This served to point up the achievement of Tudor monarchs who, in the eyes of contemporary Welsh squires, had wrought a 'joyful metamorphosis', to use George Owen's words. Having made allowance for their bias, their evidence is of lawlessness, ambush, violence and corruption. Part of the problem lay in duality of administration. Since the settlement of 1284 the Principality of Wales had been shired and was directly under the king's control, administered by his officials. The rest of Wales was under the control of marcher lords whose authority derived from conquest and who had taken over the judicial rights of the independent princes whom they had ousted. The marcher lords were virtually independent of the king's control, therefore. There were economic and social pressures in the fourteenth and fifteenth centuries. Economic recovery in the fifteenth century, from the disruption of the Black Death and the Glyndŵr rising, took place in the context of pressures from new, thrusting landowning families. Owain Glyndŵr's revolt, in which a local dispute between two marcher lords culminated in Owain declaring himself Prince of Wales in defiance of Henry IV, could not succeed because of the resources at the disposal of his English enemy and, if the rising left a legacy of inspiration, it also left division and bitterness. The Wars of the Roses, too, produced divided loyalties and the feuds which resulted echoed a long tradition of physical violence in medieval Welsh society which had not been stamped out after the Edwardian conquest. Wales was remote from the centre of government and English government was generally weak in mid fifteenth century. Where the courts were used they were often abused as private vendettas were pursued there.

The bitterness of the Welsh against the English remained, particularly in the aftermath of the Glyndŵr rising. The Welsh paid the penalty for their resistance to the English crown, particularly in the punitive legislation of Henry IV which denied Welshmen any responsible public office, the right to convict any Englishman in Wales or the right to unauthorised assembly. Neither this legislation, nor previous practice, had resulted in Welshmen being excluded from office, though Englishmen held the highest offices and, in the boroughs particularly, this bred resentment. However, from the early days of English rule Welshmen had co-operated with the English king and increasingly in the fifteenth century had become responsible in practice for much of the government of Wales. In so doing they had maintained their leadership of the local community. Examples include the forbears of the Williams-Wynne family of Peniarth, the Glynnes of Glynllifon and the Griffiths of Penrhyn. At the same time the conjunction of a fluid land market, duality of administration, disruption and devastation in time of uprising and war and pressures towards building up individual holdings of land, all combined to throw Welsh government and administration into some confusion in the fifteenth century. In all this lay the potential for greater stability. The superficial disruption of the Wars of the Roses tended to camouflage a situation in which co-operation of the Welsh in government was increasing, individual estates were being built up and economic recovery was taking place. The administrative problem, nevertheless, remained considerable. In Principality and march either the king's writ was regularly flouted or it did not run. The reign of Henry VII did not see the birth of new institutions. It did see attempts to make old institutions work.

Henry VII depended on Welsh support. Crossing from France into Wales with a small force of only some 2,000 men, his first need was not to be repulsed, his second for positive Welsh support. The climate for his Welsh reception had been well prepared, particularly by the bards who had always occupied a prestigious role in Welsh society. From Anglo-Saxon times the Welsh had been conscious of the near enemy and the theme of the emergence of a Welsh leader to take vengeance on that enemy was well worn. Since the conquest of 1282, reinforced by Glyndŵr's defeat, the theme had been constantly reiterated and embroidered. The anti-English sentiment of the poets had grown increasingly strident after the Glyndŵr revolt and was accentuated with the outbreak of the Wars of the Roses. Towards the end of the fifteenth century Welsh poets endorsed Henry Tudor as contender for the throne. This reflected a blend of genuine Welsh sentiment for a man with some Welsh blood, combined with a powerful self-interest among many of Wales's nascent gentry families whom Henry had assured would profit if he were to become king. Jasper Tudor, Earl of Pembroke, Henry's powerful, capable uncle provided not only organising ability and sure advice but also successful propaganda, so a combination of appeal to national sentiment in Wales and a consciousness of kinship with the Tudors, especially in North Wales, fused with a perennial concern with self-interest to range many Welsh gentry on Henry's side. In the wake of the Wars of the Roses, in which Welsh *uchelwyr* had allied themselves to aristocratic factions on both sides and had become increasingly accustomed to the politics of power, such a combination was a potent one. Henry Tudor's own claims to Welsh loyalties were in fact rather more secure than his claims to the English throne. He was the scion of a gentry family of North Wales which could trace its ancestry back to the days of Llywelyn the Great. A familiar blend of judicious marriage and careful estate-building in the fifteenth century had restored family fortunes after the Tudors, related to Glyndŵr, had supported the rising.

Henry VII's policy

Henry Tudor's victory at Bosworth in 1485 was by no means assured, any more than was his unimpeded progress through Wales as he proceeded to Bosworth. He had already participated in an abortive venture in 1483 when the Duke of Buckingham's attempt to depose Richard III and replace him with Henry Tudor had failed. In the aftermath Richard III had tried to strengthen his position in Wales but some important Welshmen were involved in Henry's latest preparations. With the landing at Dale, Pembrokeshire, consolidated, Henry needed the active support of the most powerful Welshmen. It was forthcoming from Rhys ap Thomas of Dinefŵr. His army and Henry's pursued their separate routes to Welshpool where they combined. Recruiting on the way, they were then joined finally on the day of the battle of Bosworth, 22 August 1485, by the troops of the Stanleys of north-east Wales. Sir William Stanley had been granted the chancellorship of Cheshire by Richard III in an attempt to consolidate that part of his kingdom.

Henry VII's most substantial supporters received the most substantial rewards. Jasper Tudor, the architect of his nephew's success, became Duke of Beaufort, Justiciar of South Wales and Lord of Glamorgan. Henry's other chief supporter, Rhys ap Thomas, knighted in the wake of Bosworth, was heaped with offices – steward and constable of the lordship of Brecknock, chamberlain of Carmarthen and Cardigan, steward of the lordship of Builth. There was nothing new about Welshmen holding office in Wales, whatever the law might decree, but now trusted Welshmen were granted office on a wider scale. Where previously there had been an element of mistrust, even of Welsh office-holders, now they became integrated into the machinery of government and an alliance with considerable implications for the future was forged between crown and substantial gentry. The change in attitude to Welshmen extended to London where Welshmen were favoured at court and in business, and to Ludlow, home of the council in the marches.

The profit of individual Welshmen, however powerful, was hardly what the bards celebrated ecstatically. The refrain was that here at last was a Welsh saviour, cast in the mould of Glyndŵr, representing victory of the Welsh over the English and revenge for a catalogue of conquest. The Welsh were once more supreme in Britain. There is no doubt that without Welsh support Henry Tudor would not have become king and he acknowledged this with his promotion of the individual Welsh interests. But it was inconceivable that even were he so minded he would allow specifically Welsh interests to assume any priority. He was heir to civil war and turmoil. Whatever Welsh expectations, and whatever the state of Wales, Henry's priority was consolidation of his position in England. But the Welsh now owed an unprecedented allegiance to the king in London, stemming from some sentiment and much self-interest; the gentry of Wales were of the same mind as their king.

There was to be no plan for the reorganisation of Welsh government and administration. Henry's policy was piecemeal, but it evolved in a benevolent atmosphere. The Welsh no longer felt themselves to be a subject people. The gentry could now consolidate the gains of the fifteenth century, whether of land or office. In the protest poetry of the bards there had been a kind of national sentiment focussed by English conquest and exploitation. That focus of discontent did not now exist to anything like the same extent, certainly in terms of racial sentiment. The co-operation of the Welsh *uchelwyr*, apparent in some measure since the conquest, was now given full rein at local and sometimes national level. These families were well content.

It is logical, therefore, that we look for the benefits Henry VII's policies brought to individuals or groups rather than to some nascent national entity. Only with hindsight do we know that Bosworth was the last episode in the Wars of the Roses. His over-riding concern was to consolidate his hold on the throne. Wales posed no immediate problem in this respect since Henry's problems in Wales were longer-term administrative complications arising from the duality of government. His position here could hardly have been stronger. His supporters were rewarded and the participation of Welshmen in government accepted and encouraged. Existing institutions of government and justice were used to restore and keep order.

Henry VII was later to do more for Welshmen. His first contribution was to restore good order in the kingdom generally, but there were specific problems in Wales. The first, the existence of penal laws against the Welsh, enacted in the wake of Glyndŵr's revolt, symbolised conquest and antipathy in the boroughs between Welsh and English citizens. The second major problem was duality of control, stretching back to the Norman conquest. The marches, ruled over by independent Norman lords who had inherited the rights of their princely predecessors, presented a problem of law and order, although the level of lawlessness in the Principality – under the direct jurisdiction of the king – was also a cause of anxiety. In both areas there was a plethora of different officials, and a combination of Welsh and English law – the legal expression of different social systems. As a result of the Wars of the Roses, death and forfeiture, numerous marcher lordships had come into the hands of the king. Even so the existence of a marcher lord as powerful as the Duke of Buckingham, virtual ruler of territory in which the king's authority was minimal, was not to Henry VII's liking. Early in his reign Henry did little to tackle either problem. After 1504 there were some pragmatic, piecemeal policies. Already, in 1501 – and active before then – a council in the marches had been formally constituted under the king's eldest son, Arthur, an evocative name for the lineage-conscious Welsh. He was to head a council whose purpose was to administer the many marcher lordships which he had been granted. Arthur's death, within months, did not stop the council's work, taken over by the king's council and the commissioners in the marches. Here was an acknowledgement of the problem. In the long term there could be no solution while the marcher lords remained outside the authority of the king's justices. Henry's approach was more conservative. He acknowledged the privileges of the marcher lords but entered into indentures aimed at stopping them affording refuge to criminals, so making lawbreakers available to the king's justices to deal with and, to a very limited degree, extending crown control into the marches. The agreement with Buckingham enjoined him to ensure that stewards in the lordship were to execute laws impartially, that tenants of the lordship should not go to any other part of the country on pain of being treated as felons, that none of the duke's officers would harbour outlaws and that they should not impede any of the king's officers who searched for outlaws, that tenants within the lordship would combine with tenants of other lordships to respect the indenture and that all suspects would appear in court and stewards would arrest offenders causing disturbances, particularly in towns.

In the Principality, Henry VII dealt with some grievances, though in a limited way. Henry IV's penal legislation was by now irksome rather than effective. Welshmen held office and succeeded despite it. Even so, it did evoke protest and, interestingly, was not repealed. Individual Welshmen had long been exempt from penal laws. Now exemption was to be on a wider scale through a series of charters which consolidated rather than innovated. Welshmen had long been moving out of Wales or moving into towns and boroughs within Wales whatever the letter of the law. Between 1504 and 1508 a series of emancipatory charters was granted to the inhabitants of the lordships of Bromfield and Yale, Chirk, Denbigh, Ceri and Cydewain and Ruthin, and to the Principality of North Wales. The charters differed in detail but essentially they exempted the inhabitants – in effect landholders and property holders – from the Lancastrian penal code. This meant that they could now legally hold crown office and land in England or English boroughs in Wales. In two charters there were concessions to estate-building gentry, either by the legal replacement of gavelkind by primogeniture as the custom of inheritance, or by granting freedom to bondmen.

In such charters – and they might well have been extended had not the king died in 1509 – Henry VII's policy is clearly delineated, and coincides with his general approach to government. He was a pragmatist who was prepared, as with the council in the marches, to inaugurate. Generally he tried to make existing institutions work more effectively. He made no effort to abolish the marcher lordships but cautiously attempted some extension of crown authority in them. Henry VII showed no particular affection for, or loyalty towards, Wales *per se*, neither did any other Tudor monarch. It has been argued that those symbolic gestures of naming his eldest son Arthur and adopting the red dragon of Cadwaladr were not seen at court as having any Welsh or 'British' significance, though particularly in the former instance this understates the impact in Wales. Certainly Henry VII was far more concerned with practicalities, with rewards for loyalty, with charters which generally legalised an existing situation. Still, the Welsh gentry class on the verge of emerging as the most powerful political, economic and social force in Wales required the imprimatur of the Tudors on the legality of their position. Penal legislation, until removed, remained a potential threat.

For the future pattern of events in Wales the most vital element in Henry VII's policy was his forging of an alliance with the Welsh gentry whose most forceful members wanted equality with the English and every opportunity to build up and consolidate their estates, translating their economic pre-eminence into office-holding under the crown. They were eager to endorse the new regime since it offered them such opportunities. A fuller reward was to come in the next reign.

Henry VIII's policies before union

There was to be no new King Arthur, recalling, if only in name, the legends of British supremacy over the Saxons enshrined in *Historia Brittonum* and the *History of the Kings of Britain*. The accession of the second son, another Henry, was a more apt comment on the processes at work in Tudor Wales. Indeed the early part of Henry VIII's reign was a postscript to that of Henry VII. There were no new initiatives between 1509 and 1525, though another group of marcher lordships came into the king's hands when the most important of the lords, Buckingham, was executed in 1521. Then, in 1525, Sir Rhys ap Thomas, henchman of Henry VII, chamberlain of South Wales, died. His reward for decisive support of Henry VII had been the award of estates, office and influence. He was the most important individual in South Wales. The king denied his heir, Rhys ap Gruffydd, his grandfather's offices – with justification since Rhys ap Gruffydd lacked experience. The king and his advisers appointed Lord Ferrers of Chartley, a major Herefordshire landowner, to succeed to the chamberlainship of South Wales and lesser offices. The influence of Rhys ap Gruffydd's ambitious wife, together with Ferrers' arrogant attitude, produced an explosive situation. It may be that Ferrers was also harrying Rhys's tenants. Then, in June 1529, at a time of national difficulty with Henry VIII involved in the 'divorce' problem, the power struggle in South Wales erupted into violence in Carmarthen when retainers of the two sides disputed lodgings at the sitting of great sessions there. For a time Rhys was held in custody in Carmarthen castle. Later, one of Rhys's rivals was murdered – probably by one of Rhys's retainers. Certainly both Rhys ap Gruffydd and Ferrers were called to London to face charges and eventually, after a period in the Tower, Rhys ap Gruffydd was executed in 1531. His was not the only Tudor execution to take place on the flimsiest of evidence. It seems likely that his real crime was to be too closely associated with Cardinal Wolsey and to be opposed to the annulment of Henry VIII's marriage with Catherine of Aragon. Rhys was widely held to be innocent but the fact remained that the premier landed-family in south-west Wales had been toppled. There was anxiety over the situation in south-west Wales with the death of the head of the house of Dinefŵr, and reports of lawlessness reached the king's council from both Principality and marches before and after Rhys's death. The Welsh customs of *arddel* and *cymortha* were being used to protect criminals, and marcher independence fostered this. Problems arose in England over the annulment of the king's marriage and the Reformation Parliament was convened. Gentry and officials in Wales, with much to gain, called for attention to the situation there. With the advent of Thomas Cromwell there was an alertness to problems of inefficient administration and lack of good order.

Cromwell was concerned with the state of Wales and measures entirely in keeping with precedent were set in train. A meeting between king and marcher lords in 1534 considered reforms in the marches. Cromwell's appointment of Rowland Lee, former tutor to his son, and Bishop of Lichfield, was more significant, though in keeping with traditional government responses and with the demands of powerful Welsh gentry who wanted a strengthening of existing institutions. Lee certainly supplied a sense of purpose. Not the best example of a devout and scholarly cleric, he had no illusions about his role in Wales as president of the council in the marches: it was to make institutions of law and order and administration work. These institutions were more effective because Lee was rigorous and ruthless, often hated but also respected. Lee was aided by a series of Parliamentary statutes passed in 1534 and 1535. One dealt with the problem of the bribery and intimidation of juries, prevalent particularly when influential members of the community were involved. The act is less significant for what it achieved than for the principle of involving an outside body, the council in the marches, in exercising some jurisdiction in formerly independent marcher lordships. Another act attempted to stop lucrative cattle- and horse-stealing by ferry across the Severn into the Welsh marches by requiring ferrymen to enter into recognisances with justices of the peace in neighbouring English shires. Again the precedent of involving justices from neighbouring counties was significant. A more important measure, the Bill concerning councils in Wales, attempted to enforce the holding of regular courts and the presence of criminals to be tried at those courts, and to ensure that any official responsible for the wrongful imprisonment of offenders should be brought before the king's commissioners or the council in the marches. The act also tried to forbid the carrying of weapons within two miles of courts and the abuse of the traditional customs of *arddel* and *cymortha*. Again whittling away the independence of the marcher lordships, the act empowered justices of neighbouring counties to marcher lordships to impose a whole range of penalties within them. This even applied, within a two-year time-limit, to criminals who had already been indicted in a marcher court. Any officer of the council in the marches might enter a marcher lordship in pursuit of lawbreakers.

These acts, and others, brought the formerly independent marcher lordships more and more into the orbit of justices of the peace of neighbouring shires. Devised as *ad hoc* responses to Lee's problems in Wales, the cumulative effect was a substantial modification of the independence of lordships. The shape of developments became firmer with the enactment of a statute providing for the eventual appointment in all the existing Welsh counties, as well as the palatine lordships of Pembroke and Glamorgan, of justices of the peace. Thus, over the whole of the Principality, the basic element in the English system of local administration was inaugurated.

The Acts of Union

Tudor policy to this stage had been firmly rooted in the political structure of the past. Henry VII's policy, and that of the early years of Henry VIII, had been to strengthen existing institutions while providing more efficient machinery, by statute, to make it work. There had been no miracle solution, lawlessness and violence were still endemic, but in pursuit of more efficient administration, increasingly substantial breaches of marcher independence ensued. This was possible because of the king's position as the major marcher lord; but it rested too on the economic and social changes of the fifteenth century which had fostered a gentry class with a vested interest in good government and restless to be responsible for its implementation, as were their peers in England. It was such developments which made possible the root and branch measures of 1536–43 also.

Those acts of Parliament relating to Wales passed between 1536 and 1543, the Acts of Union, have produced a classic controversy of Welsh history. In any nationalist perspective the integration of a smaller, less populous country with a richer neighbour, in accordance with the latter's political and administrative system, is bound to prove contentious however acceptable it might have been at the time. Among historians there has been controversy between those who have argued that Henry VIII's ultimate plan for union was visible in the legislation of 1534–5, which was an essential preliminary in restoring law and order, and those who have seen Henry VIII's policies in Wales as wholly opportunist. More recently, carrying conviction, some historians have seen union legislation as part of Thomas Cromwell's Tudor revolution in government, part of the process whereby England embarked on its modern history as a nation state, deriving strength from unity. This thesis, fathered in

G. R. Elton's assessment of Cromwell's enormous administrative talents, has been endorsed in the Welsh context in Ogwen Williams's essay, *Tudor Gwynedd* (1958).

Whatever Cromwell's role – probably it was crucial – both continuity and change were evident in union legislation. The integration of the Welsh and English economic and administrative systems had proceeded inexorably since the Norman conquest. The conquest of 1282, office-holding under the English crown, and economic changes continued to draw England and Wales into closer relationship, at least at *uchelwr* level. At that gentry level the Welsh welcomed union; the only ones – apart from Rowland Lee – who did not were stewards of the marcher lordships. who had a vested interest in the old regime.

The shiring of Wales had begun in 1284. A plan to extend this English system of government and administration to the whole of Wales was considered briefly by Henry VIII in 1531 only to be shelved in favour of an older policy of repression. It was taken up once more by Thomas Cromwell in 1536. It has been argued that his motives were to produce the administrative uniformity necessary to implement Reformation legislation and the dissolution of the monasteries in Wales, though Reformation legislation had already been passed and evoked no protest in Wales. Certainly Cromwell's approach was tentative. Indeed, the coupling of the acts of 1536 and 1543 has imposed an artificiality on interpretation which has identified a planned approach – an outline of action in 1536 consolidated by the detail of 1543. This is far too simplistic. It may be that Henry VIII until 1539 had intended governing Wales by proclamation but in that year the proclamation bill failed to become law – hence the administrative detail of the 1543 act. By that time, with pressure from Wales, some action had to be taken, but there was no inexorable homing in on the 1543 pattern. Among the options considered was the replacement of the council in the marches by a court of Chancery. More radical, and more interesting in retrospect, was the possibility that Wales might have become a separate principality ruled over by Prince Edward, with Henry VIII as suzerain.

Union legislation was to prove of the utmost significance to Wales, a scarcely planned revolution establishing a pattern which was to be maintained at least until the industrial revolution. The gentry had wanted the role in government occupied by their English compeers and this they were granted. Here was no strike at Welshness as it was understood by contemporaries. No protests emanated from the bards, certainly none from the gentry. Thomas Cromwell had no policy for upholding or destroying the Welsh language; indeed it was legislation from a later government in Elizabeth's reign which ensured the survival of the Welsh language through the translation of the Bible.

The act of 1536 united and annexed Wales with England, with the result that now all Welshmen enjoyed citizenship of the realm on the same terms as Englishmen. No longer did Lancastrian penal legislation hold any residual threat for the Welsh. English land law was substituted for Welsh – *cyfran*, or partible inheritance of land, was replaced by primogeniture, thus extending a provision of some of Henry VII's charters and confirming much of the estate-building which had already taken place. Far from inaugurating an alien system of landownership this provision legalised, to the benefit of the gentry, a situation already in existence. If, over much of Wales, primogeniture was nothing new, gavelkind did not die out overnight either, particularly among smaller freeholders.

Unity between England and Wales involved the abolition of the marcher lordships. These independent areas, dating from the Norman conquest of Wales, had long been a source of anxiety to the monarch and their abolition was a more radical extension of attempts to solve the problem. The whole of Wales was now shired, with the county the major administrative unit as in England. The former march lands now formed new counties or augmented old ones – a solution to the problem of administrative duality facilitated because so many lordships were in the hands of the crown. The counties of Brecon, Radnor, Montgomery, Denbigh and Monmouth were created. The consequence of the additional shiring of Wales was that the infra-structure of government had to be provided. For example exchequers were set up in Brecon and in Denbigh to complement those already in existence in Carmarthen and Caernarfon.

Unity of language of government was provided for in the 1536 act. The various courts of justice were to be conducted in English and persons were not to hold office unless they used the English language. Here, then, is the most contentious of the clauses of union legislation, a fact which might have surprised contemporaries since the object was to provide for uniformity of administration, not to extinguish the language, even among office-holders. Again there was continuity. Those Welsh *uchelwyr* who had long participated in English government of Wales had always needed to be familiar with English. That is not to say, of course, that the language clause was other than a major blow to Welsh.

Consolidation of local power, and participation in national affairs, was granted to the gentry by the clause which conferred parliamentary representation on Wales. Welsh members had been called to Parliament in the reign of Edward III, but now, for the first time, there was systematic representation. The immediate impact was limited but by Elizabeth's reign Welsh members had begun to play a useful part in Commons' affairs.

A clause in the 1536 act allowed the king to revoke it in part or wholly within three years. The act was not immediately implemented; indeed an act of 1539 extended the period in which the king might modify the original. In the meantime marcher government proceeded much as before. There followed two minor acts, in 1540 and 1541. By the latter, justices were appointed to those four judicial circuits in Wales which were to be established in the act of Parliament of 1543 as the courts of great sessions, with each circuit administering three Welsh counties, and each court to be held for six days biennially. Such arrangements rested on the division of Wales into twelve shires, together with Monmouthshire which was outside the great sessions organisation. The previous shiring of Wales, with minor modifications, was endorsed by the 1543 act. The judicial arrangement was not unprecedented. The north-west shires were under the jurisdiction of the justice of North Wales as before; in south-west Wales the county of Pembroke was added to the counties of Cardigan and Carmarthen under the justice of South Wales; Glamorgan, Brecon and Radnor formed a new circuit, while the three north-eastern counties came under the jurisdiction of the justice of Chester. Another administrative and judicial tier in the system, the council in the marches, was established on a statutory basis. Previously existing at the whim of the monarch, there had been periods of considerable activity in its history but it had lacked coherence and purpose. Now it was to become an integral element in the government of Wales.

The series of acts which created and endorsed the shiring of Wales also provided for the substructure of county administration through local officials. The offices of sheriff and justice of the peace, in particular, were essential to county government. Not more than eight justices were to be appointed in each county – a number soon exceeded – and the normal property qualification, that of holding land worth £20 per annum, was waived in Wales, doubtless due to the poverty of the Welsh gentry in some counties.

If the Acts of Union are seen in the perspective of the inauguration of unity rather than the imposition of union, and in the light of considerable continuity rather than sharp departure from existing practice, centrality to the history of Wales is rather less than is usually assumed. There is logic to the inexorable encroachment of the king's authority over his unruly western neighbours, first through the independent marcher lords, next by union through conquest at the end of the thirteenth century, through to a basically common system of government and administration by Parliament, council and county. None of this was inevitable, but given the military resources of the English crown it was likely.

What resulted from union? For the gentry there were benefits commensurate with the demands some of them made for union and the loyalty they showed the Tudors. The rationalisation of land-tenure legislation added legal sanction to those estates already built up, and encouraged their extension and consolidation. Gradually, closer involvement with English ports, contact with English markets and infusions of English capital meant marginally greater economic activity. However, these developments must be viewed against much more potent economic influences such as the dissolution of the monasteries which brought much land on the market, the generally fluid land market of the sixteenth century and the high rate of inflation. Far more significant was the wide-ranging role of the gentry in government and administration; and, while the Acts of Union brought much uniformity in government, they confirmed considerable differences in the manner of its execution because Welsh society remained very different from English. There were few aristocratic families. Indeed, it was precisely the decline in aristocratic power in the marcher lordships which made union possible. There was a numerous native gentry class whose ranks had been augmented by *advenae* families, particularly those of Norman origin. Such families had long served English kings in a variety of offices – constables of castles, sheriffs. Now they were to fill the offices of

Member of Parliament, deputy lieutenant, justice of the peace. They became unrivalled leaders of society and governors of their counties. Once the prerogative courts had disappeared, and certainly by the eighteenth century, they were the virtual governors of their country, too, untrammelled by major interference from London. In the three centuries following union there were changes. By the eighteenth century membership of parliament tended to be the preserve of a small elite of county families, whereas in the early days of parliamentary representation the net was spread rather more widely; this reflected a social and economic change whereby some estates in Wales had become very large by the eighteenth century. But if gradations within the gentry class were more pronounced, their basic role in government and administration remained much the same – and in the same offices – as it had been since the 1540s.

For the landowning class in Wales union brought benefits. There was unity of administration with England, and this eventually resulted in a more ordered and orderly society. The English system of government was to be administered in Wales by Welshmen. Parliamentary representation provided citizenship for the minority electorate.

What was the cost? The gentry in Wales had not lived in cultural isolation from England over the centuries; Owain Glyndŵr was only the most notable example of Welsh *uchelwyr* who had been educated at the Inns of Court in London or at the houses of English noblemen. They had co-operated with English kings and English officials in the Welsh boroughs. But they were not the custodians of culture in the medieval period. The educated classes were the clerics, in church, monastery and, later, university; and their education had much in common with that in Europe generally, and was in Latin. Welsh poetry and prose were written in the service of the Church or under clerical influence, as well as by the bards who stressed the theme of Welsh independence from the Saxons and English. Even so, in the fifteenth century, an ancestor of Sir John Wynn's was sent to England to learn English and Latin – a forerunner of the laymen who inundated universities and Inns of Court in the sixteenth century. Long before union there were hints of social and cultural change and union has to be seen in the context of movements towards lay education and Renaissance influences which would have made considerable impact. English became the official language of government, but Welsh remained the language of the people and, crucially, as a result of Tudor government action, the language of religion. The gentry needed the English language whether in administration or at the universities. There, and elsewhere, they were brought increasingly into contact with English gentry with whom they wished to establish an affinity in language, manners and education which helped distinguish them as a class. The Welsh gentry, however, saw nothing incompatible in increasing exposure to English and the preservation of what was distinctively Welsh. They continued their support for the bards, they sponsored Welsh books, collected manuscripts and it was one of their number, William Salesbury, who translated the New Testament into Welsh.

Councils and courts

Contemporary accounts would seem to indicate a fifteenth-century Wales which was lawless and violent. Marcher government, enduring traditions of an older society such as the blood feud or the corruption of such practices as *arddel* or *cymortha*, in the general context of a society far more tolerant of physical violence, made for lawlessness. The legislation passed to help Rowland Lee points to the prevalence of cattle-stealing and riotous assembly. Well into the sixteenth century those responsible for the administration of justice, Judge David Lewis, for example, point to the excessive number of unlicensed alehouses and the prevalence of gambling in them, the cause of quarrels and disorder. Immediately we are confronted with a problem of interpretation, for Lewis's strictures emerge long after the Act of Union. Other sixteenth-century writers, Sir John Wynn or George Owen, stress the good order brought to Wales by the Tudors, particularly after Union. Yet the evidence of the courts of justice, from the greatest, the court of Star Chamber, to the least, indicates that problems of government were far from solved as a result of Tudor policy. Union did not inaugurate peace and tranquillity in Wales. However, the firm rule of the Tudors, the relative success of some of those organs of government rationalised by the Acts of Union, together with the interest of the gentry in a rather more ordered society, did result in a greater degree of stability in which there was machinery, not always effective, for even the most powerful to be brought to book. This stability did not come about because of some miraculous Tudor subjugation of over-mighty subjects. The aristocracy remained the major power in the land. Their retainers, and those of the more important gentry, did not disappear, as constant clashes between rival factions in Tudor reigns demonstrates. The aristocracy were linked with gentry by a network of clientage which provided the former with their power base in the counties. The gentry were linked with the aristocracy and with each other by alliances, blood and marriage ties which complicated faction even further. The politics of the sixteenth and seventeenth centuries, particularly, was that constant jockeying for power in court and in the country which resulted in numerous disputes, often involving riot and violence as well as other time-honoured techniques such as corruption of juries, suppression of evidence and the general pursuance of private gain, legally or illegally. This was no peculiarly Welsh phenomenon. The political and social system generally, from court to country, was dominated by aristocratic and gentry faction and, while there was a greater abnegation of force, there was no transformation of English or Welsh obedience to the law under the Tudors. There was, however, an improvement in the speed and expertise of the judicial process, particularly in the more mundane cases which came to great sessions or petty sessions, though even here the strictures of Judge David Lewis and others must be borne in mind.

The machinery for good government and administration existed after the Act of Union. Over England and Wales the day-to-day administration of government was carried out by the monarch's secretaries of state and by the Privy Council. This council affected the Welsh counties because it made numerous demands on office-holders and acted as a final sanction when disputes or illegal practices were so out of control that they presented a threat to the good order of the state. The Privy Council ensured that the laws of the realm were administered in the counties and that the country's defences were adequate. If a matter of sufficient importance merited investigation in the counties the Privy Council's orders, carried by one of the forty or so messengers at its disposal, would be taken to county officials who carried out detailed investigations and made their report. In a sufficiently serious situation the Privy Council could summon peremptorily even the most important individual to London. It could also act through the council in the marches of Wales while that council existed. The Privy Council's main preoccupations were

with attempting to control the worst manifestations of faction, so
that rivalries between families did not interfere too drastically with
the maintenance of good government; with trying to ensure that the
numerous unpaid duties of local officials were attended to and
reported on; with attempting to control piracy and with trying to
ensure that men and armour were adequate for the country's
defence. The vulnerability of Wales to invasion by way of the western
ports, north and south, or infiltration by Catholic seminarists in
Elizabeth's reign, were matters of constant concern.

More Welshmen were drawn into the orbit of the London courts
in the immediate post-union decades. Those courts may be divided
into the equity and prerogative courts of Star Chamber, Chancery,
Exchequer and Requests; and the ancient common law courts of
King's Bench and Common Pleas. A vital distinction was that the
former could judge cases on grounds of equity, and thus establish
precedents, while the latter group could judge only on precedent.
There was an important difference, too, between the administration
of justice in England and Wales. The Act of Union had established
a distinctive judicial system. Twelve of the Welsh counties (Monmouthshire was excluded) were grouped into four circuits. The
justice of each circuit was to hold courts of great sessions in each
county twice every year. These courts fulfilled the function of the
English courts of King's Bench and Common Pleas and they remained
until the nineteenth century. Officials and lawyers of the common
law courts at Westminster resented this aspect of Welsh autonomy,
particularly as great sessions seem to have acquired an all-important
equity jurisdiction early on in their history. Welsh cases were still
heard at the equity and prerogative courts at Westminster. These
exercised jurisdiction over a wide range of cases, from murder and
other crimes of violence to settlement of title to land and financial
matters. Local officials in Wales often took evidence – particularly
for the court of Star Chamber – and many important Welsh cases
were heard there. The court of Star Chamber – basically the Privy
Council sitting as a court – had the virtues of strength and speed and
was able to mete out justice against powerful transgressors, including
those local officials who had broken the law which ostensibly they
were responsible for upholding. The court of Chancery administered
civil law, could cope with cases raising new legal issues and was
generally more flexible in its procedures though, by the late sixteenth

century, was hampered by the increasing demands made on it both as a court of law and an administrative body. The court of Requests was equally popular and both courts dealt with a variety of cases – land disputes, disputes over rents, legacies, loans, tithes, refusal to pass on deeds, marriage settlements. Originally the court of Exchequer dealt with cases concerning royal revenues but, by Elizabeth's reign, was giving judgments between individuals. It dealt with cases of debt owing to the monarch, recovery of lands, goods or other profits owing to the crown and it heard a large number of cases from Wales – 104 from Denbighshire, for example, was the highest number from a Welsh county in Elizabeth's reign. This is significant in view of the facilities available nearer at hand in the council in the marches and the court of great sessions. It seems that litigants used the London courts to avoid the possibility of packed juries and other local influence which might be wielded by their opponents.

One area in England and the whole of Wales warranted councils of their own – the council of the north in England and the council in the marches in Wales. After being accorded statutory recognition in the Act of Union the council in the marches developed rapidly both as a court of law and as an administrative body. As a court it had jurisdiction over the counties of Wales together with Herefordshire, Gloucestershire, Worcestershire, Shropshire and, until 1569, Cheshire. It could try cases of murder and treason, though its time was normally taken up with lesser civil and criminal cases. Its administrative concerns were extensive – the supervision of local officials, the preservation of law and order, defence of the realm, supervision of military affairs, storage and condition of armour, control of recusancy. The concerns of the Privy Council were similar, and the relationship between the two was complex, but generally the Privy Council acted through the council in the marches while it was in existence. Welshmen were thinly represented on the council in the marches and were inevitably drawn from the ranks of major gentry such as Richard Price of Gogerddan, Sir William Herbert of Swansea, Sir Thomas Mansel of Margam, Sir John Perrot of Haverfordwest and Sir Richard Trevor of Denbighshire.

The council's influence was considerable, though fluctuating. It selected local officials from among the gentry, though its influence here could be counteracted by an Earl of Leicester or an Earl of Essex, capable of ensuring the appointment of henchmen. The high point in the council's history came during Elizabeth's reign, particularly during the presidency of Sir Henry Sidney, but it was never an unqualified success. Its orders were sometimes defied for weeks, even months, on end. There were constant problems in dealing with piracy and recusancy, particularly. The council found difficulty in ensuring that those reports from local gentry officials relating to the storage and condition of armour, for example, were produced promptly and in adequate detail. Only records relating to the administrative functions of the council in the marches survive but they reveal that its role in the administration and judicial procedures was wide-ranging, particularly in the sixteenth century. Its headquarters at Ludlow attracted Welshmen, imitating on a lesser scale the role of the Elizabethan court as a centre for patronage. Lawyers, particularly, thrived there. Yet even at its most powerful, it was criticised for its inability to carry out adequately the orders of the Privy Council, for its extension of power over local courts, for the corruption of its members, for the pettiness of many of the cases brought. In the seventeenth century the council disappeared, partly due to the attacks of lawyers of the Westminster courts and gentry from the border counties, partly from inherent defects. A major impediment was regular absenteeism, accentuated in the early seventeenth century, on the part of the Lord President and some of his chief officers. When the increase in civil rather than criminal cases became evident in the 1630s a further grievance was added and the demise of the council in 1641 was not unpopular.

The courts of great sessions were held every six months in each county by a justice of assize responsible for a circuit of three counties. Twelve counties were therefore involved, Monmouthshire being exempt from the arrangement. Accompanying the justice in circuit was a protonotary responsible for organising and recording the procedures of the court. The courts dealt with a wide range of cases, including murder, robbery, theft, extortion and corruption of juries. The fullest contemporary verdict on the courts, that of George Owen, commends them for the breadth of their jurisdiction and the skill of their justices.

As with the Privy Council and the council in the marches local officials played an important part in great sessions, so once more we are reminded of the volume of unpaid administrative work contributed by justices of the peace to the judicial process. After a crime had been committed and the suspect arrested, a justice would spend up to two days questioning him and witnesses to the crime. The justice of the peace then ensured that the prisoner was present at sessions and that prosecutors and witnesses were available at the appropriate time. Great sessions remained a reasonably efficient and accessible element in the system of justice until their demise in the nineteenth century.

Next in the judicial hierarchy came the courts of quarter sessions. They were held by a justice of the peace and heard a variety of cases – trespass, riot, unlawful assembly, and had an administrative function in, for example, licensing alehouses and controlling servants' wages. County courts were held every month by the sheriff and tried cases of, for instance, debt or illegal possession of goods up to the value of forty shillings. Twice every month were held the hundred courts which dealt with similar small cases.

Local officers

Administration of the local government system was in the hands of borough and county officials. The pattern of borough government was determined by the charter granted by king or lord. The chief citizen was elected every year – the mayor or, as in Laugharne, the portreeve, would act as deputy lieutenant within the borough, as well as being coroner and a justice of the peace. He was aided by officials such as the recorder, town clerk and bailiffs and also by the constables who kept law and order. There was a whole range of town laws which governed, particularly, the trading life of the community, so that abuses concerning the weight of goods, for example, were theoretically checked. Other by-laws covered hygiene, a particular concern in the absence of adequate drainage. Boroughs enjoyed considerable independence, having their own courts, gaol and system of fines. They derived income from fines, from licences issued to traders, rents and tolls, but the state took its share through the payment of fee-farm to the exchequer and the corporation was responsible for the upkeep of public buildings.

The resemblances between county government in Wales and in England were marked but there were important differences. At the apex of county government in England was the lord lieutenant, with wide powers and high social rank. The office had been created in the wake of the Reformation to provide a military safeguard against possible rebellion. There was an appointment for each county, though not necessarily a regular one until Elizabeth's reign. In Wales there was only one lord lieutenancy, an office vested in the president of the council in the marches. The counties were served by deputy lieutenants, nominated in every county from 1586 on. These appointments were held by heads of prominent gentry families and the duties could be onerous. They were mainly military – and Wales was always regarded as vulnerable to invasion whether through Holyhead in the north or the coast near Milford in the south. Deputy lieutenants of the coastal counties bore a particular responsibility for ensuring that the county militia was adequate in numbers, training and weapons, military duties which had been taken over from special commissioners. In the later sixteenth and early seventeenth centuries another vital duty of deputy lieutenants was the control of recusants, a difficult task at some stages of Elizabeth's reign, especially when seminary-trained priests were particularly active. Still, the office of deputy lieutenant carried with it considerable prestige and such families as the Wynns of Gwydir, the Herbert branches in Glamorgan or the Trevors in Denbighshire coveted that status and distinction.

As the influence of the deputy lieutenant increased, so that of the sheriff, previously chief official in the county, lessened. The sheriff lost the responsibility of mustering men to the deputy lieutenant but was still vital to county government and judicial processes. He provided juries, levied fines and carried out sentences passed at the courts of great sessions and quarter sessions. He played a crucial role in the process of returning Members of Parliament after 1543. He convened the county court where elections were held, and declared and returned the result. He held monthly and fortnightly courts. There is no evidence that the Welsh gentry avoided the office despite the expense involved. Once more, the prestige and power were coveted and, in some instances, its holders more than compensated for their expenses by corrupt practices, including bribery and sale of offices.

The linchpin of county government was the justice of the peace. His was an ancient office, but introduced into Wales only in the 1530s. Given statutory recognition over the whole of Wales in the 1536 Act of Union, the number of justices was limited to eight in each county but this number was soon exceeded – in 1581, for example, the average number for each Welsh county was thirteen. That the maximum proved inadequate was not only because of the volume of unpaid work required. Prestige and influence accrued and appointments were part of faction struggles. Justices were appointed by the Lord Chancellor on the advice of the president and council in the marches and existing justices; but the approval of members of the council was not always sought and pressure for the appointment to office of their supporters came from those with the most influence in Wales.

The volume of work expected of the justice of the peace, who was helped only by high constables and constables, grew apace in the years following union. There was a stream of orders from the Privy Council and the council in the marches. In Elizabeth's reign there were 306 statutes which had to be made effective by justices. A single justice could gaol suspects, issue warrants to sheriffs or bailiffs to arrest offenders, examine suspects concerning theft, excessive drinking or illegal hunting. In pairs they could deal with riots, subsidy evasions and bail for prisoners. They bore a prime responsibility for holding the important courts of quarter sessions. The extent to which the state relied on such unpaid officials for the administration of justice was the outstanding feature of local government from the sixteenth to the nineteenth centuries. Below the gentry, freeholders served as high constables of hundreds and had the unpopular task of collecting county rates and apprehending criminals. Ranked below them, and involving small farmers or tradesmen, were the petty constables of parish or township who acted as policemen and tax collectors. All were unpaid.

Within limits the system of local government inaugurated by the Act of Union was successful. Its major features lasted until the scale of social change wrought by the industrial revolution rendered it wholly inadequate. In the sixteenth century the liaison between central and local government was also successful. The Welsh gentry were eager to govern their localities, to endorse the system which enabled them to translate their economic status into local adminis- trative and judicial power. When the resulting responsibilities brought divided loyalties they tended to prevaricate, but not to opt out of the system. In matters of religion, for example, those local officials with Roman Catholic susceptibilities did not allow this to bar them from accepting office, even if, as a result, they were responsible for upholding the law against recusants. The gentry were not exercised by the language issue. As we have seen, involvement in government was only one of many anglicising influences affecting their class.

The Act of Union had brought into existence a uniform hierarchy of judicial and administrative organs very different from the duality of marcher lordship and Principality. The existence of an organised system, with checks and balances did not mean a sudden transformation from lawlessness to good order. There was certainly improvement, but old habits of corruption, use of retainers, employment of force in the abuse of power and position continued. The court of Star Chamber, to take just one example, provides ample evidence of misdeeds, chicanery, abuse of official authority and criminal actions culminating, sometimes, in murder. There was laxity in enforcement of the law. As to the administrative machine, the records of the Privy Council and the council in the marches provide ample evidence of official anxiety over such a basic matter as defence. The authority of the council in the marches was sometimes flouted for long periods. The biggest defect in the system was that so often law-enforcers were law-breakers, and that, even when brought to book in the highest courts, they were either not dismissed or were soon reinstated in their offices. When Sir John Wynn of Gwydir was fined 1,000 marks for using violent methods against tenants, he had sufficient influence to ensure that the fine was reduced to £200 and he remained a justice of the peace, deputy lieutenant of Caernarfonshire and a member of the council in the marches. The council in the marches and, to some extent even the London courts, found men of Wynn's standing difficult to deal with. Yet the system worked, if imperfectly, because the gentry, from a combination of self-interest and civic consciousness made it work, despite their being untrained and unpaid. Bullying, exploitation, violence and bribery continued. The politics of faction were often contested outside the law, but the. Tudors consolidated the allegiance of the gentry class in Wales through the Act of Union. The extent of their co-operation is indicated by the range of duties which were actually performed – the troops trained, the criminals brought to trial, the piracy investigated, the recusants searched out, the county armour stored. To that extent the interests of crown and gentry coalesced.

The seventeenth and eighteenth centuries

The permanence of the system testifies to its success. Even during the Civil War in the 1640s local government in Wales did not break down. In some English counties division between royalist and parliamentarian resulted in local government falling into disarray. After war broke out in 1642–3 lawlessness increased, local risings could not be put down in the Fenlands, and in Staffordshire quarter sessions were not held. Yet in Wales both the courts of great sessions and quarter sessions continued after the outbreak of war and the officials of local government, particularly the sheriffs and justices of the peace, carried out their traditional functions. The one officer affected was the deputy lieutenant whose military duties of mustering troops and supervising the defences of the county were taken over by commissioners of array.

A major hiatus occurred with the interregnum when central government found royalist Wales difficult to administer. The detail of the way in which Cromwell and his governments tried to deal with the problem by means of county committees, sequestration committees, approvers and triers, will be dealt with in the following chapter, but such experiments were unsuccessful, and with the Restoration the familiar pattern was resumed, to remain until the nineteenth century. By means of machinery established in Henry VIII's reign the county gentry ruled Wales. In some counties – Cardiganshire, Carmarthenshire – families of Welsh origin, often tracing their pedigrees back to the days of the Welsh princes, exercised power for centuries. But in the eighteenth century here, and far more so in some Welsh counties, the ranks of the gentry changed remarkably. In Glamorgan, Monmouthshire, Merioneth and Caernarfonshire, at least, bachelordom or late marriage produced an unprecedented failure of male heirs. The ranks of the greater gentry tightened as estates were consolidated or expanded. The demarcation between greater and lesser gentry became more apparent and was reflected in the kind of office to which families might aspire, yet essentially the system of administration remained the same. Perhaps fifty or so families in each county wielded authority. The wealthiest, thirty to forty families in Wales as a whole, might aspire to membership of Parliament. Several hundred aspired to lesser office.

The involvement of the state decreased, particularly after 1688 when the prerogative courts were finally abolished. The court of great sessions continued and could decide disputes between the gentry, between landlords and tenants, during its county circuits but its effectiveness as an independent agency was limited because the leading gentry influenced appointments to it. In the eighteenth century, therefore, more than in the sixteenth, the autonomy of local government under a smaller oligarchy of great families, was very considerable. Quarter sessions performed a largely unsupervised judicial, executive and legislative role. The problem here was that, despite the increase in the ranks of justices of the peace, far fewer attended quarter sessions. In the early seventeenth century in Merioneth, for example, fourteen justices attended regularly; by mid eighteenth century sometimes only two or three appeared. The procedures and concerns of quarter sessions changed little over the centuries. After the sessions were opened by the crier, and the sheriff had returned his writ, the grand jury, members of which were subject to a property qualification, decided which cases warranted presenting in court. The range of ecclesiastical and temporal offences considered was enormous. The court might deal with sacrilege, non-attendance at church, murder, extortion, gaming, offences relating to the maintenance of bridges or highways, or the Poor Law. If the grand jury decided that the bill or presentment warranted, the case was heard in open court by the petty jury. If found guilty the criminal faced extremes of punishment. Larceny of goods worth over 12d was a capital offence, so justices regularly undervalued stolen goods. The punishment for petty larceny involved the criminal being fastened to a cart, dragged for a hundred yards, then whipped. The perennial problem of maintaining roads and bridges had to be dealt with at quarter sessions. Enforcing the annual six days of statute labour from each parishioner was, if anything, even more difficult in the eighteenth century and recalcitrant parishioners were dealt with in court.

The office of sheriff, declining in importance in the sixteenth century, continued to become less influential. The sheriff lost his military responsibilities to the deputy lieutenant in the Tudor period and in the eighteenth century relinquished his authority to keep the county gaol to justices of the peace.

The justices of the peace had always been the general factotums of local administration but during the eighteenth century their power was unprecedented. The constraints of the prerogative courts had disappeared in the seventeenth century, with the final demise of the council in the marches in 1694 particularly significant for Wales. It had been in abeyance for part of the seventeenth century and had only infrequent periods of importance in its history, yet its lord president had always been involved in the appointment of justices of the peace and the council had exercised a supervisory role. While theoretically this supervisory role was vested in the court of great sessions, in the eighteenth century active supervision was minimal. The retention of lawbreakers within the magistracy remained, as always, one of the great weaknesses of the system. Gambling and heavy drinking probably produced as much lawlessness in the eighteenth century as the affrays of the sixteenth, and gentry involvement in smuggling was still evident.

The ranks of justices of the peace in the eighteenth century actually swelled considerably since no one was dropped from the magistracy and new appointments were made at regular intervals. For example in Merioneth numbers had grown only from an original 8 to 21 in nearly a hundred years after the Act of Union, yet by 1792 there were 150. Despite this the number of active justices declined steadily. It had become a social necessity for those whose lands brought in over £100 per annum to be appointed to the magistracy, but it was the social cachet, not the responsibility of office, which appealed. Then, absentee landlordism occurred on a greater scale in the eighteenth century than previously. Of Merioneth's ninety-six inactive justices in mid eighteenth century, fifty lived outside the county, a situation brought about by the increase in the size of estates, with the consequent breakdown of what had once tended to be county units. Because of the now relatively low property qualification two new social categories of justice emerged – the younger sons of landed families, and clerics. Indeed the emergence of the squire/parson was one of the features of eighteenth-century society. Clerical justices – there were twenty-four out of 100 in Merioneth in 1776 – were the most active and indispensable.

The high constable had increased his social standing, at least in some instances, and his significance in government by the eighteenth century. He had a wide range of responsibilities, from apprehending criminals to administering the law on weights and measures. As the apathy of justices of the peace grew more pronounced the high constable's role inevitably became more vital. Yet power in the counties still rested mainly with the justices, and particularly with the chairman of the bench, the *custos rotulorum*. This office was often held by a Member of Parliament who, after 1760, might also be the county's lord lieutenant. This conjunction of offices resulted in enormous power, and testified to a considerable change in the pattern of office-holding by the Welsh gentry. The small number of very wealthy, very powerful gentry, with their immense patronage of nomination to the bench of justices and other influential posts, formed a far more obvious elite. The right of the chairman of the bench to nominate his fellow justices, nominally vested in the Lord Chancellor, went unchallenged. A marked change in community relationships accompanied this accumulation of power. The gulf between common people and gentry was accentuated as, increasingly, lawyers and stewards dispensed justice. The incidence of crime increased, poaching became more prevalent, there were threats of arson against stewards in some counties and more frequent riots. Riots over food shortages or at election time testified to the partial breakdown of traditional paternalist community involvement on the part of many of the greater gentry.

The only paid official was a clerk of the peace, but there were hints in the eighteenth century of a new dimension of professionalism and expertise, with paid officials being tagged on to the two-centuries-old traditional operation of local government. In some counties a county treasurer was appointed to relieve justices of caring for county money and a county surveyor was appointed to survey and organise the repair of roads and bridges. With quickening economic activity this became an even more pressing matter and eventually the statutory highway rate came to be levied to supplement statute labour. This improved the state of Wales' appalling roads only marginally. It would not be difficult to find examples of maladministration by justices in the eighteenth century any more than in the sixteenth. Yet it is perhaps fortunate that, at a time when even the checks and balances of the Tudor period had disappeared, their very apathy provided the most significant check to their abuse of authority. The system inaugurated in the 1530s, though modified, remained the basis both for the consolidation of gentry influence and the administration of Wales through the succeeding centuries. This local power, cemented by the wealth on which it was founded and the social pre-eminence consequent on it, has led to historians dubbing the eighteenth century the golden age of the Welsh squires.

4

POLITICAL POWER AND CENTRAL CONTROL

The working of faction

The practice of politics in Wales was the prerogative of the aristocracy and the gentry. The aristocracy exercised the greatest political power across England and Wales and maintained it by complicated political manoeuvrings and intrigues in court and across the country. They were pre-eminent due to their noble birth, their wealth and the offices they held, but it was essential for them to preserve a power-base in the counties as well as at court, and it was this that ensured regular faction struggles. Throughout the Tudor period, for example, complex political activity centred around the Earls of Worcester in Monmouthshire, Sir John Perrot in Pembrokeshire (not a member of the aristocracy but immensely powerful by virtue of wealth and court connections), the Earls of Pembroke in Glamorgan, the Earl of Leicester in North Wales and the Earl of Essex in Carmarthenshire. Robert Dudley, Earl of Leicester, provides an instructive example of the tentacles of faction in Elizabeth's reign. He was one of the Queen's favourites, enormously influential at court. In 1563 he was granted the lordships of Chirk and Denbigh, so becoming a major force in the county. In 1565 he became chamberlain of the county palatine of Chester. In the 1560s he became chief forester of Snowdon and in 1572, was granted the lordship of Arwystli and Cyfeiliog. His estates also included lands from three former abbeys, Valle Crucis, Cymer and Bardsey. He consolidated this influence by friendship with, and support from, other important families. They included William Thomas, sometime sheriff, Member of Parliament for Caernarfonshire and constable of the castle in Caernarfon and Evan Lloyd of Bodidris, sometime sheriff and M.P. for Denbighshire, Leicester's steward of the lordship of Chirk and, as commissioner for land encroachments, an extremely powerful figure. Leicester's group of clients was fostered largely through the influence of his close relative, Sir Henry Sidney, the most notable of Tudor lord presidents of the council in the marches of Wales, and the Wynn family of Gwydir, the most important of Caernarfonshire's gentry families. Leicester, like other powerful magnates with influence in Wales, did not have things all his own way. Feuds stemmed from the rivalry which his faction engendered among other powerful gentry, and opposition was led by Sir Richard Bulkeley of Beaumaris. He was not without support from other families jealous of the Leicester following.

From the time that Sir William Herbert of Cardiff was made first Earl of Pembroke of the second creation in 1551 he and his successors wielded even more influence in Glamorgan than they had done as lords of Glamorgan and owners of the largest acreage in the county. Henry Herbert, the second earl, was related to Leicester by marriage, he was a powerful figure at court and, from 1586, he was lord president of the council in the marches. He felt no qualms over using his power to the full in Glamorgan whenever his interests were at stake. He treated the borough of Cardiff as virtually his own property, and his attempts to exercise the rights of marcher lord largely dictated the pattern of politics in the county. As with Leicester, Pembroke had powerful opponents who were not afraid to cross him, notably the Stradlings of St Donat's and the Mansels of Margam.

The working of political faction was made more complex by the network of family relationships among aristocracy and gentry, since gentry families almost invariably married within their own class. The complex interplay of faction and influence meant that occasionally even the monarch might become embroiled, as happened in Elizabeth's reign. It meant that all local appointments to office were significant in the constant power struggle between families. Thus, when the Earl of Pembroke was president of the council in the marches, Herberts were appointed to deputy lieutenancies in Glamorgan, Monmouthshire and Montgomeryshire. Such favouritism could inflame relations between rival groups of gentry and sometimes result in riot.

Welsh Members in Parliament

The politics of faction was played out within a framework of national and local institutions, one of these being Parliament, though it has been pointed out that the importance of Parliament should not be exaggerated, that far too much attention has focussed on Parliamentary opposition in the sixteenth and early seventeenth centuries and far too little on the power which the crown exercised through chief ministers and spokesmen.

As a result of the Acts of Union Wales had a knight to represent each shire and a burgess to represent every borough which was a shire town. There were exceptions: the county of Monmouth was granted two Members and no burgess was to sit for Merioneth. In 1542 Haverfordwest was made a county and therefore became entitled to its own Member. Here was another ideal opportunity for the important Welsh gentry to augment their power and prestige. Despite the expense and the arduous journey to London – Welsh Members were notorious for requesting leave of absence – important county families went to great lengths to ensure their election. Gentry representation in Wales was shared among more families in the sixteenth century than later. Towards the end of the century a pattern of domination of both borough and county seats by a few of the most wealthy landed families became apparent. Contested elections were the exception since defeat was hardly to be countenanced, but there were bitter rivalries. In Anglesey in the 1540s and 1550s, for example, the borough and county seats were hotly contested by rival factions. By the 1550s the Bulkeley family of Beaumaris controlled the borough seat but contests over the county seat between the Bulkeleys and the older Welsh gentry families of the south west of the island, led by the Owen family of Bodowen and Frondeg, continued. If there was an election both sides were likely to use illegal methods to obtain votes. Elections were held in unexpected parts of the county in order to disadvantage one side's voters. Pressure was exerted on voters, force used and, most effective of all, the sheriff could be suborned. His role was crucial because the election was held in the county court, normally in the shire hall, and he was the returning officer, deciding the result on a show of hands. Some elections had to be referred to higher courts. The notorious Denbighshire election of 1601 involved a partial sheriff and the possession of pikes, staves, pistols, daggers and swords by retainers of both sides. Such elections were not concerned with national issues. In the first half of the seventeenth century there were more disputed elections in Caernarfonshire than in all but three English counties, but all were local faction struggles. The protagonists were the Wynns of Gwydir and the Griffiths of Cefnamlwch, with each faction having its network of influence both nationally at court, and locally. For over sixty years from the 1550s the Wynns were supreme but, thereafter, the Griffith faction predominated by means of a series of disputed elections, the creation of freeholders and pressure on sheriffs. Even the vital 1640 election was fought on local rivalries and was so disputed that its result was referred to the committee of privileges. They never completed their hearing.

The impact of Welsh M.P.s was limited for decades after the Acts of Union. From about 1570 bills were handed over to committees of M.P.s and Welsh Members participated in these in Elizabeth's later Parliaments. In 1597 all the Welsh Members served on the committee dealing with the Newport and Caerleon bridges bill and the bill for the inclusion of the lordship of Llandovery in the county of Carmarthen. Some Welsh members, Sir John Perrot for example, sat on rather more important committees.

Welsh M.P.s were elected and served under the same conditions as their English compeers and they were to be paid the same – 4s a day for the county Member, 2s for the borough Member, though the payment system was short-lived. The system of representation, like so much of union legislation, was experimental. In the counties, voting rights were reasonably straightforward in that they were vested in the 40s freeholders, though there were 400 different types of freehold. The borough franchise was more complicated. There were at least four major types of borough – the burgage, freedom boroughs, scot and lot boroughs, with Welsh boroughs normally of the first type. The Welsh system of borough representation was conditioned by the system of payment of Members, a concession in the Act of Union to the relative poverty of Welsh members, and a custom dying out in England. Under the 1536 act freemen of the shire towns alone were to elect M.P.s but all were to contribute to payment. It must have been that this injustice invoked protest since the 1543 act created a system of contributory boroughs voting for the burgess to represent them in Parliament. The Cardiff burgess was elected by the freemen of Cowbridge, Llantrisant, Neath, Aberavon, Kenfig, Swansea and Loughor. After 1543, then, fourteen M.P.s were elected for the Welsh counties, thirteen for the Welsh boroughs and those boroughs not included in the system were adversely affected.

Borough and county representation was dominated by landowners.

Despite the boroughs' panoply of laws and trade regulations they were not independent of the influence of the local squire whose general control of his lordship – through the manorial courts and the rents and fines associated with them – was untouched by union legislation. Therefore, either by exercising his right as lord of the manor or by holding office in the borough, the local landowner had every opportunity to control elections.

Welsh M.P.s were loyal to the crown not because of any manipulation but because of an identity of interest. This was not only true of the Tudor period; loyalty was transferred to the Stuart dynasty. There was little direct royal influence in Wales, where the most influential figure in the election of M.P.s was the Earl of Pembroke in the counties of Glamorgan and Montgomery. The constitutional issues which affected relationships between the early Stuarts and their Parliaments were less pressing in Wales than in England although the prerogative courts were resented. The council in the marches was under attack from lawyers and border gentry in the early seventeenth century for alleged corruption and the courts of High Commission and Star Chamber symbolised oppression. There was very little sympathy for Puritanism among the Welsh gentry who construed it as a threat to their own local hegemony as well as to good order in the state. The change of monarch in 1625 meant a change in the court climate for Welshmen who had been favourably treated by James I. Charles I was less generous. His policies produced a more mixed reaction among Welsh M.P.s. He had powerful supporters like the Wynn and Vaughan families but there were prominent Welsh casualties, born particularly out of opposition to Buckingham, Charles I's favourite, held responsible for the monarch's most unpopular policies, rather than arising from anti-monarchical sentiment. Sir Robert Mansel, vice-admiral, was one to suffer. Bishop John Williams, later archbishop of York, a powerful figure in North Wales, quarrelled with Buckingham and went out of favour. One of the most powerful of the Welsh aristocracy, even if absentee, was the Earl of Pembroke, another of Buckingham's opponents. There were other of Charles's policies which resulted in a diminution of loyalty to the crown. Individuals had been opposed to the various Stuart fund-raising expedients, such as forced loans, but opposition was most pronounced over ship money, paid with reasonable regularity at first but two counties did not pay in 1635, and no county paid in full in 1639, though there is no indication that this reaction was reflected in increased support for Parliament among Welsh Members. They remained loyal to the crown and there was no attempt in Wales, even by the Earl of Pembroke, to organise opposition to the king. There was some concern over religion, engendered by Laud's Arminianism and the king's perceived sympathy with Roman Catholicism. This opposition was translated into some Parliamentary protest in both the Short Parliament and the early sessions of the Long Parliament but fundamental loyalty remained, even if there was no enthusiasm at all as the crisis unfolded from 1640. When war came in 1642 very few Welsh Members supported Parliament. Even so, the importance of this minority, reflecting a rather wider minority of gentry throughout Wales, should not be underestimated. Wales was not totally royalist, though there was a good deal of support for the king. The Pembrokeshire families supported Parliament, and in Glamorgan Philip Jones, Philip Herbert and Rowland Dawkins also supported Parliament, as did the Myddelton brothers, the Thelwalls and Sir John Trevor of Trefalun in North Wales. Most Welsh counties produced at least one prominent family opposed to the king and there was certainly support for Parliament in the border counties and in some towns and ports.

Puritanism, the motive force behind so much Parliamentary opposition, had little appeal for the Welsh gentry. The interests of the gentry were generally linked with the maintenance of the Established Church, particularly when they had impropriated livings which brought them revenues and patronage. The plethora of Puritan sects in the seventeenth century, with their implications for the social order, were not to the liking of landed families.

Probably the most telling reason for lack of opposition was the underdeveloped commercial life of Wales. With industrial activity and trade playing a limited role in the economy, no mercantile class of any proportion had come into existence, so that the commercial and financial policies pursued by Charles I, which had provoked so much opposition in Parliament and among commercial interests at large, created less of a furore in Wales than in England.

Patterns of loyalty during the Civil War, despite the general loyalty to the king, are nevertheless as difficult to analyse in Wales as in England. In the last resort, allegiance was a matter of personal decision. The Earl of Worcester, based in Raglan and head of the staunchest Catholic family in Wales, fought for the king, and had his loyal gentry followers. The Earl of Pembroke fought for Parliament, and he, too, was at the centre of a network of family and political allegiances which determined some loyalties. Worcester's Catholicism worried the South Wales gentry, and Glamorgan provided one of the few examples of Puritan sympathies among the great gentry. Some gentry changed sides, objecting to Charles's alliance with the Catholics. Traditional allegiance to the monarch predetermined many loyalties. It was no sentimental attachment. It was based on the realisation that the alliance between crown and gentry since Tudor times had been a mutually beneficial one. The prospect of a clash with the monarchy, of a civil war with its concomitant disruption, its impact on the traditional instruments of good government and order, would put not only that good government in jeopardy, but also the position of those who upheld it. So the Welsh gentry were moderately royalist. Only a few – Sir John Owen of Clenennau was one – were passionately fervent in the king's cause. Far more tried to please both sides or tried to keep out of the war altogether. Royalist commanders were never too convinced of the commitment of those who traditionally are held to have supported the king so loyally. If the gentry were generally unenthusiastic, even indifferent, to the great religious and constitutional issues at stake the rest of the population were inevitably uninformed. If nothing else the language barrier in Wales saw to that.

The Civil War

Despite the lack of enthusiasm which greeted the outbreak of war in 1642, Charles relied on Wales as a recruiting ground, something impossible for Parliament, although the strategic importance of pockets of Parliamentary support in Pembrokeshire and the border counties should not be underrated. One of Charles's mistakes was that he did not exploit to the full the allegiance to his cause across so much of Wales. There was no military action in Wales during the early part of the Civil War. In the autumn of 1642 Charles visited Shrewsbury, Chester and Wrexham and sent his son to Raglan, all the while collecting troops for his projected vital assault on London. He recruited successfully, although the Welsh troops were untrained. After the first battle of the Civil War at Edgehill, in which the Welsh troops revealed this lack of training all too clearly, the king moved on to Brentford, near London, where the Welsh fought well under Rupert, only to be rebuffed and to retreat to Oxford. Charles's battle plan had to centre on the capture of London, and his failure to take it in 1642 was a grievous blow. A lesser disaster was the fate of a Welsh army recruited by Charles's commander in the west, the Marquis of Hertford, soundly beaten by Parliamentary forces at Tewkesbury.

By July 1643 the Royalists had taken Bristol with the aid of Welsh troops, and this gave them access to recruits from Glamorgan and Monmouthshire. However, for the Royalists to exploit fully the resources of the whole of Wales they needed to be in control of the whole border area. With the capture of Bristol they came close to achieving this, but in August 1643 Lord Herbert of Raglan failed to take Gloucester. This was a crucial defeat as it meant the isolation of that area of Wales capable of contributing most to the Royalist cause. The hold of Parliamentary sympathisers on parts of south-west Wales was to be vital, despite the strong Royalist advance under the Earl of Carbery in the summer of 1643 when he took control of the whole of that area except for Pembroke. Milford, particularly, provided safe haven for Parliamentary ships active in the Bristol channel in 1643 and 1644 and this enabled the Parliamentary fleet to blockade the south-eastern ports of Wales.

In North Wales the stalemate of the early months of the war was broken in 1643 when a Parliamentary army took Hawarden, Wrexham, Mold, Flint, Mostyn and Holywell before troops returning from Irish campaigns forced it to retreat. Although there was little to show for Parliamentary success, by the end of 1643 the vulnerability of the area had been revealed. By the summer of 1644 Parliament's forces had again gained the initiative in mid and North Wales after a campaign by Sir Thomas Myddelton, who took Newtown, Montgomery castle, Powys castle and Ruthin castle, proceeding into Montgomeryshire and Radnorshire.

1644 started off with Royalist forces planning the capture of the Parliamentary strategic stronghold of Pembroke but, by April, it was Parliament which was in control of much of the South Wales coast, only to have to retreat the whole way in face of a counter-offensive by Royalist forces under Gerard. However, Royalist support was everywhere beginning to crumble and in 1645 disaster followed disaster. In February, Shrewsbury fell and the way was open for Parliamentary campaigns in North Wales. Then, after the disastrous battle of Naseby, Charles came to South Wales, hoping to recruit an army from his headquarters at Herbert's Raglan castle. By now troops were difficult to recruit and demanded redress of grievances. By the end of 1645 only Raglan in South Wales and Aberystwyth on the west coast held out for the king. With Glamorgan declaring for Parliament, the other South Wales counties followed, though consolidation of Parliamentary authority in South Wales was by no means plain sailing. Early in 1646 Edward Carne of Glamorgan led a rising against Parliamentary forces but it was easily put down by Rowland Laugharne. Finally, in February 1646, Raglan castle was taken and, in the north, Chester was captured opening the way for a campaign across North Wales by the Parliamentary commander, Mytton. In March 1647, the fall of Harlech signalled the final triumph of Parliament in the north.

Wales, Royalist in 1642, was now in the hands of Parliament. The gentry, who controlled local government, had generally backed the king and, apart from a few talented trimmers like Bussy Mansel, were hardly *persona grata* with the Parliamentarians. Discontent had already been transformed into rebellion in Glamorgan in 1646. It was almost inevitable that inherent tensions in the situation would result in armed resistance. So it proved. In June 1647 there was another small rising in Glamorgan as a Royalist band marched on Cardiff demanding attention to their complaints against the administration of the county committee, but the major disturbance came not from Royalists but from Parliamentarians in Pembrokeshire. The second Civil War started with those discontents typically arising out of the termination of a war, notably the disbandment of the army. This was under way in Pembrokeshire in February 1648, and produced the inevitable grievance over arrears of pay. The governor of Pembroke castle, Poyer, took up the complaint, refusing to yield the castle to his appointed successor and announcing his support for the restoration of the king. Two other commanders, Rice Powell and Rowland Laugharne, joined the rebellion and by May had advanced across South Wales to the outskirts of Cardiff. It was there that they were confronted by a section of the New Model Army under Horton and in the biggest battle of the Civil War in Wales, at St Fagans, they were easily beaten by much superior forces. This signalled the appearance of Cromwell himself to subdue the unruly South Walians and by July the whole of the area was once more firmly under Parliamentary control. Similar grievances simmered in North Wales, combining with incipient royalism and discontent at disruption in the economy and local government, but the Royalists were easily beaten, as attempts at resistance by Sir John Owen of Clenennau and Richard Bulkeley failed dismally.

Puritan government

The confusion of war was followed by the confusion of peace, as the system of national and local government by which Wales had ordered her affairs since the union was changed radically. The Civil War was no total war and material devastation, outside those castle garrisons which had changed hands at regular intervals in parts of Wales – particularly along the north and south coasts – was limited. (Even in England, which had seen so much more fighting, there was little physical impact on the majority of small communities.) There was some destruction of property, and plunder, particularly by Irish troops, but the major dislocation was to the cattle and wool trade, basic to the Welsh economy.

During what was sporadic fighting by small numbers of troops, even at the height of the war, the basic activities of a rural economy had continued. Once fighting stopped, commercial life took little time to recover. The context of political life, on the other hand, was completely changed. A predominantly Royalist country was now governed by the Puritans. By 1648 fifteen Welsh Members had been purged from the Long Parliament and only two Welshmen were involved in the king's trial and signed his death warrant, John Jones and Thomas Wogan. The traditional governing families were on the losing side, though some, like the Wynns, had managed to remain neutral and some had supported both sides. Inevitably a vacuum was created in the government of Wales and it was filled to some extent by lesser gentry who formed the core of the county committees, that system of administration which had been set up in Parliamentary areas during the war in England and Wales. The original purpose of the county committee was that it should be the Parliamentary instrument for prompting local gentry into responsibility for county defence and any contribution to the Parliamentary military effort. With the war over, the county committee provided the obvious means of governing the localities and was given wider powers. The peace-time objective was to make it as representative as possible, so the committee tended to be large: normally over twenty men attended. Not that the Commonwealth and Protectorate ever provided an integrated plan for government in Wales. Central government was never entirely sure of the loyalty of officials and was worried about the independent stance of county committees during the civil wars. So instruments of government outside the county committee were also established. In many Welsh counties it was extremely difficult to find men of sufficient wealth and standing to choose from. In the early years of the war, with Wales so Royalist, a county committee could only be established in Pembrokeshire. In North Wales there was a Puritan faction centred on Wrexham, and Sir Richard Myddelton was a staunch Parliamentarian, but there was little sympathy among other gentry. Some gentry who had been particularly strong sup-porters of the king had their estates sequestered or had to pay hefty fines, which forced them to sell some of their land. The land which came on to the market was quickly snapped up, but the resentments caused by sequestration and forced sale, and the resulting prosperity of parvenu families, created considerable animosity which was fortified by such families being represented on county committees. Traditional governing families also resented the incursion of Englishmen into local government. Family rivalries had always been prominent and were now compounded by the bitterness of defeat and sequestration.

The committee system had started during the war to enable Parliament to control the administration and revenues of those areas which it had taken over. The system was then used by the Commonwealth and Protectorate in a variety of ways, mainly on a county basis but also, as with the committee for the Propagation of the Gospel in Wales, on a more national basis and for a variety of tasks such as sequestration and assessment. The activities of the two statutory sequestration committees, established in North and South Wales in 1649, and the county organisations under them, allowed discontent full rein. In 1650 a modified, more centralised, sequestra-tion system was established but this did not prevent accusations of partiality, corruption and misappropriation of money against the sequestrators. It was impossible in Wales, with its few Parlia-mentarians, to avoid keeping on commissioners who were known to have kept property for themselves or had committed a variety of forms of misconduct. As it was, the sequestrators were almost invariably minor gentry to whom the amounts with which they were dealing represented great temptation. The wealthier gentry were no more honest. One individual who profited was Colonel Philip Jones, member of Cromwell's Council of State, and the most influential figure in South Wales during the Interregnum. He became very wealthy, partly on fines and church money, and bought an estate at Fonmon in Glamorgan.

The county committees established for day-to-day administration were drawn from a wide range of families. The nucleus, naturally, comprised Parliamentarians such as Sir Richard Pryse of Gogerddan in Cardiganshire, already a Parliamentarian M.P., and Sir Thomas Myddelton of Denbigh. The ranks of Parliamentary sympathisers had been augmented after 1645 when Charles had negotiated with the Irish Catholics for help, though the major county families generally remained loyal to the crown. Bussy Mansel of Briton Ferry had changed his allegiance in 1645 and was subsequently placed on county and national committees, while the main branch of the Mansel family, at Margam, remained loyal to Charles. The major Parliamentary figure in North Wales was Sir Thomas Myddelton and he had a network of supporters. So, from 1647, when the first commissioners for the whole country were appointed under an assessment ordinance, some older county families served, while the bulk of the commission was supplied by middle-ranking gentry families. The national and the county committees were essentially compromises, and the nature and degree of the compromise varied from county to county. English Puritan gentry from the border counties were also used to bolster a potentially unreliable structure.

The composition of the committees changed during the Interregnum. From 1647 to 1649 there was strong representation from traditional, often Royalist, gentry. In some counties Parliamentarian gentry were at a premium, so that committees were diluted, and Royalist sympathisers had to be allowed to serve. This was the case in the counties of Cardigan, Carmarthen, Brecon and Radnor. After the second civil war some who had been involved were purged and the government attempted to reinforce loyalty by appointing lesser gentry and army officers. In North Wales about a dozen of the older families were no longer represented; in South Wales, where Royalist support in the second civil war was so widespread, there had to be a wholesale purge.

Similar problems arose with Welsh membership of Cromwell's governments. Under the Instrument of Government Welsh Members were drawn from loyalists, except for Edmund Jones and John Vaughan, both former Royalists. Opposition to the regime from fifth monarchists posed no great threat. This group, believers in the imminent arrival of Christ to establish his kingdom for a thousand years, had only a few months of real influence when, in Barebone's Parliament, 1653, four of the six Welsh nominees were Fifth Monarchists. The most remarkable of their number was the tireless Puritan itinerant minister, Vavasour Powell, who published a violently anti-government pamphlet in 1655. It did not attract widespread support and was answered by Walter Cradock. With Morgan Llwyd siding with Cradock, moderate Puritanism commanded far more loyalty in Wales and the influence of Powell and his few followers was discounted.

In 1657 Cromwell's return to a constitutional position similar to that of pre-Civil War days was foreshadowed by the acceptance of the Humble Petition and Advice. It also heralded a government attempt to reinstate a wider range of traditional governing families on the county committees. This was reflected in Wales although control still lay with loyal Cromwellians. Among those who returned was Vaughan of Llwydiarth and very significant was the re-emergence into county politics of Sir Edward Mansel of Margam, since the family had always been loyal to the king. Such traditional county families returned at the expense of left-wing members of the Propagation Commission, although this pattern of change was not even across the counties.

When Oliver Cromwell died in 1658 any hope of a permanent Puritan political settlement receded. Royalists all over Wales were returned to Richard Cromwell's brief Parliament, together with a few loyal Parliamentarians from the south. In April, 1659, Cromwell fell and the Rump Parliament was revived. Colonel Philip Jones, one of Cromwell's staunchest supporters, was forced to leave Parliament. With militia commissions issued in July 1659 to counter a Royalist threat, those families brought back into local administration in 1657 were once more dispensed with, though finding personnel in North Wales loyal to the regime was so difficult that many of the commissioners were unknown. Bussy Mansel, a remarkable political opportunist, emerged as the strong man in South Wales, replacing Philip Jones. The extreme Puritans, whose influence had so declined from the mid 1650s, enjoyed a short-lived resurgence in 1659 but the restoration of the king was widely welcomed in Wales. The followers of Morgan Llwyd and Vavasour Powell, drawn largely from the ranks of the lesser gentry in North Wales, were the only group to be destroyed by the Restoration. Only for short periods had the extreme Puritans any hope of influence – when they had filled the vacuum in government in the Barebones Parliament and again in 1659 after the demise of Richard Cromwell. Cromwell's intolerance of the extremes of Puritanism, with its revolutionary implications for the social order, were wholeheartedly endorsed in Wales – Quakerism, for instance, was opposed on all sides. Traditional governing families were involved in the vital, final county committees set up to organise the county militia in support of the restoration of the king. Some Cromwellian stalwarts, Bussy Mansel in South Wales, Sir John Carter in North Wales, accommodated sufficiently to be returned to the Convention Parliament of 1660. Moderates of both sides in Wales welcomed the Restoration.

The Restoration meant the end of the attempts to turn the Welsh into a nation of Puritans, which had started in 1650 with the act for the Propagation of the Gospel in Wales. The act was passed with as much a political as a religious purpose, though its importance as a coherent instrument of government has been overrated. Provision was made for appointing seventy-one commissioners, twenty-eight representing the North and forty-three the South, including Monmouthshire. They were not appointed on a county basis and included English militiamen who had served in Wales. They could eject clergy from livings if necessary and require pluralists to opt for one living. Vacancies were to be filled by twenty-five approvers, including Walter Cradock and Vavasour Powell. Two groups of leading commissioners emerged. In South Wales they were Glamorgan men – Colonel Philip Jones, Bussy Mansell, Rowland Dawkins and John Price. In North Wales the leading commissioners were English military men. They were zealous; 278 ministers were ejected between 1650 and 1653, on political and moral rather than religious grounds, for which in any case there were no objective criteria. Filling vacant livings proved extremely difficult. Welsh-speaking clergy were at a premium so itinerant ministers were appointed – probably about ninety, with Vavasour Powell in the van. The commissioners also founded a network of over sixty schools, but they came in for much criticism because of a general inability to achieve their purpose successfully, and for misappropriating some of the large sums of money for which they were responsible. General disillusionment resulted in the lapsing of the Propagation Act in March 1653. The approval of ministers lay with the Commission for the Approbation of Public Preachers from 1654, both in England and Wales. This absence of differentiation was in line with Protectorate policy of lessening independent provision in the provinces. There was no widespread popular support for Puritanism or for the behaviour and conduct which were some of its hallmarks. There is little evidence that the attempts of justices of the peace to enforce civil marriage, punish swearing, stamp out drunkenness, dancing round the maypole or bearbaiting were anything but unpopular. At all levels of society the Restoration was welcomed.

Government and politics after the Restoration

Occasional elements of anarchy and a plethora of experiments in national and local government had not produced anything remotely resembling that social and economic revolution desired by such Puritan sects as the Levellers or the Diggers. Though so many of the Welsh gentry had fought on the losing side in the war, the vast majority survived, with their numbers augmented by some who had profited from the more fluid land market of the Commonwealth period. The pre-war political and social structure remained intact. With the Restoration the traditional county families were restored to their position of authority in government and administration. In South Wales, more than in the North, any implicit threat to this restored order was treated very seriously. Quakers and Baptists, particularly, were persecuted, though there were gentry of Independent and Presbyterian sympathies.

Gentry power in county and borough was enormous. In Wales the gentry had always controlled most of the borough Parliamentary seats as well as county representation, and their influence in Welsh towns grew as towns expanded in the eighteenth century. In both county and borough seats the major change which occurred between the Tudor period and the late seventeenth and eighteenth centuries was the concentration of Parliamentary representation in the hands of a diminishing number of families. This reflected the social phenomenon of the concentration of economic resources in fewer hands, the emergence of a sharper line of demarcation between the lesser and the greater gentry, with the lesser gentry selling estates which served to augment greater ones. The process was moulded and enhanced in the early eighteenth century by the remarkable failure of male heirs and the resulting amalgamation of some large estates.

The proprietorial hold of important gentry on county Parliamentary seats was not achieved by direct bribery. The size of the electorate normally precluded this, since the smallest county electorate, Carmarthenshire, had 500 voters and the largest, Denbighshire and Pembrokeshire, about 2,000 each. Of course, there were various kinds of corruption, particularly involving the partiality of the high sheriff as returning officer. Even in the boroughs control was more difficult than in England because of the system of contributory boroughs unique to Wales. Some of the original contributory boroughs had been enfranchised by the eighteenth century. In the early part of the century there were five single borough constituencies, including Haverfordwest and Brecon which had always been so. In these it was relatively easy for one man to control the electorate; far less easy where there was a number of contributory boroughs.

In both county and borough, aristocracy or gentry control was the central feature. From 1689 to 1725 the Bulkeleys of Beaumaris held the county seat and Lord Bulkeley had complete control over the Beaumaris borough seat just as the Morgans of Tredegar had the Brecon seat in their pockets. The Vaughans of Corsyegedol represented Merioneth for much of the eighteenth century. In Montgomeryshire the Vaughans of Llwydiarth held the seat from 1689 to 1715. In Glamorgan the Mansels of Margam held sway before 1710, then the influence of the Stradlings, the Kemeys-Tyntes and the Joneses of Fonmon made itself felt. One of the Monmouthshire seats was always held by the Morgans of Tredegar. In North Wales in the first half of the eighteenth century the most prominent of the gentry was the Wynn family of Wynnstay. They co-operated with the Myddeltons to return the Member for Denbighshire and dominated

Caernarfon. More than this, Sir Watkin Williams Wynn, who extended an already formidable estate, managed to influence other elections in North Wales so that a solidly anti-Whig faction was elected. With his death in the mid eighteenth century this network of influence crumbled and the Wynns became just one important family influence.

Aristocratic and gentry domination did not mean that there were no rivalries or elections. Even the most influential peers, such as the Duke of Beaufort, had to tread warily. This was partly the consequence of aristocratic absenteeism, since outside interference was much resented by county gentry. Crown attempts to influence elections, which in Wales had to be directed through county families, was similarly resented. Crown influence was certainly exercised through patronage and although few Welsh M.P.s were actually given government office, one of the motives for membership was that it was through the M.P. that much government patronage was dispensed. Elections took place only as a last resort. From 1754 to 1790 there were only seventeen contested elections in the Welsh counties – the more prestigious seats – and eight in the boroughs, four of which were in New Radnor. Expense was the deterrent to elections. A candidate in the eighteenth century could easily spend £5,000 during an election, wining and feeding supporters.

The process by which political power came to be concentrated in the hands of a few wealthier families accelerated after the Restoration in 1660. In 1661 over half the Welsh Members in the Cavalier Parliament had been M.P.s previously, but the financial strain of sequestration and fines during the Interregnum left them open to bribery on a grand scale first by Clarendon, then by Danby, so that it is estimated that after 1673 twenty-two Welsh Members were receiving crown money. A few adhered to the 'country' opposition. Under Charles II three Welshmen were crown ministers – Sir John Trevor, Sir Leoline Jenkins and Judge Jeffreys, and the Court party had widespread support in Wales. This adherence drew Welsh members into similar English connections, producing an identity of interest and minimising any notion of Welsh priorities. The influence of Welsh members could only be exercised through an over-whelmingly English grouping.

In the 1670s both the Popish Plot of 1678 and the exclusion crisis in 1679 had repercussions in Wales. One of Titus Oates's accomplices was a native of Monmouthshire, William Bedloe, and he told of a local Catholic plot. This was in a county where the most prominent figure was the Catholic Earl of Worcester, whose influence was resented by neighbouring gentry, particularly after his assumption of the presidency of the revived council in the marches in 1672. In the late 1670s, in south-east Wales, there was growing opposition among the former Pembroke moderate faction to Worcester and to the court, since the moderates saw Roman Catholicism as more of a threat than Dissent.

Despite Worcester's efforts some critics of Charles II were returned from Wales in the first Exclusion Parliament of 1679, so-called because it attempted by means of an Exclusion Bill, to bar Charles's brother, James, from the succession. Charles II's direct intervention in the Breconshire election misfired and in Glamorgan Sir Edward Mansel, a staunch supporter of the king, was replaced by Bussy Mansel. At this stage there was a small majority of Welsh Members for the Exclusion Bill but by the third Exclusion Parliament the court did better, particularly in North Wales. The long tradition of electoral corruption was upheld. In Denbighshire Sir John Trevor was returned because the sheriff disqualified his opponent by referring to some obscure statute, almost certainly a well-worked ploy.

There was no opposition in Wales to James II's accession in 1685 and no support for the Duke of Monmouth's rebellion. Once more, there were Welshmen in high office – Judge Jeffreys as Lord Chancellor, Sir John Trevor of Brynkynallt as Master of the Rolls and William Williams Solicitor General. The elections for James II's only Parliament saw the Court party do well, this time in both North and South Wales. In Pembrokeshire, for example, William Barlow was returned – he was to accompany James II into exile. Bussy Mansel failed to get elected for Cardiff. However, the response in Wales to James II's pro-Catholic policies was lukewarm. When the king prepared to summon a new Parliament in 1687 it quickly became apparent that he could count on very little active support in Wales for his policy of abolishing religious tests. Even so, one of the few areas in which James could still find some sympathisers even after the birth of a male heir seemed to guarantee a Catholic succession, was Wales, with its long tradition of loyalty to the monarch. The Welsh gentry were not contemplating deserting the king at this stage but they did wish for guarantees for the Anglican Church.

As the two groupings of Whig and Tory joined to invite William of Orange to replace James II and ensure Protestantism, so Catholics in Wales rallied to James. The former Marquis of Worcester, now Duke of Beaufort, was the foremost Catholic influence in Wales and seemed prepared to raise an army. In Glamorgan Colonel Thomas Carne of Ewenni started to recruit men to the king's cause. Nationally, however, and even in Wales, James's position was actually untenable. His own prevarication gave every opportunity to his enemies in Wales, and Bishop Lloyd of St Asaph and Sir Rowland Gwynne encouraged defections. With James negotiating with Tyrconnell in Ireland and raising the old horror of an Irish invasion, even the Duke of Beaufort acquiesced in the changes in court and only a very few families – the Barlows of Slebech, the Carnes of Ewenni – held fast to the king.

The revolution of 1688 signified little for Wales except for the final abolition of the council in the marches. William and Mary were received with less than rapture in a country where Jacobite sympathies were strong. There were some practical effects. Some gentry refused to become justices of the peace and Abergavenny burgesses refused to take the oath of allegiance, but just as Welsh support for James II did not prove solid so now many Welsh M.P.s preferred the new regime. When there was an assassination attempt on the new king in 1696 it was a Welsh M.P., Rowland Gwynne of Radnorshire, who pressed for an oath of association in the king's defence. The other main feature of Welsh politics in William and Mary's reign was the closer integration of Welsh M.P.s into the major political factions, built up not on party lines but in connections and influences fostered by leading political families. A number of North Wales Members became involved with the Nottingham–Finch connection. They included the Bulkeleys, Roger Mostyn of Flint and Sir Thomas Hanmer. Richard Bulkeley was a cousin of Nottingham, and Mostyn his prospective son-in-law. One of the leaders of the Harley–Foley connection was Robert Harley, M.P. for Radnor boroughs and adherents included Sir Thomas Mansel of Margam. This fluid grouping, subject to constant change, underpinned the larger groupings of Whig and Tory, with the Tories the party of High Church and Jacobitism, the Whigs closely identified with the 1688 Revolution. When it became acceptable, in Anne's reign, for M.P.s to declare their allegiance openly, the Tory sympathies of three-quarters of Welsh Members were evident.

The pattern of eighteenth-century politics in Wales was made possible by a profoundly important social change. The size of gentry families went down and the number of men who remained unmarried increased. The majority of estates remained, often enlarged by amalgamation. One reason for this was the lack of male heirs – the male line failed in over half of Monmouthshire's gentry families between 1700 and 1780, for example. In Glamorgan, where the phenomenon was even more apparent, the political structure was changed by the arrival of three members of the aristocracy from outside Wales who married Welsh heiresses – Lord Talbot (1721), the Earl of Plymouth (1736) and the Earl of Jersey (c. 1760). Welsh families who had exercised political power since Tudor times, the Kemeyses, the Stradlings, the Mansels, disappeared. Estates were concentrated in fewer hands, the number of highly influential families contracted, and the power of those in the ruling oligarchy was commensurately stronger, and central government was in no position to curb this power. At least oligarchy made for stability. In Monmouthshire, after 1715, for examples, politics were dominated by just three families, the Morgans, the Hanburys and the Dukes of Beaufort.

With the accession of George III in 1714 Welsh Jacobitism produced individual protest but no organised opposition. Protest in the case of Lord Bulkeley or Lewis Pryse of Gogerddan took the form of non-participation, nothing more positive, and the majority of Tory sympathisers compromised. The change in the pattern of Welsh representation was evident in the 1715 election, after which the balance between Whig and Tory M.P.s in Wales was roughly equal. The Old Pretender's rising of that year made no great impact in Wales despite some ostentatious Jacobitism. James II's exile greatly modified the importance of the outstanding political issues of the seventeenth century and in the longer term gentry loyalty to the Hanoverians was assured through liberal crown patronage, sought by Tories as well as Whigs.

Those surrounding the Pretenders were more convinced of Welsh Jacobite loyalty and certainly there were gentry sympathisers in most counties – Sir Watkin Williams Wynn of Wynnstay, the Kemeyses and Lewises in Glamorgan, the Pryses in Cardiganshire, the Philippses in Pembrokeshire, the Beauforts in Monmouthshire. They met in their clubs regularly. There were accusations that such influential gentry controlled local government through their middle-ranking supporters. But since Tudor times the Welsh gentry had not been prepared for martyrdom in any cause and, although perhaps prepared to back a Jacobite certainty, they were not ready to support ill-prepared invasions.

The 1745 rebellion saw no concerted action in favour of the Young Pretender, though once more some Welshmen were implicated marginally. Sir Watkin Williams Wynn in Caernarfonshire had promised support for an invasion – but not this one, even though the Young Pretender was ostensibly marching south from Scotland to join forces with sympathisers from North Wales. There was alarm among the authorities, particularly in the border counties, but no uprising. The handful of Welshmen who attached themselves to the Pretender ended up in exile for their pains. It is uncertain whether Wynn failed to receive the Pretender's summons. He certainly did not respond. His conduct had been equivocal since he had at one stage even donated to a fund to oppose the Young Pretender. In any case, by the time of his death in 1749 the assimilation of Tories into the mainstream of government had been accomplished. Welsh Tories had already been appointed as justices of the peace after a national agreement reached between the Duke of Beaufort and the Whig administration. No new Jacobite leader emerged after Wynn's death.

One reason why the Jacobitism of Welsh gentry in the first half of the eighteenth century has interested historians is that more orthodox political participation was little in evidence. A very few Welshmen held government office but the great majority evinced no particular devotion to national, as opposed to local, politics. There was now no Welsh 'interest', since the main concern of the majority of the gentry was to integrate as closely as possible into English social life. Elections continued to be interesting, particularly as constituency politics became more organised in the eighteenth century. Tory factions were strong in Wales, with Wynn influential in North Wales and Sir John Philipps attempting a similar hegemony in South Wales. Lord Oxford was powerful in former marcher land, the Duke of Beaufort and Lord Windsor in south-east Wales. In Cardiganshire influence was wielded by the Powells of Nanteos and the Pryses of Gogerddan. But there were powerful Whig families too, such as the Earl of Carbery in Carmarthenshire.

Jacobitism waned after 1745. By 1750 the best known of the Jacobite clubs, the Society of Sea Serjeants in south-west Wales, had become a dining club and in another twelve years had disappeared altogether. The political situation was transformed between the 1740s and the 1760s as some of the estates which changed hands were inherited by Whigs, and in any case, Tories themselves were increasingly assimilated into the political system. Former high Toryism was now channelled into radical causes, particularly into support for John Wilkes who was excluded from Parliament despite having been elected three times for the county of Middlesex. Instead of allegiance being evident in Jacobite clubs it surfaced in masonic lodges, thirty-six of which were established in Wales between 1725 and 1820. Masonic ranks included, for example, the Pryses of Gogerddan, owners of an estate of over 30,000 acres, which remained intact from the sixteenth to the twentieth centuries. They were formerly extreme Jacobites. The new radicalism found expression in support for the liberty of freeholders against aristocratic corruption. There was an element of continuity between this radicalism of Jacobite origin and the transmuted radicalism of industrial Wales. Masonic lodges existed in most Welsh towns by 1820 and in such industrial creations as Merthyr and Pontypool. Their activities were linked, as we shall see, with that most radical of dissenting sects, the Unitarians, and there was some fusion of traditional county grievances with those of an emergent middle class.

Hanoverian manipulation of patronage through Whig county families was skilful and effective. This was reflected in elections. In 1727, for the first time, a majority of Whigs was returned for Welsh constituencies. In the 1741 election the Whigs made a determined attempt to end the Wynn influence in North Wales. A corrupt sheriff, appointed by the Whigs, awarded the election to Wynn's opponent only to have the return made void after an election petition carried in the Commons. However it became increasingly apparent that Tories were now interested in acquiring power through Parliament and Welsh Members became increasingly caught up in political faction. In the elections of 1754 and 1761 there was much political in-fighting in Caernarfonshire, Radnorshire and Cardiganshire, which, as usual, had little to do with matters of policy but much with appeasing important landowners and allocating crown leases. The Seven Years War (1756–63) caused some discontent in Wales because of the economic hardship it brought, and the level of peace-time taxation was no more popular. Protest centred around the cider tax, there were riots, and considerable apprehension that the southern and south-eastern counties of Wales were likely to produce outbreaks of mob violence. The issue of taxation then merged with that of John Wilkes, which evoked some sympathy in Wales. County gentry, operating in the shadows of the few favoured, had naturally opposed a system based on narrowly based influence and corruption. With the Wilkes case their radicalism linked with that of London. Indeed, with this case, and the American War of Independence (1776), the involvement of the Welsh in political issues was more obvious than had been the case since the Hanoverian succession, as we shall see in chapter nine.

5

RELIGION

The Welsh Church prior to the Reformation

Just as the princes of Wales had attempted to maintain political independence after the Norman conquest, so the leaders of the Welsh Church attempted to maintain ecclesiastical independence in the face of pressures from monarch, archbishop, Norman lords and the newly established Latin monasteries. With the fortunes of cleric and prince closely linked, the defeat of 1282 was a defeat for the Welsh Church as well as a political defeat. The intervention of the English king in the affairs of the Welsh Church, as in England, became more oppressive. From the middle of the fourteenth century the Church suffered acutely from the effects of the Black Death both in manpower and in economic terms.

Owain Glyndŵr sought to reinforce political independence with a claim to the independence of the metropolitan see of St David's from Canterbury but in the aftermath of Glyndŵr's defeat the Welsh Church was greatly weakened, economically, spiritually and culturally. As the economy of Wales revived in the second half of the fifteenth century so did the fortunes of the Church, but that recovery was relative. There was no outstanding spiritual leadership, contributions to scholarship were limited, superstition was general.

On the eve of the Reformation the Welsh Church suffered from many of the abuses prevalent in the European Church of which it was a part. In England and Wales the king was, in practice, responsible for the appointment of bishops and his concerns were always temporal, reflecting his need for bureaucrats and lawyers. The appointment of Welshmen to Welsh sees was highly exceptional. Welsh sees were so poor that English appointees regarded them as staging posts *en route* to better things. They were normally non-resident. Clergy were not appointed for their spiritual qualities. In

106

many cases the rights of bishops to appoint to livings had been granted to laymen, so making the appointment of spiritual leaders even less likely. Dioceses were administered by resident canons who, increasingly, were members of local gentry families who regarded the Church as a profitable career. Many were married and those with children were determined that their offspring should prosper, often within the Church.

Contact with the mass of the population was through the lower clergy, the parish priests, and it is difficult to be certain of their quality. With some exceptions they were poor. The valuation of Church possessions on the eve of the dissolution of the monasteries, the *Valor Ecclesiasticus*, records that a quarter of Welsh parishes were worth less than £5 per annum and the majority less than £10 per annum. The former figure, particularly, represented real poverty. Possibly half the clergy did not have livings and they would have been even worse off. Lower clergy had little education and, both in England and Wales, most found it difficult to master the Latin service, let alone the theology behind the sacrifice of the Mass. The service was recited rather than comprehended, theology transmuted into superstition. The Church, ever present in the lives of clergy and laity, was a matter of ritual, holy days, the priest, the monastery, a knowledge rooted in wooden and stone statues, pictures and stained glass. Life was short and this iconography emphasised the horrors of judgment day. Various insurances had grown up against it – pilgrimages, the cults of saints and the Virgin Mary, and those indulgences whose commercial subversion was the occasion for Luther's outburst against the Roman Church. It was superstition which led to the popularity of the indulgences which Tetzel sold in Germany and which were common to western Christendom.

At the same time there was some resentment among the laity at the financial exactions of the Church, particularly mortuary payments, and considerable anti-clericalism. Priests were not particularly pious. Many as already mentioned married, despite the theological injunction of celibacy on clergy. Sons followed their fathers into the priesthood, indeed learned Latin services from them. Neither higher nor lower clergy, and certainly not the laity, were therefore well equipped to resist religious changes which might be dictated by the state.

Compared with England there were relatively few monasteries

in Wales. There were forty-six houses: thirteen Cistercian (the wealthiest order), twelve Benedictine. Six were houses of the Augustinian canons, Talley Abbey was Premonstratensian and there was one house of the Knights Hospitallers. There were also three nunneries and ten friaries, mainly Dominican and Franciscan. The Welsh monasteries were not as wealthy as English ones. Their total net income of £3,178 in 1535 was less than that of one wealthy English house such as Glastonbury. But they were more prosperous than the secular church, with revenue from pilgrimages and justice, donations in wills and, above all, income from their large estates. Many parishes were appropriated to the monasteries which kept about 60 per cent of the tithes, while the vicar in charge of the benefice received the remainder. Since the fourteenth century it had been common for monasteries to farm out collection of tithes to laymen, local landowners, and after the dissolution they tried to get the leases confirmed. Not only had the Church therefore lost valuable income but it meant the domination of lay interests in the livings concerned and, often, neglect of the fabric of churches and the spiritual needs of the parishioners. By the sixteenth century much monastic land was leased to laymen, together with rights to mills and fishing. The revenue went into lay hands.

Lay impropriation was far more damaging to the monastic ideal than monastic scandal. Lurid accounts of gross immorality are little more than the exaggerations of Thomas Cromwell's visitors seeking to justify dissolution. Despite the activities of a coiner at Strata Florida abbey, Cardiganshire, the most glaring breach of discipline was evident in the number of sons of abbots and priors who succeeded them in office. Most damaging was the decline in numbers of monks and in the ideals of poverty and asceticism. In 1534–6 there were about 250 religious in all the Welsh houses, an average of about five to six per house. Tintern was the only abbey with a complement of thirteen, usually regarded as the minimum required to fulfil basic elements of monastic rule. Worship, teaching, preaching, training and scholarship all suffered.

On the eve of Henry VIII's Reformation outside observers regarded the Roman Catholic Church in Wales as far healthier than was in fact the case. The quality of the clergy, poverty and laicisation, were all debilitating. The control of laymen over church property and income was crucial. Although there was humanist criticism of the

Church in Wales it played little part in causing or endorsing the Reformation, just as secular motives were mainly responsible for the dissolution of the monasteries. The will of the crown was readily acceptable in Wales where, crucially, the gentry were eager to consolidate their hold over crown and monastic land. As a class they had already benefited from Tudor rule. Only a vital religious commitment would have encouraged them to risk these gains, and it did not exist.

The Reformation

Welsh involvement in the early stages of the Reformation was limited, though Bishop Athequa of Llandaff acted as Catherine of Aragon's confessor. Then, as we saw, Rhys ap Gruffydd's death may have been due partly to his antipathy towards Ann Boleyn, a dislike shared by other Welsh gentry, but their loyalty to Catherine was not the stuff of which martyrs are made. When the Act of Supremacy required an oath of loyalty only two of the Welsh clergy refused, including Athequa. At a stroke Henry VIII had neutralised effective clerical opposition, though the realisation of the significance of this was long delayed.

There was no more opposition when the monasteries were dissolved. In 1536 all Welsh houses except Strata Florida, Whitland and Neath were closed down with very little popular reaction and certainly no pilgrimage of grace. The gentry were certainly unlikely to protest. Land had been leased to them before the Reformation. This land they continued to lease or purchase with the result that their stake in the Reformation was cemented. Acquisition of monastic land did not involve commitment to Protestantism, as the eventual purchase of Ewenni Priory lands by Sir Edward Carne of Glamorgan was to demonstrate. Yet lack of resistance to the dissolution was contrary to some expectations within the Catholic hierarchy.

The pace of the Reformation quickened in Edward VI's reign. The Council of Regency – the king was a minor – had strong Protestant representation and the successive *de facto* rulers, Somerset and Northumberland, hurried along the Protestant path. The chantries were soon dissolved and Church goods pillaged, with clergy themselves – as with the canons of Llandaff and St David's dioceses – appropriating Church possessions. In 1549–50 there were attacks on images and pictures, and the replacement of high altars with tables.

These did cause resentment in Wales, although no particularly strong reaction. Most resistance came with the breaking up of shrines. The authorities were worried about reactions but the notion of strong Welsh allegiance to Catholicism was misjudged. The loyalty of the gentry to the crown was crucial because there was no equivalent aristocratic faction to that involved in risings in the north of England. We have seen that neither clergy nor laity were well-equipped to withstand centrally imposed changes.

The progress of Protestantism

The Reformation provoked no rebellion in Wales but it induced despair among those dedicated Protestants who hoped it would transform apathy towards the old religion into enthusiasm for the new, a judgment borne out by the activities of Bishop Barlow in St David's. He was a protégé of Ann Boleyn and Thomas Cromwell – it was Ann Boleyn who presented him to the Priory of Haverfordwest. There he preached advanced Protestant views and his tactlessness provoked outspoken reactions. His letters indicate that he believed St David's diocese to be a hotbed of papistry and when he became bishop in 1536 he took upon himself many of the responsibilities previously undertaken by the cathedral chapter. Barlow, safe for a few years in court and government patronage, felt free to promote extreme Protestant views, but in a national context of a Henrician quasi-Catholicism and a local context of strong opposition from chapter and clergy. His own cathedral canons soon protested officially about their bishop, and Barlow was only able to withstand such opposition because of his powerful patrons. His extreme condemnation of his diocesan clergy can be discounted, but there was superstition and ignorance among the laity and corruption among the clergy. To an ardent Protestant like Barlow the practice of pilgrimage was anathema and he preached against the shrines to the Virgin and the shrine of St David's itself, one of the most sacred places of pilgrimage in the country. Barlow realised that he would not break the tradition of devotion to the bones of the saint so he proposed moving the cathedral from St David's to Carmarthen. He also intended setting up schools for training clergy – a needed reform – but the whole plan was thwarted by the cathedral canons. Barlow was extreme and partial, but it is indisputable that the state of the diocese was a cause of grave disquiet to an advanced Protestant reformer. The old practices of Catholicism were deeply ingrained in this and the other Welsh dioceses.

It became increasingly obvious to Welsh reformers that Protestantism could make little headway without religious writings in Welsh. Protestantism was based on the notion of the priesthood of all believers, made meaningful by reading the Bible and allowing the Holy Spirit to work on its message. There was emphasis in Protestant countries on providing the Scriptures in the vernacular but there was a special problem in Wales. The vernacular was Welsh for the overwhelming majority. The first to articulate the central issue of the Reformation in Wales was Sir John Price, humanist, henchman of Thomas Cromwell, purchaser of much of the land of Brecon priory, patrons of bards, collector of manuscripts. He argued that many Welshmen who could read Welsh were unable to read a word of English or Latin and that although many Christian writings were available in manuscript, these were necessarily rare. The printing press made possible a widespread distribution of books. His argument was that those allowed to benefit should not exclude those capable of reading only Welsh. Price believed that thousands of souls were being lost because of the inadequacies of the Welsh clergy.

This refrain was echoed by William Salesbury, one of the most remarkable figures of the Welsh Reformation. The Protestant changes of Edward VI's reign were having little effect in Wales, one reason being that the first Prayer Book of 1549 and the more overtly Protestant Prayer Book of 1552 were published in English and almost certainly the majority of priests made little effective use of them. The need for religious writings in Welsh became more obvious and pressing. Salesbury, a member of the gentry class, was the first to assuage this need. His first Welsh publication was a book of proverbs, *Oll Synnwyr Pen Cymro*, in 1547. Renaissance humanists believed that Greek and Latin proverbs contained a wealth of wisdom and that vernacular languages must distinguish themselves by tapping this wisdom. Salesbury was also anxious to demonstrate that the Welsh language could serve as an adequate medium for disseminating Renaissance learning and it was this which prompted him to resort to the latinised Welsh which characterised his work. His ultimate aim was the provision of the Bible in Welsh but his next work was *Kynniver Llith a Ban*, a translation of the gospels and epistles of the

Prayer Book, intended as an interim stage in the production of a Welsh New Testament. The latter appeared in 1567, and this was intended as the preliminary to a translation of the complete Bible.

The reign of Mary Tudor

When Mary Tudor acceded to the throne in 1553 there was a reversion to the old order. She was not welcomed universally in Wales, as has sometimes been supposed. Northumberland's supporters in Wales at one time included the Earl of Pembroke, Sir Richard Bulkeley of Beaumaris and Ellis Price in Denbigh, although Pembroke, particularly, was not wholly committed. Even so, opposition was minimal and, since Protestantism had made little headway in Wales, there was little reaction to the restoration of Roman Catholicism. There were three martyrs, Robert Ferrar, William Nichol and Rawlins White and also some Welsh exiles.

In 1554 the process of depriving married priests of their livings started to take effect, and Robert Ferrar, the only married bishop in Wales, was the first to be deprived. In 1555 he was executed in Carmarthen for heresy. The many married clergy prepared to renounce their wives were allowed to take up livings elsewhere. They acquiesced if only apathetically, in other Marian changes. The martyrdoms of Ferrar in Carmarthen and Rawlins White in Cardiff, taking place in strategic centres, were intended as a deterrent. In one respect Mary's policies were doomed. Those gentry, many Catholic sympathisers among them, who had acquired monastic land were not prepared to yield it up. Apart from the restoration of some lands in Slebech, Pembrokeshire, former monastic property stayed firmly in lay hands.

The Elizabethan settlement and its aftermath

The Elizabethan settlement of 1559 produced an uneasy compromise between Catholicism and reform and once again there was little overt reaction in Wales. Some of the higher clergy appointed by Mary – Henry Morgan, bishop of St David's, Morris Clynnog, bishop-elect of Bangor – suffered, but the mass of clergy accepted the new regime as they had accepted the old. However, the events of the two previous reigns had polarised opinion among the committed of both sides, limiting scope for compromise. Morris Clynnog and other higher clergy, Owen Lewis, Morgan Phillips, Gruffydd Robert, went into exile. They were later to train as Catholic clergy and provide Catholic literature in Welsh.

There was little strong reaction among the gentry and this was to prove crucial. Sir Edward Carne of Ewenni, in Rome as Mary's ambassador, remained there but there was otherwise no open opposition among the gentry. Their loyalty to the Tudors who had consolidated their position of power in their communities was a potent factor. Lower clergy and laity alike were confused by the rapid changes. Catholic practices – pilgrimages, the use of rosaries even – carried on in Elizabeth's reign but they did not signify a basic grasp of Catholic teaching which alone might have prompted serious opposition. Such practices merely served to mislead Catholic reformers about the dedication of the Welsh to the old faith. Neither among powerful laity nor among clergy was there any propensity to martyrdom in its cause.

Quiescence did not mean any marked commitment to the new Church, but Protestant leaders in the Elizabethan Church in Wales were of high intellectual calibre and met the challenge created by general apathy towards the new church. Two Welsh bishops, particularly, were outstanding, Bishop Richard Davies and Bishop William Morgan. The majority of Welsh bishops in Elizabeth's reign were Welsh or, at least, had Welsh connections. This generally meant that they were resident in their dioceses and able to give spiritual leadership to their clergy. The provision of a Welsh Bible remained the outstanding priority, the essential tool of the reformers, but the traditional problems of the Welsh Church remained. Poverty was endemic, there was a lack of able preachers, there was the added difficulty in Wales of the language. If the clergy had received any education it would have been in English; if they were acquainted with the theological tenets of the reformers it would have been through English writings. Yet the message had to be preached in Welsh.

The reformers were well aware that the attitude of the gentry was crucial. There was a considerable residue of Roman Catholic sympathy in gentry ranks, yet its expression was muted, and paradox abounded. In Glamorgan, for example, some staunch Catholics had acquired monastic land. Not that this encouraged Protestant leaders, because it consolidated lay impropriation of livings which forced many parish priests to live on a pittance and contributed to the deterioration in church buildings.

Against such a background the lack of a Welsh Bible assumed yet greater significance. Protestant services without an order of service or the Bible in Welsh were a travesty. Elizabethan bishops not only provided Wales with the Bible but, in doing so, greatly helped to preserve the Welsh language. That was the measure of their achievement. For good measure, though on the basis of inaccurate history, they provided Welsh Protestants with a theory that their Church was the true Church of ancient Britain, which had been corrupted by Roman accretions from the sixth century.

It was wrongly believed in the sixteenth century that there had once been a Welsh translation of the Bible, and certainly none existed at the outset of Elizabeth's reign and there were formidable difficulties in providing one. A Welsh Bible required mastery of Latin, Greek and Hebrew as well as an ability to translate into a language which was not standardised. It would be an extremely expensive undertaking and the market would be limited, but Protestant humanists saw it as indispensable. Salesbury had been anxious to secure permission for a translation in Edward VI's reign and he was probably responsible for the 1561 petition to Parliament requesting that the Bible should be translated into Cornish and Welsh. In 1563 came the enormously significant act authorising translation, to be undertaken within the following four years by the bishops of the Welsh dioceses and Hereford. Thereafter, the Welsh Bible was to be used by the Welsh clergy and copies in both Welsh and English to be placed in each church. The first fruits were the appearance in 1567 of the Book of Common Prayer and the New Testament, translated mainly by Salesbury. Unfortunately, his concern with ensuring that Welsh should be of sufficient richness and beauty led him to latinise words and ignore mutations, so divorcing the written from the spoken language and making the translation much less useful to priest and layman alike. Bishop Richard Davies of St Asaph, then St David's, who had been instrumental in bringing about the act of 1563, was Salesbury's collaborator. The grander design they had of proceeding to a translation of the Old Testament came to nothing, although Davies had translated important sections of the 1567 New Testament brilliantly.

Significant though the New Testament translation was, the translation of the whole Bible by William Morgan, vicar of Llanrhaeadr-ym-mochnant, in 1588 was immeasurably more important. His prose, unlike that of Salesbury, was based on the Welsh of the great poets, though he introduced a flexibility of his own. He synthesised the work of Salesbury and Davies in a work of the highest intellectual and linguistic distinction. It was the foundation of the modern Welsh language, providing a standard reference essential now that the great medieval Welsh poets were without successors. It was a stimulus to Welsh prose writing and, in short, meant the preservation of the Welsh language. It was also part of the wider achievement of Protestantism and humanism in Wales which included religious and moral writings, works of Welsh grammar, culminating in the remarkable analysis of the language by Dr John Davies of Mallwyd in 1621 and his great Welsh Dictionary in 1632. Apart from its immense significance for the language and literature of Wales the translation provided Welsh Protestants with the essential basis for their mission. Now, with a Welsh order of service as well, Protestant teaching could be comprehensible to parish priest and laity. Few of the laity could afford to buy even the 1630 *Beibl Bach*, the first relatively cheap edition, but the impact lay in having the Bible read at church services in the language of the people. It was the key to a Protestant Wales.

Bishop Richard Davies's complementary contribution was to provide a widely believed historical account of the origins of the Protestant faith and in so doing juxtapose the great antiquity of the Welsh language and the Established Church. In his preface to the 1567 New Testament Davies made a brilliant attempt to demolish resistance to Protestantism on the grounds that it departed from tradition by arguing that, far from Protestantism being a new religion foisted on the Welsh, it signalled a return to the purity of the early Welsh Church. Interwoven with the story of the conversion of the Britons by Joseph of Arimathea within a few years of Christ's death was the notion that there had been a Welsh translation of the Bible in ancient times. A compelling advantage of the theory was that it effectively answered any criticism that the Established Church was an alien English religion forced on the Welsh. Welsh Protestant leaders were therefore able to combine priorities of humanism, religion and language to provide an effective and appealing theory of reform in Wales.

Despite the herculean labours of religious humanists the inertia of the Welsh in the face of the new Church caused great concern. A succession of bishops' reports indicated the immensity of the task facing Welsh Protestants. Humanist achievements had done nothing to counteract the essential poverty of the Welsh Church compared with that in England or the problems of lay impropriation. Poverty, accentuated by clerical marriage and inflation, meant pluralism and difficulty in attracting parish clergy of the highest quality. In 1567 Bishop Robinson pointed to the unenthusiastic response of the gentry to Protestantism. This was echoed by Bishop Richard Davies in 1570 and he also commented on the shortage of preachers in his diocese. He condemned the effects of lay impropriation and pluralism. He was no more content with the response of the masses and commented on their sexual immorality. They were lukewarm in their response to the new Church and clung to the Roman Catholic practice of pilgrimage. Davies's successor, Marmaduke Middleton, thirteen years later condemned Catholic ritual in church services, including the elevation of the host, a symbolic act of sacrifice central to distinguishing the Catholic mass from Anglican communion. Bishop Godwin's report of 1603 reiterated the theme of the evils of lay impropriation.

Yet a blend of information culled from the verdicts of Elizabethan bishops on their dioceses, and a historical tradition of sympathy for Welsh nonconformity, built on the inadequacies of Anglicanism, is bound to be misleading. The quality of the bishops in Elizabeth's reign was infinitely superior to that of many of their medieval predecessors – with the diocese of Bangor particularly fortunate. They were concerned with deficiencies, not with progress – and there had been progress by the end of the sixteenth century. Despite poverty the recruitment and quality of clergy had improved. More clergy were educated at Oxford and Cambridge and were drawn from gentry families. The gentry themselves, partly because they had impropriated tithes, were increasingly conformist. Increasingly, too, they embraced Renaissance theories of state which stressed the importance of the prince and the uniformity of institutions over which he presided. They played a crucial role in those institutions themselves. The Established Church therefore commanded at least a minimum of conformity, even among pro-Catholic families. Dwarfing these achievements was the provision of religious literature in Welsh.

In the period up to the Civil War there was further emphasis placed on preaching by bishops and gentry who made provision for it. Early Stuart governments attempted to lay down minimum standards of learning and suitability for clergy, indicated their dislike of pluralism and attempted to ensure residence of bishops in their dioceses. And, by this time, any positive threat from Roman Catholicism was more apparent than real, despite the plots of James I's reign.

The Counter-Reformation

That the Reformation and the Elizabethan settlement had produced no explosive reaction in Wales surprised contemporaries, if some Roman Catholic polemicists are to be believed. The four most notable Welshmen to promote the Counter-Reformation in Wales were Gruffydd Robert, former archdeacon of Anglesey, Morys Clynnog, bishop-elect of Bangor at the end of Mary's reign, Morgan Phillips, precentor of St David's, and Owen Lewis, of Llanfarian, Anglesey. The years following Elizabeth's accession were frustrating for Catholics, with the Pope and Philip of Spain prevaricating and, at home, increasing temptations to conform, particularly by those lay families without whose leadership protest movements in the cause of the old faith were doomed. Catholicism depended on the availability of the priesthood to the people and the celebration of the sacraments. The mass was celebrated secretly and Catholic baptism and burial continued, but not on the scale to constitute any threat to the state. In 1568 Catholic exiles founded a seminary at Douai to train missionary priests for England and Wales. Owen Lewis and Morgan Phillips joined with William Allen to establish Douai while Morys Clynnog published *Athravaeth Gristnogawl* in 1568 to provide instruction for the laity. Catholic leaders produced polemic literature early on and their secret printing presses provided the government with a grave problem.

Despite Catholic hopes, even beliefs, no serious threat to the government arose in Wales in Elizabeth's reign. It has been calculated that by 1577 there were only twelve declared recusants. Ostensibly this number had increased enormously to about 800 by the beginning of the seventeenth century, but this was at least partly due to increased government rooting out of recusants as the international situation deteriorated in the 1580s and 1590s. This was, in any case, a small number even if it did represent only the hard core. There were some important families involved, however, and it was here that any threat to the government lay because so much depended on the loyalty of deputy lieutenants, sheriffs and justices of the peace to central government. Where there was leadership, substantial groups of recusants formed – in Monmouthshire under the Earls of Worcester, or around the Edwards family of Chirk or the Turbervilles of Glamorgan. So, important groups of recusants are found in these areas, not, as might be expected, in the remotest counties.

Such groups were not given much encouragement by the Catholic authorities. The seminary at Douai sent some hundreds of priests to England in the 1570s but few came to Wales. The Douai authorities believed, even at the end of Elizabeth's reign, that Wales was a hotbed of Catholicism. They were misguided. Those who did come to Wales were men of high courage. The first Catholic martyr in Wales was Richard Gwyn, a schoolmaster of Llanidloes, who died in 1584, and William Davies of Colwyn in Denbighshire was martyred in 1593. But Wales was not the object of much missionary activity particularly after the Jesuits, opposed to Morys Clynnog's missionary methods, won control of the English college in Rome. Exiled Welshmen did go far to meet the need for Catholic literature in Welsh, with Gruffydd Roberts's *Y Drych Cristionogawl* and Morys Clynnog's *Athravaeth Gristnogawl*. In the end the efforts of priests and authors were to achieve little as gradual conformity replaced vestigial devotion to the old religion. Numerous Welsh families – and the attitude of the leading county gentry was vital – slid into conformity partly out of self-interest, partly out of genuine loyalty to the Tudor state. The estimated 800 recusants of 1603 contrast with the estimated 200,000 who conformed, whatever the quality of that conformity. Some recusant clusters remained – in 1591, for example, 160 gathered in Hafod-y-porth, Glamorgan, to celebrate mass and to christen a child brought on a two-day journey by its nurse. Priests trickled into Wales. Morgan Clynnog, nephew of Morys, came to South Wales in 1582 after training at the English College in Rome. From 1582 until at least 1619 he preached in Carmarthenshire and Glamorgan, but his was an exceptional career. Overall Welsh Catholics posed no real threat to the government.

The situation changed little up to the Civil War. Poverty remained the besetting problem of the Welsh dioceses, causing deficiencies only too obvious to early Stuart bishops. To make matters worse three of the four bishops appointed in the diocese of Llandaff between 1601 and 1640 were English and one was Scottish. The small hardcore of recusants remained untouched. The fiasco of the gunpowder plot resulted in two statutes of 1606 which increased fines for recusants and required greater vigilance from local officials. Partly as a result, numbers of recorded recusants increased — in Flintshire, for example, from 99 in 1606 to 115 in 1620 and 153 by 1624. The majority came still from the ranks of yeomen and tenant farmers who were not a major force in their communities. By Charles I's reign it was obvious that Catholic recusancy was far less of a threat to the established order than Puritanism.

Puritanism

During Elizabeth's reign the main thrust of Puritanism was towards making Protestant teaching more effective, rather than emphasising the incompatibility of the Calvinist theory of state with the Elizabethan Anglican hierarchy. It was this latter aspect which was to underpin the controversies of the seventeenth century. The Protestant desire to save souls had produced the Scriptures in Welsh but reformers were well aware of structural weaknesses, and the lack of progress of the new faith was a matter of concern. John Penry is the best known of those Welshmen conscious of the spiritual needs of his fellow Welshmen and, knowing the extent of adherence to superstitious practices and ignorance among them, he twice appealed to Parliament in 1587 and to the council in the marches in 1588. His radical beliefs included a conviction that an episcopalian system of Church government should be replaced by presbyterianism but his concern in the petitions was also to secure preaching to save souls. He was ignored, indeed arrested, accused of heresy for arguing that preaching was necessary for salvation. Disillusioned by the response of the authorities he made plain his belief that the state should not be able to determine the religious beliefs of its citizens and church membership should be restricted to those who had undergone a religious conversion.

The tensions inherent in the Elizabethan settlement, in doctrine and Church organisation, were accentuated under the early Stuarts, though the edges of Puritanism were remarkably blurred on occasion. Anglican Bishop Lewis Bayly of Bangor preached, in his *Practice of*

Piety, a markedly puritan lifestyle. Vicar Pritchard, born in 1579, Oxford graduate, vicar of Llandovery and Llawhaden, pluralist, remained in the Established Church all his life and supported the king on the outbreak of the Civil War. He was an able and caring priest and his concern manifested itself in ways reminiscent of later Methodism. He was violently anti-Papist, endorsing an extreme form of the Calvinist doctrine of predestination. He was gravely concerned with the immorality he witnessed around him and advocated, through preaching and his famous verses, published as *Canwyll y Cymry*, a puritan lifestyle – strict sabbatarianism, family prayer, Bible-reading.

Pritchard represented a growing body of opinion in the Established Church which was increasingly concerned with lack of understanding of those Calvinist doctrines believed indispensable to salvation. Some attempted to combat lay impropriation by buying up livings and using the tithe to pay preachers. The largest living purchased, in England or Wales, was that of Presteign. Financing of preaching or lecturing by unbeneficed men was a radical departure, and preaching was central to the Puritan wing of the Church. The government was well aware of the dangers, and issued preachers with licences and limited the texts on which they could preach.

Puritanism was more to the fore in the 1630s, both because of increased activity and a harder line by the government. Archbishop Laud revived the Court of High Commission after he became Archbishop of Canterbury in 1633 and in 1635 two incumbents and a curate in the diocese of Llandaff were hauled before it for misleading their parishioners – William Wroth, rector of Llanfaches in Monmouthshire, William Erbury, vicar of St Mary's in Cardiff and Walter Cradock, his curate. Cradock moved to Wrexham briefly before being forced to move on to Herefordshire, from which base he converted Vavasour Powell, at that time living in Shropshire. Wroth and Erbury, in 1639, set up the first church outside the hierarchy of the Established Church. Wroth remained rector of Llanfaches.

When the Civil War broke out the clergy, like the gentry, generally remained loyal to the king. Important Welsh puritans dispersed to England. The Llanfaches congregation went to Bristol, Vavasour Powell to London. With the war won and Parliament in power various attempts were made to show the Welsh the error of their ways. Puritanism did make some progress, particularly in the border counties and in the south-east where sufficient support came from the gentry to sustain it. The number of autonomous 'Independent' congregations multiplied and, in 1649, John Miles established a Baptist church in Ilston, Gower. This was the first of a tightly-knit organisation of five Baptist churches supervised by Miles. In the 1650s there was some more, limited, success for Puritanism, mainly the result of concerted government activity.

In 1650 the Act for the Propagation of the Gospel established a commission to puritanise Wales, a daunting task outside the border counties and the south-east. The commission, headed by Colonel Thomas Harrison, consisted of seventy-one members, a quarter of whom were English. Colonel Philip Jones of Llangyfelach, Glamorgan, who had held high rank in Cromwell's army, Colonel John Jones, signatory to Charles I's death warrant, and Sir Erasmus Phillips of Picton, Pembrokeshire, were the most notable Welshmen. Their task was to examine clergy and schoolmasters and act against clergy guilty of misconduct or pluralism. Some ministers were dismissed or ordered to surrender all but one living. In three years 278 clergy were ejected, but perhaps more remarkable is the number of clergy allowed to remain. Those ejected suffered much hardship, some were restored to their livings on appeal, some started private schools or, indeed, became official schoolmasters under the Propagation Act. In remoter areas some carried on ministering to their people as before.

Ejecting ministers was far easier than replacing them. The Propagation Act appointed twenty-five approvers – clergy themselves – to approve suitable ministers and schoolmasters in Wales. Those recommended were granted licences to preach by the Propagation commissioners, but finding adequately qualified Welsh clergy, particularly in the remoter parts of Wales, was exceedingly difficult and the commissioners had to resort to itinerant preachers. The approvers themselves performed heroically as itinerants – Morgan Llwyd travelled over much of North Wales from Wrexham; Vavasour Powell preached in mid Wales, Henry Walter in Glamorgan and Monmouthshire. They were helped by over sixty itinerants of variable quality. Often drawn from the ranks of farmers, tradesmen or even former soldiers, they were as capable of arousing hostility as enthusiasm. Their lack of education was also a handicap but the basic problem was that under this system, there could be no continuity of ministry which could alone counteract the increasingly bemusing mysteries of theology and Church organisation with which the layman was confronted. Since many of the itinerants also preached in English it was inevitable that this attempt to puritanise Wales would fail. The act lapsed in 1653.

Some Welsh Puritans were now caught up in national events as Cromwell dissolved the Long Parliament and made himself Lord Protector in 1653. The Fifth Monarchists, believing in the imminence of Christ's second coming, were appalled by Cromwell's actions and among his most prominent opponents were Vavasour Powell and Morgan Llwyd. The former had to take refuge in Wales after preaching against Cromwell, but continued his pamphlet war. There were even suspicions that Powell was leading his supporters towards armed rebellion and although there was little substance in this Powell was to spend nine of his last ten years in prison.

The mission of puritanising the Welsh became ever more complex with the various extremes of belief now circulating. Morgan Llwyd also believed in the mystic presence of Christ in men's hearts and became interested in the teachings of the Quaker leader, George Fox. Thomas Holmes led a Quaker mission to Wales in 1654–5 – through the border counties of South Wales. Fox himself made a successful tour of Wales in 1657, making converts in Glamorgan, Radnor, Montgomeryshire and Pembrokeshire. The following year John ap John made another successful Quaker preaching tour. In Flintshire the teaching of Philip Henry resulted in Presbyterianism taking hold.

In this context of a confusion of missions itinerant ministry was abandoned. The reversion to a settled ministry came with the commission for the approbation of public preachers – the triers – in 1654. Based in London these thirty-eight ministers and laymen theoretically had the power to certify ministers, though Cromwell himself and the trustees for maintenance effectively controlled the majority of livings. Most former itinerant ministers were appointed to established livings and a plan was devised for reorganising Welsh parishes to iron out the worst anomalies of size and income, though it proved difficult to make much headway with it.

Ministry under the trustees for maintenance was beset with the old problem of lack of trained, educated personnel. Many ministers could not even speak Welsh, although there were outstanding exceptions – Stephen Hughes of Meidrim or Samuel Jones of

Llangynwyd. Because of the shortage, ministers were allowed to hold more than one living, producing the usual problems of pluralism. The effectiveness of this second phase of puritanising was as limited as the first. While it may have had some impact in the border counties and South Wales it was of little effect in the North. The variety of sects and methods of mission now compounded the lack of preachers and endemic poverty in the Welsh Church. The various theological refinements of Puritanism meant little but the moral message, with its emphasis on upright behaviour, penalties for swearing and drunkenness, suppression of traditional revels like dancing round the maypole and bear-baiting, was not at all popular. So, although under the impact of a specific mission or a great preacher there was progress, the response generally in Wales was lukewarm. Radical Puritans were themselves split by 1655. Vavasour Powell's pamphlet, *The Word of God*, denounced Cromwell, but Powell had little support. Walter Cradock condemned his pamphlet and was supported by Morgan Llwyd. The moderate Puritan element in Wales proved stronger and millenarian beliefs dwindled drastically by 1660.

Puritanism as a religion was coupled with Puritanism as a state system, an unpopular one in Wales, particularly among the gentry, whose leadership was vital. The gentry opposed the ejection of Anglican clergy and the use of parish revenues to support Puritan doctrines. They resented the low quality and status of clergy appointed under the Commonwealth and, naturally, detested those changes brought about in county government and society by Cromwell's regime.

Dissent

Charles II's restoration was generally welcomed, but a smooth return to the 1640s was not possible. Puritanism had taken root in some. parts of Wales and Charles's early Parliaments were in no mood to tolerate it. Morgan Llwyd and Walter Cradock had died in 1659, but other Puritan leaders were peremptorily dealt with. The former head of the propagation commission, Thomas Harrison, was executed, Vavasour Powell was imprisoned, John Miles of Ilston emigrated to America. For over a year it appeared that the Presbyterians, at least, might be peacefully accommodated within the restored Church, but compromise became impossible after the Clarendon Code passed by Charles II's Cavalier Parliament in the years between 1661 and 1665.

The Corporation Act required those holding office to take communion in church. The 1662 Act of Uniformity required conformity with the Book of Common Prayer and the Church of England liturgy. Even before this act ninety-three Puritan clergy had been ejected in Wales, to be followed now by a further twenty-five. The act also put schoolmasters under ecclesiastical control. In 1664 the Conventicle Act tried to ensure that no more than five people – aside from families – should collect for worship except in church. This did not prevent Dissenters from worshipping together, though Bishops were reluctant to admit it. Persecution, as usual, was self-defeating, and the 1670 renewal of the act tacitly admitted as much by making penalties very severe. This merely resulted in magistrates turning a blind eye. The 1665 Five Mile Act was scarcely more successful. It was intended to stop ejected clergy establishing schools but failed. There were periods when this persecution bit into Dissent, with the situation at its worst after 1681. Quakers, particularly, persecuted not only by legislation but by fellow Dissenters, emigrated to America in large numbers. The gap between the letter of the law and its enforcement was, however, a wide one.

Despite Charles II's sympathy with Roman Catholicism its adherents suffered too, but it was on their behalf that the 1672 Declaration of Indulgence was passed, suspending the penal laws. What is interesting is the reaction of Dissenters who obtained 185 licences, 136 in South Wales. This is probably an underestimate of the number of dissenting congregations and yet gives an indication of how well they had survived under persecution. In the 1670s there were over 4,000 Dissenters in Wales and over 1,000 Roman Catholics, and as persecution of Catholics increased in the late 1670s so attitudes to Dissent grew more tolerant for a time. In response to James II's machinations Dissenters resisted promises of toleration unless sanctioned by Parliament. James II's 1688 Indulgence, suspending the penal laws was, of course, prompted by his Catholicism but resulted in his precipitate departure from England. In the reign of a successor, Queen Anne, came more attempts to stamp out Dissent with the Occasional Conformity Act for example.

Dissent, far from being wiped out in the half century following the Act of Uniformity in 1662 had consolidated, particularly in the border counties and South Wales. Its importance was greatly out of proportion to its numbers because of the dedication and conviction of members. After 1689 dissenting sects made further progress. By 1715 there were about seventy churches, with the Baptists and Independents forming the main denominations. Information from Henry Maurice indicates that there were twelve Independent churches, with only Anglesey, Merioneth and Flint not represented. These were county churches, and each might have numerous branches, with circuits to provide a regular ministry. Gathered with the Independents for about twenty years after the Restoration were the Presbyterians and Baptists, with the Presbyterians and Independents, particularly, finding common organisational cause. But by the end of the seventeenth century theological differences were beginning to divide the sects.

Licensing of ministers followed the 1672 Indulgence and the Dissenting movement became more formalised, especially after the Toleration Act of 1689. The Presbyterians and Independents established a central fund in London in 1691 to provide churches and train ministers, though this served to accentuate tensions between leaders and within churches. Notions of church democracy clashed with syndical organisation, and high Calvinism clashed with low. Within three years the Congregationalists (Independents) had started a separate fund, so creating an organisational breach healed only in 1973. There were theological differences between the different eighteenth-century Dissenting sects, though not the rigid demarcation characteristic of the twentieth century. Baptists were obviously differentiated by their insistence on adult baptism. They were also, unfairly, linked with sixteenth-century Anabaptists, and so accused of wishing to break down the political and social order. Presbyterians grew away from the Independents theologically as well as organisationally as they tended to Unitarianism. The Quakers were the most persecuted because they were felt to be most subversive – in their dress and speech, their opposition to tithes and clergy. As a result many emigrated, so weakening the sect. In the face of continued persecution the sects still had common cause and there was co-operation. However after 1689 persecution aroused anguish rather than fear – for example Dissenters were refused licences for their churches and refused burial in parish churches.

The emphasis in Dissent was on sobriety of lifestyle, hard work and lengthy instruction by sermon or lecture in unpretentious meeting-houses. Not surprisingly most adherents were drawn from well up the social scale – lesser gentry, prosperous freeholders, tenants and craftsmen. Merchants and traders in the towns were well represented, but in many congregations landless labourers formed substantial sections so that, apart from the greater gentry, all shades of the social spectrum were involved. Well into the nineteenth century both the numbers and the geographical coverage of Dissent did not seem particularly impressive. To the majority, Dissent was alien and extreme. Its concentration on intellectual analysis, and lack of emotion, precluded any mass appeal. However, the once-popular notion that there was spiritual torpor between about 1689 and the Methodist revival is untrue. Dissent was influential out of proportion to its numbers.

The Established Church after the Restoration

The Established Church had been restored with the king in 1660 but could no longer contain the Puritan wing. Penal legislation widened the breach, and produced years of bitterness. The attitude of the Church was generally very hostile to Dissent even after the Toleration Act of 1689, but the attitude of the Welsh bishops did vary. Lucy of St David's was uncompromising, while Bishop William Lloyd of St Asaph tried to persuade Dissenters to return to the Church. Because of conditioning by nonconformist historiography it has become common to regard the Church of England in Wales before the Methodist revival as increasingly anglicised, alien, lacking in adequate clergy and spiritual effectiveness. Naturally, Methodism has been concerned to contrast the spiritual poverty of the Established Church with its own religious dynamism. The shortcomings of the Church have been exaggerated, though contemporary evidence does highlight some intractable problems. In the second half of the seventeenth century most Welsh bishops spoke Welsh; some – Bishop Bull of St David's, Bishop Humphreys of Bangor – were theologians and scholars of distinction. Many of the lower clergy carried out their work effectively. Even from the hostile evidence of churchmen anxious to produce improvements – Erasmus Saunders or even Griffith Jones – it emerges that the laity were often prepared to make considerable efforts to attend church services. Early in the eighteenth century there were attempts to channel some money into the Welsh

Church, to reform services and, interestingly, to stress preaching. Some clergy were active in writing, publishing and distributing books, particularly in connection with the Society for the Propagation of Christian Knowledge. In the early eighteenth century Pembrokeshire clergy gathered for prayer and fellowship.

There is still no gainsaying the inadequacies of the Established Church in Wales, despite the case for redressing the balance. Many of these problems were endemic, particularly poverty, but in the eighteenth century they were accentuated by the contemporary climate of opinion. The eighteenth century was the 'Age of Reason'. It was fashionable to believe that science could explain the secrets of the universe and the popular religion at court was Deism. The Church was held to fulfil a social rather than a religious purpose, with its unscientific theology irrelevant. Bishops were infected by this secularism, played an increasing part in politics and were often absent from their dioceses. Welsh bishops in the second half of the seventeenth century were of higher calibre than in the first half, but they still stayed in Wales for an average of only five or six years. From 1716 to 1870 there was no Welsh-speaking bishop in Wales. Some never visited their diocese. The language problem was evident at parochial level, too. The most notorious case was the appointment of Reverend Bowles to the Trefdraeth and Llangwyfan parishes in Anglesey. He was English, which meant that only five of his 500 parishioners could understand him. Absenteeism became more common at all levels in the early eighteenth century and higher clergy often left ministry to curates who were poorly paid. There was a wholly inefficient diocesan organisation in Wales. St David's was the second largest diocese in England or Wales, and there were vast, sprawling parishes, particularly in the upland areas. Communication between higher and lower clergy was inadequate. Lay impropriation was another long-standing abuse. In the whole of Glamorgan the Bishop of Llandaff did not have one living in his gift. Lay impropriators were extremely mean in the sums they allocated for parish work. The Duke of Somerset received £900 per annum from his Carmarthenshire parishes; he allowed £70 per annum for payment of clergy. Landed society, particularly, regarded such actions as wholly acceptable. Inevitably, poverty led to pluralism and absenteeism among higher and lower clergy. By 1707 there were ninety-six pluralists in the diocese of St David's alone. In the circumstances what is remarkable is the sterling religious and educational work done by so many of the clergy.

This mixed picture of the state of the Anglican Church in Wales is confirmed in part of the diocese of St David's in the 1770s. The bishop was Shute Barrington, conscientious in his duties of confirmation, ordination and visitation. The richest livings were those in which the tithe all went to the incumbent, and the clergy in such livings often came from gentry families. Although there was pluralism the clergy were usually resident in these parishes. Poorer livings were often held as second livings, and therefore absenteeism was far more prevalent. Some curates lived in real poverty and had little education, but in most parishes there was at least one service on Sundays and in most richer parishes, two. Holy communion was usually observed less than once a month.

The Methodist revival

The Methodist revival was firmly rooted in much that had already been accomplished by Anglicanism and Dissent. The work of Griffith Jones and numerous Dissenting ministers in preparing the way for Methodist success cannot be ignored. Both Griffith Jones and the Dissenters had stressed the vital importance of preaching. By the early years of the eighteenth century most parishioners could listen to a sermon at least once a fortnight, with its religious emphasis on man's sinfulness and a social emphasis on good behaviour and the evils of drink and swearing. Dissenting ministers, not tied to parishes, preached far and wide. Baptist William Jones of Cilmaenllwyd supported a network of causes in south-west Wales virtually single-handed. The emphases were the same – Christ's saving grace in face of man's sinfulness, and the moral depravity of the Welsh in breaking the sabbath by playing games, often in the churchyard, lying, adultery, perjury, dancing, cock-fighting.

The way had also been prepared for Methodism by the large increase in the circulation of religious and devotional books in the post-Restoration period. They were written mainly by clergy and ministers, and published by the Welsh Trust, the S.P.C.K. or by subscription. From 1546 to 1660, 108 Welsh titles had been published. From 1660 to 1730 at least 545 were printed. The licensing laws restricting publication to London, Oxford and Cambridge were repealed in 1695 and provincial presses were established first at Shrewsbury then at Carmarthen, both strategically placed. Thomas Jones of Shrewsbury developed a network of book-selling agents who distributed books to general shopkeepers, though by the early eighteenth century professional booksellers set up in business. Distribution in rural areas was a problem, but partly alleviated by the establishment of parish and diocesan libraries after 1701. The motive behind publication was to supplement teaching in sermons; the books were not concerned with high theology but basic Biblical and moral truths. In the second half of the seventeenth century the most popular work was the verse of Vicar Pritchard and in the early eighteenth century about one hundred other works of verse and epigram were published. The greatest effort went into providing Bibles. Between 1660 and 1727, 40,000 copies of the Bible in Welsh were sold or given away, particularly by the Welsh Trust and the S.P.C.K. These were supplemented by the Prayer Book and catechisms. Devotional books were very popular, including a Welsh translation of Bunyan's *Pilgrim's Progress*. The themes, as in sermons, were the sinfulness of man, Christ's saving grace, the importance of conversion – all central to later Methodist teaching. Since this literature was least available to the mass of people who lived at little above subsistence level the message was also passed on orally, with verse and epigram easiest to remember. The impact of this literature was considerable. Welsh squires subscribed to devotional books, particularly gentry in the least anglicised western areas of Wales. But the more anglicised gentry, too, were keen to see such ideas of morality and social order inculcated. So patronage came not only from the important sponsors of the S.P.C.K., Sir Humphrey Mackworth and Sir John Philipps, but from the Bulkeleys of Baron Hill, the Mostyns of Flint, the Mansels of Margam, the Vaughans of Hengwrt. Dissenting ministers and Anglican clergy alike regarded possession of books as vitally important and those pillars of early Dissent, yeomen, artisans, craftsmen, shopkeepers, physicians and lawyers, all subscribed to publications. These were the people who provided the backbone of early Methodism and these, too, were the people who could provide an elementary education for their children. For those not able to do so Griffith Jones's circulating schools, with their emphasis on the Bible and reiterated themes of salvation and good conduct, paved the way for Methodist teaching and preaching.

In 1735 Daniel Rowland, aged twenty-two, was converted when listening to Griffith Jones, Llanddowror at Llanddewibrefi. His father and grandfather had been Anglican clergymen and Daniel Rowland followed the same path. He was not particularly pious in the time between ordination and conversion but, under the influence of Philip Pugh and Griffith Jones, he devoted all his energies to evangelising. Preaching the redemptive love of God and the sacrifice of Christ he drew large, enthusiastic congregations of thousands. In 1737, when Rowland took to preaching outside his parish, he met Howell Harris and they organised the basic Methodist structure of the *seiat* or society to provide an organisation of support for the converted and a basis for future mission. By 1741, however, their bickering culminated in open dispute, partly theological, partly organisational, and certainly based on the clash of two autocratic personalities. With their break complete by 1750 the first enthusiasm for the revival died away, but from 1762 the hymns of Williams, Pantycelyn wrought another revival which spread quickly and effectively. Anglican wrath caused Rowland to be deprived of his curacy in 1763, though he continued preaching regularly to congregations of over 2,000.

Howell Harris differed from Rowland fundamentally and was the main organisational force behind the movement. Born in 1714, son of a carpenter from Talgarth, Breconshire, he was educated at Llwyn-llwyd Dissenting Academy and became a teacher in 1732. In 1735 he was converted at Talgarth by the Reverend Price Davies and, after weeks of introspection, his life changed completely. His conviction of salvation released enormous oratorical and organisational energy. In 1736 he applied for ordination but was refused, not surprisingly since he had already commenced a preaching ministry. He contemplated joining the Baptists, but not seriously. From 1737 he worked with Daniel Rowland to found a movement. Harris's journeys across Wales resulted in a network of societies which established Methodism as a dynamic force within the Anglican Church, kept there largely because of Harris's loyalty to it. He was on good terms with the leaders of both wings of English Methodism, Wesley and Whitefield, but not all his friendships were as acceptable to the Methodists, particularly that with Madam Griffith, the wife of the squire of Cefnamlwch. He was himself subject to dreams which he believed to be divine revelation, and he was convinced of Madam Griffith's prophetic powers.

His personal eccentricities were partly responsible for rifts with fellow Methodist leaders but the main reason for dissension was his autocratic nature. He was a man of authority who, for a short period, had run English Methodism in Whitefield's absence, and he did not intend to be subject to the Welsh Methodist Association. But this was to deny Rowland authority in his area and the last of the united Associations was held in 1750. Harris set up Trefecca, a community of work and religion where his authority was undisputed. Frequent services punctuated a routine of work which was mainly agricultural but included building, wool-spinning and processing, shoemaking and printing. Harris brought some of the latest agricultural techniques to Breconshire through the agricultural society and he revealed his innate traditionalism by becoming an officer in the Breconshire Militia, but his importance to Welsh Methodism as brilliant preacher and organiser was immense.

In 1738 Rowland and Harris had been joined by William Williams, also educated at Llwyn-llwyd Academy, who had hoped to become a doctor. He was converted by Howell Harris and immediately began his preaching mission. Williams's father was a leading nonconformist but on Harris's advice Williams became a deacon in the Established Church, served as a curate in Llanwrtyd and Abergwesyn, but was refused ordination. His itinerant preaching was of immense influence in Methodism but Williams was far less concerned with doctrinal dogma than his fellow leaders, rejecting for example, the extremes of Calvinist predestination. He was a notable founder and organiser of Methodist societies, but his particular genius was as hymn-writer. As such he was the instigator of another phase of Methodist dynamism in the 1760s. The simple beauty of his hymns was to have an incalculable effect on Methodism and, indeed, on Dissent generally. These hymns articulated the emotional creativity of the Methodist movement which made hymn-singing central to Methodism and to Dissent in Wales. The lyrical beauty of the verse which he used to describe the Christian experience also inspired future generations of hymn-writers.

Methodism was not intended to be a disruptive movement. Whitefield and Harris, particularly, were adamant that it should be contained within Anglicanism and at no stage in the eighteenth century were societies allowed to ordain ministers. When the break did come in 1811 many deplored it. Anglicanism could tolerate many aspects of Methodism. In Wales the Methodists followed the Calvinist doctrine of the thirty-nine articles, though the emphasis on salvation was out of tune with the rationalism of the age. This applied to Methodist enthusiasm also, but the tradition of itinerant preaching within the Church was not new, though the precedents for it were not the happiest. The Church could hardly criticise the moral code enjoined on Methodists.

Methodism was, even so, a church within a church, demarcated by its local societies, its adherents subject to persecution. From the first society established in 1737 to the 400 or so established by 1750 the movement flourished, though its golden age was to come in the nineteenth century. The societies, normally ten to thirty strong, gave the movement cohesion as they met for prayer, hymn-singing and, most important, the giving of personal testimony. Leadership of cells was provided by the exhorter and his assistants, with a superintendent in authority over them. From the societies delegates were sent to monthly and quarterly meetings and, finally, to the Association, the national policy-making body. This organisation was the strength of Methodism; its weakness, perhaps, the domination of the Association by Harris, Rowland and Williams which caused disruption after the break of 1750 and a hiatus with their passing. The Methodists also had a flexible language policy – English in the English-speaking areas, Welsh elsewhere.

The seemingly common characteristics of Methodism and Dissent were more evident in the nineteenth century, but there were close links in the eighteenth century too. Dissent imbibed the enthusiasm and concentration on hymn-singing, and Methodism was the agent whereby Dissent was made a popular evangelical movement. Both Methodism and Dissent drew adherents from more prosperous members of the Welsh community – minor gentry, particularly. The local leaders of Methodism, the exhorters, were drawn from all social classes, but were often men of prosperity and education. The movement had widespread popular appeal, but poor adherents rarely achieved prominence in it. Yet what was of profound importance was that a religious change had occurred which reflected, increasingly, a social cleavage. The full impact of this was not apparent in the eighteenth century and the impact of the Methodist revival has been much exaggerated in the nation's historical memory, with far too little emphasis given to the regionalism of Methodism and the growth of Dissent. Yet the interplay of religious and social developments was eventually to be of the greatest significance. The great landed families of Wales spurned Methodism and Dissent. Many of the lesser gentry and freeholders, less powerful than in the sixteenth and seventeenth centuries, and sharply differentiated now from the large landowners, embraced them. Perhaps it compensated for their weakening economic and social position, as the cohesion of Welsh society was strained by the desire of the greater gentry to assert their superiority through monopolising parliamentary representation, disdaining things Welsh, and aping the habits of their English compeers.

There was far more to Methodism than this, however. It reached down the social scale to the artisan and landless labourer. In the end it was the identification of Methodism and Dissent with *y werin* which was to have such an impact on Welsh life in the century after 1780.

6

EDUCATION

A rudimentary education

During the sixteenth century and for much of the seventeenth only a very small proportion of the population obtained even a minimal education. The quality of popular education is difficult to assess because of lack of evidence and far more is known about the education of the upper strata of society.

There were, basically, three types of elementary education available, concentrating on the skills of reading and writing. The prosperous few could employ a private tutor; some grammar schools reluctantly taught the basics but these schools were only accessible to relatively few. Some private schools existed in which the parish priest might teach scholars, or laymen pass on their knowledge to local children for small payments. In 1574 Alice Carter turned her shop in Denbigh into a schoolroom. Some elementary or petty schools were endowed on a small scale, particularly in the early seventeenth century. Catherine Kemeys, who endowed a school in Caldicot in 1680, made her aims explicit: to educate the poor children in the parish to read the Bible perfectly and write a legible hand.

According to legislation of Elizabeth's reign, re-stated in 1603, all teachers in schools had to be licensed, so ensuring Church control over education. During the whole of the seventeenth century only fifteen such licences were issued for Monmouthshire. We know nothing of the duration of such schools, nor their size, but they must have catered for only a small proportion of the population. It is impossible to gauge their effectiveness. Literacy rates are difficult even to guess at in the early modern period. There were periods of progress and of regression in Elizabeth's reign, for example. Then, we know that literacy rates within English counties varied enormously – 36 per cent to 85 per cent illiteracy in different parishes in Essex, for example. It is certain that literacy rates were far lower in rural areas than in urban, and it is generally held that it was lower, too, in remoter areas of the country. If we add to this the fact that the great majority of the inhabitants of Wales were monoglot Welsh speakers and the availability of books in Welsh so restricted, then literacy must have been confined to the very few. It would appear that the 30 per cent to 40 per cent literacy rates which have been postulated as an average for England in the sixteenth and seventeenth centuries respectively are particularly optimistic. Given the peculiar circumstances of Wales they cannot begin to provide a guide.

Any extension of educational opportunity which resulted in more people being able to read the printed word did, however, pose problems. While Protestant reformers regarded the ability to read the Bible as essential they also realised the powerful implications. The dilemma of allowing the cultivation of such a potent skill as reading, even with press and education carefully controlled by Church and state, became even more apparent in mid seventeenth century. The Puritan schools of the Interregnum in Wales, many of them grammar schools, but others acting as feeder schools, were indication enough of the realisation on the part of the state that education served an ultimately political purpose.

Grammar schools

If provision for elementary education was limited in the sixteenth and seventeenth centuries, more advanced education was available only to the few who could afford it. One official nineteenth-century estimate – to be treated warily – indicates that there were over 500 grammar schools in England and Wales two hundred years previously. Even as an approximation this hints at considerable activity in the Tudor and Stuart period when most of them were created, usually endowed by private benefactors. The concept of the Renaissance gentleman was that of the educated polymath and this prompted interest in schooling. Puritans saw education as a fit vehicle for private philanthropy, with education an essential pre-requisite of Biblical enquiry and the propagation of religion. Voluntary effort followed on an impressive scale. Only in this way would schools be founded since there was no incentive for the state to provide schools, at least until the Interregnum, and the Established Church was more interested in controlling rather than providing education. In Wales there was a rash of foundations: Brecon (1541), Abergavenny (1543), Bangor (1557), Ruthin (1574), Carmarthen (1576), Cowbridge (1609) and Monmouth (1615) were some which survive in various forms. It has been estimated that there were twenty-seven grammar schools in Wales in the period. Endowments usually included some provision for free tuition for poor scholars, but incidental expenses meant that such schooling was not available to the vast majority.

The attitude of the Welsh gentry to the grammar schools was ambivalent. They recognised their importance in Wales, but tended to send their sons to English schools. Sir John Wynn established a scholarship in Bangor grammar school but sent his sons to Eton, Bedford, Westminster and St Albans. In the seventeenth century favourite schools were Shrewsbury, Greyfriars' School, London, and Winchester. On the other hand, some sons of gentry did go to the Welsh grammar schools, along with the sons of clergy and people involved in commerce, with a sprinkling of poor scholars. In schools whose pupils numbered from about twenty to the 120 of Ruthin, far fewer boarded than in England, most living at home or in lodgings. The Welsh schools were small, run normally by a master and usher. Some – Oswestry or Ruthin – were custom-built but others were held in churches or houses. Schooling was a long and arduous business, with the process believed to be aided by frequent birchings. Latin and Greek were the staple diet, with the day dominated by lessons in parts of speech, translations, copying down and reading from set authors. Memorising and rote-learning were vital.

There was some upheaval in the grammar schools with the Civil War and Interregnum, with problems over the collection of revenue in Bangor, and the ejection of Puritan schoolmasters and ushers after the Interregnum. The main problems were finance, administration and the fluctuating quality of staff, but the schools continued to function.

For a brief period in the seventeenth century there was a state system of education in Wales. In the Commonwealth period the Puritans implemented some of the ideas implicit in their religion, given some theoretical authority in the writings of Hartlib, Dury and Milton, for example. The Puritans were particularly concerned about Wales, which had been, from a Puritan viewpoint, so misguidedly

Royalist during the Civil War. Education, they believed, could help right these attitudes. They must also have been aware of the strictures on education in Wales. In 1595, for example, Gabriel Goodman, Dean of Westminster, had written to Queen Elizabeth protesting that the whole of North Wales had only one school to educate children in duty to God and Queen – not true, but that did not minimise the importance of the complaint.

Puritan educational and religious efforts in Wales took a number of complementary forms. There was literary effort, through Lewis Bayly and Vicar Pritchard, but the provision of education was crucial. The problem had come up in 1641 in the Long Parliament but substantial efforts came only with the 1650 Propagation Act. Colonel Harrison and seventy commissioners were appointed to act for North and South Wales and soon ordinances were issued for the establishment of schools. In August 1652, for instance, it was ordered that 'a free School be created and settled in the town of Llanbedr...for the Education of Youths in English and Latin Tongue – and that the yearly sum of twenty pounds be allowed for the keeping of the said free school'. More than sixty such schools were established, particularly in the towns, financed from ecclesiastical revenues.

In 1653–4 the system was modified when the Commission for the Propagation of the Gospel gave way to trustees and triers under the Approbation Act. The number of schools declined steadily – from sixty to twenty-one by 1660. This was not surprising when the remoteness of so many of the Propagation schools is considered. Schoolmasters sometimes entered the ministry and were not replaced. Possibly the triers were firmer in vetting schoolmasters. Certainly some schoolmasters – David Evans of New Radnor, Hugh Jones of Glamorgan, for example – had been accused of drunkenness and stopped teaching, as did Hugh Price of Brecon who had been accused of having Catholic sympathies. There was a less lenient attitude towards ejected clergy who had been allowed to teach in Propagation schools. Arrears of payment to schoolmasters also caused problems.

The demise of Puritan schools after the Restoration was inevitable but they were a forced growth and met no particular demand in Wales. They do, however, form a link with educational developments later in the century, within or outside the Established Church, because the spirit of Puritan educational endeavour did not disappear. With the Act of Uniformity and the penal legislation of 1662

Anglican control of education was reasserted. Clergy had to subscribe
to the Prayer Book and no school was allowed to function without
a licence. A large fine, £40, could be imposed for holding unlicensed
schools. Yet they did appear and the 1672 Declaration of Indulgence
must have condoned an existing situation. In 1673 Bishop Lucy's
Report listed unlicensed schools in Brecon, Carmarthen, Haverfordwest, Swansea and Cardigan. Stipends of £6 to £8 per annum were
paid to teachers who, said Lucy, were women and excommunicates,
with, he suggested, powerful patrons. The number of such schools
was still small.

Universities and Inns of Court

There was no education beyond that of the grammar schools
available in Wales, but the Welsh gentry went to the universities of
Oxford and Cambridge, and to the Inns of Court, in some numbers.
They formed part of a change in the student population which was
something of a revolution. Two particular waves of expansion, in the
third quarter of the sixteenth century and in the reigns of the first
two Stuarts, saw a large increase in the number of students – for
humanist and Puritan reasons, among others. The demands of the
landed gentry were also for some legal training and, once begun, the
trend towards the habit of university education was self-perpetuating.
It has been argued that this secularisation of education resulted
mainly in the sons of gentry going to university for social reasons
and profiting little from their stay there. There were, however, some
notable scholars among the Welsh gentry educated at both the
universities. The influx of men from the growing commercial and
mercantile classes touched Wales far less than England.

Welsh links with Jesus College, Oxford, were particularly strong,
with an estimated 250 students attending from Wales between 1571
and 1622. The college had been founded by Dr Hugh Price of Brecon,
with David Lewis from Abergavenny as the first principal. The most
important benefactor was Sir Leoline Jenkins, one time principal, who
established the links between Jesus College and Cowbridge and
Abergavenny Grammar Schools. There was one seventeenth-century
scheme to establish a university in Wales, the object being to train
Puritan ministers, but the plan foundered for lack of money. One of
the most eminent of Puritan divines, Dr Richard Baxter, was involved
in the scheme. In 1666 he sent 120 copies of one of his books for

distribution in North Wales. This preceded the efforts of Thomas Gouge's Welsh Trust and may have inspired the later venture.

The Welsh Trust

Educational endeavour in eighteenth-century Wales contrasts markedly with that of the Tudor and Stuart period. Universities and grammar schools warrant little attention; both degenerated. Some grammar schools disappeared, others declined to elementary status. They were not adapted to Welsh society and endowments became increasingly inadequate. The eighteenth-century Welsh gentry were even less inclined to patronise Welsh schools, and the commercial and mercantile classes were few in number, yet money from fee-payers and boarders was now far more vital. University education, in Oxford and Cambridge, of a particularly low standard, was available only to a small minority. Effort in Wales went into giving ordinary people a basic literacy.

The experiments of the late seventeenth and early eighteenth centuries were part of a pattern of activity evident across England and Wales as a whole. The philanthropy of the time stemmed from philosophical, religious, social and financial motives. Education was increasingly felt to be a discipline of mind and body. Puritans, in and out of the Established Church, emphasised the religious imperative of ability to read the Bible and the social purpose of improving society within the established order. Education was necessary to produce respectful and respectable citizens. In Wales the religious motive outweighed the utilitarian. Souls had to be saved. This necessitated reading the Bible and so a minimum of education was essential.

Many of the sixty or so Puritan schools of the Interregnum had disappeared before the Restoration but a precedent had been established. It seemed as if the Restoration and the Clarendon Code must sound the death-knell but some Propagation schoolmasters taught in Welsh Trust schools while two Propagation commissioners emerged as members of local committees of the Trust.

Two men particularly are associated with the work of the Welsh Trust. Thomas Gouge was an Englishman, educated at Eton and Cambridge, who had held a living in Southwark but was ejected under the Clarendon Code. He had visited the Welsh border counties in 1671–2 when he preached and gave money for teaching. He then devoted himself to providing the Welsh with religious literature and schools. Another ejected vicar, Stephen Hughes, from the parish of Meidrim was prompted to similar activity by the ignorance he saw around him. He continued to preach and eventually opened a school and began providing religious literature. A Welsh catechism, Vicar Pritchard's verses and a Welsh New Testament were printed as a result of Hughes's work. When the Welsh Trust was established in 1674 Stephen Hughes and Thomas Gouge worked together but they did not work alone. Bishops of the Established Church and ejected ministers co-operated. For example Charles Edwards, an ejected minister, helped to edit, write and supervise the printing of devotional works in London.

The twin objects of the Trust were to provide literature and found schools. Through a network of local organisations and village centres, supplied from the London headquarters, nearly 500 New Testaments, 500 copies of *The Whole Duty of Man* and, the crowning achievement. 8,000 copies of a new edition of the Welsh Bible published in 1678, were distributed in Wales – 1,000 of them free. For a short time the provision of schools was similarly impressive. Nearly 100 schools were established in the first year of the Trust, and possibly as many as 300 at one time or another. One estimate indicated that about 1,600 to 2,000 pupils were educated each year, though it was a sympathetic estimate. Gouge himself financed a number of schools but most of the money came from funds which the Trust itself built up on the lines of a joint stock enterprise. Large numbers of Welsh gentry contributed liberally, as did the City of London.

To English supporters of the Welsh Trust the provision of devotional literature in Welsh was a necessary compromise for the adult population who could not be expected to learn a foreign language. The young could have their souls saved in English. The reading, writing and catechism taught in the schools were all in English. Here we encounter at least part of the cause of relative lack of success of the Trust, though external factors also played their part. Despite the co-operation of influential nonconformists and churchmen there was opposition from bishops such as Humphrey Lloyd of Bangor and Lucy of St David's. Lloyd even accused Gouge of fostering disloyalty to the state.

By 1681 the Welsh Trust was doomed. Gouge died in that year

and with him much of the dynamism of the movement. Relative religious toleration had given way to a further outbreak of religious repression and eminent nonconformists were at best regarded once more with grave suspicion – at worst they were imprisoned. But the full explanation of decline is more complex than such immediate reasons indicate. There was a failure to train teachers. There was the increasing tendency of London philanthropists to ask that their money be spent in the city. There was at least some ineffectiveness on the literary side of the mission. One could take Bibles to the Welsh but one could not make them read. At this stage the Welsh were content, as far as can be gauged, to be without an education since there was no economic or social incentive which penetrated much further down the social scale than the gentry. Indeed the economics of the time decreed that time spent on the education of youth was largely wasted when farming tasks lay ahead. There was, as yet, no overwhelming religious incentive. Opposition to Welsh as the medium of instruction in the schools was an important handicap. Not only did this strain relations between Hughes and his colleagues but it also emphasised the alien nature of the movement. It was at least partly the product of the unwillingness of the gentry to participate in a scheme based on the Welsh language. Yet if Welsh had been the language of instruction the Trust schools, like their Puritan precursors, would still have been a scheme imposed by outside philanthropy not an answer to internal demand.

The Society for the Propagation of Christian Knowledge

There was continuity between the efforts of the Welsh Trust and the Society for the Propagation of Christian Knowledge, not only in manpower but in the siting of schools, and the Society almost certainly found Trust schools in existence when it started the next educational experiment in Wales. The S.P.C.K. was the archetypal society of eighteenth-century philanthropy. Its members were motivated partly by genuine concern for the poor in their distress and ignorance, partly by religious concern, partly out of a self-interested fear that a population not disciplined by religion would threaten social order. In England, S.P.C.K. schools have a long and generally honourable history in the education of the poor. The society concentrated its work round the Established Church and the parish unit.

By about 1760, 30,000 children were being educated in their schools. In Wales, too, the S.P.C.K. played an important part for a time. One of the founder members in 1699 was landowner and industrialist Sir Humphrey Mackworth of Neath, and Sir John Philipps of Picton Castle soon became involved. Although Welsh Trust schools had come to an end in an atmosphere of increasing acrimony between Anglicans and Dissenters, schools founded by private individuals had not, and these foundations were capitalised on by the S.P.C.K.

The Society's educational activity in Wales was directed primarily at saving souls but the social purpose, of instilling the virtues of hard work and an acceptance of the existing social order, was certainly not forgotten. Though for some years the Society had Dissenting support it was an Anglican movement. It was originally supported by the Welsh bishops and encouraged by clergy who occasionally taught in the schools. The other major prop to a movement which worked through local correspondents was the untiring work of some Welsh gentry, particularly Sir John Philipps. Finance came from English patrons, from the locality, from private patrons in Wales and from collections in church services. The finance required for providing school buildings, paying teachers and, in some instances, providing free clothing or free meals, was considerable. Where local patronage was particularly strong schools were numerous – as, for instance, in Carmarthenshire and Pembrokeshire, where there were over thirty schools. Across Wales ninety-six S.P.C.K. schools had been established by 1737.

Pupils had to learn the teachings of the Church of England and the catechism. They learned to read and write. The boys learned some arithmetic and craft and the girls some sewing, but even this rudimentary education was too much for some supporters apprehensive about the consequences of teaching pupils to read and write. Teachers were given regular employment by the S.P.C.K. but they were badly paid and untrained. Teacher-training was mooted by Sir John Philipps but rejected for financial reasons. Sir Humphrey Mackworth suggested itinerant teachers, an idea to be taken up so dramatically by Griffith Jones.

S.P.C.K. schools had considerable success in Wales from about 1700 to 1715, when sixty-eight of the ninety-six schools were established. Part of the reason was the balanced attitude to the Welsh language, rather different from that of the Welsh Trust. Though some demurred, many of the clergy advocated teaching in the Welsh language, so that the North Wales schools were conducted in Welsh while English was usually used in the South – though in places like Cardiganshire this was a considerable drawback. Even before the Hanoverian succession there was a loss of momentum in the Welsh charity school movement and after 1727 there was general decline, though many privately endowed schools were still being created. Probably Welsh education benefited more from the S.P.C.K.'s publishing efforts, which allowed a wealth of devotional literature to be printed in Welsh and distributed all over the country. This continued until at least the end of the eighteenth century. John Vaughan of Derllys was one of the originators of the idea of making libraries available to all, from diocesan level down to the parishes, although in the event only eight libraries were started, for the use of clergy only.

Discrepancies between plan and achievement characterised the educational activity of the S.P.C.K., according to some contemporaries. Griffith Jones, involved in the movement, was critical of the lack of impact on illiteracy. The schools were not a sufficiently effective agent to achieve widespread literacy, but other contemporaries were full of praise for their efforts. It is true that their scale of operation was at a different level from that of Griffith Jones's schools.

The circulating schools

From the 1730s an attack on illiteracy on an unprecedented scale resulted from Griffith Jones's inspiration. He was born in Pen-boyr in Cardiganshire in 1683 and, after attending Carmarthen grammar school, was ordained in the Anglican Church. He became a curate in Laugharne and is believed to have taught at a charity school there. He was certainly a local correspondent of the S.P.C.K. He thought of becoming a missionary in India but finally decided to take up the living of Llanddowror, in the gift of S.P.C.K. philanthropist, Sir John Philipps, whose sister Jones was to marry. He incurred the wrath of fellow clergy because he preached outside his parish and it was only the intervention of Philipps which prevented the bishops' court taking action against him. Increasingly conscious of the level of illiteracy around him preventing access to the Scriptures, he opened a school in Llanddowror, conducted in Welsh, to inculcate Anglican doctrine. More schools were established but this did not satisfy Jones who hatched up a remarkable plan for setting up a network of schools across Wales. They were normally to be conducted in Welsh, the only way to reach the mass of the population. In south Pembrokeshire, where English-speakers predominated, the schools were conducted in English. The schools were to be run by itinerant teachers, not a new idea, but never tried on this scale. They were free, so that the maximum number of scholars would enrol. The major expense was for teachers, though they were poorly paid, and the money came mainly from English subscribers who were provided with an annual report, *Welch Piety*. Editions of the Bible and other pietistic literature were provided by the S.P.C.K. The outstanding benefactress of the movement was Bridget Bevan, daughter of John Vaughan of Derllys, one of the outstanding squire–philanthropists and supporter of the S.P.C.K.

The schools were normally held for some three months in the period from September to May when there was least pressure on an agricultural population. The schoolmaster, provided with his itinerary by Griffith Jones, completed his assignment in one area, in church, chapel or house, then moved on, but schools often returned to different parts of parishes at regular intervals. During the day the schoolmaster would teach children to read from the Book of Common Prayer and the Bible. Catechising took place twice daily and pupils were urged to attend services on Sundays. In the evenings, and this was most significant, adults were taught along similar lines. In their simple objective of teaching pupils to read the Bible the schools were successful on an unprecedented scale. By the 1750s South Wales and parts of North Wales, particularly the Llŷn peninsula, were dotted with schools, though mid Wales and the border counties were less affected. Between 1737 and 1761, 3,325 schools were held, 153,835 scholars attended in 1,600 different places, though not all necessarily learned to read. It is impossible to quantify the number of adults who attended but at least 200,000 of the estimated 400,000 to 500,000 Welsh population were taught to read. This was a quite remarkable achievement and testimony to Griffith Jones's organising ability and dedication.

A religious and educational movement which expanded spectacularly in its early years attracted opposition. Although influential

Anglicans backed him, Griffith Jones found it difficult to counteract accusations that he was bolstering Methodism since he was friendly with Methodist leaders and prepared to accept help from Methodist and Dissenting sources, including the loan of meeting-houses for use as schools. His itinerant teachers were all Anglican communicants but they included some Methodists. As a result of strong opposition from the Bangor diocese, particularly, Jones had to rid himself of some of these. He tried to draw local Anglican clergy more closely into the work of the schools by using them in management and inspection. Opposition came from those who objected to the use of the Welsh language, from opponents of extending even minimal educational opportunity to the poor and from some who disliked Jones personally. The schools still flourished, essentially because the motives behind them were highly traditional. They sought to ensure the salvation of those they taught, to implant moral rectitude and to reinforce traditional social structures in that each person should know his place and be content with it. Even Griffith Jones's death in 1761 caused no essential disruption since his organisational procedures were maintained by Madam Bevan and her stewards, one in North Wales, one in South. A sadder epilogue followed her death in 1779. No one took over her organisation, Chancery took over her money – a £10,000 endowment to the schools – and decline was inevitable. Even now there was continuity in the Welsh educational tradition because Madam Bevan's money, when eventually released, contributed towards establishing schools run on monitorial lines, so taking the story into the nineteenth century.

Griffith Jones's circulating schools have become part of the folk-heritage of Wales, a mark of the hunger for education. They were certainly a unique achievement, established on a national scale and organised with genius. They influenced thinking about adult education and laid the foundation for other educational movements, particularly the Sunday schools of the late eighteenth and the nineteenth centuries. The achievement must still be seen in perspective. The schools lasted for brief periods at each location, not always with good teachers, and with a limited aim. Without the reading material provided by the S.P.C.K. they would not have been effective.

Nonconformist academies

Wales could boast of its nonconformist academies in higher education. Their origins lie in the repressive legislation of the Cavalier Parliament in 1662, reinforced in 1665 and 1713. Numbers of ejected clergy, bereft of their livelihood and with a ready-made clientele of dissenters excluded from the universities, set up academies. Conducted by serious, intent men, at first to train ministers, the academies provided a varied four-year curriculum – classics, logic, Hebrew, mathematics, natural sciences, modern languages, medicine, even practical subjects for specific vocations. Medicine was taught at the Llwyn-llwyd Academy and astronomy at Carmarthen. The academies quickly acquired a reputation for high standards and good learning which resulted in some of them attracting Anglican students, and they provided a range of education unavailable elsewhere.

The most famous of the Welsh academies was the Presbyterian Academy of Brynllywarch and Carmarthen. It was founded at a farmhouse near Bridgend by Samuel Jones, former tutor and fellow of Jesus College, Oxford. Jones himself was a man of high learning. He had been ejected in 1662 but his academy attracted Anglicans, including one of the Mansels of Margam. Before the end of the century support was received from the Presbyterians and Congregationalists and this strengthened in the eighteenth century when, after a peripatetic existence, the academy was established permanently in Carmarthen. Trainees for the Dissenting ministry were required to be able to translate from Latin into English, read a psalm in Hebrew, translate from Latin into Greek, show a knowledge of various sciences and construct a thesis in Latin. The emphasis on the depths to which higher education had sunk in the eighteenth century is somewhat misplaced. Standards of learning were, for a short period, protected not at the portals of Oxford and Cambridge but in a farmhouse at Brynllywarch, and equally unlikely edifices.

In the second half of the eighteenth century, particularly, the academies faced problems. At various times controversy surrounded Brynllywarch and Carmarthen for example. There were allegations of heresy against staff, with the result that the Congregationalists dissociated themselves in 1754. Partly as a result of such controversy the nonconformist denominations established their own academies – the Congregationalists at Abergavenny for instance. Despite the ambitious curriculum in the academies there were few staff and few books. Some teachers were outstanding, but the standard did tend to decline in the eighteenth century. Money was always in short supply, the quality of students was not always high and, with English the medium of instruction in a student body in which there was frequently a monoglot Welsh background, standards suffered. Yet despite their chequered history, common to all educational institutions of the late seventeenth and eighteenth centuries, the Nonconformist academies made an important contribution to the religious and educational life of Wales.

PART TWO

1780–1979

7

THE ECONOMY

SECTION I. 1780–1914

Population

This period saw an enormous increase in the total population of Wales and a complete change in its balance across the counties. These changes had profound implications. The population of Wales was not static before 1780. An estimated total population for Wales of about 370,000 in 1670 had increased to about 406,000 in 1700 and accelerated to about 493,000 by 1750. The rate of increase speeded up again by 1800 when the population reached an estimated 587,000. However even in 1801, according to the first census of that year, the population of the North Wales counties was only a little less than that of South Wales, in a ratio of 43:57. Although the iron industry was firmly established across the heads of the South Wales valleys its impact on population was as yet limited, and there were no very large urban centres. Glamorgan was the most populous of Welsh counties, at over 70,000, but this only marginally exceeded Carmarthenshire and Denbighshire.

In the nineteenth century the population of Wales grew from about 587,000 to 2,019,000 in 1901. The balance between North and South, and urban and rural, was revolutionised. Between 1801 and 1851 the population of Glamorgan trebled, between 1851 and 1901 it increased fivefold, to nearly $1\frac{1}{4}$ million. This was double the population of the whole of Wales in 1811. Monmouthshire's population increased rapidly to 395,000 by 1911. The contrast with the rural counties is dramatic. Anglesey's population increased from 33,000 to 57,000 in the first half of the nineteenth century, then declined to 50,000 by 1911. In the first half of the century, despite natural increase, population in Pembrokeshire, Cardiganshire, Radnorshire and Montgomeryshire also declined. Here, then, was the

151

major source of labour for industrial Wales. The trend of migration to the industrial areas speeded up dramatically from the 1850s as labour flooded the coalfields, augmented by immigration from Ireland and England. The scale of growth in some communities was staggering. One estimate has the population of the Merthyr area increasing from 24,000 in 1831 to 70,000 in 1861, though the focus of industrial activity then moved to the coal-mining areas and Merthyr's population actually declined by 18,000 between 1871 and 1911. The population growth of the Rhondda valleys dwarfed this: 1,636 in 1831, nearly 12,000 in 1861, nearly 128,000 in 1891. The balance of population within Wales changed, as did the balance within the industrial counties. Rhondda's population in 1891 was greater by far than that of any Welsh county in 1801. Concomitant changes occurred in the urban balance as Cardiff exceeded 100,000 population, with Swansea only a little less. The overriding cause of these dramatic changes was industrialisation. In the late eighteenth century 80 per cent of the Welsh population lived in rural areas; by the beginning of the twentieth century 80 per cent lived in industrial areas.

Changes on this scale changed the fabric of the nation. Migration of labour, investment of capital, creation of a mass proletariat, growth of large urban centres, the consequent strains on local government, law and order and civic institutions produced a different pattern of social and political life.

It is notable that the greatest *percentage* growth in population came in the first fifty years of the nineteenth century, not the second. Most of this increase was accommodated within Wales, in the counties of Glamorgan and Monmouthshire, though the industrial areas of Denbighshire and Flintshire also grew. Some were attracted to London and Liverpool, and the movement of population was even wider, to America and Patagonia. In the second half of the nineteenth century labour was being drawn into the South Wales coalfield at a rate exceeded only by immigration into the U.S.A. Now greater numbers were coming from neighbouring English counties, so that where 9.6 per cent of the South Wales population had originated in English counties in 1871 the percentage had risen to 16.5 per cent by 1891. This was to have an effect on language and community out of proportion to the numbers involved, as we shall see when discussing Welsh society in the period.

The land – owners, tenants, labourers

Underpinning remarkable movements in population since 1780 was the economic transformation of Wales though, throughout the nineteenth century, agriculture remained the largest single sector in the Welsh economy. At the end of the eighteenth century Wales was a country of great estates and small farms and this changed little in the following century. However the rural/industrial balance altered completely. The transformation from 1851 to 1961 was dramatic, as numbers earning a living from the land fell by 51 per cent in Wales, compared with 24 per cent in England.

It has been calculated that, in the 1870s, over 60 per cent of Welsh land was owned by 571 great landowners, all with estates of over 1,000 acres. Over 35,000 cottagers owned between them only 7,000 acres. Half of Caernarfonshire's land was owned by six landlords and a similar situation obtained in Merioneth. In 1887 only 10.5 per cent of acreage was owned by the occupier, compared with 16.1 per cent in England. The balance did not change throughout the century. Wales remained dominated by a few landed families – the Wynns of Denbighshire, Montgomeryshire and Merioneth, the Vaughans of Trawscoed, the Penrhyns in Caernarfonshire, the Pryses of Gogerddan, the Morgans of Tredegar, while the Butes of Cardiff and the Cawdors of Golden Grove represented a relatively new outside element. Their estates remained more-or-less unchanged throughout the century, though from the 1870s outlying parts of estates, particularly, came on to the market, and this market remained buoyant. It was only after the First World War that the great estates disintegrated and the process was then comprehensive.

In Glamorgan and Monmouthshire, particularly, some landowners derived most of their wealth from royalties. The outstanding example was the Marquess of Bute whose income in Glamorgan in the second half of the nineteenth century of £100,000 per annum derived largely from mineral rights. This estate was remarkable by any standards. It was based on part of the estate built up by the Earls of Pembroke in the sixteenth century and in the nineteenth century it covered an area in which a quarter of the Welsh population lived.

From a base of great wealth landowners remained the dominant figures and, however alienated they became from their tenants and the rest of the community, their grip on political life did not loosen until the last three decades of the nineteenth century. Their social and political control was in accordance with their economic strength. It was guaranteed by the tenants who worked their land, as much by ingrained attitudes of dependence and deference as by any exploitation or coercion.

Most remaining Welsh land was owned by yeomen, few in number with holdings of about 500 acres and owner–occupiers farming on a small scale, perhaps twenty-five acres, although their share decreased from the late eighteenth century. Small family farms were the most vulnerable to economic pressures and, in the agricultural depression after 1814, many owners were forced to sell out, so augmenting the estates of local gentry. Welsh agriculture had, with fluctuations, been relatively prosperous during the eighteenth century but the collapse after the Napoleonic wars was dramatic, with banks going bankrupt and ruin facing many small farmers. Numbers of small farms declined in the first half of the nineteenth century, particularly, though in the last thirty years of the century this was offset to some extent by great landowners selling freeholds to tenants. Even then the price was high and small family farmers remained in a most vulnerable position. They lived, often, in desperate poverty, practising backward farming methods and having to supplement their income by day labour.

The other main category of Welsh landowner was the cottager. There were over 35,000 of them in the 1870s, owning less than 7,500 acres between them. They, too, suffered in the nineteenth century as enclosure of common and waste either forced them to buy their small parcel of land or be ejected. Upland Wales was particularly affected by enclosure, with 500,000 acres enclosed by act of Parliament between 1733 and 1885.

The great estates, and often the land of the smaller resident owners, was farmed by tenants whose rents comprised the major part of gentry income, apart from those with income from royalties. In the 1880s, for example, approximately 90 per cent of land in Monmouthshire was worked by tenants, about 10 per cent by owners. The gentry normally only retained a home farm, as they had done since the sixteenth century, often worked unprofitably. Sometimes this was because such farms were used to attempt farming experiments and some benefits might therefore percolate through to tenants. However, when Thomas Johnes of Hafod in Cardiganshire experimented at the end of the eighteenth century with new crops, implements and breeding he found tenants very loth to break with traditional methods.

The tenures by which land was held were changing by the end of the eighteenth century. Traditional tenures, going back to the sixteenth century and before, had often been for three lives or twenty-one years. By the end of the eighteenth century tenancies were increasingly for one year, a trend which accelerated from the 1820s. In South Wales, longer leases, of fourteen or more years, prevailed, but by the end of the nineteenth century the vast majority of tenants had yearly leases and generally had not objected to their implementation. Such leases did not necessarily result in frequent changes of tenant; indeed the opposite was the case in Wales. However, from about 1870, particularly on smaller estates, the number of evictions increased and there were always aspiring new tenants. There was an inordinate pressure on holdings throughout the century.

Tenant farmers, if rather more secure than the small farmer, were subject to fluctuating climate, harvest and demand. There were periodic crises as in 1842/3 when prices fell, and in the 1880s and 1890s which were years of depression. Yet even the worst years produced no shortage of tenants, they merely perpetuated the poverty of Welsh farming. The smallness of holdings and the lack of capital meant that tenant farmers were often scarcely distinguishable from farm labourers and they supplemented their income, where possible, by working in the industrial areas for part of the year, or by pursuing a craft as weavers or tailors, for example. The Welsh small farm was a family unit, with labour provided by the family and, at certain times, by the local farming community. At haymaking, harvest or sheep-shearing, groups of farming neighbours would co-operate in a formalised system. Sometimes this involved specific work-debts where tenants of small holdings worked at crucial times in return for help with ploughing or harvesting.

The chief distinction between small farmers and labourers lay not in standard of living but in consciousness of status, with the farmer and his family enjoying a position of consequence in the local community. Status apart, it was only in parts of Denbighshire where there were few small farms, that the cleavage between farmer and labourer reflected that prevalent in so many parts of England.

Welsh farm labourers, unlike those in England, were usually resident. They became farm labourers between nine and thirteen years of age, were hired at fairs for a year and lodged at the farmhouse, partly because there were insufficient farm cottages. Hired labour was of relatively less importance in Wales than in England because of the prevalence of family farming. Even so, the labour force rose rapidly until the middle of the nineteenth century, with workers being increasingly siphoned off after that to the industrial areas. Conditions, pay and accommodation were more attractive there but most pressing was the lack of employment in the countryside. Particularly after the short-term boom at the end of the Napoleonic Wars unemployment levels in rural Wales were appalling. Distress was only partially alleviated by outdoor parish relief which, despite the hated Poor Law Amendment Act of 1834, continued long afterwards. By the end of the nineteenth century, however, the industrial areas had taken so many of the rural population that supply and demand of agricultural labour were roughly in equilibrium. Conditions of life and work in the industrial areas have often been condemned but the rural labourer was drawn to the towns by the lure of relatively high wages and better living conditions. The rural labourer worked excessive hours – fifteen hours per day in the early part of the century, ten or eleven by the end. Accommodation was appalling, in dark, dank outhouses without any sanitation. Conditions for married labourers in farm cottages were often little better and they were breeding grounds for disease, especially tuberculosis. Indeed, cottage accommodation was accounted by contemporaries to be far worse than in England.

Farming practices

Wales, as a predominantly upland country, tended towards animal husbandry, though most farmers practised mixed farming. The tendency in the nineteenth century was towards increasing dependence on animals, particularly after 1870 when the proportion of arable land fell from 42.7 per cent to 24.8 per cent of cultivated land, and the extent of grassland therefore increased. Animal husbandry employed less labour than arable farming. Oats and barley were the main arable crops, with oats comprising over 60 per cent of the Welsh corn crop by 1914. Turnips, rape and swedes were grown increasingly as the century went on and rotation of crops adopted on a more widespread basis. The main cattle strain in Wales was the Welsh Black, both for meat and milk. The breed was ideally suited to the hard conditions of most Welsh farms where lack of night housing for cattle made it difficult to introduce more productive breeds such as Herefords. The Welsh Black strain deteriorated later in the nineteenth century as insufficient attention was paid to breeding, and feeding was inadequate. There were attempts to alleviate this by the introduction of prizes and herd books, while on the more prosperous farms, Shorthorns and Herefords were introduced. There was a similar neglect in breeding other animals or in experimenting with different strains of crops. The hallmark of Welsh farming was the flocks of fifty to 2,000 sheep on the upland farms. Here again common pasturing, and lack of shelter during lambing had adverse effects, and the sheep generally remained on the upland slopes so that in winter perhaps a third of the flock might die. Fleeces from upland sheep were not of high quality and therefore not in great demand by wool-dealers. Dairy cows were vital to all farms and, apart from the upland sheep farms, butter-making was an essential activity. It was made in a primitive fashion and on a small scale, with mechanisation slow to make any impact. The Welsh were, however, noted horse breeders, especially of the cobs and ponies of upland farms.

Only the landed gentry had the capital to experiment with crops and animal husbandry on their home farms. They sponsored the agricultural societies of the late eighteenth century and continued this support in the following century. On the relatively large farms of the vale of Clwyd, east Flintshire and lowland Glamorgan tenants were more advanced and usually arable farming predominated within their mixed farms. Farmers here practised four-crop rotation in the early part of the nineteenth century, though the disadvantages of this were becoming obvious by the end of the century. They followed the landowners in using fertilisers, grew root crops, sowed by seed-drill and used modern ploughs. They took up mowing and reaping machines, while threshing machines, driven by horse or water power, were common on such farms from the 1840s, although steam-threshing machines were used only from the 1870s. Stock-rearing was more scientific on the larger farms, with better feeding, more care at lambing-time and consequently more profit. Elsewhere

Welsh tenant farmers and small farmers had far too little capital to employ on farms which were too small and they could ill-afford to experiment. They did not properly rotate crops until late into the nineteenth century, they continued to use lime as a fertiliser, at least until the 1880s and the advent of cheap superphosphates. In the middle of the century the wooden plough was still in use on poorer farms, though by the 1870s the sharp iron plough had reached most farms. Sowing was done by hand rather than corn-drill on small farms, and horse-drawn mowing machines for hay-making only became general towards the end of the century. Oats and barley were normally harvested with a scythe and wheat with a reaping-hook throughout the century. Inevitably such relatively backward practices affected relationships between landlords and tenants.

The landlord–tenant relationship

With Welsh farming characterised generally by poor land, difficult terrain, primitive methods and under-capitalisation, compounded by increasing population and consequent pressure on holdings, it is scarcely surprising that, particularly in periods of depression, there should be protest in rural Wales. This will be examined in a later chapter but one aspect of it, landlord–tenant relationships, is relevant here. In the last thirty or so years of the nineteenth century protest was channelled into Parliament, and social and economic analysis derived from the necessity to propound powerful, even dramatic, reasons for Welsh ills. Not surprisingly, that analysis proved simplistic, though it had an enormous impact on Welsh politics. By the late eighteenth century large landowners had lost touch with the Welsh language and traditions and had become increasingly anglicised. Differences with their Welsh-speaking nonconformist tenants could hardly have been more marked, though the outstanding difference was economic. From the 1880s, there were constant vituperative attacks on Welsh landlords, from press and political platform. They were attacked for economic exploitation, and threats of eviction, particularly over elections held in the previous twenty years. They were accused of charging exorbitant rents, refusing compensation for improvements, preferring Anglican and Conservative tenants and being generally unsympathetic to tenants in adversity. This Liberal–nonconformist analysis, based on the notion of an anglicised and alienated gentry, was necessary for the political campaign against tithe and Established Church and had sufficient basis in fact to make it effective. Inevitably it was exaggerated at the time and has led to a distorted view of the nineteenth century in Welsh historiography.

There were very many Welsh landlords who were thoroughly Welsh in origin, though there had been something of a transformation in the eighteenth century in some Welsh counties. They were not absentee landlords in the Irish sense of living permanently in another country, though they might be away from Wales for long periods for Parliamentary or social reasons. Landlords did not capriciously evict improving tenants, though tenants were not customarily entitled to compensation for improvements except in a very few areas of Wales, and this was not materially affected by statutory provision in the second half of the nineteenth century. Only in the nineteenth century did landlord control of tenant practices figure in tenant leases, to enforce rotation and adequate manuring of soil, for example. Their existence is no great indictment of landlords.

Far more oppressive were the Game Laws which, until 1880, allowed landlords sole right to game on tenants' land. Welsh landlords were no harsher than English in applying the laws but there was genuine outrage that landlords' sporting pleasure could result in the destruction of tenants' crops without any control allowed as rabbits and hares, pheasant and partridge wrought havoc.

The charge that Welsh landlords imposed exorbitant rents in the nineteenth century has been exaggerated, though certainly some landlords did raise rents after tenants' improvements. Others set rents below market value to take account of tenants' contribution to improvement, as happened on the Cawdor estates in West Wales and the Wynn estates in North Wales. Smaller landowners were far more prone to exploit tenants, and change of landownership always resulted in the renegotiation of rents at market value. Smaller landowners also exploited the constantly high demand for holdings, partly because they were themselves heavily mortgaged and anxious to maximise revenue. Native-born landlords were less prone to exploit tenants in this way, but landowners coming in to Wales had far less scruples. The greater landowners were least guilty of exploitation, to the extent that tenancies were not always given to the highest bidder.

Rents were the first claim on the tenant's purse. In much of Wales traditional payments in kind, either of animals or services, were commuted to money payments in the nineteenth century. Tithes, too, were commuted to money payments by the Tithe Commutation Act of 1836, and resentment at their payment steadily increased. It was an extra burden on an already hard-pressed farming population, more so because in England it was subsumed into rent. The real rub was the knowledge that the money was being used to support a church to which the overwhelming majority of farmers did not belong.

Tithes were detested by the Rebecca Rioters (see chapter nine), while in the 1880s and 1890s, at a time of depression in agriculture, protest grew more organised with the anti-tithe league. Tithe payment merged with the whole land question to grip the imagination of rural Wales and its Liberal politicians. The activities of the Ecclesiastical Commissioners, who distrained property under police protection on non-payment of tithe, inflamed public opinion. From 1891 tithe rent charge legislation meant that landlords became responsible for tithe payment, and although this was mere subterfuge, agitation became less intense. Despite the prominence of the land question, and the undoubted consciousness of grievance on which it rested, leaders of the Welsh Land League found that not all tenants were prepared to give support. From the 1880s relations between landlords and tenants were strained and the League found a ready response in the north, particularly. But across much of Wales the centuries-old bond between landlord and tenant was difficult to modify.

Land League agitation, reflected in Parliamentary activity in the late 1880s and 1890s, led by Tom Ellis, did result in a royal commission on Welsh land, 1893–5, but this achieved little. The six Liberals and three Unionists on the commission were split from the start. Welsh tenant farmers, though not farm labourers, had a full hearing and condemned landlords and their agents. Landlords defended their treatment of tenants, with some success. The report by the commission was published in 1896, with the Liberal majority pressing for a land court, though with no chance of action now that a Conservative government had come to power. With agricultural depression in the 1880s and 1890s the Welsh small farmer was hard hit. The influx of wheat from America and Russia affected him less than his English counterpart, but the collapse in animal prices in the late 1870s and again in the mid 1890s hit tenant farmers and labourers. However, from the turn of the century, prices began to recover and the problem of the relationship between landlord and tenant, in a changing economic and political climate, grew steadily less urgent.

Industry in 1780

The importance of the industrialization of Wales cannot be overstated. It transformed Wales from a poor country into a relatively rich one. That, in turn, transformed social structure and produced the wealth to provide a new Welsh culture, based, for the mass of the newly literate population, on the printed word: newspapers and books. The implications for education, politics and class struggle were as revolutionary.

Industry was well established by the mid eighteenth century – on a small scale. The potential for growth was present. In the South Wales coalfield there was iron-ore and limestone, anthracite, steam and bituminous coal, and plenty of water. There needed to be increased demand, and it was provided by the Seven Years War (1756–63). There needed to be technical change, provided by crucial developments in Watt's steam engine and, in the iron industry, by the puddling process which enabled wrought-iron to be made from pig-iron. There needed to be transport changes whereby the north of Glamorgan could be linked with the coast. Canals solved this problem in the 1790s when the Glamorganshire, Neath, Monmouthshire and Swansea canals were opened and were supplemented by linking tramroads to the iron-works.

In 1780 the iron-works across the heads of the South Wales valleys were the most obvious evidence of industrialization. Most prominent were Hirwaun, Dowlais, Plymouth, Cyfarthfa and Sirhowy, but iron was manufactured at works extending from Llechryd in the west to Blaenavon, Pontypool and Pentyrch in the east. In North Wales works had been established at Brymbo, Holywell and Bersham. Almost all iron-works were located on the South Wales or Flintshire coalfields, with coal a handmaid to iron. The iron industry involved large infusions of capital, extensive works, expensive equipment and a sizeable labour force. From the 1750s there was large-scale production, fostered by the demand for cannon. Dynasties of iron-masters were to become names to conjure with – the Wilkinsons, father and son who managed the Bersham works from 1753, the Guests who were eventually to build up Dowlais into the greatest of the works by the 1840s, with a labour force of 4,500 and eighteen furnaces working, the Crawshays of Cyfarthfa, the Homfrays from the Midlands, who managed Penydarren and the Hills who owned the Plymouth works.

With stimulated demand, some of the major works were established. The Bersham works (near Wrexham) expanded because of their ability to produce excellent cannon. The Wilkinsons supplied both sides in the Russo-Turkish war and provided the most accurate cannon used in the American War of Independence. This war prompted major developments in the 1780s when John Guest became a partner in the Dowlais works, and in 1786 Richard Crawshay from Yorkshire leased the Cyfarthfa works. After 1775, James Watt's steam engine became available commercially and, by the beginning of the eighteenth century, steam engines were in general use to drive the bellows providing the blast, so greatly increasing potential tonnage.

The Welsh coal industry went back to medieval times and mining of coal expanded from the sixteenth century. In the late eighteenth century it ministered mainly to the needs of the iron or copper industries, but the shape of things to come was already apparent when Richard Griffiths opened two coal levels in Rhondda, linked by tramroad with the Glamorganshire canal and producing coal for export. In the early part of the nineteenth century activity quickened with the exploitation of pits in lower Rhondda by Walter Coffin in 1832, in Merthyr by Robert Thomas in 1828 and in the Aberdare valley by Thomas Powell in 1840.

The North Wales coalfield in Flintshire and Denbighshire was also exploited in the late eighteenth century to meet the needs of iron-works and brick-works, but its development throughout the nineteenth century was on a limited scale compared with that of South Wales.

The copper-smelting industry was also centred mainly on the South Wales coalfield, around Neath and Swansea where there was easy access to the Bristol Channel and Cornish ores. North Wales had its copper industry at Holywell and Bagillt, but activity was chiefly centred in the south on the Neath works built up by Mackworth. In the century after 1755 the lower Swansea valley was to be dominated by copper-works at Middle and Upper Bank, Hafod, Morfa and Port Tennant. Cornish ore supplied the works until the 1770s when ore from Parys mountain in Anglesey dominated, to be increasingly supplemented after 1800 by supplies from abroad.

The last decades of the eighteenth century were notable for the remarkable entrepreneurial activities of Thomas Williams from Anglesey, who, from 1785, virtually controlled the Anglesey copper industry as well as being involved in copper-smelting at the Upper Bank works near Swansea. At the turn of the century Williams had twenty furnaces working at Amlwch and ran half the British copper industry. Thereafter came decline – by 1844 the North Wales mines had closed. The Swansea area was now to have a virtual monopoly of copper production.

The location of brass foundries was again dictated by the availability of fuel and the proximity of copper, so they were found near Swansea in the south and at Holywell in the north. At Holywell, and nearby Greenfield on the North Wales coalfield, there were also zinc works. Tin was plated at Melingriffith in Glamorgan and at works in Carmarthenshire.

Demand in the non-ferrous industries increased apace in the late eighteenth century and the nineteenth century, with war again acting as a spur. Further, the industrialisation process fed on itself. Copper was vital for use in machinery, lead for roofing and the manufacture of the zinc needed by the navy for bolts and sheathing from the 1760s.

Capital

Until the middle of the eighteenth century the money for expansion in Welsh industry came from landowners, although English capital had already been invested in the iron industry. Coal-mining was still in the hands of landowners but it was a seasonal trade, centred on sea-sale coal. From mid eighteenth century there was increased demand for iron – for use in war, particularly – and the essential technological breakthrough had already come in 1709 when Abraham Darby had succeeded in smelting iron with coke at Coalbrookdale. Not that iron-masters were drawn to the South Wales coalfield by the coal supplies. They came because of the reserves of iron-ore and timber. It was only from the late 1780s that coal replaced timber as the fuel for smelting iron in South Wales. With capital invested in metal industries, a base existed for large-scale development, but expansion could not be financed from within the coalfields so capital came with outside entrepreneurs, Bacon, Crawshay, Guest, Homfray. They brought merchant capital from Bristol and London. Some of this was loan capital from the banks of London and other big cities. Local banks, geared to the needs of agricultural communities, could not compete at this stage. Indeed banking in the late eighteenth and early nineteenth century was rudimentary. Private banks could go bankrupt, as did the Cardiff Bank in 1822. Then after 1826, the Bank of England set up branch banks, such as the one in Swansea which lasted till 1859, and later came joint-stock banks. Gradually from the 1830s, therefore, local banks, in conjunction with city banks, grew more able to satisfy capital needs. The ironmasters themselves – Crawshay, for example – ploughed back profits on a massive scale. Such entrepreneurs brought expertise as well as money and this combination enabled increased demand to be met. In 1788, 18,000 tons of iron were produced in Wales. In 1793 this had risen to 29,000 tons, by 1848 to 631,000 tons. By 1860 there were 165 blast furnaces producing almost one million tons of pig-iron, out of a total United Kingdom output of 3.6 million tons. Some of the capital generated by the iron industry helped coal and tinplate, as landowners leased their mineral rights, so here too there was quickening activity in the first half of the nineteenth century. Another industry located on the coalfield was copper, since eleven tons of coal were required to smelt four of copper ore, and English entrepreneurs and capital again played a vital part. By the end of the eighteenth century, therefore, developments in North and South Wales coalfield areas had changed the face of Wales. By 1815 South Wales produced one third of British pig-iron and in 1827 half of Britain's iron exports. Most British tinplate-works were in South Wales. In 1790 half the copper smelted in Britain came from an area round Swansea, a proportion to be increased in the early nineteenth century, so that, by 1860, seventeen of the eighteen British copper-works were located there.

Capital inflow, developing industrial activity on this scale, produced large labour forces compressed into densely populated communities. Following capital into industry, therefore, came small traders and professional men since there were money-making opportunities previously unprecedented in Wales. A middle class developed in the industrial areas. With the railway boom from the 1830s came more capital, through London merchants particularly.

Labour

The movement of labour transformed Wales. From the second half of the eighteenth century there was rapid population growth, with natural increase providing much of the needs of industry. With sustained industrial growth from the turn of the century migratory labour flooded in, especially to the industries of the South Wales coalfield. There was some movement of skilled men from England, with special skills required particularly in the iron industry. Most movement of people was over short distances. Much of the unskilled labour came from neighbouring rural counties. Merthyr drew its population early on from the Vale of Glamorgan, Breconshire and the border counties. The attraction of work and higher wages also brought in the Irish – 16,000 of them in Wales by 1861. Workers came too from the remotest Welsh counties where pressures on land forced them out, and farm labourers in adjoining areas to the coalfield tended to work seasonally in industry.

The appetite of the iron industry, particularly, was voracious for labour, and demand seems often to have outstripped supply, especially for skilled men. Even the scale of labour migration to the ironworks was exceeded in the second half of the nineteenth century as the coal industry of Glamorgan and Monmouthshire absorbed population at an unprecedented rate. Where neighbouring Welsh counties had supplied most of the inflow of the first half of the nineteenth century migration was now substantial from all over England, but from the neighbouring English counties of Gloucestershire, Somerset and Devon in particular.

The pattern of growth within Wales changed, too, as Merthyr, so rapidly expanding in the early days of the industrial revolution lost 18,000 of its people between 1871 and 1911. By contrast, the Rhondda valleys saw an increase in population from 11,737 in 1861 to 127,980 by 1891 and in the same period the population of Cardiff grew fourfold. Welsh women provided the only significant contrary trend as they sought domestic service in London, the south-west, west Midlands and north-west England.

Industrial wages fluctuated greatly according to conditions of trade. In good times skilled men in the iron industry, for example, were very well paid on piece- or time-rates. The money-wage system was supplemented by payments in kind – free housing, or food – and payment by company tokens for the truck shops complicated the picture. The truck system in its early days circumvented the shortage of cash in circulation but became a means of exploitation of workers. Even so, when trade was brisk, industrial workers enjoyed far higher wages than agricultural labourers.

High wages did not necessarily correlate with quality of life. Conditions in the iron and coal industries or the slate industry were dangerous. There was constant threat from roof falls, gas and blowbacks from furnaces. Coal and slate dust produced crippling chest diseases and workers in copper and iron were subject to contact with toxic fumes and excesses of heat which produced similar pulmonary illness. As we shall see in the next chapter the accumulation of large labour forces in industrial areas resulted not only in diseases associated with work but also communal problems of housing, health and amenity on an unprecedented scale.

The woollen industry

The oldest of staple Welsh industries was the woollen industry at Llanidloes, Newtown and Welshpool, with plentiful supplies of water available and the border centre of Shrewsbury nearby. The industry remained largely a domestic industry until the end of the eighteenth century when new machinery was introduced. Production processes such as carding were mechanised, factories were established, exports increased, particularly to America, and the small, independent producers generally replaced by entrepreneurs. This was a highly significant change since Welsh flannel and coarse cloth had been produced by spinners, carders, weavers and fullers for the local community for centuries. Each process, apart from fulling, was relatively simple and did not require complex equipment. Yielding to the new processes was slow and reluctant. Handloom weavers worked in terrible conditions and were grossly exploited by the truck system. The domestic system virtually disappeared between 1840 and 1880 as the advent of steam-driven machinery concentrated production for a time in Newtown and Llanidloes factories. The handloom weavers of Powys survived until the 1840s, sharing the discontent and occasionally the violence of their English counterparts. In the last quarter of the eighteenth century in Merioneth an employer class of cloth factors emerged and this resulted in a labour transformation as they paid piece-rate wages to former independent craftsmen. In the 1830s crisis hit the simply-woven Merioneth and Denbighshire cloth which supplied the army and slave markets. As the slave market disappeared these areas were hard-hit and ripe for discontent. In the 1830s there were riots over wages; in 1838 the first Chartist meeting in Wales took place at Newtown. Llanidloes was a hotbed of Chartism. So, after about 1825 the cloth industry in Merioneth stopped being important for exports and supplied local communities again. Many mills struggled on until the end of the nineteenth and early twentieth century in this way.

From about the mid nineteenth century prosperity in the woollen industry rested in the Teifi valley in Cardiganshire, with centres at Llandysul, Pentre-cwrt, Henllan and Drefach Felindre. Power looms were introduced about mid-century and there was great prosperity for about sixty years. This was due to the large market available for these factories which supplied shirt and underwear flannel for the burgeoning mining valleys of south-east Wales, now brought within reach by the railway network. The years from the 1880s to the end of the First World War were particularly prosperous, especially with the necessity for vast supplies of blankets, uniforms and shirts in wartime. Otherwise, there were numerous small mills which sold direct to the public and larger mills meeting orders from industrial Wales.

The slate industry

Slate was quarried in west Cardiganshire but the main location of the industry was in the Penrhyn area of Caernarfonshire, and its development furnishes a prime example of the entrepreneurial instincts of the landed gentry. Richard Pennant became squire of Penrhyn in 1765 at a time when the right to quarry slate had been leased out to numerous individuals. Realising the potential, he bought in these leases in the 1780s and established a single quarry in time to cash in on the enormous demand for slate as roofing material in housing for growing numbers of industrial workers. Pennant's activities in Bethesda were paralleled by those of the Assheton-Smiths in Llanberis. New industrial communities like Ffestiniog grew in North Wales, so that by 1881 there were 14,000 quarry workers serving a massive slate export market.

With the development of the slate industry Gwynedd was brought into the mainstream of British capitalist enterprise, just as the industrialisation of the rest of Wales brought the country from being on the periphery of Britain to a central place in the world economy. Slate was a vital element in this since in the second half of the nineteenth century Penrhyn and Dinorwic were the world's largest slate quarries and between them employed half of those working in the North Wales slate industry, while Welsh slate comprised 93 per cent of British output in 1882. The owners of both the great quarries were landowning entrepreneurs and point up a problem of differentiating between sources of wealth and status in the nineteenth century. The Penrhyn family owned more land than anyone in Gwynedd, and the third largest estate in Wales, yet their income from slate was immensely greater. The quarries made £133,000 profit in 1898. Assheton-Smith came third in the league of Gwynedd landowners. These men were also capitalists *par excellence*, owning the quarries, the land on which the houses of their workers were built and the means of communication. They wielded vast economic power and clung to it ruthlessly, but they were also paternalists who maintained hospitals and controlled sickness benefit funds.

Their workers were highly skilled and for long enjoyed a considerable degree of independence as a result, at least until it was challenged by quarry agents in the late nineteenth century. Slate was either mined underground or hewn from rock and both activities were dangerous, as was rock-blasting. The quarryman-proper needed years of experience with the slate rock of his own quarry to be able to judge precisely how the rock should be quarried and there was much skill, too, in being able to split the slate and dress it to size.

Frantic expansion in the slate industry was relatively short-lived. From mid nineteenth century there was a boom until 1879, followed by depressed demand until the late 1890s. From 1900 to 1903 came the devastating Penrhyn lock-out – devastating for men, community and industry. A workforce of 2,800 in 1900 never again topped 1,800. For Lord Penrhyn his struggle against the quarrymen's union, indeed against all those forces for change which he believed it symbolised, was more important than the economic disaster of the strike. He was well able to withstand the losses. The result was that the United States slate industry filled the gap, and never again was North Wales slate to be so important. The First World War saw the virtual collapse of the industry in North Wales, though Penrhyn quarry still works and quarry workings have become a considerable tourist attraction.

Iron and tinplate

As we have seen, the iron industry dominated the economy in the first half of the nineteenth century, with infusions of capital in works across the heads of the valleys in South Wales and, to a lesser extent, in north-east Wales, resulting in an industry producing nearly a million tons in the 1850s. Bar-iron was in steady demand and, with the coming of the railway age from the 1830s, came a boom in production.

Technological development had played an essential part since the eighteenth century in seeing that increased demand was met. In the 1780s both Henry Cort, in Hampshire, and Peter Onions, at Cyfarthfa, independently discovered the puddling process whereby impurities of carbon were removed from the molten iron which was then machine-rolled rather than hammered. Not only did this allow much increased output but it also greatly improved the quality of the iron.

It was another technological breakthrough which resulted in the most significant change in the industry in the second half of the nineteenth century. This was the change-over to steel manufacture. In 1856 Henry Bessemer's new process of extracting impurities from molten iron meant that large-scale production of steel was now possible. The Bessemer converter was improved by Sidney Gilchrist Thomas at Blaenavon and gradually steel replaced iron. The process of converting iron-works to steel production was expensive – sometimes prohibitively so – but it was put in hand at the Dowlais, Ebbw Vale, Rhymney and Blaenavon works and Welsh steel built railways in Britain, America and Europe.

The technology of steel manufacture was modified with yet another technical development. William Siemens, working at Landore, near Swansea, discovered a method of producing steel of a much higher quality than was possible by the Bessemer process and in 1868 started a works there.

By this time the implications of the breakthrough to steel production were evident. A conjunction of circumstances – the expense of converting iron-works, the dependence on imported foreign ore as demand for steel increased, intense competition from steel-works in Germany and America – meant the location of the steel industry mainly near the South Wales ports. Those iron-works which had been established in the northern part of the South Wales coalfield because of the availability of ore and coal were now in a most disadvantageous position. So came the demise of the old giants. Plymouth and Penydarren closed in the 1870s. Cyfarthfa, after a period of closure, survived until after the First World War. The Rhymney works closed in the 1890s and in 1891 the Dowlais company moved its steel manufacture to East Moors in Cardiff. Foreign competition and completion of railway networks meant a decline in the demand for Bessemer steel before the First World War but the production of Siemens steel increased tenfold in the thirty years before 1914. North Wales, too, benefited when a Siemens plant was built at Brymbo, near Wrexham in 1885, while sheet-steel was manufactured at Shotton from 1896.

There was expansion in the tinplate industry in the second quarter of the nineteenth century but then, between 1871 and 1891, output quadrupled to meet demand for canned-food containers and petrol containers. Technological development – the substitution of steel for iron as the base-plate – meant that tinplate works followed the steel industry to the coast, and clustered round Swansea and Llanelli, particularly. By 1889 there were ninety-six works producing 547,000 tons of tinplate. The McKinley tariff of 1890, placing a high duty on tinplate imported into the U.S.A., which was Wales's biggest export market, created grave difficulties and half the Welsh tinplate works closed by the end of the century. There was then a recovery so that on the eve of the First World War eighty-two tinplate works in South Wales were producing 823,000 tons, of which 544,000 tons were exported. The chief tinplate-exporting port was Swansea – over 330,000 tons were shipped from there in 1912. As we shall see, after the war the story was sadly typical. By 1937 America was producing twice as much tinplate as Britain from modern strip-mills and only in 1939 did the first of such mills open in Britain, at Ebbw Vale. The industry was also slow to capitalise on increasing chemical and metallurgical expertise.

Copper and zinc

Welsh copper-smelting was of world significance in the nineteenth century. Nine-tenths of copper smelted in Britain during the century came from South Wales, mainly from an area between Kidwelly and Neath. Over 3,700 were employed in 1911 and although copper, like tinplate manufacture, was vulnerable to world competition it remained an important industry until 1914. The Swansea area – Landore and Llansamlet particularly – was the centre of the zinc-smelting industry, with three-quarters of British capacity being centred in South Wales in 1914, while in 1902 Sir Alfred Mond constructed the world's largest nickel-smelting works in the world at Clydach, near Swansea.

The coal industry

The coal industry dominated the Welsh economy in the second half of the nineteenth century. Coal-mining had originally been in the hands of landowners or small-scale entrepreneurs. Then came the ironmasters who required coal for their industry and there was rapid expansion, because three tons of coal were required to smelt one ton of iron ore. The ironmasters were also able to manipulate the coal industry to compensate for fluctuations in demand in the iron industry.

Soon the coal industry was to develop under its own momentum, and this became even more true as railways developed. Coal was required to fuel them and trains provided the means of transporting coal. In the 1830s the coal export trade from Cardiff started after Lucy Thomas, in co-operation with George Insole, sent high-grade steam-coal from her pit in Abercanaid, near Merthyr, to London and, in the 1830s and 1840s, Thomas Wayne and Thomas Powell sank pits independently of the ironmasters.

Where, up to mid nineteenth century, the iron and coal industries together had transformed the coalfields of Wales, the rest of the century was dominated by coal as it fuelled Britain's steamships as well as supplying many of its industries and hearths. The soil which was such a barrier to prosperous agriculture concealed beneath it vast mineral wealth, enabling Wales to become, for decades, one of the most important industrial centres in the world.

The application of steam to railways and ships signalled the beginning of world significance for Welsh coal. In 1842 this was facilitated by the repeal of government duty on coal carried by British ships and, eight years later, the last barriers to free trade came down.

In 1837 George Crane and David Thomas managed to smelt iron-ore using anthracite coal at their foundry at Ynyscedwyn near Ystalyfera. This technological development meant that the western area of the South Wales coalfield, centred round the Aman and Gwendraeth valleys, could attract iron manufacture on a much larger scale. Later in the century this smokeless anthracite was increasingly used for domestic heating and in industry. Output trebled between 1895 and 1913 and placed Swansea, as a coal port, alongside Cardiff and Barry. Welsh steam-coal was found superior for British naval ships and railways had developed to take coal down to the ports of Cardiff and Newport. With the opening of the Bute West Dock in Cardiff in 1839, and a dock in Newport in 1842, facilities existed for a dramatic increase in exports. Of the $1\frac{1}{2}$ million tons going by sea in 1840 almost all was destined for Bristol or Plymouth. With the exploitation of the rich steam-coal seams of the Aberdare valley this soon changed.

The exploitation of coal seams required capital and it came not from London and Staffordshire, as had been the case with the iron industry, but largely from within the coalfield, from the ranks of that middle class created by the iron industry and consequent urbanisation. It included solicitors, shopkeepers and mining engineers, though it has been argued that outside entrepreneurs were also important. But to take one example, Samuel Thomas, father of D. A. Thomas, one of the coal kings of the Rhondda, was a grocer in Merthyr. The capital required in the early days of coal exploitation was not excessive compared with requirements in the iron industry – Welsh collieries employed about 100 people on average. From the 1860s the adoption of limited liability brought in capital from far further afield, supported by a more adequate banking system of four joint-stock banks with fifty-nine branches, as well as private banks. The most important of the companies was the Powell Dyffryn Steam Coal Company with a nominal capital of £500,000.

In 1851 the Marquess of Bute had a pit sunk in the Rhondda valley, a relatively inaccessible area in which the coal lay deep. So began a phenomenal expansion which did not end until after the First World War. By 1874 the South Wales coalfield was producing $16\frac{1}{2}$ million tons and providing 30 per cent of all United Kingdom foreign shipments. Expansion modified the industry. Mining changed from open-cast levels driven into hills to sinking ever deeper shafts of up to 1,600 yards in the 1870s. This produced ventilation problems which were particularly bad before the pillar and stall method of mining, in which pillars of unmined coal supported the roof, gave way to the 'long wall' method, by which the whole of a seam within a specified area was extracted in one continuous operation. Gradually, too, ventilation fans were introduced. Increasing depth meant greatly increased danger, only partially offset by the reluctant adoption of safety lamps by miners. There was a frightening catalogue of explosions and roof falls. Only in the wake of scores of deaths almost every year in the 1840s did the *laissez-faire* attitude of governments change and an act for the inspection of coal-mines emerge. Safety improved only slowly even then, as the mines inspector in South Wales was faced with indifference. In South Wales and Monmouthshire 738 people died in coal-mining accidents from 1851 to 1855, 20 per cent of them boys under fifteen. There was safety legislation in 1855 and 1860, though it was difficult to get mine-owners to comply. Still, there were improvements as minimum ages of employment were specified. Working hours for boys under sixteen were limited to no more than ten per day in 1872 and penalties of imprisonment could be imposed if it were proved that accidents occurred through neglect, though obtaining convictions was extremely difficult. Even so there was a marked reduction in accidents by 1875.

The South Wales coalfield was now one of the most important in the world, and the North Wales pits, too, had expanded, though at a far lower rate. Welsh collieries, in 1870, were producing 16 million tons of coal, much of it for export. By 1900 this had risen to over 42 million tons, 39 million tons coming from South Wales. In 1913 South Wales produced almost one third of world coal exports. There were 323 collieries in Glamorgan in 1913, 485 in the whole of Wales, with over a quarter of a million men working in them. In the Rhondda valley alone, 41,000 men were at work.

This expansion was achieved under the vast coal combines which developed in the second half of the nineteenth century. These combines, Powell Dyffryn, Lewis Merthyr, David Davies's Ocean Coal Company, D. A. Thomas's Cambrian Combine, were capitalist organisations of enormous wealth which gave the coalowners great power. Normally Welsh in origin, they practised a lifestyle reminiscent of the great gentry families as they built their mansions at Llanwern or Dyffryn. They distanced themselves from direct involvement in

management, which was handed over to professional colliery
managers, although a major shareholder stayed close to the administration and sales of the pits. Yet the coalowners were also highly
conventional and, in many respects, unostentatious with few
extravagances outside great houses. Profits, high in the best pits,
though not above 10 per cent overall, were extensively ploughed back
into pits, docks or railways. To produce this return costs were
rigorously controlled and, since labour accounted for 70 per cent of
costs, this meant that wages were held down. With the Coalowners'
Association so powerful, and the relative prosperity and growth in
the nineteenth century, opposition to this wage policy did not emerge
on any scale until the end of the century, with confrontation
succeeding consensus in a stoppage of six months in 1898 and a one
year stoppage in the Cambrian Combine in 1910–11.

Another implication of the development of the coal industry on this
scale was that the South Wales coastal strip became the commercial
and trading centre of Wales and a focal point of the world's economy.
The phenomenon is best illustrated by the growth of Cardiff, and
inextricably linked with one family, the Butes.

Based on the former estates of the Earls of Pembroke, who had risen
to national prominence in mid sixteenth century, the Bute estate in
Wales had been extended in the nineteenth century to over 22,000
acres. Its centre was Cardiff Castle, the Welsh residence of the family,
and its revenue was one of the highest in the kingdom for that size
of estate. This came not from agriculture but from the mineral wealth
beneath the surface of that extensive tract of land. The Butes owned
the mineral rights of much of the area of the South Wales coalfield.
The potential resources of Cardiff and the coalfield were fully
exploited by the second Marquess of Bute. His industrial enterprise
and speculative building of Bute West Dock changed the face of the
area. In 1800 the balance of economic significance lay in the west
of Glamorgan rather than the east. In 1821 Cardiff's population was
only 3,579, with twenty-six towns in Wales of larger size. By 1868
its population was 60,000, by 1900, 160,000. From 1870 it was the
pre-eminent town in Wales. Its phenomenal growth resulted from the
exploitation of coal in the Taff, Rhondda, Cynon and Rhymney
valleys. By 1850 Bute's revenue from minerals was £25,000, by
1918 it had risen to £115,000 per annum. From 1870 all this income
derived from coal royalties.

Coal from the valleys had to come down to the coast for shipment and the most convenient port was Cardiff, much of which was owned by the same Bute family. These docks made Cardiff the greatest coal port in the world for half a century. In 1839 Bute West Dock was constructed and initially attracted insufficient traffic but the growth in the coal trade, from 8,000 tons per annum in 1839 to 1.3 million tons in 1854, produced so much congestion in the dock that further space was vital. In 1859 Bute East Dock was opened only to become similarly overstretched. In 1887 came Roath Dock and only after this was the Bute monopoly broken by the opening of David Davies's Barry Docks in 1889. The rivalry which produced this challenge to Bute was typical of that which characterised relationships between industrial pioneers: Butes had tangled with Crawshay and Sir John Guest over the Taff Vale railway. Davies's Barry Docks drove the third Marquess of Bute into building the largest masonry dock in the world, the Queen Alexandra Dock in Cardiff, with which the town's dock trade reached 13.7 million tons in 1913, but after that, Cardiff's dock capacity exceeded demand. Similar dock expansion took place on a lesser scale in Swansea and Newport but Cardiff provides the example *par excellence* of how expansion in the coal industry produced a future capital city, a sprawling borough with impressive civic buildings and a commercial and trading social substructure unique in Wales.

Industry in 1914

The scale of industrialisation in nineteenth-century Wales had been dramatic, as had been its social consequences. In 1914, as we have seen, Welsh coal was of world significance. The iron and steel industry had been forced to adapt to new technological and economic circumstances but was still immensely important in South Wales, in association with the tinplate industry. Copper, zinc and nickel from South Wales were all central to British metal production.

There had been expansion in the North Wales industrial base, too, if on a considerably lesser scale. Iron, coal and steel had been developed on the Flintshire coalfield. There was also lead-smelting in that area. While there were transport problems in North Wales the area was by no means remote and peripheral, given its proximity to Liverpool and to the north-west of England. As we have seen, the slate industry, centred in Bethesda and Llanberis in Caernarfonshire and

Blaenau Ffestiniog in Merioneth, expanded rapidly with access to ports provided by the railways. Slate was crucial to the region's economy, employing over 16,000 men in the 1880s. With the substitution of tiles for slates, transatlantic competition and industrial unrest decline was evident by 1914, with the labour force down to 8,000.

Elsewhere, too, in dramatic contrast to the relentless growth of the coal industry, the industrial picture was bleaker. The copper-mines of Anglesey, the lead-mines of Cardiganshire, the woollen industry of Montgomeryshire and Merioneth were in steady decline. Even so, the prosperity of the Welsh coal and metal industries in 1914 seemed sufficient guarantee of continuing economic buoyancy. Despite foreign competition and worsening industrial relations, and lack of entrepreneurial foresight and investment in some instances, the general picture of Welsh industry in 1914 was a flourishing one. Headlong expansion had ceased, there were periods of slackening demand from the last decade of the nineteenth century, but in the first decade of the twentieth there was still expansion in the coal and metal industries while the commercial and business infrastructure associated with these primary industries flourished too.

Roads

The industrialisation of Wales and a transport revolution went hand in hand. In 1780 the main forms of transport in Wales were as they had been in Tudor times – based on roads and waterways. Road transport in 1780 was emerging from centuries of neglect under pressure from industrial demands. The drovers had dictated the routes from east to west across Wales, having used them at least since the fourteenth century, and had established shoeing points at Llandovery and Pumpsaint, for example. Other major routeways served the needs of Ireland rather than the needs of Wales. In the north there was a road from Chester to Holyhead via Denbigh and Caernarfon, in mid Wales from Hereford west to Brecon through Llandovery and Carmarthen to St David's. Finally, and increasingly important, there was the South Wales coast road.

The condition of Welsh roads was appalling in mid eighteenth century. Each parish vestry was responsible for its roads, a system which had not changed since the sixteenth century. This duty was widely neglected because, despite provision for fines, parishioners were very loth to fulfil their labour service for road maintenance. The result was uneven surfaces and prohibitive depths of mud, rocks and debris barring routes. Such primitive communications were an obvious deterrent to industrial expansion. Both people and goods travelled mainly on horses, ponies or mules and, in addition, farmers used carts and sledges.

As we saw in chapter one, the first turnpike road, between Shrewsbury and Wrexham, came in 1752. Although the turnpike trusts could acquire capital for road-building on the security of the tolls they charged, and turnpike roads spread over many parts of Wales, they provided no integrated, organised system and the trusts were under-capitalised. Roads, whether maintained by parish or turnpike trust, did improve in the second half of the eighteenth century and some coach services were inaugurated, but the short-comings in the system became ever more evident.

The inadequacy of roads, including those of the turnpike trusts, resulted in Irish M.P.s pressing for improvements to communications between mainland Britain and Ireland. A scheme for a bridge across the Menai straits, propounded in the 1780s, got nowhere but, with annual trade running at some £20 million per annum, there was more urgency among successive government committees in the 1810s. A new era in state intervention began when the government provided money to improve routes to Ireland, with the sum involved rising to £730,000 by 1830. The demands of a society in the early years of an industrial revolution, experiencing the necessity for speedier communications and better trading facilities, were too great for local administration of services. Government was forced to intervene, never to withdraw.

The engineer to the nine-man commission set up to supervise government spending on roads was Thomas Telford, perhaps the greatest of road engineers, and also a bridge and canal builder. From 1815 to 1830 he reconstructed the Shrewsbury to Holyhead road and improved the North Wales coast road from Chester to Bangor. In the process he built the Menai suspension bridge and produced a road system which not only shortened the journey from London to Ireland but also had beneficial effects for trade and industry in North Wales. His road was three times the width of the old one, firmly based on solid, hand-set stones. In 1819 a single trust was established to supervise maintenance of the road, with obvious gains in efficiency. Yet, while there were improvements, north–south communication in Wales remained very poor.

Canals

With road transport hindered by the geography of Wales water transport had always been important. The Severn estuary linked with the trading metropolis of Bristol. The Severn was navigable into Shropshire, giving access to traffic of woollen goods from Montgomeryshire and also farm produce. The Welsh coast was dotted with small ports from which goods had been carried across the Bristol, English and St George's channels since medieval times. These ports were administered for customs purposes from the three head ports, Cardiff, Milford and Chester. A substantial coastal trade remained in the nineteenth century and generated a ship-building and ship-repairing industry.

The topography of Wales was more inimical to canal building than road construction, although Welsh rivers formed the basis of a waterway system. The demand for canals, in conjunction with tramroads, was stimulated mainly by industrial development. The carriage of coal, ironstone and finished iron, as well as agricultural produce, by packhorse was slow, laborious and inefficient. As early as 1700 Sir Humphrey Mackworth had built a canal to serve his Melingriffith copper-works, but the main stimulus emanated from the ironmasters. In South Wales the main phase of canal building came between 1790 and 1820, by which time much of industrial South Wales was linked by a network of waterways. By 1810 there were nearly 150 miles of canal and 75 miles of navigable river. The famous Glamorganshire canal, linking Penydarren, near Merthyr, with the port of Cardiff was constructed between 1790 and 1794. Between 1790 and 1792 a tramway was built to link Penydarren with the Monmouthshire canal across the valleys. By 1812 the Brecon and Monmouthshire canal, linking Brecon with the port of Newport via Gilwern and Pontypool, had been completed. A branch of this canal linked Newport with Crumlin and both sections were linked by tramroads. A tramroad duplicated the canal service between Penydarren and Quaker's Yard, and it was along this stretch of tramroad that Trevithick's first locomotive inaugurated the railway age in 1804.

The canals and tramroads of eastern South Wales connected with those of the west by means of two routes. A tramroad connected Brecon with Abercrave and Ystradgynlais, linking with Swansea via the Swansea canal, constructed between 1796 and 1798. Further south a link was provided by the Aberdare canal which connected with a tramroad to Glynneath, thence to Neath and Swansea by the Neath canal, built between 1792 and 1795. Farther west still, canals were fewer and later in coming.

Canals were built by private enterprise. The Glamorganshire canal, the biggest undertaking, had seventy-one subscribers, among them the Crawshays, and it cost over £103,000. Tolls were levied on all goods and shareholders' dividends were limited to 8 per cent. Practical difficulties were immense. The fall in this canal was over 600 feet, necessitating the building of more than fifty locks – eleven in one quarter-mile stretch – and an aqueduct had to be built at Abercynon. The benefits were commensurate with the difficulties – a horse, a man and a boy could bring twenty to twenty-five tons of iron down the canal in one canal-company boat, all passing through the administrative centre at Navigation House. Not surprisingly, the canal was an immediate success, with traffic trebling between 1800 and 1820 and coal becoming an increasingly important cargo. In 1829 a similar tonnage of iron and coal was carried. Ten years later, over 132,000 tons of iron were far exceeded by 211,000 tons of coal. Such was the success of the canal in the 1830s that tolls were lowered and the canal was vital in Cardiff's development as a port.

The coming of the railways is often held to have caused the demise of canals but this was not the case. With the construction of Bute West Dock in Cardiff and the opening of the Taff Vale Railway in Glamorgan the canal was less important, but it was working at maximum capacity up to the 1870s, and only then declined. The Neath canal remained important despite the construction of the Vale of Neath railway. The coal-carrying Tennant canal boats were at their busiest as late as 1886. The Swansea canal was still profitable in 1873 when it was acquired by the Great Western Railway which operated it successfully until the 1890s. So, despite hilly terrain, freezing over in winter, thefts from barges, and particularly, the spread of railways, canals remained an integral part of the transport system for most of the nineteenth century.

Inevitably the canal network in mid and North Wales was more limited since it served mainly the needs of agricultural and woollen industries and the topography was even more daunting. Even so, the Montgomery, Ellsmere and Chester canals, built in stages between 1779 and 1819, which ran from Newtown to Chester, via Welshpool with a branch to Chirk and Llangollen, produced some of the finest canal engineering in the country, including the superb Chirk aqueduct.

Railways

Railway development was central to the economic, and later the social, history of Wales. From the 1840s there was railway mania. In 1841 the Taff Vale Railway was completed. The great iron-works were now within an hour's journey of Cardiff, growing apace to meet export demands. Railways provided a market for Welsh iron, since iron and steel were used for the rails laid not only in Wales but also across England and Europe, and even America. But a vital impetus for railway development came from the well-worn need for speedier communication with Ireland. The North Wales coast line, from Chester and Holyhead via Rhyl and Conway, was opened in 1849 and incorporated Robert Stephenson's tubular bridge across the Menai straits. South Wales was incorporated into the Great Western Railway's network with the opening of Brunel's Chepstow bridge in 1850, to link with the line to Swansea which he had already completed, and was extended to Whitland and Haverfordwest in 1854.

Railways, like canals, were built by private investment, prompted by the windfall profits to be reaped if the railway company proved successful. There was no overall co-ordination, so the railway network which developed in Wales was haphazard. Originally it was a different gauge and Brunel's South Wales line eventually had to be relaid to integrate with the rest of the country. There was some logic in the system, stemming from industrial demands. Lines ran from the northern rim of the coalfield in South Wales to connect with the main ports. Even so, railway development generally reinforced the pattern of communication from east to west, with London the focal point. Grandiose schemes for a north–south route proved abortive. Railway development also reinforced the economic supremacy of the south as difficulties of construction and lack of capital combined to limit building in mid and North Wales. Apart from the coast line the North Wales network was constructed two decades later, in the 1860s. One industrial consequence was that the woollen industry in Montgomeryshire was hard hit, first by inadequate railway links with wider markets, then by the ease of access to these markets which the railways provided for northern English counties.

The iron industry profited most from the railway boom, at least in the short term, but agriculture, too, was significantly affected, particularly in patterns of marketing. In North Wales farmers produced for the rapidly expanding markets of the Midlands and northern England while Glamorgan and Monmouthshire now provided expanding and easily accessible markets for farmers in South Wales. With accessible markets there were incentives for Welsh farmers to break away from subsistence farming. Droving largely disappeared as cattle were transported by rail. Fairs in those Welsh towns remote from a railhead tended to die out, while others – Bridgend or Lampeter, for example – prospered. Fat cattle could be bred in, say, Pembrokeshire or Clwyd for newly accessible markets. Butter, cheese and corn no longer went by small boat and Bristol, for centuries the focal point of South Wales trade in foodstuffs, lost its pre-eminence. A few market centres such as Carmarthen, Swansea and Neath in South Wales grew at the expense of many smaller centres.

Railway development, in association with faster sea transport, modified the pattern of product sale. By the end of the nineteenth century Welsh salted butter had lost out to Irish, Danish and New Zealand butter. Welsh cheese was of inferior quality to foreign cheeses. Milk production, invulnerable to foreign competition, expanded in those areas accessible to rail terminals. Remoter farms had to await the coming of the milk lorry.

The railways modified the economic activity and the social life of Wales, but they had not integrated the country or opened it up as dramatically as they might. They tended to integrate the north with north-west England and the south with areas west of London. The railways connected Wales and England far more effectively than the regions of Wales. Difficulties of communication between north and south remained and played a part in inhibiting any dynamic nationalist movement in Wales.

Ports expanded with the railways. Under pressure from the coal industry Llanelli, Swansea, Port Talbot, Barry, Cardiff and Newport grew apace. New docks were built – at Port Talbot in 1898, Swansea (King's Dock) in 1909, Barry, 1889, Cardiff (Roath and Queen Alexandra Docks) in 1887 and 1907. On the eve of the First World War the port at Barry exported 11 million tons of coal a year and had superseded Cardiff as the largest coal-exporting port in the world.

SECTION II. 1914–1979

Population

From the 1880s population movements away from rural Wales were accentuated as agricultural depression took hold, though the decline was arrested for some years after 1900. The 1920s, almost as much as the 1930s, were years of decline and depression, especially in the industrial areas of North and South Wales, though the material poverty of rural Wales continued. For the young, fit and talented there was escape to more prosperous areas of England, particularly the south-east. Nearly half a million people left Wales between the wars, siphoning off all the natural increase in population. Once again the most dramatic yardsticks are Merthyr and the Rhondda valleys, though reversing their roles as magnets of population. Merthyr's population declined by some 27,000 between the wars, while Rhondda lost 13 per cent of its population in the 1930s alone. The drift from the land continued, though now it was Liverpool and the Midlands which beckoned since there were no opportunities in industrial Wales.

After the Second World War the pattern changed once more. Economic revival centred mainly on the coastal regions of North and South Wales. The conurbations, Cardiff, and Newport especially, sprawled extensively, and the focus of economic activity centred on the southern England–Wales border – a modern version of sixteenth-century links between the agrarian economy of South Wales and the port of Bristol. In North Wales, too, links with England were evident in the growth of eastern Flintshire's population. Despite a general rise in the standard of living since the end of the Second World War population in Wales did not grow as fast as in England. In the 1960s Welsh population increased by 3.3 per cent, 2 per cent less than in the whole of the United Kingdom. The drift to England continued and was disquieting. An already sparsely populated mid Wales lost a further 2.7 per cent of its population between 1956 and 1969. Just as disquieting was the loss of highly trained personnel. Between 1920 and the 1970s more than half the teachers trained in Wales went to England. Between 1930 and the 1980s the population of Wales has varied between $2\frac{1}{2}$ and $2\frac{3}{4}$ million. Between 1961 and 1966 about 22,000 people left Wales, while a similar number came in. What was worrying was the age differential between these groups. Young people, usually well-qualified, left; older people came in, often to retire. The growth of holiday and retirement homes resulted in 25 per cent of Caernarfonshire's population having originated outside Wales. Similar trends occurred in other rural coastal counties, with serious implications for community, language and social services.

The land

From the turn of the century both the economic base of rural Wales and the popular approach to rural problems began to change. The anti-landlord campaign grew less central and the quest for the establishment of a land court was seriously questioned on grounds of its likely effectiveness and efficiency. Most important, the rural economy began to improve, with prices for dairy products increasing and more capital investment, which meant more machinery, better husbandry, increased use of fertilisers and higher productivity. Welsh farming remained relatively backward, but rural depopulation slowed down and economic issues tended to supersede politically orientated matters of landlordism and tithe.

The First World War was a watershed in the history of Welsh agriculture as in so much else. There was increased prosperity, as demand for milk, corn and livestock increased rapidly. The government, anxious to improve supplies, intervened through measures like the Corn Production Act of 1917, which guaranteed high prices for corn and wheat and gave farm labourers a guaranteed wage, and so, for the first time, a reasonably assured living.

The most profound change was that in the pattern of landowner-ship. Landed estates were being sold up in part or wholly a few years before the war in the wake of Lloyd George's increased taxes, but the war speeded up the process as tenants profited more than landlords in wartime. As rents fell – by up to 50 per cent – landlords became more eager to sell, usually to tenants eager to buy. Estates with industrial interests were sold too. In Breconshire the Beaufort estates were sold, while the long-established Margam estate in Glamorgan was sold in 1917. In the following year the Hanburys of Pontypool Park sold up. The process of sale of large estates continued after the war and owner-occupation became the norm in Wales. The social base from which landlords operated was further undermined by the acceptance of Church disestablishment and with it the end of patronage of lay livings. A very long chapter in Welsh history closed with the virtual demise of the landed gentry, though tenant purchasers inherited problems. They bought their land with the aid of hefty mortgages which had to be repaid as conditions deteriorated after the war. Wartime prosperity proved fragile. In the 1920s some upland farms benefited from the sustained profit in sheep farming but prices for other livestock were depressed and, with the end of state intervention, arable land fell out of cultivation. Land in Wales was always difficult to work and farms were under-mechanised, so they were vulnerable in adverse conditions. Such adversity came in the 1930s with world-wide Depression. The Welsh small farmer had inherited the lot of the Welsh small tenant farmer by now – poverty and struggle in a context of depressed prices and a further contraction in the extent of arable land under cultivation. Rural depopulation resumed, to the detriment of communities and the Welsh language. Only further state intervention improved the situation. In 1933 the Milk Marketing Board was established, guaranteeing farmers a price for milk sustained by government subsidy. The number of farmers engaged in milk production in Wales doubled by 1939.

War in 1939, like that during 1914–18, meant greater prosperity for the farmer, though depopulation of rural areas continued because increased prosperity also meant increased mechanisation. Unlike the situation after the First World War prosperity continued after 1945. Demand for agricultural produce, and prices, remained high. Marketing became more co-operative. The smallest farms began to be merged with larger units. But physical constraints on agricultural developments remained, of course. On only 0.2 per cent of Welsh land is there virtually no constraint on its agricultural use; on 80 per cent there are severe limitations of soil and climate which make relatively low output inevitable. So, despite big increases in milk production, in, for example, the extensive dairy farms of south-west Dyfed, or in sheep, Welsh farms remained generally small. In 1973, in an area of 3.6 million acres of agricultural land, there were over 32,000 agricultural holdings, as well as thousands more under ten acres. In Caernarfonshire 32 per cent of farms were under twenty acres. Such figures occur despite the large reduction in small farms in Wales in the 1950s and 1960s as the economic rewards became so obviously inadequate. But problems remained. Over half Welsh farms were owner-occupied in 1973, compared with just over a quarter rented, but of the smaller farms nearly half were operated on a part-time basis, an indication of inadequate return. The drift from the land continued. Rural industry hardly compensated at all, although forestry employed some. Rural Wales was badly served by government in other ways, particularly in transport policy as the Beeching Report of 1963 resulted in public transport isolation.

Welsh agriculture since the Second World War has been relatively prosperous but it has afforded employment to fewer people. The problems of the late nineteenth century have assumed a very different form. The problems of an ownership structure which had such profound social, religious and nationalist implications have been replaced with depopulation problems which, ironically, have left Wales with a more anglicised population as tourists and second-home owners have moved in, to undermine a distinctively Welsh linguistic and social base. These problems, no less than those of the nineteenth century, have had important political ramifications.

The Depression

With the end of the First World War came difficulty and eventual disaster for the woollen industry. The price of wool plummeted, hundreds of employees were sacked as mining area markets became depressed. Chain-store tailors accentuated the decline, as did out-of-date machinery. In 1926 there were over 250 woollen mills in Wales, in 1947, eighty-one, in 1974, twenty-four. The industry survived but in attenuated form, no longer supplying a basically functional product but goods for the luxury and tourist markets.

Another rurally orientated industry which declined rapidly in the twentieth century after enjoying centuries of importance was the leather industry. Producing leather, whether for boots, saddles or fine gloves was a complex and lengthy process. The ready availability of the raw materials for setting up tanneries – skins, oak bark for tanning, lime, water – had resulted in the establishment of many tanneries across Wales. Producing leather required remarkable skill and experience, together with an immunity to smells. Some of the odours of a tannery resulted from hen and pigeon or dog excreta used to make the solution which produced light boot uppers. The process of converting hides to leather, via lime pits, tanning pits and other finishing processes lasted approximately eighteen months. The market, particularly for functional products such as saddles, steadily decreased, costs of both hides and labour increased, synthetic products became available and foreign competition made increasing inroads so that both the production of leather and its retail outlets were whittled away.

The decline of the rurally based industries, particularly the woollen industry, was serious but it paled into insignificance compared with the fate of those heavy industries whose phenomenal expansion in the nineteenth century we have already observed. The First World War merely stimulated this growth as the demand for armaments required accelerated production of iron and steel. New blast furnaces had to be opened up in Blaenavon and Ebbw Vale and in the John Summers works in Shotton. Coal production had to increase in parallel.

Wartime prosperity and increased wages did not immediately die away with peace. The Welsh coal industry enjoyed a boom year in 1919, but by the end of that year depression had set in, not to be relieved until war came once more, and having all the more impact because of the frenetic pace of expansion in the Welsh economy over the previous half century. Welsh prosperity was almost wholly dependent on primary industries, coal and metal and these were worst hit. Particularly from 1926 Wales saw poverty on a scale which ate into individual, communal and national dignity. The slump, under way by 1920, hit the coal and steel industries hard, so making Wales especially vulnerable. When the British economy revived from 1934 on, particularly in light industry, there was little respite for Wales. In North Wales, Flintshire and the coastal towns escaped the worst depredations as, to a limited extent, did Cardiff and Swansea but much of Wales was devastated. By 1927, 23.3 per cent of the insured population of Wales were unemployed; by 1930, 27.2 per cent. The late twenties, then, were scarcely better than the thirties. After 1931 even this situation deteriorated. In 1935 47.5 per cent of Merthyr's population were unemployed. In Rhondda general unemployment was 40 per cent in 1935, higher still in the coal industry. The coal industry suffered most dramatically, with only the anthracite coal of the western end of the coalfield still in demand in the 1920s and even for much of the 1930s. Steam and bituminous coal were increasingly supplied by America and Germany and although demand kept up reasonably until 1924 dramatic decline was soon apparent. By 1929 coal production in South Wales had slumped to 3 per cent of world output. The geological difficulties of the South Wales coalfield exacerbated the problem by keeping production costs high. The competitiveness of industry was completely undermined by the revaluation of sterling as Churchill restored the gold standard in 1925. Demand for fuel from contracting industry was low and, increasingly, oil substituted for coal in industry and ships.

America and Germany were able to produce steel more cheaply than Wales. The plants at the heads of the valleys became even less viable and in 1921 Cyfarthfa finally closed, to be followed by Dowlais in two stages in 1930 and 1936. The social consequences were catastrophic. In the mid 1930s unemployment in Dowlais was 80 per cent; the number of working men in the borough of Merthyr fell from nearly 32,000 in 1921 to 17,500 in 1931. The Monmouthshire valleys were badly hit as Blaenavon and Ebbw Vale works closed in the 1920s. Demand for tinplate remained reasonable in the 1920s but the export trade was badly hit after 1929 and the familiar pattern of high unemployment was evident here too.

Any alleviation of a desperate economic crisis in Wales required radical change because prosperity had rested on coal, steel and tinplate. Foreign competition and government policy had exacerbated the situation. The slow return to greater economic activity was only marginally relevant to a Welsh economy resting on a disastrously restricted base. In the mid 1930s nearly half the insured population of east Glamorgan and west Monmouthshire were unemployed. Even the National government was moved to some action. But a report of 1933–4 suggested little more than that the able-bodied poor of Wales should be helped to move to areas of greater prosperity, such as the Midlands or the south-east – a route many were already taking. At last, in 1936, a Reconstruction Association was established, empowered to give grants to attract industry to depressed areas. One of these areas roughly coincided with the area of the South Wales coalfield, but practical results were very limited. Some new factories were set up but only in 1938 was there much improvement when the government took powers to buy land for new industries. In that year, too, Treforest trading estate was established and employed 2,500 people by 1939. Glamorgan and Monmouthshire local authorities helped with some public investment to create some jobs. But government intervention was on a scale which could scarcely dent the unemployment problem, and government economic policy, reinforced by banking orthodoxy, was opposed to anything like the scale of government expenditure which could have had some effect. Only in the location of the new strip-mill in Ebbw Vale was there evidence of positive government help, and this in response to *ad hoc*, if formidable, lobbying.

The economy since the Second World War

The Second World War and its aftermath solved the problem of unemployment but did not halt the decline in basic industries. Tinplate production fell by nearly a half in the war years and coal output by over a third since there were virtually no export markets. However, the war did provide Wales with a basis for remodelling the economy. A massive ordnance factory had been built in Bridgend and there were Unilever and I.C.I. factories in Merthyr. Once the war was over, demand for steel and coal revived and new technologies and new consumer demands created a range of new industries. Government intervention, with Labour in power after 1945, and with wartime precedents still fresh, was on an effective scale. So, despite general austerity, there was relative prosperity once more in Wales. In the immediate post-war years unemployment still tended to be higher in Wales than elsewhere in Britain but by the mid 1950s there was virtually full employment. Coal and steel output was up, government-sponsored advance factories were built on trading estates and elsewhere. Nationalisation of the gas industry brought investment into Wales and resulted in a petro-chemical works in the Port Talbot area. The nationalisation of the coal industry also brought new investment, as in Cynheidre. Then in the 1950s and even more in the 1960s, the story was one of pit closures. In 1960 there were

106,000 men working in the South Wales coal industry; only 30,000 in 1979. Between 1947 and 1974, 150 collieries were closed. The preference for oil as fuel hit South Wales particularly hard. It was an area of high production costs due to difficult geological features. Oil, cheaper and cleaner, fuelled domestic and industrial boilers in ever-increasing numbers until the Arab–Israeli war of 1973 heralded an embargo and a trebling of oil prices. The vulnerability of Britain to middle-east politics was evident and brought new power to the miners. Miners jumped to the top of the industrial pay league and in February 1974 brought down the Tory government. However, contraction of the industry in South Wales continued. The workforce in the coal-mines decreased by 70,000 between 1960 and 1970 and in 1979 the Coal Board planned the closure of ten more pits. The only buoyant market was for anthracite. In North Wales the industry employed only 1,250 men in two collieries by 1973. There was capital investment by the Coal Board – £200 million between 1950 and 1975 – but coal had long since ceased to be the base of a whole economy.

The outlook for the other staple Welsh heavy industry, iron and steel, seemed highly promising after the war. Ebbw Vale had already acquired its ultra-modern strip-mill. In 1947 the industry was nationalised and a large new steelworks in Port Talbot started making steel in 1951. At that time Port Talbot was the largest steel plant in Britain, and was complemented by works at Trostre, Llanelli and Velindre, Swansea. There was a boom in demand for steel and tinplate and prosperity in these areas. Government intervention had brought the works to Wales and such intervention continued, more surprisingly, under Conservative administrations in the 1950s, with car plants established in Cardiff and Llanelli as major steel customers. The 1960s started with the construction of another giant steelworks at Llanwern and there was investment at Ebbw Vale and Shotton aimed at modernising plant. The fate of steel was, however, to be similar to that of coal, though a decade later. Decline in the British car industry meant the contraction of domestic markets; world demand was falling and supply from modern plants in Germany, the U.S.A. and, particularly, Japan was rising. Ebbw Vale works closed in 1975–6; East Moors, Cardiff in 1978. By the end of the 1970s Llanwern and Port Talbot operated under the threat of closure. Since, even in the mid 1970s, metal industries in Wales employed about

25 per cent of the workforce this decline was relatively more serious than that in the coal industry. Unemployment rose to levels not witnessed since before the war.

Fortunately the Welsh industrial base had diversified steadily, particularly into light manufacturing industries, as government intervention had encouraged new enterprises in Wales by a variety of incentives. By 1979 there were 179 new factories in Wales and new trading estates had developed. On sites at Bridgend and Hirwaun, where ordnance had been manufactured during the Second World War, trading estates were established and government advance factory policy brought light industry into Cwmbran and Merthyr, particularly. Hoover established a large factory in Merthyr and the manufacture of electrical goods, insulated wire and cable, bolts and screws, clothing, toys, car components, and tyres indicates the range of industrial diversification. Milford Haven's superb deep-water harbour was exploited by the oil companies, with refineries built by Esso, B.P., Texaco, Gulf and Amoco in the 1960s and 1970s. With Labour in power, most of Wales became a development area in 1966 and more light engineering works were established. Such developments cushioned the decline in the coal industry and, later, more serious depredation in the steel industry but recession, gathering momentum in the late 1970s, showed that the Welsh industrial economy was still more vulnerable than that in many areas of England. A more secure cushion was provided by direct government employment provided by the dispersal of some government services to Wales. Outstanding among these were the location of the Royal Mint at Llantrisant, the Driver and Vehicle Licensing Centre at Morriston and Companies House in Cardiff. These services also helped boost the figure for female employment in Wales – 30 per cent of the labour force in 1969, a proportion 10 per cent below that of Britain as a whole. Women were strongly represented in those service industries which grew so strikingly in post-war Wales, to employ nearly 60 per cent of the Welsh labour force by 1973.

The disquieting feature of industrial and employment diversification was that the perennial imbalance between various regions of Wales was consolidated. The coastal areas of South Wales fared well, north-eastern areas of Wales less well. Outside these areas there was little industrial development. Tourism was one industry which did expand in rural Wales. It had started in the eighteenth century, though only with the coming of the railways, particularly the Shrewsbury line, did it develop as day trips and holidays became more common. Barry and Porthcawl in the south, Aberystwyth and the North Wales resorts of Colwyn Bay and Rhyl all developed in different ways. Since 1945 there has been dramatic expansion, facilitated by car ownership – by 1981 60 per cent of British households owned a car. In north-west Wales, tourism was producing 15.3 per cent of the area's revenue by 1973. Tourists have come in to the seaside, for pony-trekking or walking and sight-seeing in areas of outstanding natural beauty (officially designated) and national parks. Specific attractions were highlighted – Welsh castles, narrow gauge railways, slate quarries, open-air industrial museums.

Large-scale tourism brought its problems. Increasing caravanning caused environmental problems; longer stays have had more worrying implications. Attracted by the calm and beauty of rural Wales, retired couples have settled in North and West Wales. Second-home ownership has increased. In the 1970s 70 per cent of it was in coastal Wales with the Llŷn and Anglesey coasts being especially popular. Since the Llŷn peninsula is one of the most densely Welsh-speaking areas of Wales such developments awakened real fears of the dilution of Welsh culture and language, and produced legal and direct action to curb it.

Rural Wales fared relatively badly on other counts. While agriculture was comparatively prosperous, demand for labour shrank with increasing mechanisation and the population was drawn to urban areas. The slate industry, even when there was some revival in the 1970s, employed only hundreds. The Forestry Commission was only a minor employer. Nuclear power stations at Wylfa and Trawsfynydd, once built, required small labour forces. Difficulties were compounded in rural areas as railway services were axed following the Beeching Report in 1963. Government intervention attracted small-scale industrial development to Caernarfon, Aberystwyth and Llandrindod, for example, but could not compensate for the economic imbalance in Wales.

Relative to the 1930s the Welsh economy after 1945 was buoyant, employment was high, prosperity returned and social support for those out of work, for whatever reason, was immeasurably greater. But economic growth was uneven. Expansion centred on the main cities while the valleys steadily lost population, as did many rural areas. The unemployment rate was twice that of the United Kingdom. Capital investment was often in industries which employed little labour, like the oil industry. It has been estimated that, between 1964 and 1976, 100,000 jobs were lost. As in the 1930s, though of course on a far smaller scale, many of the brightest products of Welsh schools found work in England, particularly as teachers. It has emerged since 1979 that a combination of world recession and government policy can expose a worrying fragility and structural imbalance within the Welsh economy.

Transport

Only in the twentieth century has road provision fundamentally changed as buses, lorries and private cars had to be catered for and new technologies of road building devised. The growth, and eventual decline, of bus services was a major feature of rural transport. By 1914 there were eighteen bus services in Wales, owned by the railway companies. By 1950 a minimal bus service, at least, was available to all but the smallest and most remote communities. Bus companies made profits well into the 1960s but by the 1970s car ownership was so widespread that the companies required substantial subsidies. The basic pattern of road arteries in Wales was maintained so that Wales's motorway, complete between Swansea and London by 1980, inevitably reflected the trade and communication priorities of centuries.

One of the hallmarks of the First World War was increased government intervention in industry. The railways were brought under government control, so paving the way for control of the Welsh railway network by the Great Western Railway from 1923, apart from the mid Wales line which was taken over by the London Midland and Scottish. With nationalisation in 1947 Welsh railways became part of the western region of British Rail. But from the 1950s traffic on branch lines dropped and, with changing location of industry, valley lines were badly affected. The Beeching plan of 1963 recommended the closure of 274 miles of Wales's 637 miles of railway. Two vital links were preserved – the Cambrian coast line from Machynlleth to Pwllheli and the mid Wales line to Shrewsbury. There was even doubt about a major Welsh route from Shrewsbury to Aberystwyth, and railway journeys between North and South Wales became impossible.

There have, indeed, been ironic shades of the past surrounding developments in transport in recent decades. It once seemed as if growth in the railway network might break down the impenetrability of rural Wales but by the end of the 1960s the profitable routes involved the Holyhead boat trains and the Swansea to London service – routes reminiscent of those taken by the Norman conquerors of Wales.

Those who owned cars were the least concerned by the axing of railways, but rural Wales was badly served by road, too. Road improvements were concentrated as always on the major east–west arteries, although the A5 road to Holyhead remained ill-equipped to deal with the traffic loads of the 1960s and 1970s. In the south, the motorway from London to Swansea was complete by 1981, though the Severn Bridge had made access to the cities and ports of South Wales much easier from 1966. Those who suffered as the new transport priorities developed were the least mobile members of communities in the remoter parts of Wales – the old and those who could not afford cars. When the railway system was at its maximum – and it remained substantially intact until 1962 – few places in Wales were more than ten miles from a station. Now, social and community life suffered, young people had even more incentive to leave rural areas, and the concentration of industrial activity in favoured areas was made even more likely. It has even been argued that the M4 motorway and the Severn Bridge may have generated more prosperity for Bristol and Avon than for the area bordering the South Wales coast, so recalling the period we considered in Part I, when Bristol was the metropolis of the west.

8

SOCIETY

The social structure

The social hierarchy in Wales at the end of the eighteenth century and throughout the nineteenth century was dominated by the great landowners, despite rapid industrialisation. Some families of fifteenth-century or Tudor origin still owned vast tracts of land. In addition, with the high failure rate of direct male heirs between 1720 and 1760, estates had passed to more distant male relatives, often from England, and had grown larger as they were combined. Some of them had been acquired by Scottish and Irish landowners. Landed gentry like the Wynns of Wynnstay, the Powells of Nanteos, the Pryses of Gogerddan, the Vaughans of Trawscoed, the Cawdors of Golden Grove, the Morgans of Tredegar and the Butes of Cardiff were immensely powerful in their communities. In rural Wales their power was little short of feudal until late in the nineteenth century. They, or their nominees, represented counties in Parliament and expected their tenants' votes; they monopolised local government as they had done for centuries.

Landlords were not generally absentee and they had a paternalistic interest in the welfare of their tenants, helping to alleviate distress and build schools, for example. Such community involvement was vital because even the great landowners were not wholly independent. Freeholders had to be assiduously cultivated, since their support was essential at elections. From the 1830s deference to the landed classes was being slowly undermined, though it remained a potent force. Only with the inauguration of county councils in 1889 and parish and district councils in 1894 was their hold over their locality effectively ended.

The divide between gentry and tenants was manifest in every aspect of lifestyle. Anglican gentry had an increasingly nonconformist tenantry; with few exceptions the gentry not only did not speak Welsh but regarded the language as a hindrance, even though it was still the language of the majority of the population until the end of the nineteenth century. At some stage, especially in a changing economic environment, such inherent tensions would inevitably be exploited politically and nationally and a relatively static rural society find itself in turmoil.

What was to transform the role of the landed class eventually, though it was a remarkably lengthy process, was industrialisation, the most far-reaching change which has ever affected the people of Wales. The balance of population changed so that Glamorgan and Monmouthshire grew phenomenally while rural counties lost population. Industrialisation created great wealth, again particularly in South Wales. Some of it merely consolidated landed wealth, as in the case of the Butes, the Morgans of Tredegar and the Penrhyn family in North Wales, but an entrepreneurial class also grew rich on mineral profits. Some of the wealth was channelled into the communities which produced it, and went to build chapels, provide a market for books or periodicals, or support schools. Equally, industrialisation resulted in a concentration of squalor and disease and exploitation which could not, in the end, be coped with by the existing machinery of local or central government. Industrialisation produced urbanisation on an unprecedented scale. In the last quarter of the nineteenth century Wales became the first country in the world in which more people lived in urban rather than in rural areas. In conjunction with the railway system industrialisation had produced a different Wales by the end of the century. Towns had grown to serve a specifically industrial purpose – Merthyr, Pontypool, Mold, Hawarden, for example. By this time only half the towns in Wales were medieval in origin. The change in urban pattern indicated the extent to which the commercial centres of gravity had altered. In South Wales it had moved from Bristol to Glamorgan.

The urban pattern changed internally. In the old urban centres craft workshops were located in town centres and products could be sold immediately. In the nineteenth century mass production provided goods sold through specialist retailers in the town centres. where increasing numbers of professionals had their offices. By the 1870s central shopping areas were located close to railway stations. Suburban growth stemmed from a middle-class desire to use railway and tramcar to live outside the immediate town environment, an option closed to the majority of workers who had to live near their workplace.

Parts of North and South Wales had become increasingly industrialised from the 1760s. First came the growth of the iron industry, then increasing concentration on coal. Much English capital had been channelled into these developments and a new breed of dynasts had emerged. The ironmasters, Guest and Crawshay, for example, espoused a lifestyle very like that of the landed gentry and they tended to rule the communities they created in a similar kind of way. They were complete capitalists, owning the raw materials, the means of production, disposing of the finished product. They owned or leased the houses of their workmen, for a time controlled the expenditure of wages through the truck system and shared in the ownership of the transport system which conveyed iron and coal to the ports. The successful among this new breed of entrepreneurs were able to build mock-gothic castles and acquire landed estates; the lifestyle of the landed gentleman still remained the yardstick of social superiority.

The fortunes of coal-owners and copper-smelters were made in the years after 1850. The Welsh economy expanded at a rate unheralded even in the era of iron. Welsh coal was central to the world economy. Those who owned the land under which it was mined, those who managed and owned the successful pits, made fortunes. The coal entrepreneurs were usually Welsh-born or had close connections with the country – David Davies of Llandinam, coal-owner, railway and dock-builder, was a nonconformist Welshman and he and his family became closely identified with Welsh philanthropic enterprises. Their social control was in its way as extensive as that of rural landlords or early ironmasters. They were virtually sole employers in the mining valley towns, took office on boards of health and as justices of the peace. They were generally careful and orthodox, nonconformist, and philanthropic towards their churches and chapels. They were far less prepared to provide amenities in the communities which produced their wealth.

Since Tudor times there had been a small middle class in Wales, located in boroughs such as Swansea or Carmarthen, but in such numbers as not to be of great social consequence. By the end of the eighteenth century this class, still small by English standards, was growing as industrialisation increased. Entrepreneurs, lawyers, medical men, merchants, shopkeepers, middle-ranking farmers were all more in evidence. Older towns like Wrexham or Carmarthen had spawned more merchants and traders. With increasing industrialisation came lawyers, bankers, land agents and surveyors, although this development should not be exaggerated. Contemporaries were struck by the way in which the iron towns remained two-class communities – the owners, their agents and managers; and the workers dependent on them. A middle-class element was more evident later in the nineteenth century as more technical personnel were employed and government intervention in welfare, education and local concerns produced more posts. Despite this growth the political and social role of the middle class was restricted in Wales. In north-west Wales, for example, the landowning slate-quarry proprietors were virtually omnipotent despite a middle class of some social significance by the end of the nineteenth century – doctors, accountants, teachers, nonconformist ministers.

In rural Wales modification of the social structure was far less evident, with the tenant farmer still preponderant. Tenants and labourers lived in remarkably stable communities. About 40 per cent of people stayed in the parishes in which they were born, and 20 to 25 per cent of marriages were between people of neighbouring parishes. There was no sizeable class of substantial freeholders in Wales and material conditions of farmers and their labourers often reflected a similar degree of poverty. The social distinction between farmer and servant remained and it was exceptional for a farm servant to acquire high community status through, for example, becoming a chapel deacon. Rural communities, however, remained complex because, until the advent of mass production, they required service from a variety of craftsmen – bakers, blacksmiths, bootmakers, brewers, carpenters, coach-builders, coopers, curriers, glovers, hatters, maltsters, lime burners, millers, rope-makers, masons, tailors, clock-makers, stay-makers, paper-makers, weavers, skinners, thatchers, stonemasons – skills often now preserved only in folk-museum aspic.

With pressure on agricultural holdings, the surplus population had little choice but to seek employment in industry. Eventually a large industrial proletariat, originating mainly within Wales but with an English and Irish element, was created in the iron, steel and coal industries. The Welsh among them brought their language and, for long, their deferential attitudes, but here again, the homogeneity of this class must not be exaggerated. Communities of iron and coal-workers in South Wales were wealthier than the remote quarrying villages of North Wales and in both areas links with the land continued, with seasonal labour from industrial areas helping with haymaking, for example. In North Wales, particularly, this was general throughout the nineteenth century. Even so, the creation of a sizeable industrial proletariat coupled with the social problems of new communities, resulted in tensions which erupted in a variety of ways.

One source of tension, not immediately evident, was that social mobility was even more restricted in nineteenth century Wales than in England. The occupational structure was limited. In Glamorgan 40 per cent of employed men were in the iron or coal industries, fewer than 3 per cent in the professions. Only towards the end of the century were the ranks of the lower-middle class swelled as the county school products increasingly entered black-coated occupations, and this helps explain the hold which such schools had on their communities. The relative smallness of the middle class in Wales was a source of anxiety to those who regarded the perceived virtues of that class, particularly respectability, as a guarantee of order in society. To such men as Hugh Owen or Tom Ellis, indeed to the nonconformist leadership, the augmentation of the middle class, professional and commercial, was a prerequisite of national respectability for Wales, parity with England and a respected place in the great British Empire. Through the educational system, for which men like Owen worked indefatigably, much was achieved, though on English terms of individual advancement. Ironically, from the 1890s came the beginnings of breakdown in the whole Liberal, nonconformist philosophy of consensus. Notions of respectability remained pervasive, but could no longer disguise the chasm which divided the interests of employers and employees generally.

Community

These developments in industrial relations gravely dented the notion of community in Wales. Nationalist writers, in particular, have tended to couple a romanticised picture of a virtuous, law-abiding, educated (if only informally), creative *gwerin* with a corporate version of these virtues evident in small rural communities, in particular. Customs of medieval society – *cymortha*, for example – have been associated with community help. There is no doubt that there has been an element of continuity. Until well into the nineteenth century Wales was remote. The virtually universal language, one of the oldest in Europe, was regarded in England as handicapping the development of civilisation. There was inevitably a close sense of community in rural areas of small farms in which the majority of workers were local. Co-operation in such communities was essential at harvest time; common ownership of a bull or boar was equally essential, as was common ownership of some farm implements. These communities were reinforced by a considerable degree of self-sufficiency until well into the twentieth century. Farmers in pastoral upland farms, particularly, were their own craftsmen and made their own simple implements. Corn was cut with a scythe, or even a sickle in wet conditions. The range of implements required – plough, harrow, cart and a range of hand tools, was easily provided. When seed-drills replaced hand-sowing they were often co-operatively owned. It was well into the twentieth century before the tempo of farm life, and patterns moulded by it, were changed, with the coming of the tractor from the 1930s and, more especially, the general adoption of machinery after the Second World War, though community feeling remained.

Movement in and out of an area is a central factor in the existence of a sense of community and in industrial areas there were factors which militated against its emergence even though workers brought with them some of the community values of rural Wales. People flocked first into Merthyr and other heads of the valleys towns, then into the Rhondda valleys and the other coal-mining valleys in wholly unprecedented numbers. Neither ironmasters nor coal-owners provided the civil amenities which generate community values. The topography of the valleys produced housing patterns which were the antithesis of nucleated patterns. They were peopled mainly by those of a common Welsh origin but it was a floating population, with movement in and out of the area accentuated by seasonal labour. The structure of employment did not foster much community spirit, since different wage rates reflected different skills. There was no civic tradition such as existed in the old incorporated boroughs. Community problems were the result, in government, health, social integration and ultimately politics. Lack of an adequate water supply, and of sanitation facilities, resulted in widespread contagious disease, most spectacularly, cholera. In places where, especially in early days, there was rootlessness, periodic economic depression, lack of community focus in church or chapel, a truck system and lack of effective policing, violence flourished and contemporary methods of social control were stretched to their limits until after the 1850s. These areas provided fertile ground for protest whether riot, rising or Chartism.

However, in time there was much to create community feeling in industrial Wales. Common values were brought in by workers from rural Wales and they flourished in a chapel environment. In all industrial communities – the slate quarries of Penrhyn, the iron-works of Merthyr or Blaenavon, the coal-mining communities of Aberdare or Rhondda – there was danger, to individuals and to communities. Working conditions were highly dangerous, fatalities and serious accidents a part of everyday experience. In times of strike or wage-cut, accident or death, community feeling was especially strong. It was reinforced by a largely common language and religious affiliation. This in turn led to a degree of community cohesion between disparate elements – a common respectability, moral code and even lifestyle, at least on Sunday, between lower-middle and working class. There was class distinction but it was softened by a degree of cultural homogeneity in community life.

Residences

Disparities in wealth in late eighteenth and nineteenth-century Wales were enormous – between, for example, landed gentry and farm labourers or the owners of industries and their workers. These disparities were reflected in lifestyle, housing, diet, expectation of life, education and leisure activities.

There was little inspired architecture in Wales. There were some fine gentry houses, including those, like St Donat's castle, Glamorgan, of medieval origin which had been adapted over the centuries. Industrialists like Crawshay indulged their fantasies with mock-gothic creations like Cyfarthfa castle, Merthyr, in which round towers combined with Georgian windows. The new home of the Mansel-Talbots in Margam, built on land acquired at the dissolution of the monasteries, ran the gamut of neo-gothic, Elizabethan and not a little Victorian. Singleton Abbey, commissioned in 1823 and built from Vivian copper wealth east of Swansea, reflected a contemporary obsession with escapism by having each floor at a slightly different level. Most remarkable was Burges's creation for the third Marquess of Bute, eccentric Catholic convert, hero of a Disraeli novel. In Cardiff itself Burges had been constrained by an existing motte-and-stone keep but north of Cardiff he built a gothic folly of considerable exterior charm at Castell Coch. There was little distinguished town architecture. The civic centre in Cardiff was exceptional with its impressive Edwardian buildings in a spacious setting.

Tenants, in town and country, often lived in conditions of overcrowding and squalor. Country cottages were often little more than hovels. Farmhouses in the upland farms of Bute estates at the end of the eighteenth century were often made from a lime, dung and mould mix. Cottages and farmhouses naturally reflected local building materials. Where boulder clay was plentiful, as in Llŷn, cottages were normally constructed of earth mixed with straw and cow dung. In south Cardiganshire, mud walls were common until mid nineteenth century. Stone-walled cottages were common else-where – in Gwynedd, for example. Cottages sometimes comprised one living room, with partitioned-off pantry and one sleeping room though, for many, one room sufficed for living and sleeping. In the second half of the nineteenth century additional accommodation was often made available as second storeys were added to the traditional two-roomed cottages, as happened in west Wales. This made available a downstairs room as a parlour, a remote room reserved for funeral ritual and the home's treasures. Furniture was simple and locally made, except for the gentry whose houses reflected English tastes, growing increasingly sophisticated. In the second half of the century there was some surplus cash to be expended in more ornamental furniture, including clocks.

Houses in the industrial areas were thrown up by ironmasters and speculative builders to accommodate a swiftly growing population. The materials from which the houses were built were substantial enough but they were constructed quickly, and in the coal-mining areas particularly, strung out along the sides of valleys. Sanitation, for much of the nineteenth century was minimal – one lavatory to twenty-five houses being normal. A survey in Neath in 1849 revealed that 476 dwellings, housing 2,142 people, had neither wcs nor cesspools. Inevitably, therefore, the purity of the water supply was endangered. In Neath it came from four wells, contaminated by sewage draining through soil. Ratepayers in Neath and elsewhere were extremely reluctant to foot bills for reforms. Houses were overcrowded, with families and lodgers crammed together. In 1851 in no. 10, Scales Buildings, Aberdare, a workman's cottage, lived John Morris, his wife, Elizabeth, and baby son John. There were also three lodgers – not by any means a large number.

The biggest landlords in rural or urban Wales were the successive Marquesses of Bute. Residential areas developed in all directions in nineteenth-century Cardiff and Bute officials built most of Treorchy and part of Aberdare. In Cardiff, even by the end of the century, fewer than 10 per cent of the houses were owner-occupied. In the valleys owner-occupation increased rapidly in the second half of the century financed by the eighty-six building societies which existed in Glamorgan by 1891. The Bute estate remained ground landlords and the iniquities of the leasehold system were ever more apparent. It produced bitterness in North Wales, too, where there was a high proportion of home-ownership among quarry workers. Not until 1967 did leasehold reform alleviate the worst of the injustices associated with ground landlordism of domestic building.

Some social consequences of industrialisation

Skilled workers in the iron industry were well paid in good times, with a wage of about 40s per week in the 1850s, while miners and colliers earned about 12s–17s per week. Wages fluctuated dramatically. In Merthyr, for example, there were wage cuts of 30 per cent to 60 per cent in 1833, 1842 and 1847–8. Even so, industrial workers were generally far better off than their rural counterparts. Problems arose not primarily from material deprivation but from communities of unprecedented size having no social organisation.

One of the most appalling problems was the low expectation of life, due mainly to infant mortality, accident and disease. In Aberdare, in 1854, it was reported that 46 per cent of deaths were of children under five, 60 per cent of people under twenty. Those who survived beyond five years of age could expect to live to about thirty-five. Those who survived to twenty could expect to live at least as long as their rural counterparts, except when epidemics occurred. The main killers were smallpox, scarlet fever, typhoid, tuberculosis and cholera, and, although such diseases were not respecters of persons, shopkeepers, on average, lived to twice the age of labourers. Accidents were an ever-present danger. In August, 1849, fifty-two men were killed in an Aberdare colliery. In the same year a gas explosion killed sixty-five in Middle Dyffryn colliery. In the slate quarries of North Wales the conditions under which men lived – especially in their barracks – and worked, for perhaps fifty hours a week in wet conditions at extremely heavy work, produced chest and stomach diseases. The worst killer was respiratory disease brought on by constant inhaling of slate dust. A poor diet, largely bread and butter and tea, accentuated the problem.

The lot of men and women workers in industrial and rural areas was grim. Both groups worked inordinately long hours. Shop assistants in Merthyr were working eighty hours a week into the twentieth century, coal-miners in mid nineteenth century worked shifts of twelve to thirteen hours a day. Some of the worst abuses of child labour occurred in the coal industry. Children's labour was cheap but brought in an important extra wage. It was common in the 1840s for children of four years of age to be at work. Children below the age of eleven in the collieries opened and closed ventilation doors in conditions of complete darkness. Deformities resulted and their growth was retarded. Over the age of eleven boys usually hauled trams, which were too heavy for them and many were crushed to death as they lost control. Eventually, unwillingly, the government was drawn in to legislate against the worst abuses – in 1842 women, and children under ten, were forbidden to work underground. The most dramatic killer was cholera, resulting from inadequate drainage and sanitation, though for much of the century it was the smell which was thought to spread the disease. There was no sewerage system – so water from wells and pumps became contaminated – and often no drainage. In Hirwaun the same family which had built Castell Coch had put in two drains, but they worked badly. The Marquess of Bute was just as negligent of drainage in Cardiff. A statutory body of Street Commissioners had been in existence in Cardiff since 1774, but the commissioners were often Bute placemen and, in any case, extremely reluctant to spend money.

In 1848, threatened with another wave of cholera, the government reluctantly passed a Public Health Act. The Act established a board of health, consisting of a chairman and two commissioners, to advise and encourage urban authorities to establish local boards. These would appoint an officer of health and be responsible for building and maintaining drains and sewers, street cleaning and water supply, and for administering graveyards in order to prevent overcrowding. A basic weakness of the Act was that local boards could only be established where one in ten ratepayers petitioned – and they were extremely reluctant to spend their own money – or if the death rate over each of the previous seven years had averaged over 23 per 1,000 of the population.

Welsh ratepayers resisted as vigorously as any. In Cardiff, where drainage and sewage disposal arrangements, and water pollution, were appalling the Bute agent tried to stop the application of the Act, although eventually twenty-five authorities in Wales petitioned to adopt it. Related legislation was passed at frequent intervals from the 1850s but it was largely permissive until the Sanitary Act of 1866 and the Public Health Act of 1875. Even with this legislation annual mortality rates per thousand population scarcely fell throughout Victoria's reign and infant mortality rates remained appallingly high.

In rural Wales the level of disease was just as bad. Poverty was endemic, real privation only a bad harvest away. Disease associated with dietary deficiency was rife and tuberculosis and typhus endemic. This correlation between poor housing, economic disadvantage and disease continued into the twentieth century. In the 1930s the rural counties had an appalling level of tuberculosis, and local councils were reluctant to take the expensive welfare measures which would alleviate it. There was greater local government commitment in the industrial counties but the Depression conspired against any major improvement. Where the incidence of tuberculosis had previously been falling it remained static in the 1920s and 1930s.

Medical help was inadequate. During the eighteenth century doctors were becoming established in Wales and by 1817 a hospital had been built in Swansea, and a dispensary in Cardiff in 1823. Such institutions were built and maintained by subscription and were available to subscribers and those recommended by them. This system of private philanthropy in health care was completely inadequate – by 1891 there was only one hospital bed for each 2,533 of population in the Cardiff area.

Industrial frontier communities gave rise to problems of social control. Crime greatly exercised the Victorians and it was more readily obvious in fast-growing, volatile communities. It stemmed, in town and country, from both poverty and relative prosperity. As we have seen, poverty in both rural and industrial Wales could be acute. Wages fluctuated in industry and if a large works closed the outlook was bleak. When Penydarren iron-works closed in the 1850s children starved. At one point there were 7,000 people on poor relief in the Merthyr area. The Poor Law Amendment Act of 1834 was intended to change a system of poor relief, dating in essence from Elizabethan times. The workhouses built under the new Act became an enduring symbol of degradation and misery. The middle class were obsessed with social stability but it certainly was not guaranteed by the periodic prosperity of the iron towns of the first half of the nineteenth century. Merthyr Tydfil provides the most graphic illustration here because it grew so rapidly and rootlessly. The town had sucked people in, mainly from Wales but with sizeable minorities from England and Ireland, and all tended to congregate in their own enclaves. Social gradations resulted in iron-miners and colliers living in one district, tradesmen and professional people in another. The grip of the ironmasters on the community – as employers and ratepayers – was overwhelming. The Guests, for example, owned a third of the houses in Dowlais. The ironmasters were reluctant to part with their money to provide civic amenities, though the Guests' record in education is good. Organised religion – overwhelmingly nonconformist – provided an element of social control but half the population, particularly the unskilled workers, were not involved in it. They were more likely to be drawn to the 300 beer houses in Merthyr.

Crime and violence were inevitable in such communities. On fair days there were mobs, brawling, gambling. Children – at least 150 homeless, many more occasionally living rough – wandered around in gangs, prepared to steal clothes and money. Women, responsible for nearly half the recorded crime, stole clothes, food and coal. A frightened middle class across Britain pinned their hopes on the new police force. In 1841 Merthyr had nine policemen, Dowlais two; by 1864 there were sixteen in Merthyr, four in Dowlais and five in Aberdare. By that time the worst of the area's crime had been conquered. Most regular offences were stealing, gambling, drunkenness and highway robbery. Stealing from the iron-works was a major problem – wood, tools, iron and coal. Violence was never far beneath the surface. In the Monmouthshire coalfield, particularly, there was a tradition of dealing violently with blacklegs. There were tensions between English, Irish and Welsh.

Drink provided a welcome escape from the miseries of industrial society and alcoholic drink, unlike the water supply, was relatively germ-free. Pay days and weekends were notorious for offences arising from drunkenness. Gambling, cock-fighting, pitch-and-toss and thimble-rigging led to accusations of cheating, to violence and, sometimes, to manslaughter. Violence against the police and between gangs occurred regularly. Crimes of violence were associated with prostitution, practised by at least sixty Merthyr women in 1839. Some of them ended up in a House for Distressed Women in Llandaff in the 1860s.

The efforts of respectable society, symbolised by the establishment of refuges of various kinds, were all brought to bear on new industrial communities. By the middle of the nineteenth century, Victorians, spurred on by a mixture of fear, social conscience and religious teaching, were beginning to come to grips with the problem. National government involvement combined with local effort to produce an effective police-force and stern magistracy. Violent crime lessened. Drunkenness was met head-on by the temperance movement, with the Band of Hope bringing the message to the young. The respectable working class were provided with alternatives – brass bands, choirs, discussion groups, lectures. By the 1860s, Merthyr's 'China', once virtually outside the law, had been brought under social control. Such success should not be exaggerated. Later in the century, Cardiff's dockland, with its mobile population, had the reputation of being the most undesirable port in Britain, with Bute Street a byword for fleecing sailors made vulnerable because so many deserted ship in Cardiff with their agreements unexpired.

As in all aspects of social life in the late eighteenth and early nineteenth centuries the various social strata were sharply differentiated in their leisure activities. Favourite sports of the gentry were horse-racing, hunting to foxhounds, and shooting. In the second half of the nineteenth century shooting of artificially bred pheasants was the most popular of sports, and guns became safer, although there were still some nasty accidents. Game-shooting was particularly galling for tenant farmers since their crops were vulnerable to protected game.

Grand balls at large houses or at assembly rooms were one hallmark of fashionable society in the Georgian period – for the privileged. Such assembly rooms existed in Abergavenny, Monmouth, Neath, Swansea and Denbigh, among other places. One common recreational feature for all classes was gambling – gentry might lose fortunes on cards. For the masses, cock-fighting, foot-racing (epitomised in the legend of Guto Nyth Bran) and fist-fighting were popular, and gambling accompanied all these.

During the nineteenth century a Welsh popular culture divorced almost wholly from that of the anglicised, Anglican gentry developed, prompted partly by a growing middle class and endorsed by nonconformist working-class society. Industrialisation was the basic force at work here. Its chief paradox was that, as in de Tocqueville's Manchester, 'humanity attains its most complete development and its most brutish' as a consequence of industrial growth. It produced social problems on an unprecedented scale yet created wealth in Wales which was evident in thriving markets, consumer goods, grand chapels. It financed periodicals and newspapers. Sunday school and monitorial school increased literacy steadily.

The language of the press was Welsh, and its ramifications embraced large sections of the population. In the 1860s there were eight weeklies, twenty-five monthlies and five quarterlies in Welsh. Denominational and political journals predominated. The chapel infused popular culture with its ethos through prayer meetings, study meetings, literary societies and the Band of Hope. Throughout the nineteenth century, especially in rural Wales, the chapel's hold was strong, though by the 1890s ministers were becoming anxious about the spread of popular sport, and throughout the century there had been the threat of the demon drink, anathema to the nonconformist conscience. Alcoholic drink had always been consumed by all classes but in the nineteenth century the expansion of urban areas made it increasingly prevalent. It was safe, when heavy industrial work required a large intake of liquid and the public houses were more congenial than cramped, overcrowded houses. In transient, young, frontier communities drink oiled a boisterous lifestyle. To respectable society, ale-houses had always been associated with crime and anti-social behaviour. In Tudor times this correlation had been made by Dr David Lewis, but drink problems in an industrial environment were more threatening. Excessive drinking produced absenteeism – an average of a day a week – much to the chagrin of industrialists obsessed with maximising profits. Greater discipline was more vital for safety reasons. It was apparent in iron and coal mines, but self-evidently essential on the railway network. The new discipline required by the railways was symbolised by the adoption of a military-style uniform. Cyclical unemployment provided opportunities for consumption of alcohol. Employers who, through the poor rate, had to provide a subsistence level of income, resented this kind of expenditure.

The different economic order of industrialised society produced a culture change enforced by social sanctions. One of the most obvious of these was the anti-drink movement. While Rhymney ironworks built its own brewery, most employers opposed such concessions. They tried various sanctions. Long pay, at intervals of up to twelve weeks, was one. It meant that employees were in pledge to truck shops – but goods could be exchanged at beer shops. The Dowlais works tried to employ teetotallers. But the most effective sanctions were through financial or religious obligation. Employers gave advances to favoured employees who thus mortgaged their behaviour. After about 1870 a highly effective alliance was forged between industrialists – David Davies, for example – nonconformity and the respectable working class, manifested in temperance and Band of Hope movements. From the 1830s the temperance movement, imported from America, favoured total abstinence. The first society was established in Holywell in 1832 and became a sophisticated organisation with its own halls and hotels. By 1881 Wales had acquired separate Sunday closing legislation, for which there was solid support. Only a century later, in the 1982 referendum, was it evident that this issue no longer had any hold over public opinion.

Industrialisation affected rural Wales, if less directly. For example, as rural isolation broke down, centuries-old customs were modified, indeed eventually a whole lifestyle was eroded. Mass production undermined traditional crafts. Nonconformity deprecated the song and dance which had withstood Puritanism, and a more intellectual culture regarded as more respectable, developed. Christenings became, eventually, little more than chapel services; funerals became prayer-meetings rather than wakes. On the other hand there were many rural traditions very slow to die out. Until the end of the nineteenth century Christmas meant attendance at the early-morning candlelit service, the *plygain*. Christmas feasting only became a more private family affair well into Victoria's reign. New Year celebrations were more important than those associated with Christmas. Children went from house to house on New Year's morning with greetings and song, receiving *calennig* (New Year's gifts) in return, a custom which still prevails in parts of Wales. Twelfth Night was celebrated with the pre-Christian Mari Lwyd and wassail songs. Easter Monday was celebrated in parts of Wales with cock-fighting, hand-ball and stool-ball. At Mayday hiring fairs there was dancing, wrestling, singing and maypole dancing, activities frowned on by increasingly influential nonconformist opinion.

The notion of 'Welshness'

The nineteenth century saw an increasing consciousness of Welshness which co-existed, with few strains until the end of the century, with loyalty to monarch, British state and Empire. Welsh literary activity and this sense of Welshness were closely linked. It has been customary to see in the sixteenth century the beginnings of the breakdown of a bardic tradition supported by the gentry, and a historical and mythological tradition endowing Wales with ancient origins and language. The seventeenth century has been almost forgotten, sandwiched between the old society and the coming of Methodism which once more gave Wales an identity. This analysis ignores the continuity of the bardic tradition and the vital contribution of a growing, literate middle class, particularly Dissenters.

As we have seen, there was a cultural renaissance in the eighteenth century, affecting historical interpretations, poetry, music and study of the Welsh language. Towards the end of the century many books about Wales were published, including Thomas Pennant's travel books and historical works satisfying the taste of the romantic movement for forgotten legends. Then, in the nineteenth century, industrialisation helped transform the cultural scene once more, although the cultural revival associated with the eighteenth century continued its impact. Cultural imports from England – music societies (one in Wrexham in 1785) or the assembly rooms of polite society had made their way to Wales by the end of the eighteenth century. The London Welsh societies continued, though societies in Wales were now collecting historical documents and artefacts. In 1837 the Welsh Manuscript Society was founded and in 1846 the Cambrian Archaeological Society. Just as pervasive as the realities of the Welsh past were the romantic invention of Welsh costume by Lady Llanover and the attachment of the Gorsedd of Bards – an invention of the Welsh forger of genius, Iolo Morganwg – to the Eisteddfod in 1819. The Eisteddfod had been revived on a national scale in 1785, the first large gathering of poets since the 1567 Caerwys Eisteddfod. These national Eisteddfodau later attracted large crowds and expanded their competitions. The romantic view of Wales found expression in the paintings of Richard Wilson which sold well after his death in 1782. This wild, romantic notion of Wales, echoing contemporary interest in Scotland and Switzerland, spawned potent myths about the Welsh past. Iolo Morganwg's stress on the great antiquity of Wales and the Welsh language, and the remarkable contribution of men of Glamorgan, his home county, was difficult to refute because there was no institution of academic or historical critical scholarship to question his theories. Iolo's inventions, whether of the 'medieval' poetry of Dafydd ap Gwilym or druidical ceremonies in stone circles, were quite remarkable in the colourful innovation of their imaginative quality and had a lasting and highly significant influence in their contribution to a new conception of Welshness dependent on the literature and language of Wales.

Welsh heroes were re-cast in the nineteenth century to meet revised requirements. Owain Glyndŵr became the national hero who had tried to found those national institutions so dear to middle-class Welshmen – independent state, university and national church. The claims of Welsh music to great antiquity were pressed, with Welsh music supposedly emanating from druidical days. An old bardic musical tradition did go back to earlier centuries but its instruments of harp, *crwth* and *pibgorn* had died out in the seventeenth century. The triple harp, now boldly asserted to be the Welsh harp, was an Italian baroque harp which probably came to Wales in the second half of the century. The eighteenth century saw Welsh airs, so-called, published in profusion and *penillion* singing became central to Welsh musical tradition.

The industrial process gradually modified this romanticism.

Culture, for many, seemed of far less importance than politics as the Rebecca riots, and Chartism became central issues in the 1830s and 1840s. Pamphlets and newspapers were full of political and religious debate. This became even more pronounced after the 1847 report on education, 'Brad y Llyfrau Gleision' (The Treachery of 'the Blue Books'), produced a fusion of interest between Methodism and old dissent, and identified both with Welshness. This link of Welshness with nonconformity was the most powerful one in the nineteenth-century political and cultural tradition as sermons, journals, hymns and denominational histories provided Wales with a culture. Industrialisation had produced a new politics, linked with protest in rural Wales also, and the fusion of nonconformity with political involvement from the 1860s eclipsed other concerns. In industrial Wales harp and national costume seemed more and more peripheral. An increasingly influential middle class was concerned with its own, and Welsh, advancement but in English terms of career and institutions. Paradoxically, part of this process was the emergence of a new myth in the Welsh historical tradition, that of the long-pedigreed, classless *gwerin*, whose virtues distinguished Welsh society. This myth could emerge from the fusion of democracy, radicalism, nonconformity and literacy in the later nineteenth century. It has proved one of the most pervasive myths, especially among nationalist writers, because it rested on some firm educational and cultural foundations. The prominence of politicians like Tom Ellis and Lloyd George from humble backgrounds lent it additional credibility. It was a notion, too, which was essential ammunition in political battles against anglicised, exploiting, alien landlords.

Language

The most obviously distinctive element identifying the people of Wales was, paradoxically, in decline, at least in percentage terms. In 1891 54.4 per cent could speak Welsh, but the proportion was gradually decreasing. In some ways it is remarkable that the figure was as great considering the pressures against the language. It was certainly not encouraged by the gentry, and educational and political leaders were not averse to its decline, if not disappearance. English was identified with economic and material success. Yet still, because of the growth in population there were more Welsh speakers at the end of the nineteenth century than at the beginning. This was partly because population had risen most in the first part of the century when population movements had been largely within Wales. When English workers came into the industrial areas, north and south, in substantial numbers, bilingualism developed rapidly and the position of Welsh was undermined. Welsh was also the cultural language of the great majority in nineteenth-century Wales through books, periodicals, newspapers. Eisteddfod and, above all, religion. Nonconformist ministers, peripatetic for much of the century, were Welsh-speaking. But ministers themselves came to see fluency in English as the hallmark of respectability and were prepared to see Welsh as inferior. This attitude was echoed in education, in training college, university, and secondary school. The nonconformist attitude to the language was ambivalent because many saw the use of Welsh as insurance against the atheistic and secularist ideas propagated in the English language. What was propounded in Welsh was protest, but it was limited, the muted protest of nonconformist radicalism, certainly not class protest or revolutionary doctrine. In the nineteenth century the language of religion gave those who used it an identity and a culture. However, with the decline of organised religion in the twentieth century, Welsh as a language was vulnerable because it had never aspired to be the language of that social protest befitting the depression years. But before this the fate of Welsh was indicated by the diminution in numbers of monoglot Welsh-speakers – only 15 per cent in 1901. By 1961, 26 per cent of the population spoke Welsh and this had declined to just below 20 per cent in 1981. Bilingual education has been pressed as a palliative, but some have argued that bilingualism dooms the language to extinction. The dilution of Welsh with English words, whole phrases even, has been another insidious problem. It is scarcely surprising that, in face of such enormous challenges, compounded by English-language media saturation in the second half of the twentieth century, some of those who believe that Welsh is the hallmark of Welshness have employed illegal methods in their attempts to protect the language.

Literature and music

Literary achievement in eighteenth- and nineteenth-century Wales remained original and vital. In the second half of the eighteenth century William, Richard and Lewis Morris were involved in a cultural revival which encompassed music and poetry. There was a literary tradition associated with hymn-writing, particularly with William Williams, Pantycelyn. This continued in the following century, augmented by an expanding Welsh language press. There were poets of genius, such as Islwyn, and a great novelist, Daniel Owen. After 1880 there was widespread publicity for the Eisteddfodic crown and chair. In the second half of the century educational developments combined with immigration to produce an Anglo-Welsh literature.

In music there was an intermingling of Welsh and English fashions from the eighteenth century. In the seventeenth and eighteenth centuries traditional Welsh instruments were modified or replaced. As the gentry's role in patronising bards decreased a popular musical culture developed in Wales before the Methodist revival, with semi-professional ballad singers singing their highly dramatic themes at Fairs. Dissent and puritanism within the Established Church were opposed to such 'fripperies' as music and dancing and were highly effective in stamping it out, as Thomas Charles boasted.

Methodism replaced one popular musical tradition with another – hymn-singing – as, increasingly, Welsh folk-tunes were adapted to Welsh hymns and replaced English tunes. The eighteenth-century hymns were sung in unison and this remained normal until the second half of the nineteenth century. Singing in harmony stemmed from a desire to see all members of congregations participate in singing and, from the 1850s, books of hymns and choruses became available which inaugurated an era of ubiquitous choral and con-gregational singing. The other central plank in the choral tradition was the adoption, after 1861, of Curwen's tonic sol-fa notation. The *ysgol gân*, a choir practice for the *cymanfa ganu*, or singing festival, was institutionalised in Welsh life. Choirs adopted oratorio choruses from Handel, Haydn and Mendelssohn, and the former two provided popular Christian names. Brahms and Verdi requiems were popular later and from the 1860s there were Welsh choral works by Joseph Parry, David Evans and David Jenkins. Despite the numbers of choirs their repertoire was not extensive and the overall standard not high. but choral singing was a vital part of popular culture and one of the central features of chapel social life in the nineteenth century, continuing into the twentieth, when standards did improve steadily.

It is indicative of a growing concern with quality that there were criticisms of literary and musical standards in the national Eisteddfod at the end of the nineteenth century, coupled with anxieties that the invention of the *gorsedd* of bards by Iolo Morganwg, which the Eisteddfod had adopted, demeaned proceedings. Paradoxically, these criticisms heralded the emergence of remarkably distinguished literary figures. In the Bangor Eisteddfod of 1902 the chair was won by a journalist, T. Gwynn Jones. Two years before, W. J. Gruffydd, a student at Jesus College, Oxford, collaborated with R. Silyn Roberts to write a book of poetry. Gruffydd published another important volume of lyric poetry in 1906 and established an ever-growing reputation as literary historian and creative writer. Gruffydd, J. E. Lloyd and O. M. Edwards all projected a sense of the importance of the *gwerin* of Wales, the quarryman, the tenant farmer. Sir John Edward Lloyd's major achievement was a *History of Wales from the Earliest Times to the Norman Conquest*, a work of historical scholarship which, at the same time, provided a historical base for at least limited self-determination for Wales. Sir Owen M. Edwards's educational philosophy and vision are discussed in a later chapter but a belief in the virtues of the *gwerin*, the ordinary people of Wales, particularly in a rural context, informed his work as educationalist, historian and provider of children's literature. His most influential work was the provision of magazines – *Cymru*, for the general public and *Cymru'r Plant*, outstandingly influential, for children.

Edwards, strongly influenced by John Ruskin, had a romanticised, yet compelling, vision of the virtues of a rural peasantry and the rewards of craft labour. It was coupled with an anti-industrial stance, a theme which was strong in many Welsh writers and which, through the influence of Saunders Lewis in the inter-war period and after, was to enter the mainstream of Welsh political activity. The heart of the Welsh way of life for the majority of the strongest supporters of *Plaid Cymru*, which came into existence in the 1920s, was Welsh-speaking, rural Wales, the small farm and the craft skills – the antithesis of industrialisation.

In the second decade of the twentieth century new poets of distinction appeared, notably R. Williams Parry and T. H. Parry-Williams. In the latter's work, again, the strong current theme of the virtues of rural communities were emphasised. There was no war poetry but the inter-war period yielded a rich literary harvest with a plethora of poetry, short stories, essays and plays from T. Gwynn

Jones, W. J. Gruffydd, T. H. Parry-Williams, D. Gwenallt Jones, Saunders Lewis, Kate Roberts and Ambrose Bebb. Historians – William Rees in Cardiff, R. T. Jenkins in Bangor – kept up the high standard of historical scholarship set by J. E. Lloyd. Literary and linguistic scholarship in the university was safeguarded by G. J. Williams, Henry Lewis and Ifor Williams.

Sport

This manifold literary activity inevitably appealed to a minority, particularly the Welsh-speaking middle class, products of the county schools and the University of Wales. Echoing changes in society, especially industrialisation, far more closely, and reaching out to a wider audience while still manifesting Welshness, was the growth in organised spectator sport. There could be no room in populous, confined, industrial communities for the kinds of sport without rules which involved virtually all younger male inhabitants of villages – the football or 'knappan' of pre-industrialised society, for example. Sport now had to be organised and institutionalised, and this was made possible by the existence of a large potential audience with some leisure time, and able to travel. The Football Association was founded in 1863, the Rugby Football Union in 1871. In 1881 the Welsh Rugby Union was born in the Castle Hotel, Neath. In 1893 Wales won her first Triple Crown.

Some sports – fox-hunting, for example – retained a minority, middle-class image; others, boxing and association football, remained working class. Soccer, unlike rugby, was played in North and South Wales, having come in from Lancashire and Yorkshire and spread slowly south. Gradually, cricket developed a classless appeal, although internally it remained rigidly hierarchical at least until after the Second World War. Rugby football provides the most interesting social phenomenon. It was a public-school game brought to Wales through Lampeter College yet it became the working-class game of South Wales. It was remarkable for its triumph over two establishments. Nonconformist leaders held rugby to be degrading and at the time of the 1904–5 revival many rugby clubs closed in response to religious pressures. Paradoxically, it was the remarkable Welsh win over the then invincible 1905 New Zealand All Blacks which established the game as a national sport in Wales. A far more remarkable achievement was the grudging acceptance of Welsh rugby, played by steel-workers and colliers as well as the products of public schools, by the upper-middle-class controllers of the game in England, Scotland and Ireland. Cricket could segregate its amateurs and professionals. Rugby's amateurism confined it to the middle classes elsewhere in Britain and the other unions were particularly sensitive at times of Welsh success, partly owed, they argued, to the greater fitness of manual workers. One result was that the Welsh Rugby Union was sensitive to accusations of professionalism. But the economic climate of the inter-war period came to the aid of the other unions. Dozens of first-rate Welsh players went north to the Rugby League clubs to earn a living. Heroes had already been manufactured, however, in the golden age between 1900 and 1912 when Wales won the triple crown six times. They were fitting heroes, like Will Joseph, steel-worker and Swansea and Wales forward, admired for his quiet modesty and dignity in chapel and community of Morriston. In boxing Wales had its successes, too. In 1914 Freddie Welsh became lightweight champion of the world and later Jimmy Wilde flyweight champion of the world.

National sentiment was endemic in all Wales's sporting achievements but this was, and was felt to be, the ephemera of nationalism. At grass roots, anglicisation was taking place at an unparalleled rate as decennial censuses indicated. Numbers of Welsh speakers were now decreasing absolutely, education provided far more, and often the only, opportunities for social mobility and the export of Welsh talent to England. From the 1920s broadcasting expanded rapidly and patterns were set from London and in English, although a Welsh broadcasting service was eventually introduced after 1937. In hindsight the mass penetration of radio and, later, television, providing instant entertainment, news and reporting, predominantly in English, and generally reflecting the cosmopolitan values of London, was the most profound threat to Welshness, of language or lifestyle.

Post-war society

After the Second World War came another transformation. While much of Wales escaped bombing, Swansea, at least, had to be largely rebuilt. A rising population, increasing affluence and changing industrial patterns saw the expansion of urban areas and much new house-building. There was suburban spread and new towns, like Cwmbran but, still, housing stock in Wales remained older on average than in Britain generally. Wales had, not surprisingly, been less well served by the house-building boom of the 1930s. In 1966 nearly a quarter of Welsh houses had no fixed bath and 4 per cent had no wc. Relocation resulting from slum clearance also produced its community problems as rootless, vast, new estates replaced old-established communities. Even so, housing booms, private and council, in the 1950s and the 1960s saw great advances and helped to improve general health. The scale of home ownership increased as building society funds benefited from prosperity. One long-standing injustice became yet more apparent. Large areas of South Wales, Aberystwyth and Caernarfon were badly affected by the leasehold system, carried on into post-war housing developments, but partially alleviated by the Leasehold Enfranchisement Act of 1967.

Post-war Wales was an affluent society compared with the Depression years, although some communities remained worryingly dependent on a single employer – for example, Hoover in Merthyr – and the economy overall too dependent on the steel industry. One feature of increased affluence was the proliferation of service industries, including banking, insurance and finance houses. These were supplemented by large government establishments, such as Companies House, which were centred mainly along the urban areas of the South Wales coast. In turn, commuter belts and urban sprawl followed and the centre of gravity in Wales concentrated yet more firmly in the Cardiff region, consolidated by the creation of the Welsh Office in 1964.

Another consequence of growth in government and service sectors of the economy was the steadily growing middle class, increasingly produced by the expanding higher education facilities of university and polytechnic, as well as the colleges of education producing teachers. While there were increasing employment opportunities in Wales the colleges of education, in particular, produced teachers to meet shortages in England.

Proximity to England has always been the greatest threat to Welshness, and that proximity was reinforced after 1945. Economic change – the involvement of multinational companies, for example – has been mainly responsible, and the Welsh language has never been an economic necessity. By 1966 one in five of the people living in Wales were not of Welsh origin, drawn in to the urban areas to work or the rural areas to retire. The expansion of higher education in the 1960s changed the nature of the University of Wales. In 1938 95 per cent of its students came from Wales; in 1968 the figure was 39 per cent. Economic and educational anglicisation were accepted with far more equanimity than the anglicisation of the heartland of Wales through second-home ownership, which became an important political issue in the 1960s and 1970s. A sporadic campaign of arson was one reaction to this threat to the last stronghold of a language and lifestyle.

Over the nation as a whole the influence of television was more of an anglicising, even americanising, agent. From 1953 B.B.C. and later T.W.W. and H.T.V., programmes steadily penetrated the remotest parts, and television quickly became the preponderant leisure time activity. The influence of the medium has been incalculable, and attempts to mobilise it in the service of the Welsh language have met with variable success. Attempts in the 1970s to dub films such as *Shane* with Welsh words entered the folklore of disaster. Attempts at other staples of the T.V. diet were more successful. *Pobol y Cwm* was at least as good as *Coronation Street*. The 1970s produced one Welsh-speaking comedian and light actor of genius, Ryan Davies, for some years an exiled teacher, who died tragically young. With television so much a part of everyday life much emotional energy was invested in the campaign for a television channel for Wales in the Welsh language, and, after a threat by Gwynfor Evans to fast to death if the government did not adhere to its election pledge, the campaign was successful. It opened in 1982 and initially attracted higher audiences than expected.

The popular press catered increasingly for an English-language readership. In the late 1960s only 25 per cent of the Welsh-speaking population read a Welsh language newspaper or periodical regularly, and only *Y Cymro* and *Y Faner* were distributed nationally. Young people were catered for reasonably by *Urdd* publications but London daily papers circulated most widely, with the *Western Mail*, specifically Wales-orientated, selling about 100,000 copies. There was hardly a commercial market for books in Welsh nor, often, for books in English on Welsh subjects. Many books of both kinds are published, however. The University of Wales Press publishes academic works with the aid of a government grant, and the Welsh Arts Council provides aid for Welsh publishers. With the expansion of the university in the 1960s more work was done on the history of Wales and, in 1960, the important *Welsh History Review* started publication. Sadly, the considerable research and publication in Welsh history emanating from the university was not reflected in a similar scale of interest in Welsh schools although prospects improved markedly with the creation of the Association of Teachers of History in Wales in 1983.

In the literary world there was an abiding concern with Welshness and sometimes a bitter divide between those who wrote in Welsh and writers in English. There were notable writers of prose and poetry in both languages. T. Rowland Hughes remained a brilliant novelist of Caernarfonshire and its quarrying communities until his death in 1949. Kate Roberts and later, Islwyn Ffowc Ellis were both distinguished novelists. D. J. Williams, who, before the war, had been involved in the R.A.F. bombing-school fire in the Llŷn peninsula, wrote short stories deploring the effect on traditional Wales of government policies. Saunders Lewis, playwright of genius, was now an elder statesman and inspired the Welsh Language Society. From the end of the 1950s new literary figures emerged at regular intervals – T. Glynne Davies, R. Gerallt Jones, Waldo Williams, Euros Bowen, Bobi Jones and, later, Derec Llwyd Morgan and Alan Llwyd. In 1965, twenty-four new novels in the Welsh language were published, in addition to fifteen books of short stories and forty-seven new children's books.

There had always been Welshmen who wrote in English – William Williams, Pantycelyn, for example, had written his inspiring hymns and poems in both English and Welsh. In the twentieth century Anglo-Welsh literature became a genre, reflecting inexorable anglicisation. In the first half of the century Caradog Evans created a sensation by puncturing Welsh respectability with novels and short stories involving squalid, lecherous peasants in rural Cardiganshire who, he insisted, were based on real people. Just before the Second World War new talent reflected the formative influence of English language and literature through the county schools as Dylan Thomas and Vernon Watkins started writing. It was Idris Davies who, perhaps, most succinctly summed up the Wales of the General Strike and afterwards:

Before I go back to the earth
May my eyes see the end of this wrong.

Many writers dealt with the theme of the Depression – Davies himself, Gwyn Thomas, Jack Jones, Gwyn Jones, Lewis Jones. Anglo-Welsh writing after the war was not characterised by a specific theme but the flow greatly increased, and from the pens of R. S. Thomas, Gwyn Thomas, Gwyn Jones and Dannie Abse, for example, it reached the highest standards. Poetry publication was facilitated by the *Anglo-Welsh Review* from 1958, and *Poetry Wales*, while the Welsh Arts Council provided financial help. The life and poetry of Dylan Thomas continued to influence public opinion about Welsh-born poets and their poetry. He eventually became the favourite poet of an American president and acquired a place in Poets' Corner in Westminster Abbey.

From the 1950s there was an obvious tension between writers in Welsh and English, despite a strong nationalist streak in the work of some Anglo-Welsh writers. It remains that writers in the two languages had been influenced by different traditions. Indeed, before the war Saunders Lewis argued that there was no such thing as Anglo-Welsh literature and this theme was echoed after the war by Bobi Jones and Pennar Davies, for example.

Other art forms produced little which was specifically Welsh, though there were Welsh-born composers of the highest reputation for the first time – Grace Williams and, later, Alun Hoddinott and William Mathias. The last, Welsh-speaking, held that his music was suffused with Welshness but it was also in a European tradition. The University of Wales provided a base for Hoddinott and Mathias and, increasingly, sponsored performances of instrumental music. Youth orchestras in Wales benefited from an enlightened local authority policy towards school music in some areas. The Welsh National Opera Company was able to acquire an international reputation as a result of very generous grants from the Welsh Arts Council. There has been very little opera by Welsh composers for the company to perform.

Perhaps the most remarkable feature of Welsh culture since 1945 has been that unity of national sentiment, across language and class, has been found only in sport, with rugby, particularly, having been invested with a popular significance out of proportion to its centrality to Welsh life. Soccer, a more working-class sport, produced only four major clubs, Cardiff, Newport, Wrexham and Swansea. None was able to achieve either the support or the success of major English clubs, at least until the late 1970s when Swansea City football club shot from fourth division to first in four seasons, though decline soon set in. The Welsh soccer team had moments of glory but never a consistent record of success. The one Welsh first-class cricket club, Glamorgan, attracted good crowds for a time after the war – standing room only at the Australian match in 1948 – and won the county championship twice, in 1948 and 1969.

Unlike soccer and cricket teams, rugby football teams rarely fielded individuals from outside Wales and it was mainly the string of South Wales first-class clubs which provided the bulk of the national team. However, in golden years in the 1970s, J. P. R. Williams, Mervyn Davies and John Taylor played for London Welsh for part of their careers. It was in the 1970s that the hold of rugby on the national consciousness was consolidated by television coverage and national success. Wales won the triple crown in 1971 and, later in the 1970s, another four successive times. Perhaps strident national support reflected a Wales which, by the 1960s and 1970s, could afford to be far more assertive, since, through its secondary schools, it had a more effective avenue to the meritocracy than was the case in England. Symbolically, Cardiff College of Education, in the 1960s and the 1970s became the biggest single nursery for Welsh rugby internationals. Rugby spawned a subculture of its own – the cartoons of Gren, the songs of Max Boyce. Gareth Edwards and Barry John became idols of a nation. Whether such emotional investment in the defeat of England was healthy is questionable. Perhaps it reflected merely the soft centre of Welsh nationalism. It could not obscure the increasing commercialisation of the game by advertising and the purchase of blocks of debentures by large business organisations.

The devolution referendum of 1979 indicated that, for the large majority of the Welsh nation, Welshness did not consist in even limited political independence. It had not, in fact, lain in the independence of a nation state for nearly 700 years yet it remained identifiable in language, culture – Welsh and Anglo-Welsh – and attitude. In large areas of rural Wales Welsh remained the first language. The chapel and the nonconformist ministry continued to occupy a central place in such communities. Nationalism speaks with many voices. Some, foretelling doom for the language, and thus for the nation, if present trends continue, advocate direct action. Many committed Welshmen are deeply troubled by the rancour such notions generate – enmity between Welsh and English speakers, between rural and urban communities. Some analysts argue that the only hope for Wales lies in the overthrow of the economic and political system in Britain generally. None of this debate need obscure the fact that nearly 20 per cent of people in Wales speak Welsh and, according to a recent public opinion poll, 60 per cent identify with Wales first, rather than Britain. A sense of Welshness is a reality for these people. Whatever it consists of, it testifies to the permanence of a national spirit.

9

GOVERNMENT, POLITICS AND PROTEST

SECTION I. 1780–1880

Radical roots

During the eighteenth century the aristocracy and the gentry dominated local and national politics. With the franchise restricted to no more than 4 per cent of the population in any county they were able to control county and borough representation. Parliamentary seats in Wales were controlled either by the English aristocracy or by major Welsh landed families, so their interests were reflected in Parliament. In the end it was an economic revolution which brought about change in the Parliamentary system in Britain but as this industrial revolution was getting under way a political revolution across the English Channel brought Wales into contact with the Atlantic democratic revolution. There was support in Britain for the French Revolution through bodies like the corresponding societies and ideas emanating from France on the rights of liberty of individual citizens and the sovereignty of the people had implications for a society of entrenched privilege like Britain.

There had been some support in Wales for John Wilkes in the 1760s when he was elected on three occasions to Parliament but excluded. This occasioned protests from some London Welshmen too, but their reactions to the American War of Independence were more significant. Dr Richard Price, member of a minor gentry family in Glamorgan and minister of a church at Stoke Newington, ideally demonstrates the links between the old and new radicalism. He was a Unitarian, Grand Master of the Bridgend masonic lodge in 1777 and a supporter of Wilkes. He wrote important pamphlets during the American War of Independence and the French Revolution. *Observations on Civil Liberty* (1776), written in support of the American colonists, had profound implications for Britain. It argued that sovereignty was vested in the people and that king and ministers were responsible to them. Through Sir William Jones, another staunch opponent of the American war, and other pamphleteers, similar ideas spread to Wales.

David Williams, a London Welsh minister, was more radical still. A friend of Benjamin Franklin, he wrote his *Letters on Political Liberty* in support of the Americans and in it argued for principles, such as universal manhood suffrage, taken up by the Chartists. Both Williams and Price responded eagerly, though not uncritically, to the French Revolution. Price's sermon of November, 1789, 'On the Love of Country', endorsed the revolution as the destroyer of despotism and drew forth the classic conservative response from Edmund Burke. Williams was invited by the Girondists to visit Paris to draft a constitution, but when the revolution brought a tyranny of its own Williams turned critic.

Price and Williams were men of international repute and, although London based, they linked Wales with international events. They did so against a background of a Wales in which a variety of social tensions were being generated. In rural Wales there was endemic poverty. In parts of Wales by the end of the eighteenth century modern industrial capitalism had begun – in cloth manufacturing and in iron. The 1790s were bad years in the countryside and industrialisation, with its frontier communities, was bound to produce protest. There was a radical tradition of Dissent in parts of Wales and this had transatlantic links with the Welsh who had been driven to emigrate to America for religious reasons. There was another dimension to this dispersion through the legend of Madoc, the twelfth-century Welsh prince whose claims to have discovered America were stressed, on the flimsiest of evidence, for imperial reasons in Elizabeth's reign and again in the eighteenth century. Reinforced now by stories of Welsh-speaking Mandan Indians and epic explorations of North America. Madoc epitomised the notion of political freedom and gave legitimacy to Welsh settlement there. Correspondence linked Wales with events in America, ideas of civil equality circulated through parts of Wales by means of pamphlets and books, and Dissenters in the iron towns discussed these ideas. The eighteenth-century London–Welsh societies reflected some radical ideas – the Gwyneddigion particularly.

A related theme of pamphlets distributed in Wales was the neglect

of Wales, at a time when interest in its literature and antiquities –
among the London societies as well as among individual scholars –
was concentrating educated minds on its uniqueness. Even the ideas
of John Jones, Glan y Gors, with his attacks on royalty, bishops and
aristocracy, had an impact in Wales and Tom Paine's *The Rights of
Man* was well known. The London Welsh societies discussed and
disseminated radical ideas and conducted political debates as a result
of which they suffered government repression after 1794. In supporting periodicals they started a tradition which was to be important
in political development in the nineteenth century. The Gwyneddigion
supported Morgan John Rhys's *Y Cylchgrawn Cymraeg*, the first
periodical in this radical tradition. Rhys was a Baptist minister who
had written against the slave trade and was a powerful supporter of
the French Revolution. His periodical was so radical that he produced
only five numbers, before he sailed for America in 1794 to set up
his community, Beulah, as a refuge for radicals and Dissenters from
government repression. In 1795 another periodical, Thomas Evans's
Y Drysorfa Gymmysgedig, lasted for only three numbers but the
periodical tradition, in more moderate form, was re-established with
Joseph Harris's *Seren Gomer* in 1814 and David Rees's *Y Diwygiwr*
in 1835.

The link between nonconformity and political thinking is evident
at an early stage. Nonconformists suffered under disabilities even
after the repeal of the Test Acts. In the eighteenth and early
nineteenth centuries radicalism was confined to dissent, with the
Methodists very anxious to divert suspicion away from their denomination and stamp it with respectability. The extreme radicals –
Jac Glan y Gors, and Thomas Evans, Glyn Cothi – had been
neutralised by the Napoleonic wars, either through patriotism or, in
the case of the latter, by imprisonment. After the French wars, more
moderate demands for reform were more influential, since they
coincided with the emergence of wealthy entrepreneurs who were
bidding for political power. In 1814, for example, Benjamin Hall
became M.P. for Glamorgan after compelling the Marquis of Bute's
man to withdraw, and Hall's son captured Monmouth boroughs from
the Marquis of Worcester in 1831.

There was popular ferment, too, culminating in the Merthyr Rising
of 1831. The radical traditions of Merthyr and the more northerly
areas of Glamorgan had a long pedigree. Puritan ideas had taken root

there in Cromwell's day and millenarian ideas had survived. With the Anglican Church relatively ineffective in the sprawling hill parishes, nonconformity was entrenched and radical unitarianism influential. It was in such areas that the old radicalism of Dissent fused with reaction to industrial stresses to produce a potent mix of political protest.

The politics of protest

A measure of electoral reform came in the Reform Act of 1832. Wales got five of the eighty-eight seats available for redistribution, raising its representation from twenty-seven to thirty-two. Glamorgan, Monmouthshire and Denbighshire each gained another member. The Glamorgan boroughs seat was now divided into two and Merthyr obtained a seat. Welsh influence in Parliament was marginally increased, at least potentially, but the effects of the 1832 Act were limited. For example, the Marquesses of Bute, who controlled the Glamorgan boroughs seat in the second half of the eighteenth century, dominated the Cardiff boroughs seat. Given the enormous wealth of their estate, reinforced by industrial income, judicious philanthropy and patronage, this was inevitable under the restricted reforms of the Act.

In a rapidly changing and increasingly industrialised Wales the balance between county and borough representation was not changed. It remained as it had done since the Act of Union. Thirteen counties returned seventeen members, and fifteen boroughs one M.P. each. This was deliberate policy in England and Wales to reinforce the landed interest despite population changes. Wales had the smallest constituency, Merioneth, with 508 electors, but Carmarthenshire, Denbighshire and Glamorgan were above average size for England and Wales, with over 3,000 electors each.

The 1832 Reform Act produced only very limited change in the franchise. The county franchise was retained by the forty-shilling freeholder, though the freehold was not solely a landed one. In addition, the £10 leaseholders, tenants holding a lease for sixty years, got the vote. The borough franchise had always been confused and there were major changes. The main qualification now was to be property, a vote for the £10 householder whose taxes were paid and who had not received any parish relief. There had to be electoral registration in both county and borough. Individual claims were recorded and eventually printed. Here, perhaps, was the most important change since it encouraged the growth of party organisation to ensure that loyalist names were included and others deleted. Eventually, in the 1850s and 1860s, the Liberation Society, which was to play an important part in the political education of Wales, helped to ensure that eligible nonconformists were registered to vote. In the meantime the change in the borough franchise meant that there were fewer working-class voters because of the disappearance of the automatic freeman franchise. Now only property was represented. The stranglehold of the landed classes over representation was as firm as ever. For the overwhelming majority of the population of Wales the only politics possible was the politics of protest.

As we have seen, protest was central to Dissent. In the eighteenth century Dissenters were subject to penal legislation, harassment and even physical assault. At the end of the century they established a committee of deputies to work for civil liberties, and there was some contact with Wales. In the early nineteenth century Dissenters supported whichever party seemed likely to support them and tried to mobilise opinion against the Test and Corporation Acts, finally repealed in 1829. Dissenting campaigns, to be supported by Methodism in the second half of the nineteenth century, were of even sharper significance in Wales, because of the increasingly dominant position of nonconformity. With the tradition of dissenting radicalism, mixed with ideas debated at the time of the French Revolution, nonconformists had specific targets towards which principles of natural justice impelled them – abolition of tithes which supported an alien church organisation, reform of marriage and burial laws which humiliated them, access to universities which was denied them.

A second element in the politics of protest in the nineteenth century was a growing, increasingly powerful, working class. A proletariat came into being in the eighteenth century. In the flannel-making towns of mid Wales entrepreneurs set up factories. Swansea became the centre of the British copper and brass industries, and by 1800 40 per cent of the pig-iron manufactured in Britain came from Wales. There was a certain fusion of influence and interest with dissent – grievances against the existing political system and agreement on the necessity for political action to meet those grievances. But the origins of working-class protest were very different, arising from the poverty of rural Wales and the social and economic conditions consequent on industrialisation, particularly in the iron industry. There were also the pressures of modernisation evident in the cloth industries of Merioneth, Montgomeryshire and Denbighshire, as factories were established at Welshpool, Llanidloes and Newtown, with capital coming from Lancashire and Liverpool. The expression of working-class politics was different, too. Dissenting politics during and after the French wars was middle-class, moderate, against violence and, cultivating the Whig party, concerned to achieve its ends through constitutional means. Working-class politics was not only channelled into demands for political reform but, from time to time in the first half of the nineteenth century, erupted violently in response to immediate local grievances. In the coalfield areas of North and South Wales there was a rapidly increasing population, ironmasters with an enormous degree of economic and social power, an increasing number of commercial and professional personnel, a mushrooming urban workforce. There had been fluctuating markets for iron; high demand during the French wars, but, at their end, depression, unemployment, and cuts in wages. The condition of life for urban and rural workers was miserable.

In a rapidly changing society the machinery of law and order remained much the same as in Tudor times. Law enforcement was still in the hands of voluntary officers, particularly justices of the peace, with the assistance *in extremis* of the military, who could be deployed by permission of the Home Secretary, to whom the lord lieutenant had access. Four Welsh counties took up the option to establish police forces after 1839, but general policing came only with the Police Act of 1856. Policing cost ratepayers money, so counties and boroughs preferred unpaid justices of the peace, high and petty constables. Local authorities were also reluctant to use the military because of the cost of housing and feeding them. Governments were as reluctant to see the army used because its resources were stretched.

Already, during the French wars, there had been protest in rural and urban Wales. In the 1790s there was protest against the Navy Act, against enclosures and against the price of grain. In 1795 in Denbighshire, a hatred of magistrates was evident, and bailiffs and constables were even more unpopular. Magistrates were imprisoned by hostile crowds and the military had to come in to restore order. In the 1790s conditions were desperate, with pressures of increasing population, inflation and increased exploitation of agricultural holdings. Grain was short and its price rocketed. There were waves of emigration to America, with people prepared to spend weeks in misery in ships' steerage. Then there was riot – between 1793 and 1795 there were riots in Swansea, Bangor, Aberystwyth, Denbigh, Fishguard, Bridgend, and Haverfordwest. In 1795–6 riots took place in Barmouth and Machynlleth. In 1799–1800 there was another violent response to grain shortages in Merthyr, in Pembrokeshire and in North and West Wales.

There had been corn riots in Wales in the 1740s and 1750s but the situation at the end of the eighteenth century was particularly serious, with malnutrition and some starvation. Yet grain was still being exported from Rhuddlan and Chepstow. Riots were widespread; there was some looting in Dowlais. Troops had to be brought in on many occasions to restore order. There was no specific political motive, more a response to a staple food shortage, but the riots were generally the controlled responses not of the hungriest but of industrial wage-earners, craftsmen and small farmers.

After the end of the Napoleonic Wars in 1815 there was a sharp fall in the price of corn and this produced another kind of crisis. Farmers economised, shed labour and left land uncultivated. There were bad harvests, too, and a shortage of food. More rioting resulted. In 1818 in Carmarthen a crowd prevented the export of cheese. In south-west Wales there was strong opposition to enclosures. In industrial Wales the high price of bread, allied to the threat of massive wage reductions, produced a convulsion among the Merthyr iron workers in 1816. J. J. Guest barricaded himself in Dowlais House and William Crawshay took refuge in a farmhouse. Only the advent of troops dispersed a crowd of over 8,000 workers. Here, then, was another traditional response, a spontaneous search for natural justice in face of humiliation. In 1825 and 1826 the general situation was reflected in banking crises which resulted in bankruptcies. In 1830 and 1831 there was renewed agitation associated with the Reform bill crisis. There was protest across Wales – in the spinning and weaving areas of Montgomeryshire, and in the North Wales coalfield, where unionism was spreading fast, whence it caught on in the South Wales coalfield only for employers to destroy its hold by the end of 1831. Working-class energy was harnessed by the middle classes in support of the Reform bill, and there was more

traditional protest in the face of conditions which too greatly
infringed human dignity. Violence erupted in Carmarthen and, as we
shall see, in Merthyr in 1831. In Carmarthen, where there existed
a tradition of demonstrations at election time, there were fights
between rival groups of supporters in both 1831 elections, and also
demonstrations of economic discontent.

Rural and urban discontent in the 1830s were linked, and shared
some common causes, but inevitably took rather different forms. The
discontent evident in Carmarthen grew in the 1830s as conditions
did not improve and new grievances were added.

The old Poor Law was harsh, though it has been argued that its
inadequacies have been exaggerated. While its stress on the principle
of the parish providing relief for those born within it was inappropriate
for an industrialised society in which so many people moved about,
it was reasonably flexible, provided some subvention of wages, family
allowances and unemployment compensation. There was some relief
in kind, in housing and medicine. In good times in rural areas it was
an adequate system, though unpaid overseers of the poor were often
inefficient and sometimes cruel. At least relief was outdoor. Yet the
suffering and the degradation was real enough, with the young, the
old and the sick suffering most. In Dolgellau, under the old Poor Law,
if the supplicant owned a stick of furniture no relief was available.
Those on parish relief in Cowbridge were forced to wear a badge.
Parish overseers went to unseemly, cruel lengths to move people out
of parishes if they were likely to add to the ratepayers' burden of relief.
A kind of haphazard Speenhamland system existed whereby many
farm labourers in Wales had their wages topped up if they had large
families – and the system was subject to abuse.

However harshly the old Poor Law was administered the pressure
of increasing population and poverty raised the poor rate to such an
extent that a commission investigated existing provision in 1834 and
produced an array of arguments to indicate that those on parish relief
– partial relief, supplementation of wages, indeed any outdoor relief
– were being 'depressed', 'demoralised' and 'pauperised'. The 1834
Poor Law Amendment Act therefore provided that no more outdoor
relief should be granted to the able-bodied and parishes should be
grouped in unions which would build workhouses in which conditions
were to be such that they would deter all but those in a state of the
most abject poverty and degradation. In workhouses families were

split up and husbands and wives segregated in the name of utilitarian efficiency. It was some time before all unions built workhouses – Aberdare's was not built until 1853 – and outdoor relief did not stop immediately, but the 1834 Act produced outrage. It came from magistrates, clergy and nonconformist bodies as well as being a vital factor in popular discontent.

Another injustice, so small farmers felt, were the tollgates erected by the turnpike trusts. The Welsh turnpike trusts, even though they did a little to improve the appalling condition of Welsh roads, were out to make money through frequent tolls on animals and wagons, and on lime, which was a staple fertiliser on Welsh farms. The trusts were inefficient, the roads remained in a bad state and toll-farmers were hated.

Tenant farmers, squeezed on every side, and with minimal resources, were forced to pay tithes to an Established Church to which they frequently did not belong. In 1836 tithes were compulsorily commuted to money payment, increasing the pressure on farmers. The discussions by which the rate of tithe was settled brought to the surface the underlying bitterness caused by this exaction.

Such grievances were accentuated by the increasing gulf evident between the mass of the people and those who wielded authority over them. The gentry and clergy were natural allies in a propertied, established society. As magistrates they were responsible for administering laws reflecting their own interests in a society increasingly divorced from them in religion and community. In 1838 and 1839 festering protest once more led to violence. In January, 1839, Narberth workhouse was set alight. On 13 May 1839 the tollgate at Efailwen was destroyed. It was re-erected but was destroyed for a second time by Rebecca and her 'daughters' – men dressed in women's clothing. The Llanboidy gate, also belonging to the Whitland Trust, was destroyed in similar fashion some nights later. After a lull for over three years there was a further, major, attack on the gates of the Whitland Trust, an attack which spread to the three western counties. The attack widened, clergy and magistrates were threatened. Then in June 1842 over 300 horsemen, augmented by rioters from the town, ransacked the workhouse in Carmarthen. Rebecca's activities spread into east Carmarthenshire and Glamorgan. A gate in Pontardulais was attacked, though three rioters were caught. Rebecca then attacked a gate at Hendy and the old woman gate-keeper was shot. The authorities captured two ringleaders, John Jones and David Davies, and sentenced them, along with the Pontardulais rioters, to transportation. There were subsequent riots in Radnorshire but now Rebecca's protest waned. She and her followers, aided by sympathetic coverage of rural grievances in *The Times*, had achieved much. County roads boards took over the turnpike trusts, a uniform system of tolls was introduced and the lime toll halved.

There were many links between rural and urban protest. For example bad harvests affected not only the small farmer but put up the price of bread in the towns, too. There were common spokesmen for Rebecca and for Chartism. There were of course, very different dimensions to the urban problem. The iron towns – Merthyr, Dowlais, Ebbw Vale, Hirwaun, Pontypool, Brynmawr – were transformed parish communities, ruled by ironmasters and generating intractable social problems. There were minimal amenities, dangerous work, high risk of disease and appalling infant mortality. Between 1821 and 1830 in Merthyr, of children under five, there were 479 burials per thousand baptisms, though life expectation after five was higher than in rural areas of Glamorgan. Wages, good when trade was good, fluctuated violently. Social controls in rural areas were lacking, there was no civic tradition and the parish vestry could not cope with the scale of problem. The ironmasters filled the power vacuum – they paid the men and owned their houses, operated a truck system and wielded power in the community as magistrates or through the parish vestry.

In the raw conditions of new communities, in an environment of danger, when human life in iron-works or coal-mine was cheap, there were regular reactions to extremes of injustice. Wage-cuts produced forty strikes between 1800 and 1831. Two rioters were hanged in Merthyr in 1800. In 1810 there were riots because of a shortage of bread. With the slump in demand for iron after the Napoleonic wars there were wage reductions which provoked strikes or riots. A riot at Tredegar iron-works in 1816 saw one rioter killed and troops called in, but the wage reduction was withdrawn. Riots followed in Nantyglo, Blaina and Ebbw Vale. In the 1820s came the Monmouthshire colliers' strikes and the Scotch Cattle, a movement rooted in Monmouthshire which involved direct action and attempts to control blacklegs and profiteers. The movement sprang up in Monmouthshire and Breconshire after 1816 and operated particularly in the colliery villages where there were similar grievances to those in the iron industry – fluctuations in demand for coal leading to wage reductions, the truck system, payment of wages in goods, long periods between payment which meant constant debt, abuse of the contracting system of hiring labour. In response, the Scotch Cattle operated just like a rural secret society in the 1820s and 1830s when colliers, dressed in women's clothing, masks and cattle skins, were led by a man rigged out with a horned bull's head. They operated not against industrialists but against contractors, landlords, bailiffs, 'blacklegs' or workers prepared to work for low wages. They destroyed furniture, sent out warning notes, attacked houses, burned tools and wagons. They were very difficult to track down because they operated in secret and engendered intense loyalty as well as fear. They were also highly organised.

The Merthyr rising

A more remarkable working-class protest took place in Merthyr in 1831. For four days, between 300 and 400 armed men, with thousands of supporters, held the iron town of Merthyr. They were dispersed only with the aid of 800 troops and afterwards were starved into submission by Guest of Dowlais and Hill of Plymouth, the ironmasters. It is not surprising that there should have been a confrontation in Merthyr. It had a tradition of radicalism from the 1790s but with little scope for action based on such ideas. The ironmasters were in control of the town and they allied with shopowners in institutions like the court of requests, established in 1809 to deal with debtors. Merthyr's growth from a small community of farmers and craftsmen into the main iron-producing centre in Britain had imposed severe strain. By 1830 it was producing 40 per cent of British pig-iron. Over 9,000 men were employed at the four great iron-works.

The attitudes of deference of rural Wales had been transferred from rural to industrial Wales, translated from deference towards landlord to deference towards ironmaster. This was not surprising in view of the economic grip ironmasters exerted, but it reinforced a sense of natural hierarchy based on a centuries-old relationship in rural Wales. At the same time workers from rural counties brought with them a tradition of direct action. There was a history of riots and strikes as in 1800 and in 1816. Fluctuations in demand were reflected in variable wage rates and sometimes the traditions of protest in the face of provocation, expressed in the activities of Rebecca or the Scotch Cattle, came to a head. In the major strike against rising food prices at a time of reducing wages in 1816, troops had to be called in to suppress the rioters. In the Merthyr context, with its long-standing radical discussions, rooted in strong unitarianism, pamphleteering and political Eisteddfodau, working-class action took this form of direct action rather than that of the Scotch Cattle.

Wage fluctuations produced a volatile situation. The skilled men of the iron industry, puddlers or rollers, were valued workers and well paid when trade was good. They were dismissed only as a last resort. But with wage reductions of 40 per cent in 1816, for example, reaction was inevitable. There were other consequences of wage variation. Ironmasters were involved in the community because their actions produced the need for increased poor relief in bad times, hence increases in the rates from which they and their fellow ratepayers suffered. Wage cuts also resulted in widespread debt. Out of such concerns grew an identity of interest among the ironmasters which did not stem from inclination. The ironmasters – Crawshays and Guests, for example – were very different in personality and outlook. William Crawshay was a radical, prepared to tolerate trade unions. Guest was an orthodox proprietor, philanthropist and paternalist. There was a natural identity of interest between ironmasters and Merthyr's middle class of shopkeepers, auctioneers, clerks and lawyers in times of economic crisis, too, because of the increased scale of workers' debt, and there were always clashes between workers and shopkeepers at such times.

From 1830 economic crisis in Merthyr combined with agitation over the Reform bill to produce an inflammable situation. The depression in iron had grown worse since 1829. Production was reduced, wages eventually cut. Debts grew, credit increased, shopkeepers felt the crisis. The court of requests ruthlessly pursued debtors and distrained goods. There was grave distress, a high poor rate and crisis in the select vestry which controlled the town's affairs. With truck acts and reform being discussed in Parliament there was a wider context to the immediate crisis.

In April 1831 the Reform bill was stopped and the situation in Merthyr began to get out of control. There had already been large reform meetings, now there were more. A mass meeting of 2,000 workers took place above Dowlais on 30 May 1831. It was both a reform meeting and a protest meeting against the court of requests. The following morning, bailiffs of the court tried to distrain property of Lewis Lewis, 'Lewsyn yr Heliwr'. They were stopped. On 1 June an insurrection began. Merthyr was held by the workers, who went from house to house restoring goods taken by the court of requests to their former owners. The magistrates sent for the Argyll and Sutherland Highlanders from Brecon. Outside the Castle Hotel there was a confrontation between troops and workers. Troops opened fire, about twenty-six of the crowd were killed, sixteen soldiers wounded, six badly. The Government were alarmed and sent in more troops. The Swansea yeomanry were disarmed and forced to turn tail but by 6 June the insurrection had collapsed.

Twenty-eight miners, colliers, artisans and labourers were brought to trial for raiding homes, violence or seizing arms. Two men, Lewis Lewis and Richard Lewis (Dic Penderyn) were sentenced to death. The former's sentence was commuted to transportation. The latter, though there was much evidence to indicate that he was not guilty, was hanged at Cardiff gaol in August 1831 allegedly for having stabbed a soldier, Donald Black, in the thigh. Colliers' union lodges were spreading across the coalfield in the same month. At Dowlais and Plymouth iron-works the masters told their employees to renounce the union. By October, through near-starvation, the men were forced to submit. But the events of 1831 in Merthyr had brought together both a whole array of grievances and working-class activity in the fight for an element of justice. Politics and protest were to remain central in Merthyr's history, and, through events in Merthyr, in Welsh radicalism.

Chartism

In 1836 the Working Men's Association was established by William Lovett and Henry Hetherington. The latter was a close friend of Hugh Williams of Carmarthen. He was a solicitor who drew up Rebecca's petitions and defended participants in her riots. In 1837 Williams became secretary of a Working Men's Association branch in Carmarthen. In 1838–9 about fifty branches of the W.M.A. were established in the South Wales coalfield. The industrial working class was evolving a new kind of protest. In 1838 the People's Charter was published. The grievances which had prompted the 1831 rising had not disappeared; indeed, the Poor Law Amendment Act had accentuated them. The Chartists' aim was political democracy, universal male suffrage, annual Parliaments. Chartist support was widespread in Wales in the 1830s – in Wrexham, Ruabon, Carmarthenshire, Swansea and, the Chartist stronghold, Merthyr, which published two Chartist newspapers. Another stronghold was mid Wales where Newtown, Welshpool and Llanidloes provided fertile ground because of the difficulties of the cloth industry. The first Chartist demonstration was held in Newtown in 1838, attended by 3,000 to 5,000 people. Here was a reform movement which commanded the support of all radical elements, unionists, Scotch Cattle and more cautious radicals. The Unitarians, especially strong in Merthyr, added a particularly radical element. There were leaders of high calibre – Hugh Williams of Carmarthen, Thomas Powell of Newtown, Charles Jones of Welshpool, John Frost of Newport and Zephaniah Williams of Blaina. In 1838 there was a meeting in Merthyr at which Hugh Williams was elected delegate to the Chartist convention. In January 1839 a torchlight procession took place in Carmarthen. There was an attempt to burn down the workhouse in Narberth. Later in 1839 came serious violence in Llanidloes. The cloth industry was depressed, the all-embracing truck system and the new Poor Law caused grave resentment. Provoked by the presence of three London policemen sent by the Home Secretary, the cloth workers acted spontaneously and responsibly. They held the town for a week before soldiers restored order. Despite underlying grievances the uprising had been provoked by the authorities to silence Chartist leaders.

In May 1839 Henry Vincent, the Chartist leader, was imprisoned in Monmouth gaol. A demonstration, involving about 30,000 people, followed in Blackwood, Gwent. One of the leaders of this protest was John Frost, tradesman, former mayor of Newport, justice of the peace, another of Welsh Chartism's middle-class leaders. Also involved, and mistrusting Frost, was Dr William Price, the eccentric leader of Pontypridd Chartism.

The Newport rising followed in November. Three groups of demonstrators were to converge on Newport, from Blackwood, Ebbw Vale and Pontypool. John Frost led the first, Zephaniah Williams the second but William Jones's third group did not keep the rendezvous at Risca. The first two groups did reach Newport, though in low spirits because of the torrential rain which had drenched them. Those who arrived came down to the Westgate Hotel only to be fired on by troops stationed there unbeknown to the demonstrators. The crowd fled, the leaders were arrested, tried and deported. Almost certainly the Newport affair was a demonstration, not an attempt to seize Newport. There is some evidence that Zephaniah Williams intended it to be part of a general insurrection in Cardiff, Newport, Brecon and Abergavenny timed to coincide with uprisings in England and Scotland. On the other hand, an insurrection was contrary to the traditions of Welsh Chartist leadership, particularly that of John Frost who was a 'moral force' Chartist. The Newport rising was a failure, it merely demonstrated the extent to which government would go in defending its interests. Chartism did not disappear, however. A Chartist periodical appeared in Merthyr from 1840 to 1842. A petition to Parliament in 1842 contained 36,000 signatures from Glamorgan. There were meetings in Merthyr, and Guest and Crawshay dismissed Chartist workers. At precisely this time the Rebecca movement, sharing some common causes with Chartism, was in full spate in west Wales. But Chartism was far more than an industrial version of Rebecca, or a twin to the Scotch Cattle. Its political objectives, and especially its moral force dimension, attracted a wide variety of support from the middle class and the respectable working class, often leaders in their communities, who condemned violence. Such people did not forget their ideals, they continued to play an important part in their communities, they held meetings and heard lectures for years after Chartism is supposed to have died out. At the same time Chartism had played a vital part in moulding a class consciousness among the working class in Wales. The government and employers were well aware of this and, along with government coercion, went attempts by employers to divert working-class energies into, for example, education through works schools or even brass bands.

The 1868 election – background and aftermath

There was now a return to more piecemeal industrial protest, normally against cuts in wages. In 1843 Swansea copper-workers were defeated, as were Aberdare's miners in 1857 in face of a 15 per cent reduction in wages. But, generally, working-class activity and protest were far more sporadic than in previous years, largely due to increased prosperity in the 1850s and 1860s. This was particularly evident among skilled workers, of whom there were high proportions in the copper, tin and iron industries. Still, a pattern of working-class protest had been established, with a variety of elements in it. From the 1790s to the 1840s there were instinctive reactions to injustice – appalling physical conditions or large wage-cuts. Radical ideas of political change and democratisation were fed in through pamphleteering and discussion from the time of the French Revolution. There were links with Dissent, particularly the radical Unitarian denomination so strong in Merthyr. There were traditions of community action and instant justice evident in the Rebecca and Scotch Cattle movements. After the 1850s a different pattern of politics developed which was to result in forty years or more of Liberal domination and, broadly, consensus politics. At the same time militant action re-emerged in the 1870s as unionism took root, coalowners combined and there was periodic depression in the coal trade. There were stoppages in 1870 and 1873. Wages were twice cut by 10 per cent in 1874 and, in 1875, a five-month stoppage resulted in a further large wage-reduction. It also produced the sliding scale which tied wages to the price of coal, but with a minimum and maximum. What was to become so contentious later was at this stage welcomed more by the colliers than the owners, but, with the price of coal falling in the 1870s, the drawbacks of the scheme soon became apparent.

Working-class political activity was channelled into radical causes in a variety of ways. From the 1840s Dissent went on to the political attack from pulpit and in press, and a consensus of radical, liberal, nonconformist activity and leadership, normally middle class, emerged. Methodism, too, was drawn in to some extent after the publication of the Education Report of 1847, but the resultant radicalism was limited. With nonconformity such a dominant influence through its press and pulpit, its ideas permeated political life and, in general, secularist and socialist ideas did not circulate in a Wales insulated by its language. This helped to mould a more quiescent pattern of politics and protest in the second half of the nineteenth century.

The context of political activity after the 1840s had been irrevocably changed by working-class organisation, the growth of nonconformity, the press and, above all, industrial change. The vested interests to be confronted were, even so, as powerful as ever. The hold of the landed gentry over a system of Parliamentary representation which had not changed much since the Act of Union was still as strong in the counties and nearly as strong in the boroughs. Only in Glamorgan was the new industrial wealth represented, and even here the distinction between land and industry as a source of wealth was an artificial one. About one in sixty of the population had the vote; about one-third of the land in most counties was owned by four or five families. The hold exerted over their tenantry was enormous, and reinforced by the deference of centuries. The orthodox politics of local and central government was denied to the mass of the rural and industrial population. Nonconformity provided an avenue to political action, though still in the 1850s there was no great desire to use it. In the small towns of rural Wales or the growing boroughs of industrial Wales there was a rather different social structure and the potential for political growth was greater, particularly if a middle class of professional and trades people combined with the skilled working class.

Confrontation eventually came, therefore, in orthodox political terms as well as through protest. It came not in the new industrial towns but in a rural town, as we shall see. While Merthyr presented all the preconditions for spontaneous action there was an insufficiently large middle class to bring political pressure on the ironmasters. Only with the vote could the vast potential power of the working class there be mobilised. Even then a secret ballot was required before workers could vote against their employers, just as tenants were then liberated from the threat of eviction. In town as well as county it was also difficult to break down the deference to employers which was characteristic of that rural Wales from which most workers in the industrial areas had come. Indeed, when there was a breakthrough in 1868 in Merthyr, it was followed by very moderate political activity. The entrenched power of wealth and economic domination was first challenged successfully, then, in a remote rural county by a combination of Calvinistic Methodist leadership, from the most politically conservative of the nonconformist denominations, and a tenantry which was prepared to sacrifice livelihood for principle.

The *annus mirabilis* of Welsh politics has always been seen as 1868, when the election of Henry Richard for Merthyr fused Liberalism and nonconformity into a potent force. In fact specifically Welsh nonconformist grievances were not at issue in 1868, and a number of Welsh M.P.s were already both radical and Liberal. Members of Parliament had already campaigned over nonconformist disabilities, particularly in education.

The 1868 election is perhaps best seen as both a culmination and a beginning. As we have seen, Dissenting attitudes were only slowly radicalised, despite many grievances. Only Merthyr's Dissenters were actively involved in the campaign for parliamentary reform in 1831, and the 1832 act hardly changed the balance of political power. The grievances of nonconformists in the 1840s were traditional – tithes, exclusion from the universities and endowed schools by religious tests, exclusion from burial in consecrated ground. Then, in 1847, the report of the commissioners on education aroused the political consciousness of nonconformity, and this time even the Calvinistic Methodists, traditionally so politically aloof, were incensed. At the same time a new type of leader emerged in Methodism – Thomas Gee, for example.

From 1840 the Liberation Society provided nonconformity with a vital element of organisation as branches were established in many parts of Wales in the 1850s. From 1862 there was a specific campaign, led particularly by prominent nonconformist ministers, to press for civic rights for nonconformists. In 1859 Thomas Gee, one of the movement's leaders, started the most influential radical periodical, *Baner ac Amserau Cymru*. The society also organised the collection of statistics and encouraged electoral registration. Throughout the 1850s other factors drove nonconformist opinion to greater involvement in ideas of reform. The Church of England was putting its house in order rather too effectively for nonconformists' liking, with the appointment of reforming bishops and increasing provision of elementary education through the National Society. British Society schools were proving no substantial answer. Trade depressions were more frequent in the 1860s, so pointing up yet more clearly the poverty of rural Wales and fluctuations in wages in industrial Wales. Long before the 1868 election the centuries-old hegemony of the squire was under attack. Evictions of tenants who voted against their landlords assumed enormous significance, as in 1859 when W. W. E. Wynne evicted tenants on his Rhiwlas estate for having voted against his representative. By 1868 newspaper articles called for the overthrow of landlord domination and the Liberation Society provided the organisation by which this might be achieved.

The tensions and pressures in Welsh society could result in action because of the 1867 Reform Act. There was only one significant change in the Welsh constituencies – Merthyr was to return two members. There was no fundamental change in the county franchise but there were important modifications of the borough franchise. The enfranchisement of householders had a remarkable impact in some parts of Wales. In Merthyr, most dramatically, the electorate increased from 1,387 to 14,577.

The results in the 1868 election were evidence of a quite remarkable change in Welsh politics, but they conceal a subtle mixture of religious, social and political influences which varied from county to county and certainly between rural and urban Wales. The scale of change is evident in Merioneth. The domination of the landed gentry had been complete – through the Vaughans of Corsygedol in the eighteenth century, then Sir Robert Williams Vaughan of Nannau and Hengwrt, Sir Richard Richards and W. W. E. Wynne of Peniarth. The relationship between landlord and tenant was one of obligation and deference. Tenant support for his landlord at election time was taken for granted – by both sides. There was no scope for orthodox political activity. The county was dominated by its gentry – eighteen of them owned nearly half the county's land. Freeholders and tenants found it difficult to do more than subsist in a county of poor land, but relations with landlords were not based on any great animosity. The county's landlords were not absentees, they did not exploit their tenantry. There was no marked political consciousness. There was, however, heightened political awareness – among more prosperous freeholders and the intellectual leaders of theological colleges when Bala recovered its chartered borough status – but it was after the 1859 election that the real political response came. The largest landowners in the Bala area, R. W. Price and Sir Watkin Williams

Wynn, ejected some of the tenants who had voted against their
interest. The ensuing resentment provoked a potent alliance of
Methodist leaders, larger freeholders and Bala townsmen. With an
organisation in existence to ensure that all voters eligible to vote
registered, and a genuine sense of outrage at the actions of Price and
Wynn, the preconditions of victory in 1868 existed. They were
reinforced by the 1867 Reform Act which gave the vote to householders in the growing slate-quarrying areas of northern Merioneth.
This meant that the pressure which landlords were able to bring to
bear on tenants – influential in the 1865 election despite the sense
of grievance and a growing political awareness fostered by the
Liberation Society – was far less effective. Again, all reforming
elements in the county were united over the great issue of the 1868
election, the disestablishment of the Irish Church. In 1868, therefore,
the Liberal David Williams saw W. R. M. Wynn retire from the
contest because he realised that a Liberal victory was inevitable.

There were similar habits of deference to landlords in Cardiganshire, too, a county in which five families owned a third of the land
and a further forty-eight families another third. Not surprisingly, the
landed gentry exercised a stranglehold over Parliamentary representation. Only in Cardigan and Aberystwyth was there a small class
of tradesmen, craftsmen and professional people with a potential
alternative political power. Nonconformity, into the 1860s, was
politically quiet. The seemingly remarkable result of 1868 was
achieved because the election was fought over the one issue which
could provoke the nonconformists into action, the disestablishment
of the Irish church. In Cardiganshire the result was that the Liberal,
Evan Matthew Richards of Swansea, won the county seat, with a
small majority of 156 votes. This victory did not mean that old
loyalties were dead, or that a new politics based on a different kind
of political relationship within the community had arrived.

On the surface, the result of the 1868 election in Denbighshire was
remarkable. In Denbigh boroughs Watkin Williams, a Liberal,
defeated the Tory, Townshend Mainwaring. In the county, George
Osborne Morgan defeated Colonel Biddulph of Chirk Castle. Head of
the poll, however, was Sir Watkin Williams Wynn, epitomising the
old order – great landowner, head of a family whose origins went
back beyond Tudor times, a paternalist of the old order, and highly
respected by his tenantry.

These were beginnings of a changed political situation in Wales. It was the product of the 1867 Reform Act, the politicisation of nonconformity, the impact of the Liberation Society in ensuring the effectiveness of a thorough registration of nonconformist voters, and some fusion of middle-class and working-class protest in respectable nonconformist radicalism. The change was most obvious in Merthyr with its long tradition of working-class action. The significant feature here was not so much that the Liberal nonconformist was elected, but that the sitting member was ejected by the working class. That member was Henry Austin Bruce, whose impact on educational history, as Lord Aberdare, was to come a dozen years later. He came bottom of the poll behind Henry Richard and Richard Fothergill. That Bruce, a trustee of the Dowlais works, a coalowner, an M.P. for sixteen years representing Merthyr, with a good record on liberal issues, should have been so overwhelmingly defeated is remarkable. It was partly that the 1867 Reform Act, which had given Merthyr a second seat, had enfranchised resident householders, so giving workers the vote. There was some fusion of middle-class and working-class radicalism fostered by nonconformity in a town with eighty-four places of worship, seventy-one of them nonconformist. The Liberation Society had been active in ensuring registration. Henry Richard himself was an outstanding figure; a prominent critic of the Education Report in 1847, a leading figure in the Liberation Society and the Peace Society. His nonconformist appeal could not have been greater, and, as we have seen, there was a national issue, the disestablishment of the Church in Ireland, around which to unite. But Richard benefited crucially, too, from the working-class vote which Bruce forfeited because miners showed that his stance on safety in the mines, and working conditions, was suspect. So local issues blended with national ones, an alliance of working-class and nonconformist interests existed. Bruce's fate was sealed, and Henry Richard became one of the outstanding spokesmen in the Commons on nonconformist and working-class issues.

It is possible to exaggerate the actual changes wrought by the 1868 election. Almost all the Welsh Liberal M.P.s were Whigs. The landed interest was still represented by ten Conservative M.P.s and some Liberals. Only three of the thirty-three Welsh members were actually nonconformists – Henry Richard, Evan Mathew Richards and Richard Davies. The last was a self-made man, though now, as shipowner and ironmaster, very wealthy. Even in Merthyr the second seat had been won by an ironmaster and in 1874 a miners' leader, Thomas Halliday, was beaten there. Still, with all the caveats, 1868 was the start of a fundamental change.

SECTION II. 1880–1979

Liberalism – achievements and problems, 1880–1914

There was increasing identification of Liberal and nonconformist interest as the Liberal party grew more radical. Eventually the radical element in the Liberal party predominated and the Whig element split off over the issue of Home Rule for Ireland. Party allegiance across Britain became more manifest and Wales identified with the Liberal Party, an identification which seemed to be complete by the 1880s. M.P.s were forced to become far more aware of national issues too and, especially after the widening of the franchise in the 1884 Reform Act, to take notice of the issues which concerned their constituents. Already the Ballot Act of 1872 had made the vote secret. In all, constituency feeling was now important and party organisation in constituencies vital. It existed already to some extent for the Liberals through chapel leadership. The divide with Conservatism was accentuated by that party's habit of meeting in public houses. The 1880s were crucial in the development of Liberal Party organisation in Wales as, under the influence of Stuart Rendel, Welsh Liberals developed a programme of educational reform, disestablishment, land reform and devolution which was taken up by the British party. Organisation improved with the establishment of two Liberal Federations, one for North Wales, one for South. The party established a Welsh National Council in 1887 and the Parliamentary committee of Welsh M.P.s was reorganised.

Welsh allegiance to the Liberal Party remained steadfast from 1868 until 1922, largely immune to the fluctuations of English politics. A predominant feature after 1868 was that Welsh M.P.s determined to press for solutions to specifically Welsh problems. Their solution meant radical measures in British terms – undermining the traditional power of the landed class, disestablishing the Church of England in Wales. It was pressure from Welsh M.P.s which was partly responsible for getting the Ballot Act of 1872 – pressure resulting from the spate of evictions of tenants brave enough to vote counter to their landlords' interests.

After 1868 there was a strong radical, nonconformist political tradition. In 1884 the Reform Act enfranchised the working class and, for the moment, their aspirations for reform were largely contained within the orthodox Liberal radical framework. Liberalism and nonconformity had the grievances on which to thrive. The position of the Established Church remained provocative for economic, religious and emotional reasons. It was propped up in Wales by those landed classes who were now increasingly, and stridently, branded with exploitation of tenants and especially with having evicted them on political grounds for having voted according to the dictates of a nonconformist conscience. The notion of disestablishment went back decades but only after 1868 did it become politically feasible, since the campaign had to be supported outside Wales. In 1870 there was actually a vote in the Commons on disestablishment but at this stage there were only three Liberal M.P.s in Wales to vote for it. By 1887 it was a part of Liberal policy, though it was not until 1914 that it was actually secured; the high point of Liberal radical nonconformist achievement in the nineteenth and early twentieth centuries.

Welsh involvement with Gladstonian Liberalism was more marked after the 1886 election. Gladstone himself was sympathetic to Wales on many issues, but sympathy and political expediency were linked because Gladstone realised the value of Welsh Liberal allegiance, especially on the issue of Home Rule for Ireland. After 1886 there were new and more militant leaders in Wales – particularly Tom Ellis and Lloyd George. They steered Wales to a position of greater importance than ever before in British politics, resulting in disestablishment becoming a high priority in the Liberal Party programme nationally in 1891. The Welsh land question, too, became prominent through skilful propaganda and the genuine poverty of tenant farmers, accentuated by the 1880s depression.

Between 1892 and 1895 Welsh Liberalism achieved great things – a charter for the University of Wales, a royal commission into land and a disestablishment bill. Lloyd George and Tom Ellis were powerful figures and the latter was particularly influential as chief whip of the Liberal Party. With the fall of the Liberal Government in 1895 came some disillusionment with Welsh radicalism and especially the *Cymru*

Fydd movement for home rule, which carried within it the seeds of its own destruction.

Despite a cultural awakening at the end of the eighteenth century there had been no political dimension to cultural nationalism. Wales merged into England, and only towards the end of the nineteenth century qualified for separate legislative treatment. The radical issues in the later part of the nineteenth century like disestablishment, the land question and education, had political implications. Welsh radicals wanted parity with England and recognition of Welsh rights, rather than independence. There had been injustices for Wales – often as with the 1847 Blue Books, deeply felt – but they fell far short of the starvation which had been inflicted on Ireland, for example. In Wales, the most striking differences between it and England were linguistic and religious. The pre-eminence of Welsh nonconformity made tithe and disestablishment live issues, dominating much of Welsh political life in the later nineteenth century. Nonconformity dominated the language of politics, too, moulding its gradualist and moderate tone.

There was an emphasis in Wales on cultural nationalism which became increasingly evident later in the century. It led to an emphasis on the virtues of the Welsh peasantry, a notion streaked with romanticism and reflecting a strand of Victorian thought which glorified craft work. Welsh distinctiveness was recognised in the last decades of the century. The strength of nonconformity and its association with the temperance movement led to a Sunday Closing Act in 1881. There was also the Welsh Intermediate Education Act in 1889. Both these provided a precedent for progress with the disestablishment issue. Educational legislation was linked with cultural nationalism through, for example, the pressure for a national museum and a national library. O. M. Edwards, a short-term politician, supplied Welsh adults and children with literature in their language and pressed for the teaching of Welsh and Welsh history in schools. Beriah Gwynfe Evans, of the Society for the Utilisation of the Welsh Language, was equally keen.

The quest for higher education had always rested on the desire for parity with England. There was a constant striving to meet deficiencies manifest in English terms. England had her universities, public schools and grammar schools to train leaders and a middle class.

Wales had no university and few grammar schools. In time, the university and intermediate school movements were able to capitalise on popular support, attuned to this notion of the desirability of parity with England. The education movement is often held to be an example of Welsh distinctiveness, and there was certainly separate legislative treatment, but it also showed up the limitations of nationalism in Wales. The Education Act of 1902, with its aftermath of the Welsh Revolt against rate aid to predominantly Anglican denominational schools, indicated priorities. There was an underlying acceptance of the fusion of the educational systems of England and Wales. The creation of a Welsh Department of the Board of Education in 1907 conferred a very limited autonomy.

The one movement which attempted to fuse cultural and political nationalism was *Cymru Fydd* ('Young Wales') between 1894 and 1896. It was supported at first by the great names of Liberalism in Wales – Tom Ellis, Lloyd George and D. A. Thomas. For two years Welsh Liberalism came close to being taken over by the movement and Welsh Home Rule made a Liberal objective in a way similar to Irish Home Rule. *Cymru Fydd* was actually founded on shifting sand because of deep divisions between the commercial, rich, cosmopolitan southern seaboard and the rest of Wales. Anglicised industrialists like D. A. Thomas, leading figure in the South Wales Liberal Federation, were not prepared to countenance Welsh control of commerce and industry. There was a short-term crisis for Welsh Liberalism with Lloyd George's failure to secure support for *Cymru Fydd*, but pressure for independence was so limited that the crisis passed. Subsequent attempts to achieve support for Home Rule just before the First World War and in the inter-war years were yet more unsuccessful. Welsh influence was, paradoxically, most in evidence as part of British politics.

After the defeat of the Liberals in the 1895 election, Liberalism in Wales lost much of its dynamism in the aftermath of the breakdown of *Cymru Fydd*. More tensions resulted from the Boer War as Liberal opinion in Wales was divided between imperialists, like Brynmor Jones, and pro-Boers, like Lloyd George and Herbert Lewis, though far more unity was evoked by the atrocities perpetrated against the Boers. And, fortunately for Welsh Liberalism, there was an issue, the Education Act of 1902, round which it could unite. Lloyd George's opposition to rate aid for denominational schools under that Act was precisely the kind of nonconformist–Liberal issue which best fused the two forces.

The Liberal election triumph of 1906 would seem to have provided another opportunity for Welsh influence at the highest level. Indeed, there were many achievements between 1905 and 1915 – a Welsh Department of the Board of Education, a National Library, a National Museum, a Welsh Insurance Commission, a National Council for Wales for Agriculture and a Welsh Church Act. These achievements nevertheless concealed a malaise. Liberalism had no social policy – in fact, attitudes to trade unionism and socialism were unsympathetic. Socialism provided a potential alternative political influence. There were no longer radical leaders of Welsh Liberalism – Lloyd George was now engrossed in government in Whitehall. The Liberal Government had no need of Welsh support since its majority was so great. Just before the First World War there was a flicker of interest in Welsh Home Rule once more, and E. T. John presented a bill in the Commons, but it was not a live political issue.

Most fundamental to Welsh politics in the twentieth century was the evolution of distinctively working-class political structures. Nineteenth-century Welsh political radicalism had commanded massive working-class support but it was not directly a working-class movement. It represented best the professional class, the lower-middle class, and industrialists. It was extremely successful in uniting opinion behind a programme of rectifying very real injustices and had achieved its main educational, religious and cultural objectives by 1914. It had never directly ministered to the needs of industrial Wales, and Home Rule policies had never been a sufficiently prominent issue to fire national enthusiasm. This continued to be the case after the war and it was only after 1925, with the foundation of *Plaid Cymru*, that the movement for Welsh independence took on a different aspect, though the party had very little support at first.

What Wales had achieved was first an awareness of, then action on, a variety of its own deeply felt grievances and this was the achievement of radical Liberalism. It was made possible by a remarkable Liberal domination from the 1880s to the First World War. In 1880 Liberals won twenty-nine of the thirty-three Welsh seats. The landowner domination of Welsh politics, going back to the Acts of Union, was no more, though landed influence in local government and the administration of justice continued for the moment. The 1884 Reform Act brought more changes. Householders in the counties now had the vote; new constituencies were formed in populous industrial areas. Glamorgan had five members, not two, Monmouthshire an extra member. Five old borough seats, like Haverfordwest, disappeared and with them some traditional Whig members. In the rural areas tenant farmers and labourers were enfranchised, though 40 per cent of men, and all women, still had no vote. The new voters were solidly Liberal so that only in the anglicised border areas, or the vale of Glamorgan or south Monmouthshire, were the Conservatives able to mount a challenge. In the 1885 election thirty of the thirty-four Welsh seats were won by Liberals. From 1892 to 1895 the solid phalanx of Welsh Liberals held the balance of power in Parliament. With a Conservative government in office from 1895 to 1906 Liberals lost influence and some seats; but in the 1906 election there was a remarkable result. In the aftermath of the campaign against church schools after 1902, the Liberal party won thirty-three of the thirty-four Welsh seats. The only seat lost went to Keir Hardie for the Labour Representation Committee in Merthyr.

Since the 1880s Wales had also produced Liberal leaders of remarkable ability. In the 1880s a new, more radical, Liberalism emerged, to the disquiet of the older generation of Henry Richard and Osborne Morgan. Their allegiance had been to British Liberalism but this was far less so, at least for a time, with Tom Ellis and Lloyd George, who pressed Welsh issues from a Welsh base. Tom Ellis was born in Bala, with its strong radical tradition. His uncle had suffered eviction from his farm. Ellis was educated at New College, Oxford, he was a brilliant orator, a nationalist, particularly in a cultural and literary context, and an enormously talented politician who became Liberal chief whip. He was much criticised for accepting this government post but wielded far more influence on behalf of Wales in government than he would have done outside it. D. A. Thomas, M.P. for Merthyr Tydfil from 1892 to 1922, owned the Cambrian collieries in the Rhondda and spoke for the commercial interest of south-east Wales. He was a nationalist, instrumental in establishing *Cymru Fydd*, more influential in destroying it. He was an interesting political phenomenon – coal-owner and reformer, a Liberal who came to be hated in the coalfield. Lloyd George was the most complex of politicians not only of his own time but of any. He became M.P. for Caernarfon Boroughs in 1890. He had already been involved in tithe disputes and nonconformist grievances over burial rights when in local government on the new Caernarfonshire County Council. He was rooted in rural Wales, like Ellis, and lived in Llanystumdwy from the age of one until he was seventeen. He knew of nonconformist grievances at first hand. Brought up a Baptist, he had to attend a church school. The Church was one symbol of oppression, the squire the other, and Lloyd George's nationalism centred around these symbols of inequality. He became the leading Welsh spokesman in Parliament on disestablishment and led the revolt over the 1902 Education Act with remarkable success. For a time he linked these issues with support for Welsh political independence through the *Cymru Fydd* movement, or his demand for a Welsh National Council for Education.

The achievements of these Welsh Liberal leaders, working from a base of solid support across the country, were equally remarkable. In 1881 the Welsh Sunday Closing Act was the first recognition of a separate political existence since the Acts of Union. The 1889 Welsh Intermediate Education Act was an even more formidable political achievement, wresting money from the Treasury for a state system of secondary education where none existed in England. At an important phase in the history of this Act, Conservative support came from Lord Salisbury and Sir William Hart-Dyke, so it was a bipartisan recognition of Welsh distinctiveness. Later, the strength of Liberalism and nonconformity in alliance was demonstrated in another educational issue, when Lloyd George's leadership of the opposition to rate aid for church schools led to most Welsh local authorities being prepared to administer the 1902 Act only under their own conditions.

The last quarter of the nineteenth century saw the politicisation of the Welsh land question. There were specific grievances which had motivated Rebecca – land hunger and tithes. Tenants had been ejected from holdings in the 1850s and 1860s for having voted contrary to their landlords' interests and although propaganda exaggerated the scale of the grievance it was real enough and a gross injustice. There were problems of compensation for improvements. From the 1880s depression sharpened the land question and a model for Welsh aspirations had come into existence in Ireland in 1881 with the passing of the Irish Land Act, conferring security of tenure, compensation for improvement and a land court to determine fair rents. In the event, Wales got a Royal Commission on land. It sat from 1893 to 1895 and produced two separate reports reflecting the social and political affiliations of its members. With a Conservative government in power from 1896 no action was taken and, in any case, there was some economic improvement in rural Wales as prices rose.

The disestablishment of the Church in Wales, finally guaranteed in 1914, was not only a remarkable political achievement but another recognition that here was a peculiarly Welsh injustice, closely linked, through the necessity for tithe payments, to the land question and rural poverty. In 1891 the tithe question was settled in unsatisfactory fashion by a Tithe Rent Charge Act, which charged tithe to the owner not the tenant. Disestablishment still remained the goal, though ironically, by the time it came, the political world of which it had seemed such an integral part was fundamentally changed.

From the 1880s Welsh Liberalism, which had achieved so much, seemed impregnable. There was no Conservative opposition in Wales since Conservatism represented the interests only of a tiny landlord class, whose power had been wrested from it by Ballot Acts and changes in local government. The socialist challenge had not yet become effective, though the signs were there. After 1898 Independent Labour Party branches were set up in places like Merthyr, Swansea, and Wrexham, and by 1905 there were twenty-seven branches in South Wales. In 1900 Merthyr elected Keir Hardie as its M.P. and by 1905 there were five Labour councillors in Swansea. As yet, the challenge was potential, not actual. Where industrial confrontation did take place the political complexities were evident, and showed cracks, even chasms, in the Liberal consensus. In 1898 there was a strike in South Wales coalmines. The men were defeated and the confidence of moderates like Mabon (William Abraham) shaken. Out of the 1898 strike the South Wales Miners' Federation was born – with moderate leaders, William Abraham himself, William Brace, Thomas Richards.

There was confrontation in North Wales in the slate industry. The two largest slate-quarries in the world, Penrhyn and Dinorwic, were owned by Lord Penrhyn and the Assheton-Smith family, major Welsh landowners. In the face of such overwhelming, concentrated economic power, there could be no countervailing middle-class political influence capable of standing against these families locally on directly economic and social grievances. The small middle class supported the moderate, constitutional, national challenge to land-lordism, a Liberal programme endorsed by quarry workers steeped in similar traditions of language and religion.

Eventually the mould broke. Lord Penrhyn was content with nothing less than the deference traditionally accorded him as landowner. Still, after one abortive attempt, a North Wales Quarry-men's Union was established in 1875 though, with such a scattered workforce and the strength of the employers, it was difficult to maintain its momentum effectively. There was also some blurring of issues between the bargaining objectives of the union and the struggle, which union leadership endorsed, of the Liberal Party against landlordism and the Anglican Church. In the 1880s and the 1890s there were defeats for the union in Dinorwic and Penrhyn. Then, from 1900 to 1903 came the climactic confrontation at Penrhyn. Lord Penrhyn realised full well that this represented a struggle for power more basic than Liberal campaigns. There had been a management victory in 1897 followed by victimisation. On 22 November 1900, 2,800 men walked out; 1,000 never returned. Not until November 1903 did the men go back. They lost because Lord Penrhyn had the economic resources from land to allow him to forego slate revenue, and because he realised that the dispute was fundamentally about the position of men like himself at the apex of society.

The quarrymen had minimal resources and were pushed inexorably towards starvation. But the quarrymen's fight was important. They fought not as representatives of traditional Welsh radicalism but as workers in an industry. They fought from a socialist base, though one often defined in traditionally radical terms. The common cause of Welsh Liberal radicalism and the quarrymen was soon to be won, despite short-term defeat. The First World War, which saw the virtual destruction of the slate industry, was followed by disestablishment and the accelerating break-up of the great estates by means of which landlords had dominated Wales for centuries.

These portents of change are more obvious in retrospect. Liberalism had a firm grip on public opinion, the backing of nonconformist leaders and congregations, the support of a middle-class backbone of farmers, shopkeepers, solicitors and ministers of religion until the First World War. The Local Government Act of 1888 had revolutionised local government, so Liberals took control from the landed gentry in the county councils, and a centuries-old domination disappeared with the creation of urban and district councils in 1894. A variety of newspapers and periodicals lent support – the only Tory paper in Wales was the *Western Mail*. In North Wales only 85 of the 260 councillors were not Liberals. In South Wales 215 of the 330 councillors were Liberals. Local politics reflected national politics in that Liberal councils worked for a degree of social equality based on belief in the harmony of interest between middle and working classes. As at national level, Liberal councils had no coherent economic or social policy and were far more in tune with rural than urban society. Local Liberal Associations were reluctant to endorse working men, even leaders, as Parliamentary candidates. Yet the Labour movement, in the first decade of the twentieth century, continued to acquiesce in endorsing Liberal politics. Miners' leaders like Tom Richards or William Abraham shared a belief in class harmony, and Keir Hardie himself identified with Liberal causes like disestablishment and land reform. Welsh Liberalism in the Commons was less influential when the Liberals were in power after 1906 than it had been in the 1880s and 1890s, largely due to the fact that it no longer held the balance of power, and that leading figures such as Lloyd George and Herbert Lewis were in the Government. But the popular base seemed secure. In the two elections of 1910 Liberals were returned for all but two or three Welsh seats and Lloyd George was a Welsh hero as he attacked landlords through his People's Budget. Welsh issues were also less central now. The major social problem traditionally had been landlord exploitation of tenants economically and politically. The countryside was now relatively more prosperous and political exploitation could no longer occur. The Welsh Sunday Closing Act took the sting out of temperance reform agitation in 1881 and the Welsh revolt over the 1902 Education Act fizzled out with the return of a Liberal Government in 1906, though three Liberal bills to modify the system foundered on House of Lords opposition. It soon became apparent that the financial problems of the Anglican Church in providing schools had only been alleviated by the 1902 Act and gradually they transferred many of their schools to local authorities. By 1913 there were twice as many state provided schools as non-provided schools in Wales.

The Liberal Government viewed the traditionally paramount issue of Welsh disestablishment with no great enthusiasm, partly because until the Parliament Act the Lords could veto any bill. Disestablishment did become law in 1914 under the provisions of the Parliament Act and, although this did not engender the rapture which it would have done twenty years previously, it was a remarkable achievement.

The rise of Labour

There was no rupture between Liberal and Labour parties in Wales before 1914 but it was obvious that there was an increasingly influential new force in Welsh politics. The Labour Party grew in influence in industrial Wales, especially in the South Wales coalfield, with the Liberal Party indifferent to specifically working-class concerns. On many issues such as education and, up to a point, labour relations, a consensus approach made sense. Within this consensus, Lib.–Lab. approach, Lloyd George's New Liberal measures – on unemployment, and health insurance – appealed widely in Wales, though he derived his inspiration from Germany, not from his native land. It became obvious after the 1906 election, however, that the mould of Lib.–Labism was breaking. Keir Hardie, M.P. for Merthyr, strongly advocated divorce from the Liberals. Branches of the Labour Party were established in the industrial areas of North and South Wales. After 1908 miners' M.P.s joined the Labour Party in the House of Commons. There were more militant miners' leaders in the South Wales coalfield – Vernon Hartshorn and Charles Stanton. Both of these stood at general elections and Labour candidates stood at local elections. Nonetheless, there was still enormous working-class loyalty to the Liberal Party. Labour was not electorally very successful and its organisation was rudimentary. But there was, formally, a divorce between the parties, which derived much of its rationale from endemic problems in industrial relations. The dispute in the Penrhyn quarry demonstrated the political complexities of such confrontation but it had many of the elements of a socialist dispute. In 1910 the Tonypandy riots in South Wales indicated beyond doubt that the consensus had broken down. There had always been conflict in the coal industry, and the sliding scale for determination of wages produced frequent wage reductions and consequent bitterness. The miners eventually won an eight-hour day, to operate from 1909, but the issue of a minimum wage was still unresolved. It became periodically apparent that not enough of the wealth of coalowners like D. A. Thomas and Sir William Lewis was spent on safety. In 1913, 439 men died in the worst-ever mining disaster, the explosion at Senghennydd colliery, an unforgettable reminder of the human sacrifice involved in the industry.

In 1910 miners refused the rates to be paid at a seam at the Naval Colliery, Penygraig and they were locked out. By October all the Cambrian Collieries' miners, 12,000, were out on strike. By November 30,000 miners were out. The employers brought in blacklegs, there were riots between police and strikers and a miner died from a fractured skull. Winston Churchill, the Home Secretary, authorised the sending in of troops and they remained in Pontypridd for weeks. The strike continued until August 1911. At the same time the class war was starkly underlined by the national railway strike. In Llanelli troops shot and killed two railway workers.

In 1909 the Marxist, Noah Ablett, an orator and pamphleteer of great ability, founded the Plebs League in the Rhondda, committed to the overthrow of capitalism by direct action. Ablett and other militants injected a new steel into the South Wales Miners' Federation. They also set up their own unofficial reform committee in 1911 and from this committee came *The Miners' Next Step* in 1912. It called for a seven-hour working day and an 8-shilling per day minimum wage, as well as workers' control of the mines, to be achieved by militancy, strikes and industrial action.

Not all militants supported the syndicalism advocated in this influential pamphlet and even in the South Wales coalfield there was strong support for the gradualist approach. But the climate of industrial relations was changing. Influential Welshmen of the old Liberal school tried to reverse this trend to confrontation politics. Most notable of them was Thomas Jones, one of the most successful of Welsh bureaucrats, secretary to the National Insurance Commission before he moved to the Cabinet secretariat in 1916. In alliance with M.P.s like David Davies of Llandinam and fellow bureaucrats such as Percy Watkins he campaigned for moderate trade unionism and consensus politics – a 'respectable' working class. He founded *Welsh Outlook* in 1914 and, later, Coleg Harlech to propagate these ideas.

The First World War

When war broke out in 1914 it was generally popular. It was strongly supported by the Liberals and by some of the most militant of the miners' leaders, by preachers and intellectuals. Recruitment was proportionately higher in Wales than in England or Scotland. Pacifists across Britain were badly treated and the few in Wales who stood out against the war were no exception. They opposed popular sentiment and a long tradition of Welsh loyalty to Britain and her wars. Liberal opposition to the Boer War, as opposed to Lloyd George's personal opposition, had come only in its latter stages. During the First World War Welsh jingoism was as extreme as any. Hermann Ethé, a professor at Aberystwyth, was hounded because of his German nationality. George Maitland Lloyd Davies and Morgan Jones, the future Caerphilly M.P., were imprisoned. As the slaughter increased and the incompetence of the generals became more obvious so opposition to the war built up, but only on a small scale, and it was of cultural rather than political significance. There were some crises of conscience among nonconformists and Liberals over conscription but, in general, support for the war and Lloyd George, after he became Prime Minister in 1916, was wholehearted. Lloyd George himself was surrounded by prominent Welsh Liberals in Government. Not only individual Welshmen but Welsh Liberalism seemed particularly influential at this stage, with disestablishment achieved, the great landed estates breaking up and landed influence in political life eroded beyond recognition.

The war saw fundamental changes in Welsh politics, hastening trends already apparent. Liberal causes had been won but there were no new ones on the agenda, particularly in terms of industrial problems. Total war meant state intervention on an unprecedented scale, there was public control of mines – of particular significance to Wales – and railways, and an increasing dependence on workers in industry which was reflected in a rise in real wages in some industries. Trade union membership doubled between 1914 and

1929, and the Labour party assumed growing importance as labour played such a vital part in the war effort. Workers and Government realised the power which resulted for workers. The miners won wage increases and the South Wales Miners' Federation became more militant. The Miners' Federation of Great Britain embraced a policy of nationalisation of the mines. Some of the miners' militancy in South Wales was channelled into politics through the Labour Party. The Labour Party, in South and North Wales, reflected the increasing class consciousness of industrial workers. There were constituency parties and full-time agents, and during the war the party became a political force.

At the end of the war Lloyd George called an election – the Coupon election of 1918 – in which endorsed candidates, Liberal and Conservative, and a few Labour supporters, were given letters of approval. Lloyd George's supporters won an overwhelming victory. In Wales they won twenty-five of the thirty-six Welsh seats, including that of Aberdare with the Patriotic Labour candidate. Charles Stanton. Far more significant was that Labour won ten seats and 30.8 per cent of votes. Nationally, the Liberal Party was now split between followers of Asquith and supporters of Lloyd George and had no real social policy with which to answer the Labour challenge. Only in the late 1920s did Lloyd George advocate policies to meet the grim economic problems then confronting Wales and the wider nation, by which time it was too late. Neither did Welsh Liberalism have a nationalist policy for which to work now that the great battles of the nineteenth century had been won.

Politics in the inter-war years

The discontinuity between the old and the new Welsh situation was emphasised at the end of the war by disestablishment and by the break-up of the Welsh landed estates. Between 1918 and 1922 a quarter of Welsh land was sold. In Glamorgan an estate originating in Tudor times, that of Cefn Mabli, was sold for over a quarter of a million pounds and the house was turned into an isolation hospital. The Baron Hill estate in Anglesey went for over £200,000. Former tenants bought small freeholds but mortgaged themselves up to the hilt in order to do so.

Political discontinuity was confirmed in the 1922 election when

Labour successfully challenged the Liberals. Labour won Llanelli, Aberavon – where Ramsay MacDonald became M.P. – Swansea East, Neath, Aberdare and Merthyr in South Wales, and Wrexham and Caernarfonshire in North Wales. Altogether, Labour returned eighteen M.P.s, Conservatives six, Liberals eleven. Labour seats were rooted in industrial areas, Tory seats in the commercial south-east and Liberal hegemony was now generally restricted to the rural areas. The growth of Labour influence was remarkable. It was accompanied by disillusionment in Liberal ranks. This had been apparent during the war; it was reinforced by growing unease with Lloyd George's coalition Government. At least in the early days of this Government the alliance with the Conservative Party did not prevent some progressive reforms in housing and in education – a Housing and Town Planning Act in 1919 and reforms in teachers' pay and pensions with the Burnham committees. But there was considerable Liberal disquiet over the deployment of the Black and Tans to coerce Ireland. Soon, boom slid into slump so that, after 1920, Liberal disquiet became more pronounced. The Welsh Liberals who opposed the Government – most supported Lloyd George – formed a Welsh Liberal Federation in 1921 and there was a bitter election in Cardiganshire in 1921 when there were two Liberal candidates. Disillusionment was evident, too, in local Liberal associations whose efficient organisation was essential for electoral success.

With Lloyd George's fall from power, and Labour success in 1922, it was apparent that in industrial Wales the future lay with the Labour Party and the days of Liberal monopoly were past. Labour won twenty seats in the 1923 election, sixteen in the 1924 election after the scare of the forged Zinoviev letter. In 1924 the Conservatives won only two fewer seats than the Liberals. The Liberals won only eleven seats – all in rural Wales. This represented an immensely important change in Welsh politics. Although Labour in Government did not attempt to implement revolutionary policies – and would not have done even if it had enjoyed an absolute majority – its base in industrial Wales was very different from that of traditional Liberal radicalism. The whole ambience of working-class politics was different, with syndicalism in the Rhondda valleys and militancy in the coalfield. S. O. Davies, Arthur Cook and Arthur Horner were Marxist miners' leaders. Miners soon came to realise the depths of the Depression which had hit the industry. They realised how they had been outmanoeuvred over the Sankey Commission of 1919 which had recommended public ownership of the mines. There was resentment at callous management attitudes over constant tragedy in the mines. Even when there was no major disaster there was a steady death and injury toll. Miners accepted the dangers and were themselves responsible for circumventing safety procedures sometimes. But this did not alleviate the sense of injustice against the owners who, at Powell Dyffryn, for example, tried to cut across the traditional miners' early leaving to attend a fellow miner's funeral. Owners and colliery officials also got off lightly in court whatever breaches of mine safety they had allowed. They were also adept at delaying compensation payments.

The grievances expressed in the South Wales coalfield were channelled more effectively than before through an effective working-class education programme. The railwaymen and the miners sponsored tutorial classes through their unions. Men like Ness Edwards, future M.P. for Caerphilly, and James Griffiths, future M.P. for Llanelli and member of Labour cabinets, were educated at the Central Labour College in London which stayed in existence until 1928. From 1919 to 1921 Aneurin Bevan was a student there.

The dominant issues in Welsh politics in the 1920s had far more to do with Labour issues than those traditionally associated with Liberalism – the miners' strike of 1921 and the 1926 General Strike, for example. Unemployment, depression and industrial relations were the foci of attention. Neither Home Rule for Wales, nor more limited devolution had such appeal for the parties, and did not provoke much feeling in Wales. Lloyd George offered token support for various devolutionary schemes but the Speaker's Conference of 1920, which recommended either local parliaments or regional grand councils, did not arouse much interest. There was pressure for the establishment of a National Council for Education for Wales but it was sporadic. In 1922 a Government of Wales bill was presented in the Commons but did not get past its first reading. The only devolutionary measures of any note were the establishment of the Welsh Board of Health in 1919 and a Welsh Department at the Ministry of Agriculture and Fisheries, but the real authority exercised was as slight as that wielded by the Welsh Department of the Board of Education.

Whitehall's tentacles stretched as far and gripped as firmly as ever. Bureaucracies centred in Bristol or Liverpool emphasised the demarcation between north and south rather more than devolutionary measures emphasised unity.

The nationalist vacuum was filled politically by the Welsh Nationalist Party, *Plaid Genedlaethol Cymru*, created in 1925 by the Revd Lewis Valentine, Moses Gruffydd, H. R. Jones, Fred Jones, D. J. Williams and Saunders Lewis. The last-named was the most distinguished, as academic and writer. The founders represented a wide spectrum of views, from traditional nonconformist radicalism to Saunders Lewis's conception of Wales as part of a long-lost medieval European civilisation. This variety of viewpoints produced clashes. For example W. J. Gruffydd, another of Wales's foremost academics, very sympathetic to Welsh nationalism, attacked Saunders Lewis and Ambrose Bebb for their anti-democratic views derived, he alleged, from French Catholic right-wing ideas. Certainly, there was an authoritarian strand in Welsh nationalism and this derived from Anglican opinion in the nineteenth century. The Anglican response to the propaganda battle with nonconformity in nineteenth-century Wales, which it comprehensively lost, was that, far from being a classless society, the Welsh Liberal radical middle class exploited the working class for its own ends in the cause of anti-landlordism and disestablishment. They saw the democracy and industrialisation which made this possible as evils which undermined traditional social authority as it had been exercised for centuries. Anglican opinion saw state intervention, especially in education, as consolidating this erosion of traditional social sanctions. Traditional authority had to be reasserted in Wales. This could not be done by the state, since it represented a new and dangerous trend towards centralisation, it could not come from the middle class, who embraced radical Liberalism and nonconformity. Industrial Wales was a new society with new values. Leadership, on this theory, could only come from a cultivated literary elite within rural Wales. Such an endorsement of authoritarianism was best reflected in Saunders Lewis, and naturally offended traditional radical nonconformists within the party. What *Plaid* members did agree on was the prime importance of preserving the Welsh language but the party's influence in the pre-1939 period was very limited.

Welsh influence in British politics was more limited than it had been for decades. From 1922 to 1929 a Conservative administration was in power except for a short-lived Labour administration in 1924. Government policies were often positively detrimental to a Wales caught in the grip of economic blight. Treasury orthodoxy meant a rigid policy of balanced budgets and low public expenditure which ensured that there would be no alleviation. Winston Churchill's decision to return to the Gold Standard in 1925 made matters worse. There were alternatives proposed, particularly after 1929, when Lloyd George's pamphlets advocated imaginative programmes of public expenditure to bring down unemployment. The Government was unmoved. They considered other solutions, such as wholesale movements of miners to other parts of Britain.

The Conservative Government was more concerned about the 1926 General Strike in which Labour-dominated South Wales played a significant part. Labour achieved an ever-increasing share of the vote in General Elections – up to 43.9 per cent in 1929. The largest county councils, Glamorgan and Monmouthshire, were Labour. But political radicalism found no outlet at national level in the inter-war period. Labour formed a Government only for a short time in 1924 and again in 1929 until overwhelmed by financial crisis in 1931. Up to 1920 Welsh industrial society was thriving. From 1920 on it was a different story. Industrial Wales was decimated. The youngest and fittest went into permanent exile in England. Government policy towards the unemployed was demeaning. In 1929 Boards of Guardians could no longer cope with the relief of poverty and were replaced by Public Assistance Boards formed by local authorities. In 1931 there was a 10 per cent cut in benefit and means testing of families. In 1934 Neville Chamberlain decided to standardise payments to curtail the 'excesses' of Labour-controlled authorities in Wales and elsewhere who had put a liberal interpretation on the amount of benefit they were able to pay. The result was a direct action protest when the Unemployment Assistance Office in Merthyr was raided and its records burned. This action actually changed the Government's plan. In the 1930s the misery of the mining communities seemed permanent. It was calculated in 1934 that 80 per cent of children in Monmouthshire were physically deprived in some way. Twenty per cent of miners had been out of work for over four years in 1934. School pupils were encouraged to look to England for employment. Tom Jones suggested sardonically that everyone should be evacuated and Wales turned into an industrial museum. Yet the industrial communities preserved their dignity along with their choirs and institutes. They participated in hunger marches and once, over Chamberlain's unemployment assistance plans, they defeated the Government.

The politics of protest were hardly less rewarding than conventional party politics. The 1926 General Strike seemed to indicate the height of the class struggle. It followed the defeat of the miners in the 1921 strike, with wage cuts of up to 75 per cent. Between 1921 and 1936, 241 mines were closed. The miners in the anthracite areas were defeated in 1924 in a strike which involved imprisonment for rioters and victimisation of strikers. In 1926 the miners were already bitter over wage cuts, defeats and assaults on traditional working practices. The Government refused to go on subsidising the coal industry. Only the miners stayed solid when the leaders of the other unions capitulated. The General Strike lasted for nine days; the miners stayed out for months until starved into submission. When the strike was called off on 3 May 1926 the rank and file of the other unions in Wales were resentful of their leaders, but only the miners did not return to work. It was a traumatic period of near starvation, educational opportunities blighted, victimisation, blacklegging and abject poverty. Community support was outstanding and soup kitchens and concerts were organised to provide some money. In the end, there was disillusionment as the men were forced to surrender. The South Wales Miners' Federation lost money and much support. An 'industrial union' was founded – in fact a company union – and some owners insisted on their employees joining it. The influence of advocates of direct action had been undermined and advocates of a gradualist approach – James Griffiths, Arthur Jenkins – were more influential.

Labour remained the dominant political force in Wales throughout the 1920s despite something of a Liberal revival in the latter part of the decade. Lloyd George had widespread popular support and Welsh Liberal members provided a high proportion of Liberal representation in the Commons – ten of the forty members in 1924, for example. Lloyd George's programme for meeting unemployment provided Liberals with a new programme, untrammelled by relics of nineteenth-century causes. Electorally, however, Labour domination was reflected in the polls in 1929. While the Liberal share of the vote increased to 33.5 per cent, the party suffered from the 'first past the post' system and lost three seats to Labour. The Labour Party also won six seats from the Conservatives, while the Liberals won three Conservative seats. The Labour Party had successfully projected a more moderate image after the episode of the Zinoviev letter in the 1924 election and after the General Strike. The party now rejected the radical programmes of the Independent Labour Party and Communist Party attempts to affiliate. The image of moderate constitutionalism prevailed in the 1929 election despite the efforts of the Conservative *Western Mail*. There was a hint of the former Lib.–Lab. persona about some Labour M.P.s in their chapel- and community-roots image as the Labour Party took over as the radical party of Wales. One who did not fit into old categories was Aneurin Bevan, elected for Ebbw Vale for the first time in 1929 and to become one of the Labour Party's most influential politicians as well as one of the finest orators of the century. Again in 1929 the Aberavon seat, once occupied by Ramsay MacDonald, was taken over by W. G. Cove, one of the youngest-ever presidents of the National Union of Teachers, one of the foremost champions of comprehensive education on grounds of social justice and unfortunate in not becoming Minister of Education in the Labour Government of 1945, perhaps because he did not get on with Clement Attlee.

Labour's gains in Wales were part of the wider success which brought the party to power in 1929 as a minority government. There were attempts at reform. In education, for example, there were abortive bills aimed at raising the school-leaving age to fifteen. The Coal Mines Act of July 1930 cut a half-hour from the working day, though the owners refused to implement the agreement in January, 1931. Generally Wales did no better; from late 1929 the depression in Wales got worse. If the 1920s had been bleak in Wales, the 1930s were disastrous. The pound collapsed in the summer of 1931. The Labour Government gave way to a National Government among bitter recriminations which split the Labour Party completely for a decade. In 1929 there had been 289 Labour M.P.s. In the 1931 election only forty-six Labour and five I.L.P. candidates were returned. Sixteen of Labour's M.P.s came from Welsh constituencies. Liberal Wales was split between supporters of three rival groups and was dead as a powerful political force.

The economic situation in Wales was desperate. Rigidly orthodox fiscal policies allowed for no programme of public works to help boost employment. Even the meagre targets of coal production set by the

1930 Coal Mines Act were not reached. The depression was worst in the heavy industry which formed the basis of the Welsh economy. In parts of Britain, particularly the south-east, the economy picked up after 1934 but in much of industrial Wales unemployment remained above 30 per cent. The bleakness of the situation emerged officially in the *Report on the Investigation into Industrial Conditions in Certain Depressed Areas* published in 1934. It revealed that over 45 per cent of the insured coal-miners were unemployed as were 40 per cent of iron and steel workers. The Government did react with some modest initiatives – a Special Areas (Development and Improvement) Act in 1934, a Special Areas Reconstruction Association in 1936. There was some financial incentive to attract industry to the depressed areas. The practical effects were limited. Economic improvement was confined mainly to Cardiff and Swansea until 1938 and 1939, when a trading estate opened in Treforest. In 1938 a new, up-to-date steel and tinplate works opened in Ebbw Vale after pressure from Lloyd George, Aneurin Bevan and other Welsh M.P.s resulted in Prime Minister Baldwin taking the initiative with steel-makers Richard Thomas.

Conventional political action produced nothing more. Direct action, particularly in the form of marches of unemployed people, merely testified to the spirit of the depressed areas. There were marches to Bristol and London against unemployment and the means test. Aneurin Bevan tried, briefly, to set up para-military anti-fascist groups but although some were established he soon distanced himself from them. In the North and South Wales coalfields the miners won modest wage increases in 1934 and 1935 despite the economic climate, but the signal victory came when the South Wales Miners' Federation defeated company unionism by 1935.

In the 1935 Parliamentary election the Welsh Labour Party won eighteen out of thirty-six seats. It was strongest, naturally, in the industrial constituencies of north and south but its influence also spread to rural areas such as Anglesey and Carmarthen. In local government the county and urban district councils in the industrial areas were solidly Labour. In rural Wales Liberal or Independent councils, reflecting the domination of the more middle-class vote, were the norm. The political division reflected different attitudes and policies. On social legislation – education, housing, health – it was the Labour-controlled authorities who were progressive in outlook and generous in spending. The result was that, despite grinding poverty, South Wales fared better in health, housing and education and this despite the poverty of the councils themselves. They were invariably low-rated and saw their income fall during the depression. Carmarthenshire, Glamorgan, parts of Monmouthshire and Wrexham provided free school meals, for example, while such provision was exceptional in most of North Wales. The move towards expanding secondary school places to be filled on merit was far more evident in Labour-controlled authorities. The Inquiry into the Anti-Tuberculosis Service in 1939 drew attention to the efforts made by local authorities in the industrial areas to combat poor housing and the deprivation of depression, while condemning Montgomeryshire, Merioneth and Anglesey Councils for complacency towards disease, insanitary conditions and bad housing.

The Second World War and its aftermath

What finally lifted Wales from depression – and its concomitant social stress – was the outbreak of the Second World War. There was general acceptance in Wales that it was a just war, and opposition was sporadic. Proportionately, there were more conscientious objectors in Wales than in England or Scotland and some cases were dealt with in a way reminiscent of the First World War. For example, Dr Iorwerth Peate was dismissed from his post at the National Museum. Up to 1944, sixty-seven conscientious objectors were imprisoned, but generally their treatment was far more enlightened than in the earlier war. The downfall of Neville Chamberlain in 1940, helped by lobbying from Liberals Clement Davies, particularly, and Megan Lloyd George, produced more identification of interest with a government which now included a powerful Labour element.

Such a total war inevitably produced analyses of how society should change when the war was won, and the focus of discussion was sharpened by the grim experiences of the previous twenty years. The Second World War counterparts of Lloyd George's Ministry of Reconstruction were the Beveridge Report and the Education Act of 1944, though Prime Minister Churchill could hardly have been more lukewarm about both. James Griffiths, M.P. for Llanelli, led Labour's criticism of Churchill for reacting unfavourably to Beveridge. Aneurin Bevan wanted full-blooded socialism and public ownership and was far more concerned with centralised planning than with any Welsh dimension. James Griffiths, with some support, was more sympathetic to specifically Welsh concerns, but generally there was no movement for devolution. Welsh M.P.s were more committed to preserving those wartime improvements which had stemmed from the establishment of ordnance factories in Bridgend, Hirwaun, Glascoed, Pembrey and Marchwiel near Wrexham. The Bridgend factory alone employed 37,000. In 1945 a Distribution of Industry Act empowered the Board of Trade to direct firms to set up in Wales. The war transformed the coal industry. It now reverted to playing a vital part in the country's economy and, for the first time since 1920, miners had strong bargaining power. As a result they won a national minimum wage in 1944, for example. The parameters of a potential new Wales arose from increased industrial demand, unprecedented state intervention, a demand for social justice, and the programme of a new national welfare scheme. Britain endorsed these notions in 1945 in an election which saw Labour win 58.5 per cent of the vote and twenty-five seats in Wales. Though Liberals managed to win seven seats this was no longer of much political consequence. *Plaid Cymru* fought eight seats but lost seven deposits. *Plaid's* history had not been auspicious. It had come to prominence over the incident in Llŷn, Caernarfonshire, when three of its leaders, including Saunders Lewis, had symbolically burned down part of an R.A.F. bombing school. The government handled the case ineptly in transferring it to the Old Bailey, so provoking an outcry among numerous shades of Welsh opinion at the accusation that a Welsh jury would not return an objective verdict. The result was a boost to the party's membership. But during the Second World War, *Plaid* encouraged conscientious objection, a highly unpopular move, and the party's performance in the 1945 election was not impressive. The Conservatives held four Welsh seats in 1945.

Post-war politics

Labour, in power from 1945 to 1951, established the welfare state, nationalised the coal and steel industries which were still of such importance and helped start a change in the Welsh economic base. In the fifties, and particularly the sixties, there was affluence. New industries came in, old ones were modernised. Welshmen were in government. James Griffiths was Colonial Secretary in Attlee's administration, Ness Edwards was Postmaster General and Aneurin Bevan was one of the most prominent members of the cabinet until he resigned over National Health Service charges in 1951. Despite Labour's fluctuating fortunes – out of power for thirteen years following the 1951 election – Wales was Labour-dominated. The Party won twenty-seven seats in the 1951 election. In 1955 Labour held on to these seats and in 1959 only lost the marginal Swansea West seat from this number. When Labour returned to power in 1964 Welsh members were once again influential in government. James Callaghan was Chancellor of the Exchequer, John Morris was at the Ministry of Power, Cledwyn Hughes at the Commonwealth Office and James Griffiths the first Secretary of State for Wales. In the 1966 election Labour's triumph in Wales was complete. Out of the thirty-six Welsh seats Labour won thirty-two.

Welsh nationalism had by now become a political reality, after having made very little headway in the inter-war period. Even after the Second World War, when Irish and even Scottish nationalism were making progress, there seemed little hope for *Plaid Cymru*. They made no great impact in the 1945 election, although Wynne Samuel polled 20 per cent of the vote in the 1946 Aberdare by-election. Aneurin Bevan, Wales's most influential M.P., was implacably opposed to devolution in any form, though there were Labour members, such as James Griffiths, who were far more sympathetic. In 1948 the Government set up an Advisory Council for Wales, though it did not have wide responsibilities. The Conservative Party was also averse to devolutionary measures yet, remarkably, went further than Labour. The Conservative Government which came to office in 1951 appointed a minister for Welsh Affairs. Presumably because there were so few Welshmen with the right background they appointed a Scotsman, Sir David Maxwell-Fyfe, though a Welsh-speaking Welshman, Gwilym Lloyd George took over in 1954, to be succeeded three years later by one of the less charismatic Tories, Henry Brooke. In 1961 the Ministry was entrusted to Sir Keith Joseph and he set up the Hughes–Parry committee to examine the status of the Welsh language in law and government.

In the 1950s and 1960s industry was prosperous to an extent inconceivable during the inter-war years, and was being restructured. However, from 1958 there was a run-down of one of the staple industries, the coal industry, with as little consultation as there would have been in the days of private ownership. Wales shared generally in the 'never had it so good' years, but discontent remained at many levels. *Plaid Cymru*, of course, stood for Home Rule. A 'Parliament for Wales' campaign, begun in 1949, attracted some support from all parties, but there were organisational weaknesses and inadequate popular support so the movement broke up. *Plaid Cymru* made some electoral headway, polling over 10 per cent of votes cast in the 1959 election but seventeen of their twenty candidates still lost their deposits.

There were issues in the late 1950s which focussed attention within and outside Wales. The community of Tryweryn was wiped out as the valley was flooded to provide Liverpool's water. This led to nationalist direct action. As the danger to the survival of the Welsh language became ever more apparent the Welsh schools movement became established, and progressed, in the anglicised counties of Glamorgan and Monmouthshire. In 1962 the language issue hit the headlines with Saunders Lewis's B.B.C. radio lecture 'Tynged yr Iaith' ('Fate of the Language'). He argued that the Welsh language was more important than self government and it might be that direct action was required to preserve it. As a result The Welsh Language Society, *Cymdeithas yr Iaith Gymraeg*, was created in 1962. Direct action increased during the 1960s and it brought results. Government offices, nationalised industries, universities, even, in the end, British Rail, adopted bilingual policies. In 1967 a Welsh Language Act gave Welsh parity of official status with English. The most obvious manifestation of direct action was green paint liberally daubed on road signs and *Plaid Cymru* was galled to see the harm done to its constitutional image. For a time in the 1960s there was a more sinister fringe movement, the Free Wales Army, which posed a threat to security when the investiture was staged in Caernarfon castle in 1969.

Plaid Cymru achieved less success through the polls. In neither the 1964 nor the 1966 election was there any sign of a breakthrough. Shortly afterwards there was a by-election in Carmarthenshire. The party's immensely popular president, Gwynfor Evans, was elected amid scenes of wild popular enthusiasm. This was a remarkable victory and served to indicate, at last, that *Plaid* could break the deadlock of the party system. In by-elections in Rhondda West and in Caerphilly in 1967 and 1968 *Plaid Cymru* produced incredible 30 per cent and 40 per cent swings. This was in the industrial, Labour heartland, not in rural fastnesses. For thirteen years, until the devolution referendum, *Plaid Cymru* remained an important political force in Wales.

It was difficult to keep the euphoria of 1966–8 going and harder to translate a substantial popular vote into seats. *Plaid* still continued to be supported by many sections of the electorate. It was strong traditionally in rural Wales, with nonconformist support, especially that of ministers of religion, and backing from a professional middle class, especially teachers and lecturers. Young people tended to be enthusiastic and vociferous in support. In the 1960s *Plaid* broadened its appeal to the predominantly English-speaking industrial south-east and this seemed an important breakthrough.

Devolution

The Labour Government had given Wales a Secretary of State in 1964 and, in the second half of the 1960s, had to face the fact that, if the *Plaid* bandwagon continued, none of the seemingly impregnable Labour seats in Wales was safe. The Welsh Office had some power and some successes though these could not disguise the continuing Welsh dependence on Whitehall. Then, from the mid 1960s, the idea of an elected Welsh Council found more favour. With Cledwyn Hughes at the Welsh Office in the Labour Government after 1966 there was progress. He mooted the idea of a council with legislative powers in a White Paper but he faced powerful opposition. George Thomas was at the Welsh Office from 1968 and he was far less sympathetic towards devolutionary plans, but local government reform was under discussion in Britain generally with the Redcliffe–Maud Report of 1969. The result was a royal commission on the constitution set up in 1969, with one of its major tasks to consider devolutionary options for Wales and Scotland.

It is difficult to know how seriously the Labour Government took the Crowther/Kilbrandon Commission. In any case Labour were replaced in government by the Conservatives after the 1970 election, an election in which *Plaid Cymru*'s performance was disappointing. They fought all thirty-seven seats but won none, even though they obtained 11.5 per cent of the vote. Labour won twenty-seven seats, but lost four seats to the Tories. Welsh issues were now less important; the Secretary of State for Wales, though a Welshman, sat for Hendon South.

In 1973 the *Kilbrandon Report* was published and devolution became an important political issue because a majority of the commission recommended an elected assembly for Wales, though not with legislative powers. Nearly half the members of the commission wanted far more than this – an assembly with wide powers of taxation and a whole spectrum of administrative responsibilities. In 1974 Labour were returned to power, though without an overall majority. The Welsh result in 1974 made it virtually certain that the government would take careful note of Kilbrandon since, although they won twenty-four seats, they captured less than half the vote for the first time since before 1945. The Conservatives did well, winning eight seats, Labour lost Cardiganshire to the Liberals and, of most immediate significance, *Plaid Cymru* won two seats from Labour in rural, Welsh-speaking Wales – Caernarfon with Dafydd Wigley and Merioneth with Dafydd Elis Thomas. Gwynfor Evans failed by three votes to win back Carmarthen for *Plaid Cymru*. The party had tried to widen its appeal since the 1960s by developing coherent economic policies and by trying to demonstrate that it was a party for all Welsh people rather than specific interests. This, of course, meant some difficulty over the language issue which, for many members, was the most important one. It also came up against the lack of widespread support in Wales for even limited political independence. Still, with two members in Parliament after 1974 the party was able to keep Welsh issues alive. More important, with Labour in a minority in the Commons, the attitudes of small parties such as the Scottish or Welsh Nationalists was a matter of major significance for the Government. In September, 1974, the White Paper, *Democracy and Devolution*, postulated elected assemblies for Scotland and Wales. In October 1974 *Plaid Cymru* retained its two seats and added Carmarthen, which Gwynfor Evans won back.

Despite strong opposition from many Welsh Labour M.P.s – Neil Kinnock, Donald Anderson, Leo Abse, for example – the Government had little choice but to accept that a head of steam had built up over the devolution issue. The introduction of legislation was fraught with difficulties. In December 1976, the devolution bill passed its second reading but the Government had been forced to concede referenda. It was not until the end of July, 1978 that what had now become two devolution bills, one for Scotland, one for Wales, passed their various stages. There was now at least the possibility of an elected assembly for Wales, with limited powers, certainly, but of great symbolic significance. The referendum took place eight months later, on 1 March 1979. It had been preceded by acrimonious debate across party lines. Officially, the Labour and Liberal parties, as well as *Plaid Cymru*, who were prepared to accept half a loaf, were in favour of devolution. The Welsh Conservatives were hostile. In the event Labour endorsement of devolution made little impact, far less than that made by loquacious South Wales opponents. There was public dread of more reorganisation following local government changes in 1973, which had replaced Welsh counties in existence at least since the Acts of Union with far larger units. This had proved very expensive without being notably efficient. Fears reminiscent of the 1890s cropped up again as Leo Abse conjured up pictures of an assembly dominated by Welsh-speakers from rural areas. This was a highly effective, if entirely irrational, analysis.

The referendum was a disaster for the pro-devolutionists. 243,048 voted for an assembly, 956,330 against. There was a majority against the assembly in every Welsh county, even in Gwynedd. The Scottish result was far more of an embarrassment to the Prime Minister, James Callaghan, and was instrumental in precipitating an election in May 1979. It produced a Tory Government and a swing to the Tories in Wales. Labour held twenty-one seats, the Tories eleven. Two Welsh Nationalists held their seats but Gwynfor Evans lost Carmarthen and the *Plaid* share of the overall vote, which fell to 7.6 per cent, reflected the impact of the referendum. Wales was now far less Labour-dominated and the only nationalist cause which prospered was that over the Welsh television channel when, faced with Gwynfor Evans's threat to starve himself to death, the Government decided to honour its election pledge after all and provide a fourth television channel mainly in Welsh for Wales.

Despite the devolution referendum, Welshness, that sense of difference from other countries in Britain, that sense of shared experience, of a common heritage, of history, of a communal emotion, of commitment to the concept of Wales, remained, varying in intensity from individual to individual, from community to community. Its political configuration was certainly changed by the devolution referendum, both within the conventional party structure and outside, but it was still a reality.

10

RELIGION AND EDUCATION

Nonconformity and Anglicanism

The eighteenth century saw a regeneration of religious activity in Wales and it is invariably associated with the Methodist Revival. This emphasis on Methodism does a disservice both to the many conscientious, concerned Anglican clergy and to Dissent. Baptists and Independents were as buoyant elements in religious activity as Methodists, and were heirs to a long-standing radical tradition which led them to question the institutionalised hierarchies of Anglicanism and, by implication, those of a wider society. Anglicanism was the religion of the landed class; Dissent and Methodism were increasingly taken up by lower orders, though Dissent had not always appealed to the labouring classes. By the end of the eighteenth century the social and religious cleavage was distinct in Wales, with Anglicanism representing continuity of the kind of society which the gentry desired because of their dominant position in it.

A transformation was beginning in Wales through industrialisation. New communities were created and grew so rapidly that they produced grave social tensions. The Established Church found it very difficult to meet this challenge, while nonconformity made headway. The social strains imposed on Welsh society in the eighteenth century, as landowners became increasingly divorced from the community through anglicisation in language and lifestyle, was now compounded by the dislocation caused by population movement on an unprecedented scale into communities with no amenities. Evangelical religion, with its emphasis on rebirth and the rewards of the next world, had an obvious appeal. Again, the social cleavage was evident, with ironmasters, like landlords, almost invariably Anglican, their workers nonconformist, if they belonged to a religious denomination at all. The growing middle class, too, tended towards

272

nonconformity. The linguistic divide was reinforced here, since Welsh was the language of nonconformity while that of the Established Church, certainly at the highest level, was English. The first Welsh-speaking bishop since the mid eighteenth century was appointed in 1870. Anglicanism was strongest in the most anglicised areas of Wales – Pembroke, Monmouth, Chepstow, Montgomery and Wrexham.

Between 1800 and 1851 the population of Wales nearly doubled. Places of worship grew in number from about 1,369 to 3,805. The Anglican rate of increase was 16 per cent, the nonconformist 51 per cent. Inevitably the 1851 census showed that Wales was a predominantly nonconformist nation. The religious census of 1851, the only one of its kind, provides invaluable information about the worshipping habits of the people of Wales. There are problems in interpreting the information because generally the figures provided by clergy and chapel officials seem to have been estimates rather than head counts and, above all, no attempt was made to number those who attended one service and those who attended two, or three. It is therefore impossible to be certain of the precise percentage of the total population who attended a place of worship. The census is, nevertheless, revealing. In terms of accommodation Wales was far more religious than England. In churches in Wales there was seating capacity for over 75 per cent of the population. Even the most densely populated counties – Glamorgan and Monmouthshire – were near this figure, while in Merioneth and Breconshire there were more seats than people. In England the Church of England was the largest denomination; in Wales it provided only one-third of the seating accommodation. In South Wales the Independents provided nearly one-quarter of the accommodation, in North Wales the Calvinistic Methodists nearly one-third. In a few areas the Anglican Church was on a par with nonconformity – Chepstow, Hay, Presteigne, for example. But, outside particularly anglicised areas such as the border, nonconformity was preponderant, often overwhelmingly so. It was less fragmented than in England. Calvinistic Methodists (in North Wales and Cardiganshire), Independents (from Pembrokeshire eastward to Bridgend) and Baptists (from Bridgend eastward, as well as Llanelli and Merthyr) predominated. Unitarians were strong in the Merthyr area and Quakers provided 2 per cent of seating capacity in South Wales. There were twenty-one Roman Catholic churches and thirty-one Mormon congregations. Nonconformity, then, was largely comprised of three denominations, and on census Sunday provided 87 per cent of the total number of worshippers at all services.

The problems of the Established Church

Part of the reason for nonconformity's hold lay in the shortcomings of the Church of England. Despite inroads made by Dissent in the eighteenth century, it was industrialisation which demonstrated the organisational weakness of the Established Church. Its organisation and financial system were centuries old, designed for a predominantly rural society. It could not adapt quickly to rapid growth in population nor its redistribution. The local administrative unit was the parish, and in Wales parishes were relatively poor. In upland Wales they were also very extensive in area – some of them over 50,000 acres. In upland Glamorgan and Monmouthshire, parts of which were to become so heavily industrialised, parishes were over 20,000 acres. Parishes could only be sub-divided by Act of Parliament. As a result, in the extreme case of Merthyr Tydfil, there was church accommodation for 2,500 for a population of over 50,000.

The diocese of Llandaff, covering the area most heavily industrialised in the nineteenth century, was poor, and this posed problems for clergy. Lay impropriation had diverted funds out of the Church since before the Reformation and in the 1830s over a fifth of Church income went into lay hands, £67,457 from a total rent revenue of £304,563. In the diocese of St David's seventy-five out of 115 benefices were not in ecclesiastical hands. Laymen often had the right to appoint clergy – in the diocese of Llandaff the bishop could appoint directly to only one parish. Normally these laymen were concerned to spend as little as possible on clerical stipends, and pluralism resulted. In a diocese like St Asaph, where the bishop did have much more control, he and some other senior clergy held numerous livings themselves and kept most of the revenue. While the bishop of Llandaff had to administer his diocese on £924 per annum the bishops of Bangor and St Asaph were far more affluent. Their dioceses were not faced with industrialisation on anything like the scale of South Wales. There, too, the traditional handicaps of pluralities and lay impropriation were less in evidence – four-fifths of tithes were in Church hands in Bangor diocese. Yet, where the

Church was financially most secure and social change least evident, it lost ground to nonconformity just as surely as in the industrialised south. Indeed the take-over pre-dated industrial development.

After 1832 the Ecclesiastical Commission of the Church of England was empowered to create new dioceses. None was created in Wales until 1920, after disestablishment. There was some attempt to meet the challenge of changing patterns of population with new churches after 1840, but there were no Welsh-speaking bishops until 1870. Still, slowly, rural church buildings were restored and new ones built in areas of growing population. In Cardiff, Swansea and Newport, and in the industrial valleys, first temporary buildings, then permanent ones, met part of the need. By 1910 about £3,330,000 had been spent in Wales on building work. Clergy numbers doubled between 1850 and 1910 – from 700 to 1,543. The worst of pluralism, non-residence and, more slowly, lay patronage were whittled away.

Many parish priests in the eighteenth century were younger sons of landowners, placed in livings by lay impropriators. Such priests were wholly unsuited to nineteenth-century circumstances and a new breed of clergy, more dynamic, often evangelical, emerged, with St David's College, Lampeter providing training. Reforms in personnel, training and administration led to a resurgence in the Anglican Church by the end of that century. It had reacted positively to the challenge posed by nonconformity and adapted to a new kind of society.

While the Established Church dealt with its pastoral problems adequately it remained the religious arm of the state, a political force, and this led to a more intractable problem in Wales in the second half of the century. Nonconformity, at this stage, was also a political force, in mesh with a burgeoning national Liberalism, and the campaign for disestablishment was a political, religious and national movement. It became a major political issue in the last quarter of the century, not only in Wales but in British Parliaments, when Liberal Governments were in power. In May 1870 a bill for disestablishment was introduced into the House of Commons, moved by Watkin Williams, M.P. for Denbigh district and an Anglican. By the time a disestablishment bill was introduced by Asquith in 1894 the accent was on the Anglican Church as an alien body in Wales, and a focus for national resentment. Liberal politicians had stressed the link between

Anglicanism and the class of landowners who were held to exploit
small farmers and had become divorced from community and nation.
The disestablishment campaign became linked with that against the
landlords.

The educational monopoly of church schools in so many parts of
rural Wales fuelled resentment. There was a greater sense of injustice
when nonconformist burials were forbidden in church precincts and
over the exaction of tithes from a poor population to maintain a
church to which it did not normally belong. Campaigners for
disestablishment were able to fasten on to abuses which had
characterised aspects of the work of the Established Church in the
eighteenth and early nineteenth centuries. With a little historical
juggling it was easy to identify the church as alien, nonconformity
as Welsh. Bishops like Basil Jones of St David's did not help their cause
– he said in 1886 that Wales was little more than a geographical
expression.

On the surface it would appear that the Established Church was
defeated overwhelmingly when the disestablishment bill pursued its
stately way through Parliament to become law in 1914, though not
to be implemented until 1918. Disestablishment was actually a
liberation for the Church in Wales. While, in retrospect, it is clear
that Welsh Liberal nonconformist radicalism, seemingly triumphant
in 1914, rested on shaky foundations, the Anglican Church had
revived considerably. At the time of the 1904 revival it was only
one-third as strong as the combined nonconformist denominations,
but this represented recovery. There were clergy of higher calibre
than previously, and the Church was more closely identified with the
people of Wales. It was nonconformity which was to suffer more from
increasing secularisation, general anglicisation and an increasing
emphasis on social Christianity. Politically, it was to suffer from the
gradual erosion of Liberal influence.

The nonconformist dynamic

This was a far cry from the situation which obtained towards the
end of the eighteenth century and during the nineteenth. The
dissenting sects – Independents, Baptists – had a long tradition in
Wales. Relatively few in numbers until the nineteenth century, they
exercised an influence out of proportion to their numerical support

because they tended to consist of solid citizens in their communities. Towards the end of the eighteenth century they were involved in discussion, printing and dissemination of radical ideas. Dissent was inevitably political because it had started from an alternative view of the relationship of church and state in the seventeenth century. Some Dissenters had left Britain to try to found new social organisations. Late in the eighteenth century some were caught up in the ferment of debate accompanying the Atlantic democratic revolution in America and France. There was constant doctrinal debate in Dissent. The Independents produced a strong growth of Unitarianism in their academies, a radical sect which became particularly strong in Merthyr. Methodism was far more disciplined in theology and politics than Dissent, reluctant in the eighteenth century to leave the Established Church and, in the first half of the nineteenth, to become embroiled in politics.

The Methodists' break with Anglicanism came in 1811 when they began to ordain their own ministers. For the rest of the nineteenth century Dissent and Methodism together met the spiritual needs of the mass of Welsh men and women. As we have seen, part of the reason lay in social and economic change, part in weaknesses inherent in the Established Church, but it would not have happened without the inner dynamism of nonconformity.

Compared with England the Welsh denominational structure, as we saw when considering the 1851 census, was a simple one. The three preponderant denominations shared a generally common theology of moderate Calvinism, a gradualist approach to improvement in social conditions and a commitment to involvement in the affairs of the community. Despite constant theological disputation there was a basic strength in this shared evangelical theological base. Welsh nonconformity therefore escaped damaging denominational splits and preserved a common religious and social commitment towards and, in a sense against, the world outside. This made possible a remarkable impact on society generally as it meshed with the needs of a society under strain, whether through the dramatic increase in population or the profound problems of the new industrial communities.

There was dynamism, too, in the way in which the nonconformist message was conveyed. The Independents, Baptists, Calvinistic Methodists and Wesleyans all produced their great preachers in the nineteenth century – Christmas Evans, John Elias, William Williams, Y Wern. Settled pastorates were not normal for much of the century so gifted orators were itinerant and often preached to vast congregations out-of-doors. The finest preachers, normally of humble origin and little formal education, possessed gifts of acting, oratory and inspiration which brought congregations to a high pitch of emotional excitement. Such preaching was a Sabbath highlight for those whose lives for the rest of the week were dominated by inordinately long hours of hard physical work. Not all nonconformist preaching was inspirational, but preachers of lesser ability were able to imitate the style and 'hwyl' of the famous. At times of revival the best orators dominated their communities. Local revivals punctuated the century and on three occasions, in 1840, 1859 and 1904, there were revivals which spread across large areas of Wales. They differed. The revival of 1859 was profoundly theological while that of 1904 was dominated by deeply felt emotion, often accompanied by remarkable scenes of large-scale conversions. The Evans Roberts revival of 1904–5 is said to have increased chapel membership by 90,000, leading to a total membership in 1906 of 549,000. Reinforcing revival, and part of the fabric of chapel life, were prayer meetings, Bible studies and singing festivals. For many, conversion in the 1904 revival was to prove permanent, but by this time the nature of nonconformity had changed in Wales. It now had an establishment, indeed even a hierarchy, of its own, and the respectable elements were rather suspicious of the fervour and emotional intensity accompanying this last widespread revival – yet it was from precisely this kind of regular renewal that nonconformity derived its strength. Developments in education, anglicisation and scientific theorising made this kind of message unlikely to ripple through Wales again.

The Sunday school was one of nonconformity's most important assets. It provided a basic education in reading the Bible for younger children and a more general forum for discussion for adults, and, in the latter aspect, nonconformity was unique. Incidentally, this literary education through the Bible was of immense significance in preserving standards in the Welsh language. Adults taught and learned in Welsh Sunday schools; they also participated in church government, as deacons or merely members of sovereign congregations in some cases. This was in strict contrast to the hierarchies of Anglicanism. Nonconformist government reflected far more closely the new social realities of the nineteenth century. Chapels in Wales were neither totally egalitarian nor classless. They had their own hierarchies, particularly that of the 'sêt fawr' or diaconate. It tended to be drawn from the middle-class and skilled working-class personnel who provided chapel leadership. Even so, the Independents and the Baptists practised direct democracy. Individual congregations built chapels, elected deacons, appointed a minister – and dispensed with him if they wished. Such democracy brought its own tensions. When ministers came to be permanently appointed rather than part-time they could suffer from disagreements among sectional interests in their congregations. The 'split' to found a new cause was common – indeed it was a feature of growth. But, with a leadership drawn from the people in the community, democratic government was one of the abiding strengths of nonconformity, especially since it was not to be found in political life until the 1880s.

For nonconformity there was strength in the printed word. Lewis Edwards founded the quarterly *Y Traethodydd* in 1845 and provided a forum for discussion of English and German theological and philosophical ideas, including those of Kant. From the 1860s Welsh theologians got to grips with the implications of Darwinism, more rigorous Biblical scholarship and scientific discovery. *Seren Gomer* (Baptist, founded 1814), *Y Dysgedydd* (Independent, founded 1821) and *Y Diwygiwr* (Independent, founded 1835) all provided a forum for religious issues.

Political discussion was muted. Any revolutionary Dissenting characteristics apparent at the end of the eighteenth century were eschewed. Dissent became more cautious, overtly political only when national events made this inevitable, as in 1868. Methodism was even more conservative, and therefore denominational journals were rarely strictly political. The language of debate was restrained, deferential, traditional, ready to compromise, and this moulded political attitudes. Still, there were constantly causes for which to fight – the 1847 education 'Blue Books', nonconformist disabilities, disestablishment – and, especially in the latter cases, these were cast inevitably in a political mould. Later in the nineteenth century, the alliance between Liberal politics and nonconformity was based on common ground over tithe, landlordism, the land question of the 1880s and education in church schools.

Such political participation followed after 1868 when nonconformist superiority could slowly be translated into effective political action. After the 1868 election there were sufficient numbers of evictions from agricultural holdings – forty-three in Cardiganshire, for example – to fuel a genuine sense of outrage at the injustice, and a highly effective propaganda campaign. The tithe question, particularly the distraint of goods from non-payers, produced similar outrage. Nonconformist Liberalism kept the disestablishment issue to the fore in the later nineteenth and early twentieth centuries, as we have seen.

Symptoms of decline

Not all the people of Wales had attended chapels in their heyday. In mid nineteenth-century Merthyr, for example, about half the inhabitants were outside the orbit of organised religion. But the whole population was affected to some extent by the social conscience bound up with nonconformity, the temperance movement, a popular culture moulded by notions of respectability. The chapel vestry in the nineteenth century, and into the twentieth, provided education, a respectable kind of entertainment, hymn-singing, meetings, discussion groups. The chapel provided instant social judgments on offenders against its puritan code, articulating the sanctions of a community on unfaithful husbands and wives – those who were found out – and illegitimate children.

In the later part of the nineteenth century the nature of nonconformity altered. One feature of this was that the language of religion, once almost wholly Welsh, changed to accommodate ever-increasing numbers of monoglot English people. English-language chapels were built in the towns and two of the major English-language denominations, the Independents (Congregationalists) and Baptists, became part of administrative unions covering England and Wales.

By the 1870s and 1880s there was a consciousness that the grip of nonconformity was not quite as firm. There were worries over the general adoption of full-time pastorates. The pioneering days, when chapels had sprouted regularly, had inevitably given way to more order. More affluence had produced nonconformist cathedrals, architecturally unimaginative but in a combination of styles – classical, gothic and baroque – with ornate interiors colourful in gilt and a variety of pastel shades mixed with the traditional discomfort of wooden pews, now varnished. The ministers here were pillars of the local community. In industrial Wales coalowners sponsored chapels, and the deacons who occupied the segregated area at the foot of the pulpit – the 'sêt fawr' (big seat) – provided an influential middle management. There was no dynamic to be derived from revival between 1859 and 1904. There was increased secularisation. Yet symptoms of decline were hardly apparent in numbers. Membership of nonconformist chapels – 434,000 before the Evan Roberts revival, 300,000 Welsh-language – rose to over half a million in the two years after 1904. There were preachers at work who became legendary – Herber Evans, Thomas Jones of Libanus, Morriston, and, perhaps the most outstanding, Elfed Lewis. We have seen that there were elements in nonconformity which were theologically and morally stultifying and part of its strength was derived from opposition to the Church of England, but its centrality, through a variety of activities, to the educational and cultural life of Wales was unmistakable.

The Evan Roberts revival, sharply declining in influence by 1908, was the last great manifestation of nonconformist fervour. For a few years it had spread like wildfire in a still prosperous South Wales, in communities experiencing large-scale immigration from rural Wales and from England. It may be that the revival tapped desires to restore the community values of Wales in a new environment. Its impact on chapel attendance, on adherence to temperance movements, in numbers of converts, was enormous.

If the fire had gone out of revival by 1908 it was the First World War which saw a marked change of direction in the story of organised religion as in so much else. Paradoxically the achievement of disestablishment in 1920 heralded a period of decline in nonconformity while the new Church in Wales proved more effective than its predecessor. The new church was financially secure, courtesy of a £1 million Treasury grant, skilful management of its finances and purchase of land and property. It reorganised, creating the diocese of Swansea and Brecon and the diocese of Monmouth. The Church withstood increasing secularisation better than the nonconformist denominations. The impact of nonconformity in Wales remained. Membership did not fall below 400,000 in the 1920s. Chapels were well attended, theological colleges attracted talented students, ministers of religion remained respected figures in the community. Sunday schools, *cymanfaoedd canu*, youth clubs, chapel Eisteddfodau flourished. But nonconformity had to change its stance. The message became more socially conscious, yet the image of respectability, tinged with hypocrisy, remained. Events of the twenties and thirties tended to blunt the edge of organised religion. The 1920 census revealed that the total number of Welsh speakers had declined for the first time. In 1931 only 37.2 per cent of the population were Welsh-speaking. By 1951 there had been another large decrease. Numbers of Welsh speakers declined most in the largest centres of population. This decrease particularly affected nonconformity which was predominantly Welsh-language. Unemployment in the 1920s and 1930s forced thousands to leave Wales – and they left from rural as well as industrial areas. The Depression hit the chapels hard. Membership in the Rhondda valleys fell by 70 per cent between 1921 and 1935. Morale and finances were affected. English cultural influences increasingly provided alternatives to chapel-dominated recreation. Newspapers, books, radio and cinema broke down linguistic divides and cultural isolation to an increasing degree.

After the Second World War – particularly from the 1950s – a new pattern of religious observance became apparent in Wales. The large chapels emptied, combined, closed. Membership dwindled, bills mounted, pastorates joined. The decline was fast now, with an ageing population supporting the old style of prayer meeting and Sunday school. Theological colleges in Carmarthen, Brecon and Swansea closed as few students were attracted. The mass culture of the 1960s overwhelmed sabbatarianism in its traditional chapel form. In rural, Welsh-speaking Wales the chapel and its associated cultural norms still exerted a strong hold but in the populous industrialised areas young people felt little affection for chapel values. There were public defeats for the chapel ethos. Cinemas in Wales opened on Sundays – from 1950 in Swansea, for example. Under the 1960 Licensing Act counties and county boroughs in Wales held referenda to decide on Sunday opening of public houses. The battle which followed was symbolic rather than practical since dedicated drinkers had always used clubs to circumvent the law, but the symbolic significance for nonconformity, with its traditions of sabbatarianism and temperance, was considerable. Results reflected a divide in Wales between those areas where nonconformity remained particularly strong – rural, Welsh-speaking Wales – and the industrial, most anglicised areas which voted for Sunday opening. Seven years later only Anglesey,

Caernarfonshire, Merioneth and Cardiganshire held out for the 'dry' Sunday. Organised religion in Wales differed less and less from that in England. Old animosities between Church in Wales and nonconformity diminished in increasing waves of ecumenicism. English-language Independents (Congregationalists) combined with the English Presbyterian Church in 1972 to form the United Reformed Church. In 1982 that United Reformed Church was prepared to vote for a covenant with the Established Church of England which would have involved the creation of nonconformist bishops had it been acceptable to the Anglicans. In that same year the leaders of all nonconformist denominations in Wales accepted an invitation to meet the Pope in Cardiff.

The Sunday schools

We saw in chapter six that Dissenting religion made a vital contribution to education in Wales in the eighteenth century through the academies which provided advanced education in a country largely devoid of it. The other outstanding educational movement of the century was the circulating school, and in its early days this movement, too, involved some nonconformist teachers and criticism of Griffith Jones for fostering Methodism. The outstanding contribution of nonconformity to mass popular education came with the Sunday schools. They capitalised on the lack of alternative provision, on the remarkable expansion of nonconformity in the nineteenth century and on elements of a pattern of education laid down for over a century in Wales, starting with the Welsh Trust. The circulating schools had provided the basic education in reading and catechising which was to characterise Sunday schools.

The pioneer of the Sunday school movement was Robert Raikes of Gloucester whose work led to the establishment of the inter-denominational Sunday School Society in London. Schools were established in Wales and, as the result of the efforts of an Independent minister, Edward Williams, there were Sunday schools in Holywell, Bala, Denbigh, Caernarfon and Llanfyllin by 1789.

A more unlikely pioneer of the Sunday school movement was Morgan John Rhys, best known for embracing radical causes in the wake of the Atlantic revolution. He backed the French Revolution, republican America and Negro emancipation. He founded a radical journal, *Y Cylchgrawn Cymreig*, which government repression killed off in 1793 and in it he pressed for Sunday schools and described how they should be organised. Rhys's radicalism so upset many of his contemporaries that his contribution to the Sunday school movement was, for long, unacknowledged.

Thomas Charles's early Sunday schools were appendages to the day schools to which he was at first devoted. Only gradually did the usefulness of Sunday schools, open for only a couple of hours a week, become obvious to him. In 1798, as a result of contacts which he established, the Sunday School Society in London set up a fund to provide for Welsh needs.

As always in Wales these needs were conservative, and the more pressing because of the poverty of the country, its scattered rural communities, its language and communication problems. The schools were held where congregations gathered – chapels, barns or farm-houses. Books were essential and here the support of the Sunday School Union was crucial – in 1801, 1,000 New Testaments in Welsh were provided. Teachers were unpaid, and required little more than the ability to read since this was the staple skill to be passed on. Catechising – question and answer on denominational texts – followed. It was repetitious rote-learning and produced prodigious feats of memory.

The heyday of the Sunday school came in the first seventy years or so of the nineteenth century, with much of the appeal stemming from social activities, thus reinforcing educational achievement. Recreation tended to centre round the chapel for masses of people and Sunday school parades, outings and teas punctuated the learning grind. Children also recited and sang what they had learned at Sunday services and quarterly meetings. The education available was a limited one, but it touched the lives of very many children for whom no other was available. Educational provision until after 1870 was voluntary, with only small injections of state aid, and methods of teaching were no more enlightened in day schools. The participation of adults in the Sunday schools was unique. At its best this provided opportunities for adult education unavailable in any other way, and it reinforced the hold of nonconformity. It was the Sunday school which was partly responsible for creating an appetite for periodical literature. The language of both was Welsh. It has been argued that leaders of opinion in Wales would have done greater service to the

Welsh language by pressing for day-school provision in Welsh in the second half of the nineteenth century, instead of accepting that sufficient safeguard existed through the Sunday schools, but this presupposes an awareness and an attitude generally absent when national aspirations were so bound up with an attempt to attain respectability on English terms, through the English language. The appeal of the Sunday school lay in its integration with nonconformity in a society with limited formal educational provision until well into the second half of the century. Its role in fostering Welsh literature and preserving the Welsh language was only evident later.

The graph of Sunday school activity rose with that of nonconformity, expanding in the early decades of the nineteenth century and not declining in numbers until the following century. Its teaching methods changed little, neither did the recreational activities associated with it. From the 1870s more order came into curricula as Sunday school committees and unions planned schemes of work and examinations, and supplied the material for the work. Up to 1870 they were central to educational provision generally, but after that, state provision catered for the three Rs, although Sunday schools continued to augment that education.

National, British and works schools

Religion and education were not only linked through the Sunday schools. The other organisations which provided much of the elementary education of the nineteenth century were religious bodies – the National Society founded by the Church of England and the British Society sponsored by the nonconformists. The National Society was far more successful in terms of numbers of schools and pupils – paradoxically, it might seem, given the religious affiliations of most Welsh people. By the middle of the century there were 375 National schools, fewer than fifty British schools. National Society schools received more than £13,700 in grant and were distributed all over Wales. The National Society for promoting the Education of the Poor in the Principles of the Established Church was founded in 1811 to establish schools on the monitorial principle. It was in direct line with the charity schools organisation of the previous century since the Society was sponsored by the S.P.C.K. Its aim was to establish a school in every parish in England and Wales, an ambitious

scheme which could be contemplated if only one master was required
to transmit information to monitors who would then instruct the
younger pupils. They were to educate the poor – private schools were
available for those who could afford them – and the object was to
inculcate the virtues of humility, honesty and hard work into the
lower orders, and to teach them to accept their station in life, so
guaranteeing social harmony. They appealed to philanthropists,
therefore, on grounds of religion, thrift and self-interest. The education provided was minimal, not only for reasons of expense but also
in order to ensure that pupils did not get ideas above their station.
Religious indoctrination was deemed essential to prevent pupils
succumbing to nonconformity. The first schools to be established in
Wales were two in Flintshire, built and maintained by Lord George
Kenyon. Thereafter, through the work of individuals and diocesan
committees, expansion was rapid – thirty-three schools were built or
affiliated between 1811 and 1817, with the main concentration in
North Wales. Landed gentry were generous in their donations of land
and financial gifts but the running of the schools proved expensive.
Some of the early schools were free but normally parents paid about
a penny a week for each child. This very limited income had to be
supplemented with local collections and gifts, but it still proved far
from easy to pay schoolmasters their small salaries – about £40 to
£50 per annum usually. Despite the problems, 146 schools, catering
for over 13,000 pupils, had been established in Wales by 1833. In
that year state money was channelled to the societies and expansion
was more rapid. But Wales was badly catered for. In 1833 some of
the big urban areas – among them Swansea and Cardiff – still had
no National school and there were only three British Society schools
in the whole of Wales. With the rapidly expanding population it
became ever clearer that the voluntary societies could not cope even
with providing a rudimentary and cheap education, which aimed at
teaching just the three Rs and paid teachers a pittance. It was a system
provided for the working class by those who counted themselves their
betters in every respect. Since there was no real incentive for the
recipients the small fee payable was a considerable deterrent. Some
schools gave instruction in Welsh but the lack of recognition of the
need to teach in Welsh merely added to the lack of impact. National
Society schools formed only a small proportion of church schools in
Wales – there were over 1,000 of these by mid-century. Altogether

there were nearly 1,400 schools in Wales linked to the Church of England, supplying most of the elementary education in a predominantly nonconformist society.

British Society schools, also run on monitorial lines, were inaugurated by Joseph Lancaster, a Quaker. Until the 1840s the effect of the non-sectarian British and Foreign Schools Society was minimal in Wales, though schools for boys and girls were established in Swansea in 1806 to provide the basic three Rs, together with religion and morality. Later, schools opened near Cardiff and at Neath, Wrexham, Tremadoc and Abergavenny, usually with the help of Quaker philanthropists, but only fifteen schools had been opened by 1820, another nine by 1833. There was strong opposition from many nonconformist leaders even when state money became available from 1833. The Independents, particularly, objected to state aid for education.

In 1843, anxious over the lack of schools in Wales, Hugh Owen, in his 'Letter to the Welsh People', proposed that a network of schools be set up across the country. The response was so positive that Owen asked the British Society to send agents to Wales. In North Wales thirty-one British Society schools were established in three years. In South Wales the Voluntaryists kept up their opposition to the use of government money, though not to British Society assistance, and they started a Normal school for training teachers in Brecon. It was obvious that such efforts, with or without state money, were inadequate. It was estimated in 1845 that over 40 per cent of men and nearly 70 per cent of women were unable to write their own names – though this did not mean necessarily that they were unable to read.

Some industrial philanthropy was channelled into another category of school – the industrial schools run by proprietors, with subventions from employees. By 1870, 134 works schools had been established, with the majority connected with ironworks or collieries. Largest, and catering for the widest age-range, was the institution founded by the Guests at Dowlais – providing for infants to adults.

'Brad Y Llyfrau Gleision'

The educational system as it developed in Wales – and in England – in the first half of the nineteenth century was haphazard and sporadic. Landed proprietors and industrialists were happy to see their offspring educated at the public schools. There was an insufficiently large middle class to support the old-established grammar schools which, as a result of social and economic changes, were now far from the main centres of population. There was a consciousness of the inadequacy of provision of both elementary and secondary education. What turned this into a central concern in the history of Wales was the investigation of the commissioners into the State of Education in Wales who produced their report – the Blue Books – in 1847. Welsh leaders across the denominations condemned the 'Treachery of the Blue Books' – *Brad y Llyfrau Gleision*. In fact the commissioners represented contemporary middle-class attitudes towards Wales. The Welsh language was deemed a handicap to progress, and the majority of the Welsh were to feel the same way for a century. The commissioners who investigated the Rebecca riots were the first to speak of English as 'the language of promotion'. It was an attitude which underlay much of the educational development of nineteenth- and early twentieth-century Wales.

The investigation of the commissioners into Welsh education started against a background of growing unease among the Welsh middle class, and exiled Welshmen, over the ineffectiveness of mainly voluntary effort. The investigation was initiated in Parliament by William Williams, a Welshman who had made a fortune in London before becoming M.P. for Coventry. He was convinced that private enterprise could not be adequate in Wales, and a state system of education was essential. The gentry and industrialists were not prepared to contribute sufficient funds, there was no adequate system for training teachers, there were no adequate means by which the Welsh could learn English. Williams got his enquiry.

The commissioners, Lingen, Symons and Vaughan Johnson, have become bywords for unsuitability – upper-middle-class Englishmen, educated at Oxford and Cambridge, and Anglicans. Seven of their ten assistants were Anglicans. They took evidence from 334 witnesses, 80 per cent of whom were Anglicans. In fact, on educational matters, their judgments were balanced. They drew attention to the in-adequacy of Welsh education even by low contemporary standards. There was praise for the Sunday schools, particularly from Vaughan Johnson. He regarded them as a civilising influence and an effective means of religious instruction because they used the Welsh language.

What the commissioners did not allow for was the difficulty of teaching monoglot Welsh children through the medium of English with books in English. In only one day school in the counties of Brecon, Radnor and Cardigan was the Welsh language taught. There was no outrage at criticisms of the Welsh language, nor of the condemnations of conditions under which schools were held. There was a violent reaction to gratuitous sideswipes, entirely commensurate with contemporary English attitudes, at Wales as a kind of primitive backwater, ignorant and immoral. Anglicans and nonconformists alike were outraged, even though it was nonconformity which was associated with immorality in the report. This was largely the result of interviewing a large majority of Anglicans.

The Blue Books became enormously important symbolically. They helped sharpen the edge of radicalism and nonconformist opinion already incensed by the Tithe Commutation Act of 1836. Despite Anglican condemnation of the Blue Books it was nonconformist outrage which was most obvious. Differences between older Dissent and Methodism were less evident as the Methodists reacted angrily. The Blue Books helped foster a sense of nationality through outrage in the face of insult. The aim now was respectability through redress, but hardly on Welsh terms. The small wooden rectangle hung around the necks of pupils lapsing into Welsh – the Welsh 'Not' – was already in use in 1847. As with the Blue Books controversy, the Welsh 'Not' has generated a mythology of its own. Yet that piece of engraved wood symbolised the victory of the Blue Book commissioners in their view of Welsh education.

Elementary education and the state

There was growing concern across England and Wales in the 1850s and 1860s that education was inadequate for an industrialised society increasingly challenged by European competitors. The 1870 Education Act indicated an acceptance that voluntary effort could not adequately provide a national system of elementary education. Baptists and Independents in South Wales had resisted state provision. There was now strong opposition to the notion of state-supported schools providing denominational religious teaching. In England, after the Liberal gains in the 1868 election, a group of Birmingham radicals campaigned for locally elected school boards to provide a free elementary education supported by Treasury grant. Societies set up in Wales to support this National Education League pressed for a more radical solution – a secular system of elementary education not only in areas of special need but nationwide. In January 1870 a Welsh Educational Alliance was established in Cardiff to campaign for this but did not achieve its aim then or subsequently. The Forster Act of 1870 gave increased aid to the National and British Societies, and time for them to 'fill in the gaps' in provision. The gaps which remained would be filled by locally elected school boards. There was strong nonconformist opposition in Wales, with its large preponderance of Church schools which were still giving denominational instruction under the Act. The clause allowing parents to withdraw their children was something of a mockery in such a situation.

The school boards were democratically elected and the Welsh Educational Alliance, denied its secular education system, turned its attention to trying to get on to school boards. It faced determined opposition, and often tactical defeat, at the hands of both Anglican and Catholic clergy. Even so, by the end of the nineteenth century, over half the 320 school boards in Wales operated either a policy of wholly secular instruction or Bible-reading without comment. While there were only seven school boards in England with a secular education policy there were fifty in Wales. There still remained at least 300 districts in rural Wales with only Anglican schools. Yet in some rural areas, at least, about 85 per cent of children attended school and a majority of these stayed to fourteen before this became a legal requirement.

Nonconformist fury erupted once more in 1902. In the meantime elementary education had become compulsory and virtually free. School boards had prospered; denominational schools had found it ever more difficult to find money for upkeep and expansion. The return of a Conservative Government in 1896 had resulted in an awareness of the threat to Anglican provision and apprehension over the activities of the school boards, regarded by the Tories as dangerously radical, though in parts of Wales they were the preserve of the middle class. Under the 1902 Education Act the school boards were abolished and control of education vested in the county councils which the Tories regarded as far safer. Former voluntary and board schools were brought under state supervision and rate-aided, but the non-provided or voluntary schools were still able to offer their own brand of religious instruction. In Wales, because of the dramatic dichotomy between Anglican and Nonconformist, the reaction was particularly strong and was orchestrated by Lloyd George into the Welsh revolt.

Within a few weeks of the bill becoming law in December 1902, Lloyd George encouraged illegal opposition to it, but he also very nearly reached a compromise with the Bishop of St Asaph, though other Church leaders were not even prepared to discuss the issue. Lloyd George therefore encouraged the Welsh local authorities, overwhelmingly Liberal, to operate the Act only under certain conditions. When the Conservative–Unionist Government was defeated in 1905 some Welsh councils were still defying the Act. With the return of a Liberal Government in 1906, and a commitment to meet nonconformist grievances, the Act was administered. Attempts at legislation came to nothing but what was emerging was a growing realisation that the denominationalism of elementary education was becoming a less important issue. Financial pressures on the Established Church saw the surrender of control of 151 Anglican elementary schools, out of 800, between 1903 and 1913. Thenceforward elementary education was far more influenced by government policies. It came under the control of the Welsh Department of the Board of Education, created in 1907. The *Hadow Report* of 1926 spurred on the development of central and modern schools, with a break at the age of eleven, but there were difficulties in implementing such reorganisation in rural Wales, particularly. In industrial Wales, progressive plans were not easy to introduce in such adverse economic conditions as prevailed in the 1920s and 1930s. Still, the quality of elementary education undoubtedly improved in the inter-war period and there was a more enlightened attitude to the teaching of Welsh.

After 1944 Welsh practice was closely in line with that of England. The Butler Education Act of 1944 implemented three stages of education, primary, secondary and further, so finally doing away with the old parallel system whereby the only education open to the majority was an elementary one. In industrial Wales, particularly, the primary schools were little different from those in England. In 1961 only 17.6 per cent of Welsh children between the ages of five and fifteen could speak or understand Welsh. But now the issue of the Welsh language was becoming increasingly important. In 1967 came the report of the Welsh Central Advisory Council for Education, the *Gittins Report*. It found that only three Welsh authorities had no bilingual policy, and half the authorities introduced Welsh as a second language at the age of five: 6,478 pupils out of 250,000 were being educated in Welsh-language schools. Gittins attached over-riding importance to fostering the Welsh language in primary schools and added impetus to the Welsh schools movement.

Grammar schools and county schools

There had been grammar schools in Wales since Tudor times but the system had never rested on a secure social base. By a variety of expedients the schools survived – Carmarthen, Swansea, Cowbridge, Bangor, for example. Ruthin took boarders mainly from England and others did elementary work. By the second half of the nineteenth century a growing middle class and professional element in the population was not being adequately catered for according to the priorities of the day and convention decreed that their needs must be met by a secondary-school system. They had 'long been left without any better means of instruction than those which are accessible to the children of the poor'. So Hugh Owen, who best reflected the concern with which middle-class Welshmen viewed education as a means to respectable nationhood, pressed for an in-vestigation into higher education. The Aberdare committee reported in 1881 and showed how few grammar-school places were available to non-Anglicans in Wales. Eventually, in 1889, came a dramatic response – a state system of secondary education confined to Wales, and financed partly by local funds but partly by the Treasury. The latter involved inspection, so the Central Welsh Board was established for the purpose in 1896 to inspect and examine the schools by means of certificate examinations. By 1902 ninety-five schools had been established under the Act, with rural Wales particularly well catered for. The county schools soon settled into a pattern of providing an academic education, the main function of which was to enable pupils to surmount examination hurdles and acquire a school certificate at age sixteen. Since the universities used the credit pass of school certificate as a matriculation standard this became the real hallmark of success. The schools were therefore geared to the bright pupils who were assessed on a narrow range of academic subjects decided by the universities. As a result, there was strong criticism of the county schools before the First World War because, it was alleged, they were not providing the education which Welsh children needed, nor providing cultured and skilled leaders who would set the tone of their local communities. However, there were fine achievements to the credit of the county schools, and those municipal schools founded after the 1902 Act to fill in some of the gaps in the system. They reflected a more egalitarian society than England. From the earliest days they were more open to working-class talent, with nearly 90 per cent of their pupils coming from the state elementary schools by 1909. The schools indicated that a poorer, somewhat less class-ridden society could compete on English terms of individual achievement. They demonstrated, too, that such competition could only be on English terms in a strictly capitalist, achievement-orientated meritocracy. A school certificate, particularly a matriculation certificate, provided a ticket, often out of the local community, the county, even the country, to a desirable black-coat job. In the most industrialised parts of Wales Labour-dominated councils successfully tried not only to increase the number of secondary-school places, even in Depression years, but also worked towards providing them free, and therefore on merit, rather than allowing in a substantial proportion on payment of fees. By 1932 substantially over 60 per cent of places were free, a far higher figure than in England. For the sake of £35,000 over seven years, the National Government in 1932 replaced free places with means-tested special places, so sacrificing one of the most progressive elements in the Welsh system. Poverty in inter-war Wales conspired to defeat the Government because means-tested free places dropped only marginally below previous figures. Progressive authorities used the 1932 controversy at least to secure the maximum number of special places possible, so that access to the secondary system became dependent largely on talent rather than ability to pay.

The Welsh secondary system was, then, more open to talent and fundamentally fairer than the comparable English arrangement. Yet critics remained, because the function of the secondary school in Welsh society had never been wholly clear even to the pioneers. Hugh Owen had wanted to provide a suitable education for the burgeoning Welsh middle class which would add an essential element to social stability. O. M. Edwards, the remarkable inaugurator of *Cymru* and *Cymru'r Plant* who had progressed from material, though not spiritual, poverty to a glittering academic career culminating in a fellowship at Lincoln College, Oxford, had a more romantic vision of both the secondary schools and Welsh society. He hoped that the sons of tenant farmers would come to the schools, imbibe the culture and history of Wales and, of course, its language, and return to their native community as leaders, while pursuing their ennobling craft labour. In 1907 Edwards became Chief Inspector at the Welsh Department of the Board of Education, so was in a position to try to implement some of his ideas, but found himself enmeshed in the social and educational values central to the English secondary school with its priorities ordered by the Board of Education. The examination system of School and Higher Certificate, which Edwards constantly criticised, was central to this competitive system ministering largely to the needs of the middle class in England, and catering for its social and occupational aspirations. Welsh parents, fully appreciating the role of the secondary school in social and economic mobility, endorsed the system.

The Welsh secondary school was an anglicising force not only in terms of language but, more fundamentally, in cultivating attitudes and distinctions which existed in England. There was more concentration on teaching Welsh after the early days of the schools but almost invariably in the inter-war period it was set against French as an examination subject. Parents on the whole believed French to have a higher status. More significant, the Welsh secondary schools, becoming grammar schools after 1944, were modelled in their early days on English public schools in terms of team games, house systems, prefect systems and uniforms, reinforced by government and Board of Education policy. Their social function was to cultivate a middle-ranking meritocracy. With rare exceptions, the highest-ranked occupations, filled by the products of the English public schools, were not available to Welsh pupils, but access to the middle-rank occupations in the professions was made available through the county and municipal secondary schools. In 1911–12, for example, 15 per cent of boys and girls from such schools in Wales went on to further education, 23 per cent of girls, far fewer boys, went in for teaching, 42.5 per cent of boys, 9 per cent of girls, entered professional, clerical or commercial employment, 7.5 per cent of boys and 0.3 per cent of girls went into some form of rural or agricultural work. The schools therefore trained their pupils for occupations which were hardly available in rural Wales and which, between the wars, were at a premium in Depression-ridden South Wales, too. So, a flow of talent left Wales.

After the *Hadow Report* of 1926, which advocated the establishment of central or modern schools wherever possible, problems arose in the organisation of such schools in Wales, especially in the rural areas, since it made no sense to duplicate facilities and buildings for the eleven-plus age group. Circumstances therefore drove the Welsh Department of the Board of Education to press for a multilateral solution, even a comprehensive solution, whereby all pupils would pursue a common curriculum for two years and share the same facilities after that. Such a prospect was anathema to the Board of Education. Wales had to wait over thirty years for its comprehensive schools. While the Welsh secondary-school system would un- doubtedly have developed differently during the inter-war years if it had not been for the radical implications which changes suited to the Welsh situation would have had for government policy generally, the secondary schools had achieved a great deal. They had the backing of local communities, chapels, and Labour councils which wanted to make secondary opportunities available to more and more pupils. They often provided a high quality of education through dedicated teachers. They provided opportunities for talent to be channelled into achievement on an unprecedented scale.

The integration of the Welsh and English systems of secondary education was virtually complete after the 1944 Education Act which legislated for free secondary education for all pupils over eleven. The various religious denominations and the Central Welsh Board were more concerned over matters of denominational instruction when they met R. A. Butler than with the form secondary education should take. That form over most of Wales, was a bipartite one, with a system of grammar and secondary-modern schools. There was a pious hope that there would be 'parity of esteem', soon shown to be impossible when the economic prospects for grammar school products were so obviously superior. Anglesey was allowed to develop a comprehensive system but plans were blocked elsewhere by the Ministry of Education, usually with parental approval. Still, a far higher percentage of Welsh pupils continued to find places in the secondary–grammar schools than was the case in England – the figure reached 55 per cent of the age group in some areas – though the corollary was that secondary-modern schools tended to be neglected.

Since 1944 Welsh educational development has been in line with government policy. After Crosland's Circular 10/65 pressed the comprehensive solution to secondary organisation, the Welsh local authorities acted quickly, many of them having been committed to the principle before. Wales became a nation of comprehensive schools. The debate on the quality of the schools still centred around examination results, as it always had done, amid accusations that the grammar-school tradition in Wales decreed that too much attention was paid to the brightest pupils and too little to the less able. A far more enlightened attitude developed towards the Welsh language. The development of Welsh-language comprehensive schools at Ystalyfera, Rhydfelin and elsewhere testified to this.

Higher education

A similar integrative process overtook the University of Wales. The expansion of the universities in the nineteenth century, through provincial universities or colleges, was confined to England until the 1870s. Only the Anglican ecclesiastical foundation of St David's College, Lampeter, came to nonconformist Wales. The indefatigable Hugh Owen, having founded Bangor Normal College to train teachers, returned to his main purpose of seeing a Welsh university college come into existence. His efforts culminated in the opening of Aberystwyth University College in 1872 to provide an intellectual and vocational education, with a scientific bias appropriate to an industrial society. Despite the myth of the 'pennies of the poor', the enterprise was heavily dependent on philanthropists like David Davies of Llandinam, a coalowner, and was conceived not as a university for Wales, but primarily for North and mid Wales. Despite traumatic early years the university movement was eventually successful. The Aberdare Committee in 1881 recommended a college for South Wales and a college for North Wales, and Cardiff and Bangor colleges were founded in 1883 and 1884 respectively. Government grant was made available not only to these colleges but also to Aberystwyth, and a charter was granted to the University of Wales in 1893.

From the first it was essential that the colleges achieved recognition through the quality of their work and this remained essentially an international activity. The Cardiff college adapted to the mercantile, commercial ambience of the area and Bangor was not really rooted in the tradition of the ordinary people. Aberystwyth, given its struggle to survive and the collections taken on its behalf from the ordinary people of Wales, was more of a symbol of national achievement.

The University drew more than 90 per cent of its students from Wales until the 1920s and, even after the Second World War, remained a much more local university than those in England. It continued to be a national university with federated colleges, strengthened by the endorsement of the Haldane Royal Commission in 1918, the addition of Swansea college in 1920 and the creation of the University of Wales Press and the Board of Celtic Studies in 1922. A serious attempt to defederalise the university in 1964–6 was thwarted, but the expansion of universities after the Robbins Report in 1963 made the University of Wales far more cosmopolitan. The Welsh colleges still drew more of their students from their own region, and more of those students were working-class in origin, than was the case in England. Yet, whereas 95 per cent of University of Wales students came from the principality in 1938, thirty years later that number had gone down to 39 per cent. One response in the 1970s was to press for a college for Welsh speakers, with little success. Direct action to try to limit the number of students from outside Wales was also unsuccessful.

The training colleges originated with the founding of Carmarthen by the Anglicans in 1848, followed by recognition for the Caernarfon college which moved to Bangor in 1855. The first nonconformist college, largely the work of Hugh Owen and the Methodists, opened as the Bangor Normal College in 1858. A British Society college for women opened in Swansea in 1872. With the 1902 Education Act, and local authority provision of teacher training, colleges were set up in Barry, for women, and Caerleon, for men, while a special training school in cookery was established in Llandaff in 1891. In the 1950s two more colleges, at Cartrefle, Wrexham and Cardiff were founded to help meet an unprecedented demand for teachers. In the 1960s and 1970s the colleges of education, as they had now become, were caught up in a maelstrom of expansion and curricular experiment but although localised in intake, very many of their products found teaching posts in England. The James Report, *A Framework for Expansion*, published in 1972, heralded a period of contraction in the colleges within a few years and they were forced to amalgamate and diversify in order to survive. Barry college did not manage to do so.

Success and failure

Whether as tribute to the notion of Welsh national needs in the 1880s or as part of dramatic expansion in England and Wales generally in the 1960s there have been elements of success in the story of Welsh secondary and higher education in the last century. Schools, training colleges and the university widened access to the professions dramatically and trained distinguished servants of Wales across a whole range of occupations. The regard for education in Wales has been real, born of a variety of social and political pressures. Any advantage, for individuals or for the nation, was not gained lightly. The political struggles for the implementation of the Aberdare Report in the 1880s gave way to constant battles in the 1920s and 1930s against government economy measures which bore hard on the Welsh system. Some Welsh local authorities, particularly those in industrial areas, emerged with real credit in the fight to preserve the formal educational fabric and extend provision for students from working-class families.

The fight against central government policies of neglect and attack on financial resources provided one touchstone of success. In the schools, either through the scholarship/eleven-plus or the School Certificate/'O' and 'A' levels, examination success provided an immediately relevant and concrete measure for parents, teachers and pupils. Current debate in Welsh education has again, in the late 1970s and early 1980s, been overwhelmingly concerned with this indicator of standards.

It is understandable that schools, colleges and university should have developed in the way they did, constrained by legislation, financial considerations and institutional traditions impelling them to seek parity with their English counterparts. It is perhaps less easy to understand why the general debate on educational standards, initiated in the 1970s by James Callaghan's Ruskin College speech, should have been reflected in Wales in an obsession with the seeming shortcomings of schools in their ability to provide their pupils with as many Certificate of Secondary Education passes as their English counterparts. Since 1945 the distinctiveness of Welsh education has been analysed almost wholly in terms of language, where earlier in the twentieth century discussion of the language issue was combined with a wider social analysis. There was discussion of the implications of geographical mobility – the drain of talented, qualified young people from Wales – and social mobility – the kind of education appropriate to the career gradations felt suitable for Wales.

Outside the mainstream

It is salutary to recall that many of the outstanding political and trade union leaders – Aneurin Bevan, James Griffiths, Arthur Horner, for example – had little orthodox state education. They provide a timely reminder of the influence of more informal educational movements. The Workers' Educational Association reflected the Liberal tradition in Wales, radical but not revolutionary, wide-ranging in its appeal across the political spectrum. The National Council of Labour Colleges endorsed a more revolutionary approach to class and society. In 1906 the South Wales branch of the W.E.A. was formed. Concurrently, the South Wales Miners' Federation provided scholarships for some of its members to attend Ruskin College, Oxford, a college for trade union and working students established in 1900. In 1909 a Central Labour College was founded, dependent largely on the support of the South Wales Miners' Federation. It lasted only until 1916, but it helped create a clientele for Marxist-orientated evening classes in the coalfield, meeting a demand which the W.E.A. had not filled.

The W.E.A., after the First World War, endorsed the message of class co-operation under the influence of establishment figures like Thomas Jones, Percy Watkins and Daniel Lleufer Thomas. While sympathetic to many aspects of working-class aspiration they saw education as a means of fostering social harmony. During the First World War, however, independent workers' education classes had proved far more popular as they concentrated on Marxist political and economic analysis. After 1918 there was a resurgence of interest in the W.E.A. and during the 1920s it played an important part in trying to alleviate some of the effects of unemployment, especially in providing non-vocational classes for working-class students. It was helped by government support after it became an approved association under 1924 regulations. The Labour College was revived in 1919, to survive until 1929, during which time Aneurin Bevan, Jim Griffiths and Ness Edwards, all future Labour M.P.s, attended, but it was the moderate W.E.A. which prospered, despite the efforts of the *Western Mail* to smear it as Bolshevik. By 1933 there were over 4,000 W.E.A. students in Wales, in over 200 classes. After the Second World War adult education expanded in a much more encouraging environment. The W.E.A., university extra-mural departments, and technical colleges mounted an ever-wider range of courses, supported by government and local authorities. From 1971 the Open University in Wales provided a 'second chance' for many students without any formal qualifications. Coleg Harlech, a residential college for working men, opened in 1927. The motive force behind it was Thomas Jones and much of the money came from David Davies of Llandinam. It was founded in the belief that such a college could help reconcile worker and capitalist and counteract seemingly increasing alienation. Despite early difficulties the college thrived, expanded and went on to make an incalculable contribution to working-class education in Wales.

In conclusion, it is equally salutary to contrast the ethos and achievements of the secondary schools with those of a youth organisation, *Urdd Gobaith Cymru*, the Welsh League of Youth, founded in 1922 by Sir Ifan ap Owen Edwards. His father, O. M. Edwards, tried to start a children's organisation in 1896, with little success. The son's efforts were remarkably successful. Conscious of the crisis which confronted the Welsh language, Edwards started the Urdd as a children's language movement, but he intended it to encompass much else he felt to be of value in Welsh life.

As a result of its branch organisation the Urdd movement spread rapidly. In 1924 came penetration of South Wales and in 1925 the famous goodwill message of the children of Wales to the children of the world. By 1927 there were over 5,000 Urdd members in eighty branches, and in 1928 the summer camps started. The following year came the first Urdd Eisteddfod. Both activities have maintained popularity and momentum ever since. The ideals which informed the movement challenged Welsh youth when they were formulated by Sir Ifan ap Owen Edwards in 1929. They have continued to do so:

The aim of the *Urdd* is to create an undefiled Welsh Wales – not for its own sake, not in any way to make Wales superior to other countries, but in order that Wales can play its part in bringing peace to a world which today is too ready to display a spirit of antagonism and of war...If Wales is to develop and present its own contribution it must cherish elements which are characteristic of the nation at its best – its literature, its tradition, its religion and its language.

11

◆◆◆▶

CONCLUSION

Challenges to members of *Urdd Gobaith Cymru* to preserve the literature, tradition, religion and language of Wales contained, implicitly, a judgment on the elements of Welsh nationality. For practical, as well as moral, reasons, Ifan ap Owen Edwards did well to eschew any notion of Welsh superiority. In the second half of the nineteenth century Wales could boast of her economic importance but this never seriously carried with it the aim of extending it into political independence or even devolution. By the time the *Urdd* was founded the Welsh economy had been undermined and, with it, national self-confidence.

The English frequently use 'England' to mean Great Britain – and are understood. It would, of course, be nonsense for the Welsh to imitate them. Common parlance points to the assumed lesser role of the satellites – Wales and Scotland, particularly – in relation to the greater neighbour. This reflects political realities. The political independence of parts of Wales disappeared with Norman and English conquest in the twelfth and thirteenth centuries. Present elements of administrative devolution, particularly the Welsh Office, were granted by Whitehall. The Welsh themselves rejected an elected Welsh assembly in 1979. The Welsh sense of nationhood has not lain in political independence over the last five centuries.

Half a century on from the inception of the Urdd Edwards's other criteria of nationhood appear far less relevant. Nonconformist allegiance, with its moral and spiritual sanctions over so many Welsh communities in the nineteenth and early twentieth centuries, has become marginal; all too often a catalogue of empty chapels and ageing memberships. The Welsh language has remained a vital touchstone of nationality for many. Even at the end of the nineteenth century, with the most remarkable reorientation of the nation's history through industrialisation, half the population spoke Welsh.

302

Largely because Welsh had been the language of religion, Anglican in the sixteenth and seventeenth centuries, nonconformist in the eighteenth and nineteenth, Welsh did not meet with the same fate as Cornish. It is still spoken by nearly 20 per cent of the population. Yet Welshness is not a function of language alone.

In citing tradition, Edwards pointed to a pervasive element in the consciousness of Welshness over the centuries. The folk memory of the nation, its history and its *sense* of history, have been vital. A variety of custodians of tradition have been aware of this and provided an exotic blend of myth and reality. The bards were honoured recounters of the achievements of princely and gentry patrons. Geoffrey of Monmouth gave new life to old legends of the ancient descent of the British race from the Trojans and prophecies of future glories. The bards reinforced the notion of the emergence of another Arthur in their image-laden poetry which eventually settled on Henry Tudor as the Welsh hero.

In the sixteenth century Geoffrey of Monmouth's 'history' was undermined by Polydore Vergil and other critics but bardic prophecies had culminated in the coming of the Tudors and the merging of Welshness into a wider allegiance. In Elizabeth's reign new myths were born of new necessities. The sanction of the past was necessary for Elizabethan foreign and religious policies. So, the notion of the discovery of America by the Welsh prince, Madoc, had no significance for any sense of Welsh nationhood, at least in the sixteenth century. The Protestant reformers' view of the history of the Welsh Church was persuasive and pervasive. Its purpose was religious, not national-istic, but it endowed Wales with a claim to have fostered the true Church brought to Britain within some thirty years of Christ's death.

In the eighteenth and early nineteenth centuries, a variety of influences, some emanating from rare scholarship, others from inventive imagination, combined to depict Wales as heir to the most ancient language in Europe, endowed with an aura of mystery, romance and literary achievement by a past world of Celts and Druids that still survived in modern Eisteddfodau, a wealth of musical inspiration and a spurious national costume.

In the late nineteenth century Welsh princes and rebels were resurrected to provide the authority of history for the great causes of the day. Owain Glyndŵr, for example, was portrayed as an enlightened advocate of an independent Welsh government, university and church. There was stress, too, on the lower orders, the *gwerin*, respectable, law-abiding, religious, culturally gifted, who gave the lie to contemporary English accusations of backwardness and handicap caused by an irrelevant language and culture. The ordinary people of Wales, and their middle-class champions, had much to do. It was entirely comprehensible for a Welsh bishop to maintain that Wales was no more than a geographical expression, or for the *Encyclopaedia Britannica* to record: 'For Wales – see England'. In terms of political independence, so vital a criterion of nationalism in the nineteenth century, Welsh claims to nationhood were tenuous.

There was some truth in the myth of the *gwerin* but it ignored, or was antipathetic towards, that most vital element in the history of modern Wales, industrialisation. There was no myth which, as yet, incorporated industrial Wales – nor could there be for so patently recent a revolution. Liberalism, whose hallmark was cultural nationalism, the incorporation of national respectability for Wales through educational and religious achievement, and which encapsulated in its political achievements much of the *gwerin* tradition, did not embrace the social causes of industrial Wales.

The predominance of rural tradition, coupled with a theory of rural leadership, was reflected much more in literature than in politics in the twentieth century. Mainstream politics, Conservative and Labour particularly, were hardly wedded to notions of Welsh distinctiveness. University historians, rigorous in their methodology and stress on primary sources, no longer purveyors of popular tradition, were influenced by contemporary stress on the politics of the nation state – which hardly helped the Welsh cause since her political independence had ended in 1282–3. Historical fashions changed later in the twentieth century. Economic and social history came to attract as much attention as political history. This served Wales well, since at so many points Welsh society was so patently different from English. The history of Wales became, and has remained, a more popular and vital study than ever.

Welshness, and a sense of Welshness, have had a variety of constituents over the centuries. The most obvious mark of nationhood – political independence – has not been essential to allegiance to Wales. Those who have lived in Wales have normally deemed themselves Welsh, though they have combined this allegiance with others. That sense of Welshness is sufficient claim to nationhood. It has always been sustained by a sense of the past.

ILLUSTRATIVE DOCUMENTS

(Grouped in chapter and topic order.)

PART ONE

1. Agriculture in Pembrokeshire in the time of Elizabeth I

So this little county of Pembrokeshire is not without plenty of God's blessing as well for sufficient means for the people to live in good and plentiful sort, as also to vend and send into other countries thereby bring in money, to procure such necessaries from other countries as the same wanteth. Among the chiefest and greatest commodity that this shire uttereth, I take corn to be a commodity that of all other deserveth most to be cherished and the procurers thereof most to be favoured...

This commodity of corn is the chiefest that bringeth in money to the country, being a country more apt for tilling than for breed, the soil being naturally dry and fit for the plough work, but this differeth much in some part of this shire from other...

The second and next commodity that this country sealeth is cattle as oxen, steers, bullocks, heifers and kine of the country breed, which of late years is greatly increased more than in times past: as a commodity that (particularly) yieldeth profit with less charge to the owner, but generally not so commodious for the commonwealth as the tillage, by reason it procureth depopulation and maintaineth less people at work: this trade of breeding cattle is used much in all parts of the shire but most in the welsh parts and near the mountains, where their land is not so apt for corn and where there is larger scope of the ground...

The third commodity that helpeth this shire to money is wool whereof there is great quantity yearly sold, beside that which is spent in the country for their necessary uses of clothing; the country aboundeth with sheep, more at this present than heretofore, and yieldeth great profit with little charge...

The sheep are but small of body, and the wool coarser than the english wool, and therefore yieldeth less price as most commonly between or about eight shillings and ten shillings the stone, weighing 17 li. but the flesh of these muttons is found to be very sweet in taste, wholesome and good meat, seldom or never infected with the rot...

The lower part of the shire vend and sell their wool to Bristol men, Barnstaple and Somersetshire which come twice every year to the country to buy the wool: The upper parts as Cemys and Cilgerran sell their wool weekly at the market of Cardigan which is bought by Northwales men, and wrought by them to white cloths which they sell to Shrewsbury men.

The fourth principal commodity that this country yieldeth is butter and cheese, whereof there is greater store made now in this shire than in times past, and the same is uttered especially, the butter by sea but this may not be known; so is the cheese to the countries adjoining and sometimes to Ireland for provision of the Queen's garrisons there...

The lower parts as the hundreds of Narberth and Rhos make some gain by selling of Seacoal by sea to Ireland and France, but generally the country people dislike with the selling of this commodity, lest in time it grow so scarce that the country shall want it, being the greatest fuel, as it hath already enhanced the price thereof...

The manner of tilling the ground in this shire is in two sorts: the englishmen use most sowing of wheat, Rye, barley, peas and beans. The welshmen being the worser husbands apply more the tilling of oats, and some cause there was, which caused this in former times, which now being taken away the welshmen are become the better husbands: the englishmen before Christmas fallow for wheat and rye, and having given it the first breaking it lieth so till Mid may after barley sowing when they harrow it and turn it. and then it lieth till the latter end of July, and then again harrow and turn it, and so it resteth till harvest be led in; at which time they dung and sow it under furrow, by this kind of tilth the land yieldeth goodly corn...

One other cause was the use of 'gavelkind' used among most of these welshmen to part all the fathers patrimony among all his sons, so that in process of time the whole country was brought into small pieces of ground and intermingled up and down one with another, so as in every five or six acres you shall have ten or twelve owners; this made the country to remain Champion, and without enclosures or hedging, and winter Corn if it were sown among them should be grassed all the winter and eaten by sheep and other cattle, which could not be kept from the same: for all the winter long the sheep, horses, Mares, colts and so many cattle as are not housed do graze all the fields without restraint over all the country...

The welshmen plough commonly with two oxen and two horses before them, their land being shallow and light by reason of this ill kind of tillage used among them: among the english diverse have plows of horses alone and oxen also but commonly six beasts in their plough...

> From: George Owen, *The Description of Pembrokeshire*, ed. Henry Owen, Cymmrodorion Record Series, no. 1, London, 1892, pp. 54–63.

2. An Alderman's Will, 1716

CHRISTOPHER MATHEWS, Alderman of Cardiff.

1716/7 February 25.

To wife Deborah use of various articles in his house at Cardiff; (*inter alia*) of "a Stilling for a Mashing vate in the brewhouse." Also, 1,000 of Cornish tiles. Also a bedstead in "the little forestreet chamber, six black chairs, one case of drawers......one fire grate with tongs, slice & pooker," the white curtains belonging to a bed in the same chamber, commonly called the Parlour Chamber; "one small oval wallnut-tree table one midleing looking glass usually in the window of ye s^d Chamber"; feather bed in the inner room of the said chamber, and a small "skreen"; one larger chair "with arms & its cushin"; one low black chair, one small oval table "most an end"; all the china ware, tea tables, teapots and all earthen ware, coarse and fine, in parlour, closets, larder or kitchen. (Three closets within the parlour.) My pewter alembick; one powdering tub; pewter dishes; two deep trenchers marked with wife's name and mine; brass chafing dish; two upright brass candlesticks, one brass hanging ditto, one old flat ditto; a pa[ir of snuff]ers with its pan and frame; one large brass ring with its heater; one ham (?) toaster with its hooks and "tinnin" dripping pan; spit; beat box; slice or fire shovel; bellows; copper stew pan; copper coffee pot; brass ladle; brass skimmer; flesh fork; "one midleing brass pott one Copper pott with it's Cover & Ladle of the same; one bell mettle Skillett"; basting stick, in the kitchen. Item to wife my best pillion and cloth; 6 silver forks, 2 silver salts; one silver snuff box; one case of knives. My second best periwig to my kinsman John Lewis of Llantrisant. To father-in-law James Mathews my best hat and the mourning band about it. To Henry Williams, of Cardiff, currier, "one old hat, my best light coloured coat & one druggett wastcoat, a pair of leather britches, a pair of leather spatter dashes & a kersey riding coat." To servant maid Sarah Bembrick my old night gown and a pair of black gloves...

To son William furnace, boiler, mashing vat, stilling and brewing tubs in the Brewhouse; large trough for salting of meat, in the Larder; flat brass candlestick with a handle to it, copper chocolate pot, tin coffee pot, "one

3. Customers' and Controllers' Entries, Port of Milford, 1566–7

Date	Name of Ship	Master	—	Merchant	Cargo
10 April.	Le Peter de Aisheforde	Thomas Bowe	Barnstaple	Henry Downe	2 t. iron, 1 fardel linen, 40 pieces calico, 4 lb. cinnamon, 1 cwt. white soap.
30 April.	Le Trenete de Teuxeburie	Rice Umfrey	Bristol to Haverfordwest	Rice Passe of Teuxbury	8 w. barley malt.
29 May.	Le Katerynge de Tenby	Thomas Kynge	Bristol	John Sinet of Haverfordwest	3 cwt. hops, 3 cwt. white soap, 3 cwt. madder, 5 doz. *crassum*, 4 burdens steel, 1 frayle spurs, 2 packs 1 brl. divers goods, 1 frayl horseshoes, 2 brls. 1 kn. black soap, 1 t. iron.
11 June.	Le Thomas de Portu Milforde	John Bran	Barnstaple	Oliver Hearde	5 t. iron, 3 cwt. pitch.
29 July.	Le Savior de Milford	Philip Pollett	Bristol to Haverfordwest	Thomas Thomas of Haverfordwest	8 cwt. old brass.
"	Le George de Millforde	Philip Pollett	Bristol	Edward Pegis of Lansey	1 t. iron, 1 cwt. hops, 3 hhd. oil, 3 brls. drywares.

| 31 July. | Le Kateringe de Tenbi | Thomas Kynge | Bristol to Tenby | John Launsdon of Tenby | 1 t. 1 p. iron, 5 cwt. hops, 6 brls. drywares, 3 hhd. vinegar, 1 kn. butter, 4 brls. black soap, 1 brl. oil, 5 cwt. white soap. |
| ,, | Le Anne de Portu Milforde | Thomas Follande | Bristol | Morice Walter of Haverfordwest | 5 t. iron, 5 t. train, 2 hhd. vinegar, 6 packs and 8 fardels linen, 5 cwt. hops, 8 brls. drywares, 8 kns. black soap, 5 chests 2 hhd. dry wares, 6 doz. dikers tanned hides, 2 doz. calfskins, 1 t. 'shomake.' |

From: E. A. Lewis, ed., *The Welsh Port Books (1550–1603)*, Cymmrodorion Record Series, no. XII, London, 1927, p. 98.

bright Defender or Toaster, wth it's fork &c., one spitt, a pair of pott hangings"; one dog wheel, a yew tree chair, in Back Kitchen. My timber "at the place called the Ruins & Cathays." One back of cast iron in his (my son's) manservant's room. In Hall: 2 great chests, large stand, pewter still, clock with its case, twigging chair, large sea chest, livery cupboard, desk, window curtains, rods and hangings. Jack for roasting of meat. My box of large sea instruments for surgery, and a box of new steel pocket ones, with its lancet case and salvatory; box of silver pocket instruments with its salvatory; cases furnished with "best lawncetts & Incission knives," three choices "Raizors." "All my Study of books in my Closett or elsewhere particularly Queen Ann's Comon prayer done in her Reign & the large Bible bought at Bristoll." Silver tankard, pair silver shoe buckles, [silver] tobacco box, my camlet cloak.

From: J. H. Matthews, *Cardiff Records*, vol. III, Cardiff, 1901, pp. 156–8.

4. Recreation in Pembrokeshire in the time of Elizabeth I

The foot company thus meeting, there is a round ball prepared of a reasonable quantity, so as a man may hold it in his hand and no more, this ball is of some massy wood as box Ewe, crab or holly tree, and should be boiled in tallow, for to make it slippery, and hard to be holden, this ball is called Knappan, and is by one of the company hurled bolt upright to the air, and at the fall, he that catcheth it hurleth it towards the country he playeth for, for goal, or appointed place, there is none neither needeth any, for the play is not given over until the Knappan be so far carried that there is no hope to return it back that night, for the carrying of it a mile or two miles from the first place, is no losing of the honour, so it be still followed by the company, and the play still maintained, it is often times seen the chase to follow two miles and more, in heat of course both by the horse and foot; The Knappan being once cast forth, you shall see the same tossed backwards and forward, by hurling throws, in strange sort, for in three or four throws you shall see the whole bodie of the game removed, half a mile and more, and in this sort it is a strange sight to see a thousand or fifteen hundred naked men to concur together in a cluster following the Knappan, as the same is hurled backward and forward...

You shall see gamesters return home from this play with broken heads, black faces, bruised bodies, and lame legs, yet laughing and merrily jesting at their harms, telling their adversaries how he broke his head to an other that he struck him on the face, and how he repaid the same to him again, and all this in good mirth, without grudge or hatred, and if any be in the arrearages to the other they score it up till the next play, and in the mean time will continue loving friends, whereas if the least of these blows be offered out of this play, it presently breedeth unquenchable quarrels.

From: George Owen, *Pembrokeshire*, pp. 273–7.

5. The Plague in Haverfordwest, 1651/2

LETTER FROM THOMAS DAVIDS, MAYOR OF HAVERFORDWEST, TO THOMAS PARRY AND THOMAS JONES, ESQUIRES, OR EITHER OF THEM, 25 FEBRUARY 1651/2

Gentlemen,

Last night a warrant was brought unto me by the constables of Prendergast signed by Button Ormond one of the high constables of Dongleddy hundred, whereby they were required by him not to permit any to come into the town or any townsman to come hence by reason of the sickness of the plague here. Myself and the rest of the Aldermen of the town directed our certificate unto them and the rest of the justices of the peace of the county certifying the state and condition of the town but conceiving it came not to your hands (being delivered to Mr Sampson Lorte the next day after the date), I have sent you a copy of it enclosed, desiring your considerance thereof and your care therein. Thanks be to God the town being as touching the sickness in as good or rather better condition than when we certified the same. Your care whereby the preventing of the dispersing of the sickness is commendable. So that you will be pleased that provision of victual may be provided for the inhabitants being upon 3,000 souls which must starve if food be kept from them, I make bold to write these few lines unto you only being told that the original warrant (if any be) came from yourselves. There hath not four died this last week and I cannot learn of any one that is at present sick. So not doubting of your Christian and charitable care therein I rest

Haverfordwest the 25th of February
1651

Your kinsman and servant
Thomas Davids Mayor

I shall desire you that you would cause your servant to deliver the enclosed summons as is directed with what speed may be To the

worshipful his most honoured friends Thomas Par(ry) and Thomas Jones esquires these or to either of them present.

From: Matthew Griffiths, ed., *Sources for Welsh Towns*, The Open University in Wales, n.d., p. 79.

6. The Antiquity of the Welsh Language. An eighteenth-century view from Griffith Jones

"The greatest philologists of England and France (says a great antiquarian, Edw. Llwyd) have maintained that to be the chief remains of the Celtique which is spoken in Wales, Cornwall, and Bass Bretagne." Monsieur Pezron's authority confirms the same; "That the language of the Titans, which was that of the ancient Gauls, is, after a revolution of four thousand years, preserved even to our times; and now spoken by the Armonican Britains in France, and by the Ancient Britains in Wales." This learned man adds; "These are the people who have the honour to preserve the language of the posterity of Gomer, Japheth's eldest son, and the nephew of Shem; the language of those princes who passed for great deities among the ancients."

From: W. M. Williams, ed., *Selections from Welch Piety*, Cardiff, 1938, p. 48.

7. The Acts of Union, 1536–43

A.D. 1536   27 Henry 8, c. 26

AN ACT FOR LAWS AND JUSTICE TO BE MINISTERED IN WALES IN LIKE FORM AS IT IS IN THIS REALM

"Albeit the Dominion Principality and Country of WALES justly and righteously is, and ever hath been incorporated annexed united and subject to and under the Imperial Crown of this Realm, as a very Member and Joint of the same, whereof the King's most Royal Majesty of Meer Droit, and very Right, is very Head King Lord and Ruler; yet notwithstanding, because that in the same Country Principality and Dominion divers Rights Usages Laws and Customs be far discrepant from the Laws and Customs of this Realm, and also because that the People of the same Dominion have and do daily use a Speech nothing like, nor consonant to the natural Mother Tongue used within this Realm, some rude and ignorant People have made Distinction and Diversity between the King's Subjects of this Realm, and his Subjects of the said Dominion and Principality of WALES, whereby great Discord Variance Debate Division Murmur and Sedition hath grown between his said Subjects"; His Highness therefore, of a singular Zeal Love and Favour that he beareth towards his Subjects of his said Dominion of WALES, minding and intending to reduce them to the perfect Order Notice and Knowledge of his Laws of this his Realm, and utterly to extirp all and singular the sinister Usages and Customs differing from the same...

That his said Country or Dominion of WALES shall be, stand and continue for ever from henceforth incorporated united and annexed to and with this

his Realm of England; and that all and singular Person and Persons, born or to be born in the said Principality Country or Dominion of WALES, shall have enjoy and inherit all and singular Freedoms Liberties Rights Privileges and Laws within this his Realm, and other the King's Dominions, as other the King's Subjects naturally born within the same have, enjoy and inherit.

And that all and singular Person and Persons inheritable to any Manors Lands Tenements Rents Reversions Services or other Hereditaments, which shall descend after the Feast of *All Saints* next coming, within the said Principality Country or Dominion of WALES, or within any particular Lordship, Part or Parcel of the said Country or Dominion of WALES, shall for ever, from and after the said Feast of *All Saints*, inherit and be inheritable to the same Manors Lands Rents Tenements Reversions and Hereditaments, after the English Tenure, without Division or Partition, and after the Form of the Laws of this Realm of England, and not after any Welsh Tenure, nor after the Form of any Welsh Laws or Customs...

Also be it enacted by the Authority aforesaid, That all Justices Commissioners Sheriffs Coroners Escheators Stewards and their Lieutenants, and all other Officers and Ministers of the Law, shall proclaim and keep the Sessions Courts Hundreds Leets, Sheriffs Courts, and all other Courts in the English Tongue; and all Oaths of Officers Juries and Inquests, and all other Affidavits Verdicts and Wagers of Law, to be given and done in the English Tongue; and also that from henceforth no Person or Persons that use the Welsh Speech or Language shall have or enjoy any Manner Office or Fees within this Realm of England, WALES, or other the King's Dominion, upon Pain of forfeiting the same Offices or Fees, unless he or they use and exercise the English Speech or Language...

A.D. 1542–3   34 & 35 Henry 8, c. 26

AN ACT FOR CERTAIN ORDINANCES IN THE KING'S DOMINION AND PRINCIPALITY OF WALES

First, That his Grace's said Dominion, Principality and Country of WALES, be from henceforth divided into twelve Shires; of the which eight have been Shires of long and ancient Time, That is to say, The Shires of Glamorgan, Caermarthen, Pembroke, Cardigan, Flint, Caernarvon, Anglesey and Merioneth; and four of the said twelve Shires be newly made and ordained to be Shires, by an Act made at the Parliament holden at Westminster in the twenty-seventh Year of our said Sovereign Lord's most noble Reign, that is to say, the Shires of Radnor, Brecknock, Montgomery and Denbigh, over and besides the Shire of Monmouth, and divers other Dominions, Lordships and Manors in the Marches of WALES, united and annexed to the Shires of Salop, Hereford and Glocester, as by the said late Act more plainly appeareth...

Item, That there shall be and remain a President and Council in the said Dominion and Principality of WALES, and the Marches of the same, with all Officers, Clerks and Incidents to the same, in Manner and Form as hath been heretofore used and accustomed; which President and Council shall have Power and Authority to hear and determine, by their Wisdoms and Discretions, such Causes and Matters as be or hereafter shall be assigned to them by the King's Majesty, as heretofore hath been accustomed and used.

Item, That there shall be holden and kept Sessions twice in every Year, in every of the said Shires in the said Dominion and Principality of WALES, that is to say, in the Shires of Glamorgan, Brecknock, Radnor, Caermarthen, Pembroke, Cardigan, Montgomery, Denbigh, Flint, Caernarvan, Merioneth and Anglesey; the which Sessions shall be called the King's great Sessions in WALES...

Item, Over and besides the said President and Council, and Justices, there shall be Justices of Peace and Quorum, and also one *Custos Rotulorum*, in every of the said twelve Shires...

Item, That there shall not exceed the Number of eight Justices of the Peace in any of the said Shires, over and besides the President, Council, and Justices aforesaid, and the King's Attorney and Solicitor...

Item, The said Sheriffs shall keep their Counties monthly, and their Hundred Courts for Pleas under 40s., as is used in England; and shall take for the entering of Plaints, Process, Pleas and Judgments in the said Shire-courts and Hundreds, such small Fees as is used to be taken in Shires and Hundreds in England, and not above...

From: Ivor Bowen, The Statutes of Wales, London, 1908, pp.
78–117.

8. Summoning Quarter Sessions, 1552

John Wyn ap Meredydd, esquire, and his associates, Justices of the lord king assigned to keep the peace in the county of Caernarvon and to hear and determine divers felonies, trespasses and other misdemeanours perpetrated in the same county, to the sheriff of the same county, greeting. On behalf of the lord the king we order you that you omit not on account of any liberty in your bailiwick but that you enter it and cause to come before us on Monday namely the 18th day of July next to come at Caernarvon twenty four free and lawful men from each hundred, trithing, wapentake and each borough of your aforesaid bailiwick to do there what shall be enjoined upon them on behalf of the lord the king. You are also to cause all stewards, constables, subconstables and bailiffs within hundreds and of the boroughs aforesaid that they shall then be there having with them all the names of artificers, labourers and servants within their bailiwicks taking excessive [*wages*] against the form of the ordinances and statutes sufficiently engrossed. Moreover you are to cause it to be proclaimed that all those who both on behalf of the lord king and on their own behalf wish to complain or prosecute against these artificers, labourers and servants any actions according to the form of the ordinances and statutes aforesaid that they shall then be there before the Justices ready to prosecute therein. And you yourself are to be there then with the bailiffs of the hundreds, liberties and boroughs aforesaid having with you all the names of the stewards, constables and subconstables, jurors and this precept. Witness being the aforesaid John Wyn at Gwydir on the 28th day of June in the sixth year of the reign of the lord Edward the Sixth by the grace of God of England, France and Ireland, King, Defender of the Faith, and on earth Supreme Head of the English and Irish Church. *Footnote:* by me Owen Wyn, Clerk of the Peace.

Endorsement: Return of Hugh Peeke, esq., sheriff of the county of Caernarvon, to this writ. By virtue of this writ I cause to come before the within written Justices at the day and place within written both twelve free and lawful men from each hundred and liberty within written and twenty four free and lawful men for the body of the county of Caernarvon to do as this writ demands and requires. The names of ministers of the county of Caernarvon are shown in a certain schedule annexed to this writ.

From: O. Williams, ed., *Calendar of the Caernarvonshire Quarter Sessions Records*, vol. I, 1541–58, Caernarvonshire Historical Society, 1956, pp. 94, 95.

9. Quarter Sessions Indictment, 1558

1558 April 7. Rhydderch ap Hywel ap David ap Hywel of Cwmllannerch, yeoman, (Margaret ferch David Lloyd ap Meredydd, his wife, gent.) and Geoffrey ap Richard of the same, gentleman, at Cwmllannerch made an assault and affray upon David Lloyd ap Llywelyn ap John and did maltreat him and drew blood. And the said Geoffrey with a staff which he held in his hand struck the said David Lloyd upon his arm and gave him a great wound so that he did and still does languish in danger of death.

From: O. Williams, *Calendar*, p. 170.

10. The Council in the Marches as a Court of Law, 1594

This Council, although it bear the name of Council, is not so much occupied in matters of Council, as it is in hearing and determining of matters of right.

For it is now used and grown to be an ordinary Court of Justice for every man to sue in; and is much like in authority to the Court called the Chancery in Westminster, which is a court of equity to mitigate the vigour of Law in divers causes. The authority and jurisdiction of this Council is not certainly known: for they are to judge and determine of such matters as the Queen of England shall authorise them from time to time by way of instructions, and their authority is not certain. But most commonly they deal for all manner of misdemeanours, as assaults and affrays, riots, routs, forcible entries, briberies, extortions, comorthas, exactions, and all manner of outrages and misdemeanours committed within their commission. And therein they resemble much in authority the high and noble Court of Star Chamber at Westminster. They also deal in mitigating, as I said before, of all extremities and rigorousness of the Common Law of this land, as extreme dealings upon penal bonds and such like. It also determineth detaining of evidences where there is no remedy at the common law. It examineth the title of lands, depending upon the same; it taketh order for the speedy trial and pleading of matters at the common law: also it holdeth plea for debt without specialty, detaining of goods or chattels: it forceth evil dealing tutors to yield account to fatherless infants of their goods and debt: it examineth witnesses to remain of record *ad perpetuam rei memoriam*; and which is most beneficial of all other matters, it taketh speedy remedy for restoring or stalling of possessions of lands or tenements, which otherwise would be long ere they might recover their lawful possessions by ordinary course at the common law. It also punisheth the vices of incest, adultery and fornication. And generally it is the very place of refuge for the poor oppressed of this country of Wales to fly unto. And for this cause it is as greatly frequented with suits as any one Court at Westminster whatsoever the more for that it is the best cheap court in England for fees: and there is great speed made in trial of all causes. For they divide their sittings for matters in hearing into four terms, agreeable to those for England in number, though not agreeable in time...

This court is it which at the beginning brought Wales to that civility and quietness that you now see it, from that wild and outrageous state that you shall read of. And although some think it an unnecessary court at this present, considering the obedience that Wales is now brought unto, and fitter to be dissolved than continued, doubtless they are far mistaken therein, unless there were some other courts of like authority erected for punishment of divers the offences aforesaid...

From: George Owen, *Pembrokeshire*, pp. 21–4.

11. Quarter Sessions Depositions, 1762

DEPOSITIONS: INFORMATIONS

Humphrey Thomas, John David, and David Davies, deponents, said on oath
that Jane the wife of John Griffith of Bala, shopkeeper, had upon several
market days in Bala within the past year 'bought several pounds of bacon
and butter and several quantitys or loafs of different sorts of bread' and that
she had 'particularly on Saturday the tenth day of this instant bought six
pounds of butter or thereabouts and immediately after exposed the same to
sale the same day, and sold what she could sell off for a greater price, to the
prejudice of the poor in general' and the deponents in particular.
At the foot: Ordered that an indictment or an information be brought against
her at the next quarter. By the court.

From: K. Williams-Jones, *A Calendar of the Merioneth Quarter
Sessions Rolls*, vol. I, 1733–65, Merioneth County Council, 1965,
p. 214.

12. Parish responsibility – indemnification in a case of illegitimacy

13 *July* 1762

To Lewis Nanney, esquire, one of his majesty's justices of the peace in and
for the county of Merioneth.
Whereas Mary Jones of Penygilan in the county of Montgomery, single-
woman, hath in and by her voluntary examination, taken in writing and
upon oath before the said Lewis Nanney, declared that she is with child, and
that the said child is likely to be born a bastard and to be chargeable to the
parish of Llanwryn, and that one John Thomas, now of Cyldydd in the said
county of Merioneth, yeoman, is the father of the said child, we, the
churchwardens and overseers of the poor of the said parish of Llanwryn,
do therefore certify unto your wordship (*sic*) that Thomas Richard, David
Rees, and the said John Thomas have entered into their joint and several
bonds to us, bearing equal date herewith, for the indemnification of the said
parish of Llanwryn from all manner of costs, taxes, rates, assessments, and
charges whatsoever for or by reason of the birth, education, and maintenance
of the said child. Witness our hands this thirteenth day of July 1762.

Griffith Tudor, curate of Llanwryn.
William Hughes, churchwarden.
John David, Lewis Owen, overseers.

From: K. Williams-Jones, *A Calendar*, p. 215.

13. Parliamentary Representation, Acts of Union

And it is further enacted by the Authority aforesaid, That for this present Parliament, and all other Parliaments to be holden and kept for this Realm, two Knights shall be chosen and elected to the same Parliament for the Shire of Monmouth, and one Burgess for the Borough of Monmouth, in like Manner Form and Order, as Knights and Burgesses of the Parliament be elected and chosen in all other Shires of this Realm of England, and that the same Knights and Burgesses shall have like Dignity Pre-eminence and Privilege, and shall be allowed such Fees, as other Knights and Burgesses of the Parliament have been allowed...

And that for this present Parliament, and all other Parliaments to be holden and kept up for this Realm one Knight shall be chosen and elected to the same Parliaments for every of the Shires of Brecknock, Radnor, Mountgomery, and Denbigh, and for every other Shire within the said Country or Dominion of WALES; and for every Borough being a Shire-town within the said Country or Dominion of WALES, except the Shire-town of the foresaid County of Mereoneth, one Burgess; and the Election to be in like Manner Form and Order, as Knights and Burgesses of the Parliament be elected and chosen in other Shires of this Realm; and that the Knights and Burgesses, and every of them, shall have like Dignity Pre-eminence and Privilege, and shall be allowed such Fees, as other Knights of the Parliament have and be allowed; and the Knights' Fees to be levied and gathered of the Commons of the Shire that they be elected in; and the Burgesses' Fees to be levied and gathered as well of the Boroughs and Shire-towns as they be Burgesses of, as of all other ancient Boroughs within the same Shires.

From: Bowen, *The Statutes of Wales*, pp. 89, 90.

14. A Forthcoming Merioneth Election, 1571

At Ludlow, 14 March 1571.
Whereas the Council is informed that there is great labour and suit in Merionethshire concerning the next election of Knights of the shire for Parliament, and danger that by outward signs and tokens of brag a proper election will be prevented. The Council had thought wise to commission certain people to be present and take note of every one who should infringe the laws against rioting and carrying arms in assemblies and thereupon to report to the Council. But on consideration of the authority and charge of the Sheriff and Justices of the Peace, the not doing of their duties not being had in suspicion before some trial thereof, it is decided to trust to them. Therefore letters are to be sent out rehearsing this and commanding the Sheriff to make proclamation at the time of the election against any breach of the peace and especially against the carrying of weapons on pain of penalties provided by statute. If any disturbance should arise the Sheriff and

Justices are to use correction therein as the law has appointed and after being thus warned they will be held responsible for any disorder.

From: R. Flenley, ed., *A Calendar of the Register of the Queen's Majesty's Council in the Dominion and Principality of Wales and the Marches of the Same*, London, 1916, pp. 94, 95.

15. Petition of the Inhabitants of Haverfordwest to the Army, 1650

To the right Honourable the Committee for the Army

The humble petition of the Inhabitants of the Town and County of Haverfordwest

Sheweth

That your petitioners since the beginning of the War have been firm to the Parliament continually and in the year 1644 maintained a garrison therein upon their own charge against the late King's party, and for this their fidelity to the Parliament have been plundered of their estates, and many of them taken prisoners and forced to redeem themselves by paying great sums of money. That during the siege against the Town of Pembroke, being nine weeks or thereabouts, your petitioners assisted the Parliament's forces, being under the command of the then Lieutenant General Cromwell, the said forces being then on free quarter, and your petitioners have been heavily burdened with the relieving of prisoners of the Parliamentary party taken by the late King's forces, and maintaining of sick and wounded soldiers, and demolishing the Castle of Haverfordwest by the Lieutenant General's order, and by paying only the monthly assessment, and the assessment for Ireland, being in the said assessment raised from £10 a month to £45 a month, although the Army in August and September last in their march to Milford Haven to take shipping for Ireland were maintained by your petitioners for the most part upon free quarter, and continued a long time on them there, and do daily quarter as they go, and by reason hereof your petitioners are brought very poor, and most of the inhabitants of this town not able to maintain themselves and families, and many of them are forced to leave this town by reason of the said heavy assessment, which assessment should it be continued any longer, will be to your petitioners' utter undoing.

May it therefore please your honours, to take the sad condition and intolerable suffering of this town into consideration, and to take some order herein, whereby your petitioners in future assessments may be freed from paying any. Or at leastwise eased.

And your petitioners shall ever pray, etc.,

William Bowen Mayor	Thomas Arnold
John Davids	Jenkin Howell
William Davids	Roger Beavons

From: Matthew Griffiths, *Sources for Welsh Towns*, p. 78.

16. Bishop Richard Davies on the Coming of Christianity to Britain

Richard can rat DYW Episcop Menew, yn damuno adnewyddiat yr hen ffydd catholic a gollaun Evangel Christ i r Cembru oll, yn enwedic i bop map eneid dyn o vewn ey Escopawt...

y mae yn dra salw genyf dy welet ti wlat Cembru, a vu ryw amser gyntaf, yr owrhon yn dyvot yn olaf ynghyfryw ardderchawc oruuchafieth a hynn...

Dwyn cof a wnaf am vn rhinwedd ragorawl a gydbwysa yrhei vchod oll, ath harddai gynt, ac a rodday yt ragorfraint a goruchelder, sef crefydd dilwgr, crystynogaeth bur, a ffydd ffrwythlon ddiofer. Can ys dowait Sabellius historiawr ddarvot i ynys Prydain dderbyn ffydd Christ yn gyntaf vn or oll ynysoedd, ac nid heb achos: o blegit yn y ddecfet flwyddyn ar vgain ar ol derchafiad Christ i doeth i r deyrnas hon y Senadur anrhydeddus Joseph o Aramathya discybl Christ ac eraill discyblon crystynogaidd dyscedic gidac ef: y gwyr hynn megis ac i derbyniasont wr'r ffydd a'r crefydd ar crystynogaeth can Christ i hun, ay Apostolion, felly y pregethasont, ac i dyscasant yn y teyrnas honn. Nit bychan y goruchafiaeth hynn, cael cenadwyr dyscedic ffyddlon i osot sail a dechreuad sprydol edeiladaeth ffydd Christ ymplith pobyl. Y cynnyrch hwn a ffrwythawdd ac a chwanegawdd rhyd y teyrnas hon o ddydd i ddydd, ac o flwyddyn bigilydd, eithr heb i gadarnhau trwy gymeriad cyffredinawl a chyfraith y teyrnas hyd yn amser Lles vap Coel, rhwn a eilw y Lladinwyr Lucius, hwn a teyrnasai pan oedd oed Christ 180...

Translation

Richard, by the grace of God Bishop of St David's, wishing the restoration of the old catholic faith and the light of Christ's gospel to all the Welsh, especially to every human soul in his episcopate...

it is a great sadness to me to see you, the land of Wales, which was once first now last in so excellent a supremacy as this...

I will remind you of one excellent virtue outweighing all these others, a virtue which once adorned you and gave you privilege and supremacy, that is an uncorrupted belief, a pure Christianity and a fruitful faith. Because Sabellius the historian says that the island of Britain received the Christian faith first of all the islands, and not without cause: because in the thirtieth year after Christ's ascension there came to this kingdom the honourable senator Joseph of Arimathea, a disciple of Christ, and with him other learned Christian disciples: these men just as they received the truth faith and belief and

Christianity from Christ himself and his apostles so they preached and taught it in this kingdom. This was no small privilege, to have faithful and learned missionaries to lay the foundation of Christ's faith among people. This bore fruit and increased throughout this kingdom from day to day and year to year, though it was not confirmed generally by law until the time of Lles, son of Coel, called Lucius in Latin, who ruled in the year of Christ 180...

From: G. H. Hughes, ed., *Rhagymadroddion, 1547–1659*, Caerdydd, 1951, pp. 17, 18.

17. Religion in the Diocese of St David's, 1721

As the Christian Service is thus totally diffus'd in some places, there are other some that may be said to be half serv'd; there being several Churches, when we are but rarely, if at all to meet with Preaching, Catechising, or Administring of the Holy Communion; In others the Service of the Prayers is but partly Read, and that perhaps but once a Month, or once in a quarter of a Year; nor is it indeed reasonable to expect that they should be better serv'd while the Stipends allow'd for the Service of them are so small that a poor Curate must sometimes submit to serve three or four Churches for Ten or Twelve Pounds a Year, and that perhaps when they are almost as many miles distant from each other...

There is, I believe, no part of the Nation more inclin'd to be Religious, and to be delighted with it than the poor Inhabitants of these Mountains. They don't think it too much when neither ways, nor Weather are inviting, over cold and bleak Hills to travel three or four miles, or more, on foot to attend the Public Prayers, and sometimes as many more to hear a Sermon, and they seldom grudge many times for several hours together in their damp and cold Churches, to wait the coming of their Minister, who by Occasional Duties in his other Curacy's, or by other Accidents may be obliged to disappoint them, and to be often variable in his Hours of Prayer...

And yet not withstanding these discouragements, there are, God be thanked, several clergymen among us, that by their Vertue and steady Application, surmount the Difficulties they meet with, find Means to be well accomplished, and to adorn their Station for the sake of Well-doing, and to be no less Eminent for their Pastoral Care and Diligence, than others are for their Neglect and Scandal...

From: Erasmus Saunders, *A View of the State of Religion in the Diocese of St. David's*, London, 1721, University of Wales Press, Cardiff, 1949. *Topics in Welsh History*, Schools Council Committee for Wales, 1980, no. 8.

18. Howell Harris's Preaching Journeys, 1748

From a letter dated 20 October 1748 to Thomas Boddington

Tis now about 9 weeks since I begun to go round South & North Wales, & this week I came Home from my last journey Round North Wales – I have now visited in that time 13 Counties & travaild mostly 150 miles every week, & Discoursed twice every Day & Sometimes three & four times a Day: & this last Journey I have not taken off my Cloaths for 7 nights & travaild from one morning to ye next evening without any Rest above 100 miles, Discoursing att 12 or 2 in ye morning on ye mountain, being oblig'd to meet at that time by Reason of Persecution – one man being made ye week before I went there to pay 20£ near Wrexham, to Sr. W.W. Wynne, & Several of ye Hearers 5£ & som(e) 10£ yt had pd before, this being ye 3d time Poor people have been servd thus yt neighbourhood for assembling together;...I had in another Place, viz Bala, a Blow of my Head with Violence enough to slit my Head in two but I Recd no hurt – such crowds I never saw coming to hear & more Glory among ye People, many Hearts & Doors have been lately opened; & several Lately which we know of have been awakened, & ye Lord seems to turn His Face towards ye Rich, Several of them have been this Journey to hear me, & Several more talk with affection to come & hear Mr. Whitefield when He comes.

From G. M. Roberts, *Selected Trevecka Letters*, 1747–94, Caernarfon, 1962. *Topics*, Schools Council, no. 1.

19. Hymns by William Williams, Pantycelyn

(i) O'er those gloomy hills of darkness
Look, my soul; be still, and gaze;
All the promises do travail
With a glorious day of grace:
    Blessed Jubil
Let thy glorious morning dawn.

Kingdoms wide that sit in darkness,
Let them have the glorious light;
And from eastern coast to western
May the morning chase the night
    And redemption,
Freely purchased win the day.

Lord, I long to see that morning,
When Thy Gospel shall abound,
And Thy grace get full possession

Of the happy promised ground;
   All the borders
Of the great Immanuel's land.

Fly abroad, eternal gospel,
Win and conquer, never cease;
May thy lasting wide dominions
Multiply and still increase;
   May thy sceptre
Sway the enlightened world around.

(ii) Iesu, Iesu, 'r wyt Ti'n ddigon,
'R wyt Ti'n llawer mwy na'r byd;
Mwy trysorau sy'n dy enw
Na thrysorau'r India i gyd;
Oll yn gyfan
Ddaeth i'm meddiant gyda'm Duw.

Y mae gwedd dy ŵyneb grasol
Yn rhagori llawer iawn
Ar bob peth a welodd llygad
Ar hyd ŵyneb daear lawn;
Rhosyn Saron,
'Ti yw tegwch nef y nef.

(I am grateful to Beryl Thomas for providing me with a copy of the Welsh hymn.)

20. John Wesley in Wales, 1739 and 1763

I returned to Bristol. I have seen no part of England so pleasant for sixty or seventy miles together as those parts of Wales I have been in. And most of the inhabitants are indeed *ripe for the gospel*. I mean (if the expression appear strange) they are earnestly desirous of being instructed in it, and as utterly ignorant of it they are as any Creek or Cherokee Indians. I do not mean they are ignorant of the name of Christ. Many of them can say both the Lord's Prayer and the Belief. Nay, and some all the Catechism. But take them out of the road of what they have learned by rote, and they know no more (nine in ten of those with whom I conversed) either of gospel salvation or of that faith whereby alone we can be saved...

FRIDAY, 19. I preached near the market-place, and afterwards rode over to Trefeca. Howell Harris' house is one of the most elegant places which I have ever seen in Wales. The little chapel and all things round about it are finished in an uncommon taste, and the gardens, orchards, fish-ponds and mount adjoining make the place a little paradise. He thanks God for these things and looks through them. About six-score persons are now in the Family – all diligent, all constantly employed, all fearing God and working righteousness. I preached at ten to a crowded audience, and in the evening at Brecon again, but to the poor only, the rich (a very few excepted) were otherwise employed...

From: A. H. Williams, ed., *John Wesley in Wales*, Cardiff, 1971, pp. 5, 63, 64.

21. S.P.C.K. Schools – an answer to critics

TO THE REV MR PYE AT MONMOUTH   16 Sept 1710

Reverend Sir,

I receiv'd yours of the 19th and 28th of August both which so far as relat'd to the Society were communicat'd to them and they are very much pleas'd with your Resolution, Constancy and Success under the difficulties you have met with upon the score of Charity Schools. The Calumny you mention was, I believe, the first upon the design of Charity Schools that ever was heard of in the Society, and I am well satisfy'd is altogether groundless: I hope the Author of this unchristian reflection, whoever he be, will live to be convinc'd that they are the best friends to Religion in general and to the Church of England in particular, who wish all to be taught from the greatest to the least.

If Poverty and Meaness in the children of Charity Schools were a sufficient reason to justifie the neglect of 'em, Moses himself might have been left to perish on the Stream, and Pharaoh's daughter, instead of acting a generous part, had act'd very imprudently. But can they need to be vindicat'd who have above ten thousand living advocates in this Island – – – and may their number still encrease till the Knowledge of God shall cover the earth as the water cover the sea.

From: M. Clement, *Correspondence and Minutes of the S.P.C.K. relating to Wales 1699–1740*, Cardiff, 1952, p. 325.

22. The Circulating Schools

Many of the masters now are such as have themselves been taught in these schools; and all of them have it in charge, to teach their scholars to read, to sing psalms, and to pray with them morning and evening, and to make it always part of their devotion, to pray for their benefactors, and for the blessing of God to prosper their labour of love in these infant seminaries. They are to exhort their scholars to pray by themselves at home, and (if they are able) to set up the worship of God in the families they belong to, and not to neglect the public worship on the Lord's day. The masters are likewise to catechise and inculcate the principles and duties of religion, and admonish them against the reigning vices of the times, twice every day. In most of the schools, the adult persons do make about two thirds of the number taught in them. In some places, several who, for old age, are obliged to wear their spectacles, come into them...

I cannot but apprehend myself obliged humbly to offer what I think a sufficient answer to what is objected in England against these charity schools in Wales. They have now pretty well got over such prejudices that we were afraid would be most fatal to them; as, "The disagreeable novelty of setting up schools in the Welsh tongue, which had hardly been heard of at any time before; the harshness of expecting old people to learn to read, and men and women to be publickly taught and catechised in the principles of religion," etc. But all this prevailed little, the schools at present are earnestly desired in more places than we are yet able to supply...

From: W. M. Williams, *Selections from Welch Piety*, pp. 35, 37.

PART TWO

1. The Land Problem in the Nineteenth Century

But though there are these points of difference between the condition of Ireland and the condition of Wales, yet there are many points of resemblance. There is the same land hunger exhibited in almost if not quite as great a degree. There is the same attachment to the native land, and to the pursuit of farming under the same general traditional conditions. There is much of the same divergence in temperament, idiosyncracy, and habits between the actual cultivators of the soil and the aristocratic class who own the land. There is the same hostility, more veiled, but not less felt, to the agents of the landlord. Religious and social differences between the cultivators and the owners are just as well marked in Wales as they were in Ireland, if, indeed, not more highly developed. There is the same fear among the tenants that they may be ousted from homes to which they are passionately attached. There is the same conviction that the pressure of legal rules and economic circumstances is depriving them unjustly of the fruits of their labour. Besides these general points of resemblance, there is the important fact that, when the circumstances of the formation of the holdings are considered broadly and in the light of the past, it cannot be denied that a very large part of the improved value of the land is due to the work and the capital of generations

2. Dowlais Iron

Prices of Iron at Dowlais-Works, Glamorganshire, October 3 1816

		£	s.	d.
Squares Five-eighths Inch Diameter and Upwards, per Ton Short Weight		8	–	–
Half Inch Ditto	per Do. Ditto	9	–	–
Three-eighths		12	–	–
Round Bolts ¾ Inch Diameter and Upwards		8	–	–
Five eighths		9	–	–
Nine-sixteenths	}	11	–	–
Eight-sixteenths				
Seven-sixteenths				
Six-sixteenths	}	13	–	–
Five-sixteenths				
Four-sixteenths.	}	15	–	–
Common Flats, assorted to One and a Quarter Inch by a Quarter Inch per Ditto		8	–	–
One and an Eighth Inch by a Quarter Inch		9	–	–
One Inch by Half an Inch		9	–	–
Ditto by Three Eighths of an Inch		9	–	–
Ditto by Quarter-Inch.		9	10	
Seven Eighths by a Quarter Inch		10	–	–
Casement Iron	per Ton long weight }	9	–	
Nail Rods, Common, assorted .	per Ton long weight }			
Best		11	10	

	per Ton short weight
Hoops, Inch wide and upwards }	12 –
...... Seven-eighths	14 –
...... Three-quarters	12 –
Plough Plate Iron . . . . }	15 –
Box and Chest Plate, No. 1 to No. 11 Wire Gauge .	
Sheet Iron, Singles, No. 12 to No. 18 .	17 –
.... Doubles, No. 19 to No. 22 .	19 –
.... Trebles, No. 23 to No. 25 .	25 –
.... Four-fold, No. 26 .	13 –
Boiler Plates .	12 10
Hammered Uses, Axles, &c. .	
Planished Iron......extra per Ton, £0. 10. 0.	
Best Iron, or No. 3 extra, per Ton, £2. 0. 0.	

Delivered free on Board at Cardiff.

Payable by Acceptance (in London) at Six Months.

From: M. Elsas, ed., Iron in the Making. Dowlais Iron Company Letters 1782–1860, Glamorgan County Council and Guest Keen Iron and Steel Company Ltd, 1960, p. 111.

of cultivators who have never received adequate compensation in respect of
what has been done, but who, year after year, have felt that the power of
the landlord has enabled him to appropriate without acknowledgement the
additional value of the land due to the cultivators' exertions, by arbitrarily
raising rent.

From: *The Report of the Royal Commission on Land in Wales and
Monmouthshire*, 1896, pp. 911–12.

3. The Glamorganshire Canal

Navigation House [Glamorgan], November 4th 1823

I beg to inform you that the Canal is now ready to admit Boats to navigate
thereon, with a burthen of 25 Tons each, but there being very few Boats
prepared to carry that weight, and some part of the Banks being very recently
puddled and consequently not sufficiently settled to bear the additional
pressure, without incurring some risk, it is deemed best to raise the water
for the winter Months to navigate 23 or $23\frac{1}{2}$ Tons only, and which loads you
may forward at Your earliest convenience as the water in the Canal will from
henceforth be regulated accordingly.

From: Elsas, *Iron in the Making*, p. 154.

4. The Economy of South Wales during the Depression

The Coal Industry

Exports have dropped every year since 1929, from 29.9 million tons to 19.1
million tons in 1935; and the position has worsened not only absolutely but
relatively to the rest of the country. The percentage of South Wales exports
to United Kingdom exports has fallen from 37 per cent in 1929, to 35 per
cent in 1935...

If the royalties payable in South Wales had not been greater than the average
for the country, the ascertained loss of the industry in 1933 and subsequent
years would have been changed to a slight profit...

It is no longer disputed that the maintenance between 1925 and 1931 of
the pre-war gold value of the £, however much it may have assisted other
industries or interests, affected very adversely the coal exporting districts, and
especially South Wales, which exports a very large proportion of its total
output and finds its chief market in France, a country whose currency was
undervalued at a time when the £ was overvalued...

In the area as a whole the average percentage of unemployed men in the
coal-industry was 32.5 in 1931, rose to 42.4 in 1932, and fell steadily in

subsequent years to 34.4 in 1935. Expressed in numbers these percentages represent 65,853 in 1931, 81,507 in 1932, and 62,155 in 1935...

Numbers of Coal-miners (men only) insured (July), Unemployed[1] (June), and approximate numbers employed in June of each year from 1931 to 1935

District.	Status.	1931	1932	1933	1934	1935
Monmouth,	Insured	39,253	37,031	36,587	35,410	33,974
East and	Unemployed	8,988	16,252	15,644	15,969	9,313
West	Employed	30,265	20,879	21,943	20,441	24,661
Rhymney,	Insured	57,716	55,011	54,414	54,017	51,689
Merthyr and	Unemployed	21,554	28,355	27,168	29,258	20,266
Aberdare	Employed	36,162	26,656	26,246	24,759	31,423
Rhondda and	Insured	69,237	65,770	65,075	63,090	59,943
Port Talbot	Unemployed	34,586	39,610	32,940	31,995	26,511
	Employed	34,651	36,160	32,135	31,095	33,432
Neath, Swansea,	Insured	36,002	34,198	33,723	34,111	34,769
Amman	Unemployed	7,880	5,590	5,361	5,934	5,232
	Employed	28,122	28,608	28,362	28,177	29,537
	Insured	202,208	192,020	189,790	186,728	180,275
Whole Region	Unemployed	72,608	89,816	80,913	83,146	61,332
	Employed	129,600	102,204	108,877	103,582	118,943

[1] Wholly unemployed and temporarily stopped.

Projected solutions

The following general conclusions therefore emerge from the review of industries and population contained in this volume. Firstly, further State aid in the encouragement of new industries in South Wales would be economically justified. Secondly, some transfer of labour to other parts of Great Britain should still continue. Thirdly, certain new industries could be successfully located in South Wales without any need for special assistance, though it may be necessary to offer them certain inducements in order to overcome unjustified prejudices against location in this Region. Fourthly, the establishment of trading estates is justified as a method of ensuring the success of new industries. Fifthly, the success of new industries will depend upon the width of the market to which they can easily obtain access; and for this reason an improvement in the transport services connecting the Region with the rest of the country is desirable.

From: *The Second Industrial Survey of South Wales*, Cardiff, 1937, pp. 37, 38, 51, 64, 69, 402.

5. Early Nineteenth-century Caernarfon

The market here, which is held on Saturday, is most excellent, and affords in abundance of butcher's meat, poultry and garden stuff. The supply of fish might be better, but the establishment of a fishing boat with trawls within the last few years promises to improve the market in this respect, as the bay of Caernarvon abounds with the superior sorts of flatfish. A market house, handsome and substantial, is a recent erection and a great accommodation, although it be somewhat deficient in a full exposure to the air. Above it are kept the arms of the local militia, amounting to about seven hundred men. The town is copiously supplied with water from conduits of an excellent quality, so that the place cannot but be regarded as a very eligible residence for families which wish to unite at once comfort and economy. There are accordingly in general many strangers here, chiefly from Ireland. The shops also are numerous and well supplied, and of good medical assistance there is no deficiency. In no respect perhaps is the present generation more advantageously conditioned beyond any preceding one than in the widespread diffusion of medical advice and chirurgical assistance. Besides numerous public houses, there are in Caernarvon no less than four inns which keep post chaises.

Ship building was once carried on here to a considerable extent, but the decay of the accessible timber, together with the general circumstances of the Kingdom, has diminished it so greatly that I do not remember to have seen more than one small vessel at a time upon the stocks.

The harbour may be considered as formed by the mouth of the Seiont, which flows along the quay below the castle, and at high water is capable of floating the largest class of brigs. Vessels, however, lie in the Strait or above the town, and their numbers are generally so great as to imply a considerable traffic. The exports are slate, the chief branch of trade; some provisions, copper, a few bales of paper made in Llanrug, and a small quantity of coarse cloth. The imports are groceries, liquor, the various articles of supply for the shops, and coals.

From: Matthew Griffiths, *Sources for Welsh Towns*, pp. 13, 14.

6. Living in the Industrial Towns

William Taitt to Thomas Guest, 17/1/1799

One thing I must insist on, that we pay our Men only once a Month in future which will save us 3 broken days in the Month besides those drunken Combinations. Give the men Notice tomorrow so that they may prepare themselves accordingly...

Josiah John Guest to James Wise, 26/5/1826

I am sorry to have so bad an account of the Colliers. Bedlington must take two or three of the worst of them before a Magistrate & punish them by *committal* for neglecting their work. Our works consume a regular daily quantity of Materials & there is no good reason why the supply should not be regular & the Colliers work every day in as regular a Manner as Pudlers or any other class of Men...

John Evans to Lady Charlotte Guest

Dowlais, 20th September 1854

We have had twenty one deaths since Saturday and the disease [cholera] is spreading. The people are so frightened that they are leaving the place in droves, especially the Irish, amongst whom so far it has been most fatal.

It attacks all the dirty courts and gulleys and the over crowded houses. There are very few that survive many hours when once attacked. God grant that in his mercy to us that the heavy scourge may soon pass away. All that can be done for to aleviate their distress shall be strictly attended to. We shall remove a lot up to the Barn to day, and further provision is being made for the reception of a larger number. It is very distressing to see the state of excitment which prevails amongst the men. It is with the greatest dificulty that we can carry on the Mills & other departments. The men are leaving the place altogether...

When a child first goes into the pits he is taken down by father, or some friend who has employment in the work; he is usually put to keep an air-door, or to some light work. In examining the boys few would own that they felt much fear or distress on entering the pits, and all say they very soon became used and reconciled to their work...parents...lured by the wages, are never backward in sending their Children to the pits as soon as they can get them into employ, so that no sooner is a collier's son able to exert a little muscular force than he becomes an underground machine, destitute of the slightest mental cultivation.

Drawing or pushing the coal-wagons, which in North Wales are called pyches, forms the principal employment of Children and Young Persons in the pits. Drawing is performed by means of a chain passing from the pyche between the boy's legs, and fastened to a girdle around his waist; being thus attached to the load he draws it by stooping down, proceeding along "all-fours". Some push the pyches from behind, which is done by the hands and forehead. The Children describe it as immaterial to them which method they persue. In low works, where the seams of coal are very thin, they draw, as they can stoop lower than in the attitude of pushing.

At first the chain in drawing...sometimes causes so much soreness as to oblige the boys to leave off work for a day or two; but no other evil arises from this unnatural and in appearance brutal mode of working boys; and custom reconciles...them to their wretched fate...

Accidents at Coal Pits. – There have been numerous and very fatal accidents in the course of the last four years from explosions in coal pits. In July 1845, there was an explosion at the Upper Dyffryn Colliery, by which 29 persons lost their lives; in August 1849, an explosion took place at the Lletty Shenkin Colliery, by which 52 lives were lost; in December 1850, an explosion took place at the Middle Dyffryn, which resulted in the death of 8 persons. In the summer of 1851, 14 persons lost their lives from the breaking of a chain at the Wherfa Colliery. The last great accident was occasioned by an explosion of gas at the Middle Dyffryn Colliery (May 1852), when 65 persons were killed...

2. The deaths under 5 years of age have been at the rate of 46 per cent upon the whole number of deaths; and the deaths under 20 years of age have been 60 per cent of the whole mortality...

Mr. *Thomas Price* states, –

"A large number of the houses between this and Aberamman, and also in the town itself, have cesspits without any outlet. Bute-street is in this state; and in many cases the liquids have overflowed already, and even run into the houses. Many of the houses here are newly built, and the nuisance is not so bad as it will be in the course of a few years. Scores upon scores of houses are in this state. A very large proportion of the houses upon Lord Bute's property are so circumstanced – Bute street, Wrgan-row, Hirwain-row, Club-row, and others."

Robert Parsons, serjeant of police, states, –

"The overcrowding is excessive. In one small room there are five beds. It is common to find three in a bed, and mostly quite naked – male and female in the same room. The roof or ceiling is so low that in one case there is not room for one to sit up in bed. There is no drainage whatever, and no privy; nor, indeed, the right to the use of a privy to any of these houses.

WATER SUPPLY. – There is no public provision for water supply. In a very few cases there are wells sunk in private premises; but the great bulk of the inhabitants, indeed the whole of them (with the exception of those having wells), are supplied from natural springs or spouts, which are scattered at great distances apart...

Under the best circumstances the people here have to fetch their water from places above a quarter of a mile distant, and at times they have to go a mile and upwards...

Mr. *Thomas Price* states,

"There is much waiting at the spouts; three hours for a turn is no uncommon time. People have been known to go for water immediately after their dinner at twelve o'clock, and return at six o'clock without any, their turn not having come round. They get up frequently at two or three o'clock in the morning to go for water. A hundred jugs in a row are at times seen at the spouts. There is much immorality at the spouts, from people waiting there, and having nothing to do..."

> From: Elsas, *Iron in the Making*, pp. 24, 73; *Report of the Royal Commission on the Employment of Children in Mines*, 1842, Schools Council, no. 34; Rammell's *Report on Aberdare*, H.M.S.O., 1853.

7. Housing and Health between the Wars

An analysis submitted by Mr. Tomley of the mortality from tuberculosis (all forms) in the counties and county boroughs of England and Wales for the seven years 1930–6 shows that, in the 83 county boroughs, the average mortality from tuberculosis was 968 per million; three county boroughs in Wales exceeded this figure viz. Cardiff, the worst of the Welsh county boroughs, which came seventh on the list, Newport which came twelfth, and Merthyr fourteenth, but Swansea (thirty-first on the list) showed a mortality below the average for county boroughs.

The Welsh counties showed up badly. The average tuberculosis mortality for the counties of England and Wales for the seven year period was 724 per million. Welsh counties occupied the seven highest places in the list, viz., Caernarvon with average mortality 1,283 per million, Merioneth 1,196, Anglesey 1,153, Cardigan 1,104, Pembroke 956, Glamorgan 938, Carmarthen 918; Brecknock came tenth on the list, Monmouth thirteenth, Denbigh fifteenth, Montgomery sixteenth, Radnor twenty-second, whilst Flint only (twenty-sixth on the list) showed a mortality figure below the average for all counties, its mortality being little more than half that of Caernarvon.

Mr. Tomley's table brings out very clearly how greatly the tuberculosis mortality in the rural counties of Wales exceeds that of the rural counties in England, and how even such industrialised counties as Lancashire and the West Riding of Yorkshire have tuberculosis mortalities considerably lower than the rural counties of Wales...

According to Dr. Cox, in Anglesey not only was there serious overcrowding generally, but a large proportion of tuberculous persons were occupying the same room as other persons and actually sleeping in the same bed. In 104 beds there were sleeping 104 phthisical patients and 113 other persons, which means that in some instances a tuberculous person shared the same bed with at least two other persons...

It is obvious, from the particulars already given, that the Local Authorities in Wales have not taken the advantage that they should have done of the powers and assistance given to them by Parliament. The figures show that the number of new houses erected in Wales since 1919 compares unfavourably with the number for England and Wales as a whole. A more detailed examination of the figures, moreover, shows that the best use of the powers and assistance given by Parliament has been made in Flint, Swansea, Denbigh, Newport, Cardiff, Carmarthen, Monmouth, Caernarvon and Glamorgan, and that there is a very marked falling off in the efforts made in the remaining eight counties and county boroughs...

It is well known that the difficulties of the rural areas are great, and witness after witness directed our attention to these difficulties. In particular, they pointed to the poverty of the Authorities, and the small incomes of the inhabitants in the rural areas. The low wages of the agricultural labourer form also the standard on which the wages paid to other workers in the rural areas are based, and as the general spending power is small, the amount earned by the shopkeepers and others is also small...While being well aware of these difficulties and giving them due weight, we are, nevertheless, of opinion that the Authorities in those counties have fallen far short of their duties and of their obligations. We find that they have had insufficient regard for their powers or their duties or the advice which was tendered to them by their officers. In fact, they have failed in their trusteeship as guardians of the health and welfare of the people who elected them...

Evidence was given as to a type of house found in Anglesey, Caernarvon, Carmarthen, Cardigan and Pembroke, which was designated by Dr. Glyn Cox as the old-fashioned Celtic type. The house may stand alone on the countryside or it may be one of a row in a village or small town. The following is a fair description of it: –

The house is stone-built with no damp course. The walls and roof are often lime-washed and from the outside have a not unattractive appearance. The building is about 24 ft. long by about 9 ft. deep. There is one entrance which is in the middle of the front wall. There are two windows – one on either side of the door. The height of the house to the eaves is about 8 ft. The roof is usually a gabled one. On entering the door, it is found that the house is divided into two rooms by a thin partition. One is the living room or kitchen and the other is the sleeping chamber or "siamber." In South Wales, one room is called the "pen-uwch" and the other the "penissa." There is a grate in the living room or kitchen, with, sometimes, an oven attached. The floor is of earth, or mud and lime, or stone or slate. Then often, in order to provide further sleeping accommodation, boards have been put across from wall to wall above the sleeping chamber. This is to provide another room called a grog-loft. The height of such a loft at the apex of the roof varies from about 5 ft. to 6 ft. and, of course, it tapers down to nothing at the walls on either side. Sometimes, but not always, there is a small skylight in the roof, which seldom measures more than about 18 ins. by 15 ins. and which does not always open. The grog-loft is reached by a ladder which is sometimes movable and sometimes fixed. Further, so we were told, in some of these houses there is a puddle which was made originally as a well. This is sometimes open and sometimes has a cover... We should like here to pay a tribute to the women who have occupied such houses as these. We ourselves observed, and we heard a great body of evidence showing, that cleanliness was most marked. The furniture and clothing, bedding and linen in these hovels are, for the most part, kept spotlessly clean, and one can only imagine what the cost has been for the women, and wonder how they kept their faith and their spirit in such adversity...

Speaking of Cardigan, Dr. Ernest Jones said: –

"The main diet is tea and bread and butter. Sunday is the only day when fresh meat appears on the table. Country products such as milk, eggs, garden vegetables and fruit enter very little into the diet of the people, and the milk-oatmeal foods (i.e. porridge, flummery, and oatmeal cake) once so characteristic of Welsh farm life, are rarely seen even in outlying farms. The garden and its products are fallen into neglect, and the art of vegetable cooking has largely disappeared. In many villages milk cannot be obtained at any price."

From: Ministry of Health, *Report of the Committee of Inquiry into the Anti-Tuberculosis Service in Wales and Monmouthshire*, H.M.S.O., 1939, pp. 24, 35, 138, 139, 142, 143, 210.

8. The Chartist Rising, Newport, 1839

'At about nine o'clock the cheering of many voices was heard in the distance, from the direction of Stow Hill, producing the utmost alarm...In a few minutes after, the front ranks of a numerous body of men, armed with guns, swords, pikes, bludgeons, and a variety of rude weapons, made their appearance, and wheeled round the corner of the hotel, from Stow Hill, with more observance of regularity in movement than it is usual for rioters to display; an observer who saw the movement down Stow Hill, calculates that this body of Chartists must have amounted to five thousand men. When the head of the column arrived at the Westgate…they appeared to be almost twelve abreast. The leading ranks then formed in front of the house, and a large body made an attempt to enter the yard leading to the stables, but found the gate too strongly secured against them. Then they wheeled to the portico of the inn, holding their guns and other weapons in a menacing manner…The heat of the conflict lasted about a quarter of an hour, when the defeated Chartists took to their heels in all directions – throwing away their arms, and abandoning the dead and dying…'

From: *Monmouthshire Merlin*, 9 November, 1839; Schools
Council, no. 37.

9. The Unions, 1831

John Maughan junior to Josiah John Guest

Mostyn, Holywell [Flintshire], November 8 1831

I hope you will excuse the liberty I am about to take in addressing you, but my acquaintance with Merthyr & the honor of a slight acquaintance with yourself have caused me to be deputed by the Magistrates here to ask a question in regard to the State of the *"Unions"* in South Wales, which is, have you or any of the Coal Masters in your District been able to break down the Unions & to persuade the men to dissociate themselves from them?

We have a very stubborn Contest going on here now & one very likely to make much disturbance in the Country, growing out of the overbearing Conduct of the men in the Union belonging to the Mostyn Colliery. Messrs. Eyton, the Lessee, has been provoked to declare that he never will suffer a man connected with the Unions to work in his Pits. The men have complied with everything required of them, except the abandonment of the Union, & they affirm that their Unwillingness to yield upon this point arises as well from the Solemnity of some oath they have taken, as from an apprehension that, if they were to give way & relinquish the Union, they would never be able to get employment elsewhere. It has been stated to the Magistrates that in South Wales the Unions have been overcome & that the men have for the most part given them up. The men, however, flatly contradict this. If you could affirm the statement it is thought that it would do much towards disposing these men to separate from their Union. They are exceedingly destitute. They receive scarcely any supplies of money & they are most anxious to go to their work. If their consciences in regard to the oath could be appeased, & if their apprehensions in regard to the safety of their persons could be overcome, it is thought here that they would throw the Union overboard. The Contest has been going on 5 weeks.

From: Elsas, *Iron in the Making*, pp. 62–3.

10. The Disestablishment Issue

'We ask for Disestablishment not only as an act of political justice, but also in the interests of the religious life and social peace of Wales. The representatives of rural England here today, need not be told how the Establishment embitters and impoverishes the life of your villages. You know its baneful influences. But in Wales, every one of these influences is accentuated, and so exercised as to affect most prejudicially the life of the people...

With all its phenomenal activity under threat of Disestablishment, the Church is still a small minority in almost every parish in Wales. It is anti-national in its sympathies. It strains the exercise of its legal and social principles so invidiously here and so wantonly there, as to create heartburning and irritation. Nay, more, its continued maintenance as an Establishment is a degradation...Welsh nationality has outlived Castle oppression. But an equally degrading yoke remains.'

From:T. E. Ellis, *Addresses and Speeches*, Wrexham, 1912; Schools Council, no. 50.

11. Lloyd George's First Commons Speech

14 June 1890

Shortly after I wrote my letter of yesterday to you I got up & spoke for the first time in the House of Commons....There is no doubt I scored a success & a great one. The old man & Trevelyan, Morley, Harcourt appeared delighted.

Tom Ellis who is genuinely delighted because one of his own men has succeeded – told me that several members had congratulated *Wales* upon my speech.

From: Kenneth O. Morgan, ed., *Lloyd George Family Letters 1885–1936*, Cardiff and London, 1973, p. 29.

12. Cymru Fydd

21 November 1895 (from Swansea)

Last night's demonstration was simply *immense* – that is the word. Nothing like it in the Rhondda – not in the memory of the oldest inhabitant has anything to equal it been seen. Crowds from all parts of the Rhondda came down. Hundreds of D. A. Thomas' own colliers amongst them. Mabon looked blue. I talked Home Rule for Wales & all the nationalist stuff which the Mabon crew so detest – but the people cheered to the echo. The Rhondda has been captured.

16 January 1896 (from Newport)

The meeting of the Federation was a packed one. Associations supposed to be favourable to us were refused representation & men not elected at all received tickets. There were two points of dispute between us. By some oversight they allowed me to speak on one & we carried it – as it turned out not because the majority of the meeting was with us but because they went to the vote immediately after my speech & I can assure you the impression made could be felt. I simply danced upon them. So they refused to allow me to speak on the second point. The majority present were Englishmen from the Newport district. The next step is that we mean to summon a Conference of South Wales & to fight it out. I am in bellicose form & don't know when I can get home.

From: K. O. Morgan, *Lloyd George*, pp. 92, 94.

13. The Penrhyn Lockout

We make an appeal on behalf of Old Men, Widows, and Orphans who are already suffering great hardships in consequence of the Lock Out.

We who are on the spot, and are sufferers ourselves, know full well the justice of the men's cause, and the oppression they have suffered every since the present Lord Penrhyn came into possession. The good feeling that existed between his late noble father and his workmen was destroyed at a stroke by the present lord within three months of his coming into the property, and all his dealings with them ever since have been tyrannical. He terminated at a month's notice the conditions under which they worked with his noble father...He did all this without consulting the wishes of the men to whom it was of vital importance. He has by his actions endeavoured to create ill-feeling in the quarry between Unionist and Non-unionist workmen...

On behalf of the Relief Committee,

W J Parry, Chairman
G Roberts, JP, Vice-Chairman,
Daniel Lloyd, Treasurer
Rev W W Lloyd, General Secretary
6 February 1901.

From: Schools Council, no. 53.

14. The Alternative Politics of 'The Miners' Next Step'

It becomes necessary then to devise means which will enable this new spirit of real democratic control to manifest itself...

Programme

That the organisation (a centralised British union of mineworkers) shall engage in political action, both local and national, on the basis of complete independence of, and hostility to, all capitalist parties, with an avowed policy of wresting whatever advantage it can for the working class...

Alliances to be formed, and trades organisation fostered, with a view to steps being taken, to amalgamate all workers into one national and international union, to work for the taking over of all industries, by the workmen themselves.

Policy

The old policy of identity of interest between employers and ourselves be abolished, and a policy of open hostility installed.

Objective

Every industry thoroughly organised...to fight, to gain control of, and then to administer, that industry. The coordination of all industries on a Central Production Board (to overcome production and distribution according to need)...leaving the men themselves to determine under what conditions and how, the work should be done. This would mean real democracy in real life, making for real manhood and womanhood. Any other form of democracy is a delusion and a snare.

> From: Unofficial Reform Committee, *The Miners' Next Step*, Tonypandy, 1912. Included in David Smith, 'The Tonypandy Riots', *Wales, 1880–1914*, The Open University in Wales, 1984.

15. A Secretary of State for Wales

Wales has her Secretary of State after a campaign of 60 years. But at first sight his responsibilities, as outlined yesterday by Mr. Wilson, do not seem to make up a significant devolution of authority. Since 1951, when the first Minister of Welsh Affairs was appointed, Cabinet representation for Wales has been linked, first, with the office of Home Secretary and, more latterly, with that of the Minister of Housing and Local Government. As Sir Keith Joseph was quick to point out in the House of Commons yesterday, the only additional executive responsibility beyond housing, local government and town and country planning given to the new Secretary of State concerns roads. The Labour Party's 1963 policy document, Signposts to the New Wales, which was endorsed by their election manifesto promised that education, health and agriculture would also fall under his authority.

On this score there will, of course, be disappointment among many Welshmen – clearly, the Secretary of State for Wales will not have the same power as his Scottish equivalent.

From: *Western Mail*, 20 November 1964.

16. A Plaid Cymru Victory
Plaid soar to great win

Evans doubles vote

The Carmarthenshire by-election produced a major political sensation when the Welsh Nationalists gained their first-ever seat in Parliament early this morning.

President of the party, Mr. Gwynfor Evans, aged 54, ended the nine-year Labour dominance with a win over Labour's Gwilym Prys Davies, a Pontypridd solicitor.

Plaid Cymru turned a 9,000 Labour majority into a 2,436-vote victory with the Liberal Hywel Davies polling 8,615 votes, and Simon Day, the Tory, 2,934. The Tory candidate loses his deposit.

Outside the hall the result – announced shortly after 1.05 a.m. – was greeted with a tremendous roar from Welsh Nationalist supporters singing Welsh songs.

From: *Western Mail*, 15 July 1966.

17. Devolution

Wales and Scotland must have their own directly-elected assemblies. That is the unanimous view of the Kilbrandon Commission on the Constitution, though its 13 members are deeply divided on what those assemblies should do.

The commission, as expected, emphatically rejected any notion of separatism for both countries, because it feels they would be materially worse off outside the United Kingdom, and because the vast majority of people just do not want it.

But it does present four alternative schemes of devolution ranging from advisory councils to virtual domestic Home Rule. And Government action is sure to be influenced as much by the public debate that is bound to follow as by the commission's arguments.

The demand for a measure of legislative self-government for Scotland and Wales tends to fall into one of two traps. If the nationalist movements are quiescent, the answer is that no one wants any change.

If the separatist parties are winning votes, the answer is that there may be case for devolution but to concede at this time is to encourage people to demand more and more until nothing is possible but total separatism.

From: *Western Mail*, 1 November 1973 and 20 May 1974.

18. An English view of the Welsh Language, 1847

My district exhibits the phenomenon of a peculiar language isolating the mass from the upper portion of society; and, as a further phenomenon, it exhibits this mass engaged upon the most opposite occupations at points not very distant from each other; being, on the one side, rude and primitive agriculturists, living poorly and thinly scattered; on the other, smelters and miners, wantoning in plenty and congregated in the densest accumulations. An incessant tide of immigration sets in from the former extreme to the latter, and, by perpetuating a common character in each, admits of their being contemplated under a single point of view. Externally, indeed, it would be impossible to exhibit a greater contrast in the aspect of two regions and the circumstances of their inhabitants, than by comparing the country between the rivers Towi and Teifi, with Merthyr, Dowlais, Aberdare, Maesteg, Cwm Afon, and the vales of Neath and Swansea. Yet the families, which are daily passing from the one scene to the other, do not thereby change their relative position in society. A new field is opened to them, but not a wider. They are never masters; and, if the rural portion of them does not grow in numbers, nor manifest any fresh activity, while the other portion is daily augmented and put upon fresh or more extended enterprizes, the difference is to be sought in the classes to which they are severally subjected and not in themselves. It is still the same people. Whether in the country, or among the furnaces, the Welsh element is never found at the top of the social scale, nor in its own body does it exhibit much variety of gradation. In the country, the farmers are very small holders, in intelligence and capital nowise distinguished from labourers. In the works, the Welsh workman never finds his way into the office. He never becomes either clerk or agent. He may become an overseer or sub-contractor, but this does not take him out of the labouring and put him into the administering class. Equally in his new, as in his old, home, his language keeps him under the hatches, being one in which he can neither acquire nor communicate the necessary information. It is a language of old-fashioned agriculture, of theology, and of simple rustic life, while all the world about him is English.

From: *Report of the Commissioners of Inquiry into the State of Education in Wales*, London, 1847, pp. 2, 3, 4.

19. Sunday Schools and Works' Schools, 1847

Whatever such Sunday-schools may be as places of instruction, they are real fields of mental activity. The Welsh working-man rouses himself for them. Sunday is to him more than a day of bodily rest and devotion. It is his best chance, all the week through, of showing himself in his own character. He marks his sense of it by a suit of clothes regarded with a feeling hardly less Sabbatical than the day itself. I do not remember to have seen an adult in rags in a single Sunday-school throughout the poorest districts. They always seemed to me better dressed on Sundays than the same classes in England. By the denomination "Workmen's Schools," I intend to designate schools directly connected with particular works, and maintained (wholly or in part) by a stoppage from the people's wages employed in those works, the proprietors usually providing the site and the school-room.

I found 24 such schools. The stoppages upon the people's wages vary considerably in amount, as $\frac{1}{2}d.$, $1d.$, or $2d.$ per week; $2d.$, $4d.$, or $6d.$ per month; $\frac{1}{2}d.$, $1d.$, or $4d.$ in $1l.$, (in the latter instance the sick fund is maintained from the same source). For these payments, books, but not stationery, are generally found. The stoppage is compulsory, and is made irrespectively of the number of children sent to school, or of a man's having any to send.

From: *ibid.*, pp. 4, 12.

20. A Private School, 1847

This school is held in a ruinous hovel of the most squalid and miserable character: the floor is of bare earth, full of deep holes; the windows are all broken; a tattered partition of lath and plaster divides it into two unequal portions; in the larger were a few wretched benches, and a small desk for the master in one corner; in the lesser was an old door, with the hasp still upon it, laid crossways upon two benches, about half a yard high, to serve for a writing desk! Such of the scholars as write retire in pairs to this part of the room, and kneel on the ground while they write. On the floor was a heap of loose coal, and a litter of straw, paper, and all kinds of rubbish. The Vicar's son informed me that he had seen 80 children in this hut. In summer the heat of it is said to be suffocating; and no wonder.

From: *ibid.*, p. 16.

21. The Religious Census of 1851

Northop Township.
Popn. 355 males, 364 females; total 719.

ST. PETER'S CHURCH NORTHOP (LLANEURGAIN).

Endowed: by tithe rent charge.

Space: free 213; other 462.

Present: morn. 100*+55 scholars; aft. 90+20 scholars; even. 140.

Average: morn. 150*+50 scholars; aft. 90+20 scholars; even. 180 to 200.

Remarks: To account for the difference between the morning congregation of March 30 and the average, it shd be stated that the morning service is *Welsh & English* on alternate Sundays. On March 30 the morning service was *Welsh*, when the congregation is much less. In the average a mean is taken. Also the evening proved unfavourable, the congregation was less than the average.

Thomas Jones Hughes.   Curate.

[Remarks on a separate sheet:]

In estimating the *Church* [crossed out] attendance at divine worship at Northop Parish Church it is important to bear in mind, that Northop being a *Border Parish* is peculiarly circumstanced, two languages, *Welsh* and *English*, being spoken in it. To meet this difficulty, *three* services are provided, the morning and afternoon interchanging Welsh and English on successive Sundays, and the evening being always English. The numbers cannot be added as the services are held at different parts of the day; but if the object of the return be to ascertain the number of *different persons* who attend Divine Service at Church on Sunday this may be done with some stylish deduction and taking one service attendance only of the Sunday Scholars, as the difference of language under the congregations with few exceptions totally different. I mention this circumstance as the return does not seem to contemplate parishes situated as Northop is.

[Dated at Northop April 2nd. '51]

EBENEZER. WESLEYAN METHODIST.

Erected 1841.

Space: free 40; other 250; standing 30.

Present: morn. 8 scholars; aft. 38; even. 31.

Average: morn. 30+10 scholars; aft. 45; even. 35.

Thomas Hughes.   Manager.

SALEM. WELSH CALFINIST.

Erected 1778.

Space: free 20; other 48; standing 120.

Present: morn. 60 scholars; aft. 86 scholars; even. 151.

Average: morn. 53 scholars; aft. 72 scholars; even. 138.

Robert Roberts.   Steward.

DWLLIN CHAPEL. METHODIST NEW CONNEXION.
Erected 1834.
Space: free 90; other 90.
Present: morn. 15 + 91 scholars; aft. 56 + 23 scholars; even 65 + 23 scholars.
Average (12 *months*): morn. 15 + 96 scholars; aft. 80 + 120 scholars; even. 100 + 40 scholars.
Thomas Attbury.
Local Preacher and Leader.
Northop Colliery.

> From: I. G. Jones, ed., *The Religious Census of 1851 A Calendar of the Returns relating to Wales*, vol. II, Cardiff, 1981, pp. 109, 110.

22. Secondary School Deficiencies, 1881

In the Report of the Schools Inquiry Commissioners estimates are given which indicate that about 16 boys in every thousand of the population should be receiving education higher than elementary.

Taking the population of Wales and Monmouthshire to be about 1,570,000, and reducing the estimate in consideration of the exceptional conditions of Wales from 16 to 10 per 1,000, intermediate school accommodation should be provided for 15,700 boys, and that number ought to be in attendance.

In contrast to this our returns show accommodation in the public schools for less than 3,000, and that accommodation to a great extent unsatisfactory. They also show an attendance of less than 1,600.

After taking into account the trifling provision made by the proprietary schools referred to above, and the numbers in attendance in private schools, as to the efficiency of which in respect of accommodation and instruction we have no complete information, there still remains a great and deplorable difference between the number who ought to be receiving intermediate education and the number who are in receipt of it...

The industrial conditions of many parts of Wales, the ordinary requirements of trade and agriculture, and the tastes and aptitudes of the Welsh people themselves suggest to us the importance, in any course of instruction prescribed for intermediate schools, of giving prominence to various branches of natural science, especially in their practical application to commerce and manufactures.

We suggest, therefore, that in places where there is a considerable population requiring education superior to that which can be provided in an ordinary elementary school, but unable to avail themselves of a higher school, advanced elementary schools for boys and girls should be established, and that the instruction in such schools should be adapted as closely as possible to the characteristics of each place, and to the educational needs of the inhabitants.

From: *Report of the Committee appointed to inquire into the Condition of Intermediate and Higher Education in Wales*, H.M.S.O., 1881, pp. xvi, lv and lx.

23. College Provision, 1881

On this ground we recommend that for the present only one college in addition to that already existing should be provided. It would, we believe, be almost unanimously agreed that such new college should be placed in Glamorganshire, though there might be some difference of opinion as to the rival claims of Cardiff and Swansea, to be regarded as the most suitable site.

Cardiff, and the places within reach of it, supply, within a given area, the larger population, while Swansea and its neighbourhood are the seats of more varied industries.

The Glamorganshire college may be expected for some time, at all events, to meet the requirements of South Wales, and the college at Aberystwith, whether retained on its present site or removed to Carnarvon or Bangor, must be accepted as the college for North Wales.

From: *Report on Intermediate and Higher Education*, p. lxvi.

A NOTE ON FURTHER STUDY

Further investigation into any aspect of the history of Wales might involve work on a wide variety of, first, secondary, then primary, sources. It would start with the compilation of a bibliography. The most detailed resource – the *Bibliography of the History of Wales* – was published in 1962 (Cardiff). Four supplements have been published in the *Bulletin of the Board of Celtic Studies*, 1963, 1966, 1969 and 1972. A new bibliography is currently being prepared by the Board's History and Law Committee and is very near completion. There is an important literary bibliography available, *Llyfryddiaeth Llenyddiaeth Gymraeg*, edited by Thomas Parry and Merfyn Morgan (Cardiff, 1976).

Some standard works carry extensive bibliographies, the best example being that in K. O. Morgan, *Rebirth of a Nation, Wales 1880–1980* (Oxford and Cardiff, 1981). There is a substantial list of books and articles, both English- and Welsh-language, in Geraint H. Jenkins, *Hanes Cymru yn y Cyfnod Modern Cynnar, 1530–1760* (Cardiff, 1983). A short bibliography has just been published by the Historical Association, *The Teaching of Welsh History in the Secondary Schools of Wales* (1983). Its author, Hugh Thomas, has provided a most useful introductory list of textbooks, monographs and articles. Major texts and monographs should be available in the majority of school and reference libraries. All such works are normally available in college and university libraries. County libraries have a service whereby books held by the county can be made available at any branch, normally within seven days. Increasingly, this service is computerised.

Articles on Welsh history appear in British journals, as with Peter Roberts's 'The Union with England and the Identity of "Anglican" Wales', in *Transactions of the Royal Historical Society* (1972). The source of many major articles on the history of Wales is the *Welsh History Review*, first published in 1960 and currently published twice a year. It carries seminal articles and performs two other signal services. These are the publication of substantial reviews of all new books which have some relevance to Welsh history, and the annual listing of articles on Welsh history which have appeared in the previous year. A similar list also appears in *Archaeologia Cambrensis*. The majority of these articles are published in national journals which appear annually, such as the *Transactions of the Honourable Society of Cymmrodorion* or *Llafur, the Journal of Welsh Labour History*, or a whole range of journals published by county and local history societies. For instance the county journals of the historic counties of Cardigan, *Ceredigion*, and Glamorgan, *Morgannwg*, appear annually and contain important articles and reviews. County libraries normally subscribe to the major historical journals and hold them for reference. University and college libraries subscribe to a wider range.

Articles published in journals are normally the fruits of original research, predominantly by professional historians. Some of this research appeared first in thesis form. Students of the University of Wales who complete master's degrees or doctorates deposit one copy in the National Library of Wales, Aberystwyth, and one in their own university library. They are available for consultation in either place. Students at other British universities sometimes choose Welsh themes, and special arrangements have to be made before Oxford and Cambridge theses can be consulted. Lists of theses on Welsh subjects are published regularly in the *Welsh History Review*. There are lists in Vol. V, No. 3, 1971; Vol. VII, No. 1, 1974 and Vol. IX, No. 1, 1978. The National Library of Wales publishes *A List of Dissertations submitted and accepted for Higher Degrees in the University of Wales*. The list goes back to 1899 and the latest volume takes it up to 1979. Particularly important theses tend to form the basis of monographs. This practice is currently being actively encouraged by means of the *Studies in Welsh History* series of monographs being published by the University of Wales Press under the auspices of the Board of Celtic Studies and the general editorship of Ralph A. Griffiths, Kenneth O. Morgan and Glanmor Williams.

The 'grass roots' research which results in theses, articles and monographs involves investigating a bewildering variety of primary sources. The bulk of these are printed and documentary sources but, for the more recent past, photographs and oral history, for example, loom large. Extracts from a small sample of the available printed documentary material are reproduced earlier in this book. They include Acts of Parliament, government reports, court records, censuses, diaries, antiquarians' descriptions and newspapers. This kind of material provides invaluable intentional record and unwitting testimony about the period to which it relates and requires rigorous analysis of bias, reliability, insight and relevance to yield its full quota of information.

Many books of printed documents are transcriptions of manuscripts, provided either in calendar form, in which the editor has extracted that information which he feels is most relevant, or in full. Calendars, especially, require careful use because the editor has to exercise fine judgment as to what he feels the researcher might need, and reflect his own priorities and biases. The original material remains sovereign. This even applies, in a different sense, to books of photographs, now proliferating. They are invaluable, but include only *some* of the rich photographic collections available. Oral history is significant for the student of the twentieth century. The richest collection in Wales is at the South Wales Miners' Library of University College, Swansea and is currently being augmented by video recordings. Academic journals such as the *National Library of Wales Journal*. *Archaeologia Cambrensis* and the *Bulletin of the Board of Celtic Studies* carry documentary material and commentary, while valuable calendars have been produced by the Board of Celtic Studies in its *History and Law Series*. Ideal for school use are the eleven short volumes of documents in the *Llygad y Ffynnon* series, in English and Welsh, published by the University of Wales Press between 1972 and 1978 under the general editorship of Hugh Thomas, and the Schools Council Committee for Wales pack of documents published in 1980, *Topics in Welsh History*.

Manuscript material relating to Wales is available in so many locations that it is impossible to list them all. The chief repositories outside Wales include the Public Record Office, either at Chancery Lane or Kew, London, the home of central government records. Here there are documents as diverse as star chamber cases relating to Wales from the sixteenth and seventeenth centuries, and records of the Welsh Department of the Board of Education from 1907 to 1944. Documents relating to Wales, like all those at the P.R.O., can only be consulted when they are at least thirty years old. The British Library, the House of Lords Record Office and the newspaper library at Colindale hold material essential to the researcher.

The chief repository within Wales is the National Library of Wales at Aberystwyth, with its fine collections of manuscripts, prints and maps. Records of the courts of great sessions are held there, as are the papers of many great landed estates and the bulk of Welsh diocesan records.

The records of the county of Powys are deposited in the National Library of Wales. All other Welsh counties have their own record offices housing the papers relating to local government and a whole range of other material including parish records, estate and industrial records and documents relating to education. City and county libraries often have excellent collections of pamphlets, newspapers, documents, photographs and maps which are indispensable for the national and local historian. A *very* preliminary indication of holdings can be found in the Historical Association's *Material for Theses in Local Record Offices and Libraries* by F. G. Emmison and W. J. Smith but this needs to be supplemented by reference to the published guides to individual record offices. All the record offices have produced some collections of material, in booklet or archive teaching unit form, which might be of use in the preliminary stages of an investigation, while the National Museum of Wales has published books of illustrations.

Library resources vary but can be excellent. The Cardiff Central Library has a nationally significant collection of documentary sources, as do some of the university college libraries. The bigger reference libraries in Wales all have a variety of useful material. For instance, Swansea Central Library has a comprehensive reference section and a wide range of periodicals. Articles from journals to which the library does not subscribe are normally made available in ten days or so. There is extensive material on the history of Swansea and west Glamorgan which includes manuscript material. The library retains files of twenty-seven newspapers, dating from 1804, and *The Times* on microfilm. In addition there is a large collection of old maps and photographs of Swansea and district. The main county libraries, in fact, are ideal places from which to start more detailed investigation into themes in Welsh history.

INDEX

Index